THE OPIOID EPIDEMIC AND US CULTURE

THE OPIOID EPIDEMIC AND US CULTURE

EXPRESSION, ART, AND POLITICS IN AN AGE OF ADDICTION

EDITED BY TRAVIS D. STIMELING

West Virginia University Press / Morgantown

ISBN
Cloth 978-1-949199-70-3
Paper 978-1-949199-71-0
Ebook 978-1-949199-72-7

Library of Congress Cataloging-in-Publication Data

Names: Stimeling, Travis D., editor.
Title: The opioid epidemic and US culture : expression, art, and politics in an age of addic-
        tion / edited by Travis D Stimeling.
Description: Morgantown : West Virginia University Press, 2020. | Includes index.
Identifiers: LCCN 2020011805 | ISBN 9781949199703 (cloth) | ISBN 9781949199710
        (paperback) | ISBN 9781949199727 (ebook)
Subjects: LCSH: Opioid abuse—Social aspects—United States. | Opioid abuse—Social
        aspects—Appalachian Region. | Artists—Drug use—United States. | Artists—
        Drug use—Appalachian Region. | Drug abuse in art. | Drug abuse in literature. |
        United States—Social life and customs—21st century. | Appalachian Region—So-
        cial life and customs—21st century.
Classification: LCC RC568.O45 O77 2020 | DDC 362.29/3—dc23
LC record available at https://lccn.loc.gov/2020011805

Cover and book design by Than Saffel / WVU Press

Contents

PART II

If You Lived Here: Representing the Opioid Epidemic from Within

PART III

New Day Dawning: Recovery, Sobriety, and Post-Opioid Futures

The Opioid Crisis and Expressive Culture

Travis D. Stimeling

A crisis. An epidemic. A public health challenge of epic proportions. An economic drain. A moral failing. A blight on the neighborhood. A burden.

Such is the language used to describe the devastating impacts of opioid and opiate addiction on communities all across the United States, from the rural coal camps of southern West Virginia to the streets of Las Vegas.[1] Opioid addiction has been a transformative force for more than two decades, killing tens of thousands of people, many of them under the age of forty, and contributing to the first decline in life expectancy in the United States since World War I.[2] Or, as a recent study indicated, more Americans have died as a consequence of opioid abuse in 2016 than were killed in the most devastating year of the Vietnam War in 1968, with a disproportionate number of opioid casualties occurring among people between the ages of fifteen and forty-four.[3] Children, too, have felt the consequences of opioid addiction, with an increasing number of infants experiencing prenatal exposure to opioids and minors of all ages entering the foster care system as parents and guardians struggle to gain control over their addictions.[4] And hidden to many observers are the many people—friends, family members, social workers, and many more—whose lives have been indelibly changed as a consequence of their interactions with people struggling with opioid addiction.[5]

Sometimes, the best way to convey the impacts of opioid abuse on people in the United States is to amass statistics. But what is often lost in the frequent reporting of statistics are the individual human impacts of opioid abuse. Documentary filmmaker Elaine McMillion Sheldon's made-for-Netflix documentaries *Heroin(e)* (2017) and *Recovery Boys* (2018) and journalist Laura Macy's book *Dopesick: Dealers, Doctors, and the Drug Company That Addicted America* (2018) have, by contrast, personalized the opioid crisis, focusing attention on the individual people who are fighting their own addictions, supporting others in their struggles, and trying to maintain some semblance of normalcy in a situation that often resists rational explanation.[6] *The Opioid Epidemic and US Culture: Expression, Art, and Politics in an Age of Addiction* seeks to contribute to these efforts to humanize the opioid crisis by focusing our attention expressly on the ways that creative people have engaged with opioid addiction, recovery, and loss in a variety of media, from music to memes and everything in between. The essays in this collection operate from the fundamental assumption that expressive culture is both a tool through which people can make sense of their struggles and a means to challenge dehumanizing assumptions about addiction and recovery. As such, *The Opioid Epidemic and US Culture* supposes that, even amid the anesthetic effects of opioid addiction, aesthetics matter.

THE OPIOID CRISIS IN *OVERVIEW*

Although opiates have been a significant concern in the West for centuries, the use and abuse of prescription opioids is predominantly a recent phenomenon, emerging during the late 1990s, when pharmaceutical manufacturer Purdue Pharma developed the opioid-based pain reliever OxyContin and built an extensive marketing and education campaign to convince physicians to prescribe the drug for the relief of chronic pain.[7] Initially targeting doctors working in rural areas and with working-class populations, Purdue Pharma misused limited scientific data to falsely argue that OxyContin was a nonaddictive pain relief option that could far exceed the analgesic power of conventional prescription painkillers.[8] As physicians increased their prescriptions for OxyContin, it quickly became clear that the drug was addictive, and illicit trade of the drug became commonplace, as did the arrival of "pill mills" that offered prescriptions for high doses and large quantities of OxyContin with only limited medical evaluation and oversight.[9] In addition to pain clinics that served rural populations directly, large operations also opened in major urban centers, which served people who drove or flew from hundreds of miles away to obtain the pills they needed to meet the demands of their own addictions and, in many cases, to sell illicitly upon their return home.[10] Between physicians prescribing opioids for medical purposes, pill mills prescribing opioids on the margins of medical best practice, and the illicit trade of the drugs, any efforts to stem the tide of the opioid epidemic from public policy and law enforcement perspectives were quickly proven to be ineffective in preventing both opioid abuse and its related crimes.[11] As evidenced by the *Washington Post*'s July 2019 release of a Drug Enforcement Administration database of opioid sales and distributions, "the cumulative data shows . . . [that more than seventy-six billion] oxycodone and hydro-codone pills were distributed across the country" during the seven years between 2006 and 2012.[12]

As Macy has implied in her work, the emergence of this addiction crisis in rural working-class communities may have kept the opioid epidemic out of view of national policy makers and media outlets. She observes, for instance:

> When a new drug sweeps the city, it historically starts in the big cities and gradually spreads to the hinterlands, as is the cases of cocaine and crack. But the opioid epidemic began in exactly the opposite manner, grabbing a toehold in isolated Appalachia, Midwestern rust belt coun-ties, and rural Maine. Working-class families who were more tradi-tionally dependent on jobs in high-risk industries to pay their bills . . . weren't just the first to experience the epidemic of drug overdose; they also happened to live in politically unimportant places, hollows and towns and fishing villages where the treatment options were likely to be hours from home.[13]

As a consequence, opioid addiction has frequently exerted devastating, but nationally unnoticed, impacts on rural and working-class communities—par-ticularly among the white population, but also devastating Native Americans, the Latinx community, and African Americans.[14] The *Washington Post*'s re-porting provides supporting data for this argument, showing that some rural counties in Appalachia received more than 150 opioid pills per resident between 2006 and 2012.[15] But by the first decade of the new millennium, opioid abuse had found its way into the suburbs, where its impacts were felt in middle-class homes thanks to the easy availability of prescription opioids and the use of opioids as a party drug, particularly among people under the age of thirty.[16] As federal regulators began to crack down on excessive pre-scribing practices, law enforcement increased arrests for possession and traf-ficking, and legal settlements required the reformulation of OxyContin and other prescription opioids in the early 2000s, many prescription opioid users turned to other opioids and opiates to satisfy their physiological cravings. As such, the markets for heroin and other drugs, including the deadly fentanyl and carfentanil, increased dramatically, resulting in the importation of drugs from Mexico and China and connecting the opioid epidemic to a global network of producers and traffickers, many of whom exploit people on the margins of society at multiple points in the system.[17] Perhaps not surprisingly, it was at this point that the opioid crisis began to draw national attention, generating a host of news stories in mainstream news outlets and garnering the attention of policy makers, including both presidents Obama and Trump.[18] At the same time, pharmaceutical companies that thrived as a consequence of the manufacture and distribution of opioids also worked closely with government regulators to create more hospitable regulatory environments for them as recently as the Obama administration.[19]

Even with increased national attention, efforts to support the recoveries of people struggling with opioid addiction have yielded mixed results and have been met with resistance at local, state, and federal levels. Medically assisted treatment, in which patients are provided a pharmaceutical remedy to stave off cravings, remains difficult for many people to access, particularly those living in rural areas, and the drugs that are used in such treatments are easily abused. Residential treatment centers are even harder to come by, particularly for patients without private medical insurance or the cash to pay for a bed out-of-pocket.[20] Twelve-step programs, as well, are often incapable of providing adequate support for people in recovery. Moreover, lawmakers in some states have proposed and passed legislation that mandates drug testing for recipients of state and federal aid for low-income families, arguing that governments should not use taxpayer moneys to assist people with addiction.[21] Similarly, harm reduction programs—including needle and syringe exchanges, free access to the overdose-reversing drug naloxone, and safe injection sites—have met mixed public responses, with uneven and inconsistent adoption in communities around the United States spurred by fears that such programs will attract people with addiction to their cities and towns, despite the abilities of such programs to prevent the spread of blood-borne pathogens and overdose deaths.[22] And perhaps most disturbingly, recent reports indicate that, despite the availability of new drugs to assist in saving the lives of people with opioid addiction, pharmaceutical manufacturers—the very source of the opioid epidemic—continue to find ways to limit access to these medications through patent protection and price hikes.[23] Such systemic barriers to harm reduction, rehabilitation, and recovery programs consistently highlight the dehumanizing attitudes that political, financial, and industrial gatekeepers hold about people fighting addiction: that is, people with addiction are widely seen as a problem that results from bad choices made by people with weak moral fiber rather than as people who are caught in a vicious cycle that, in many cases, was started by the very political, financial, and industrial gate-keepers who want to prevent them from recovering.[24]

EXPRESSIVE CULTURE AND THE OPIOID CRISIS

Expressive culture—whether created by people with addiction and in recovery or by people whose friends and loved ones have struggled with addiction—challenges dehumanizing attitudes toward the individual people caught in the opioid crisis.[25] Paintings, photographs, short stories, songs, dance concerts, and film draw audiences into the stories of individuals, using the tools of a particular medium to force audiences to engage directly with the perspectives of those people most directly affected by drug addiction and challenging stigmas about opioid abuse. Expressive culture often foregrounds the experiences of individuals in the timbre of a singer's voice, brushstrokes on a canvas, or the movements of a dancer's limbs, and communion with these traces of humanity can challenge preconceived notions of what addiction looks like. Such was the case with an August 2018 concert performance in Knoxville, Tennessee, in which concert pianist and recovering opioid addict Kris Rucinski used his critically acclaimed talents to raise funds for Tennessee Overdose Prevention in a program he described as "A Musical Message of Remembrance and Hope."[26] Similarly, Marshall University's ongoing efforts to document and share recovery stories—Movable: Narratives of Recovery and Place—challenge viewers to engage meaningfully with individual experiences of the opioid crisis as a tool "to combat stigma and promote recovery," as project member Kristen Lillvis noted.[27]

At the same time, expressive culture also provides an avenue for individual and collective protest against the structural factors that have contributed to the opioid epidemic. In 2018, amid growing furor about the role of Purdue Pharma—and the Sackler family, which owns the company—in spawning and exacerbating the opioid crisis, a group of artists organized under the banner of Prescription Addiction Intervention Now (PAIN) and led by Nan Goldin launched protests in art museums that have been recipients of the Sackler family's philanthropy, including the Metropolitan Museum of Art, the Smithsonian Institution, and the Harvard Art Museums.[28] In recent months, museums and other cultural organizations have increasingly turned away from the Sackler family's patronage as a consequence.[29] In another act of public artistic protest in June 2018, sculptor Domenic Esposito and gallery owner Fernando Luís Alvarez delivered a massive "steel sculpture of a bent, burnt heroin spoon" to the Purdue Pharma headquarters in Stamford, Connecticut, leading to widespread news coverage and criminal charges for Alvarez; since then, his Opioid Spoon Project has delivered several such sculptures to corporate headquarters and other spaces associated with the opioid epidemic.[30] Such work not only spurs important conversations—in some cases because the artists involved "come out" about their own fight with addiction—but also serves as a powerful challenge to the marginalization of the people most directly affected, speaking truth to power.

Expressive culture has also played a key role in the daily lives of people experiencing the opioid epidemic in a variety of ways. During the 1990s, for instance, Purdue Pharma armed its sales force with compact disc compilations of swing music as a giveaway item to entice physicians to prescribe OxyContin, making for a bizarre soundtrack to the primary source of this deadly addiction crisis.[31] Television viewers, too, are regularly confronted with discordantly upbeat advertisements for opioids and other drugs that are tied to opioid abuse (including a number of drugs intended to address "opioid-related constipation"), ads that depict people smiling, laughing, and easily inhabiting their bodies as a consequence of those drugs. And government officials have recently attempted to utilize digital media to target younger audiences that might be susceptible to opioid abuse.[32] Expressive culture can, therefore, also be seen as a contributing factor to the opioid epidemic, and, as such, its power to do harm must also be considered.

The essays in this collection, then, deploy techniques honed in humanistic inquiry and creative practice to come to terms with the ways that expressive culture influences both the opioid crisis and our understandings of it. The authors in this volume represent a broad cross section of perspectives, both within the arts and humanities and vis-à-vis the opioid epidemic. Although many of the contributors to this volume hold advanced degrees in literature, musicology, art history, folklore, and other disciplines, still others have developed their insights with little aid from higher education, which often serves to marginalize the voices and perspectives of people who are not deemed acceptable by white middle-class society. Some of the authors here have openly spoken of their own battles with opioid addiction, while others have no personal experience with drug use at all. Urban, rural, and suburban perspectives also work in dialogue here to demonstrate the uneven effects of the opioid crisis on the national landscape. And this book also highlights the voices of people with diverse identities and sexual orientations, revealing in the process the ways that privilege and power influence the ways that individuals experience the opioid crisis.

The Opioid Epidemic and US Culture is loosely organized around three perspectives. The first section explores some of the ways that the opioid epidemic has been represented by creative individuals working on the periphery. These essays engage with narratives surrounding opioid use, addiction, and recovery that are generated and propagated by people looking in, narratives that, these authors suggest, sometimes exert a negative influence on the short- and long-term recovery of individuals involved in the opioid crisis more directly. In the second section, authors consider the ways that artists and artistic communities who are living in the midst of the opioid crisis use expressive tools to present work that humanizes addiction and loss and that highlights grassroots efforts to support recovery and harm reduction at the local level. Particularly noteworthy here are community efforts to bring people together to discuss their shared experiences and to point toward better futures. In the final section, authors turn their attention toward those futures, futures that will require sustained engagement with recovery and harm reduction for many decades. In these essays, the authors reveal how creative endeavors might simultaneously reveal the limitations of recovery efforts while also providing spaces within which people can continue to build community to support one another through the work of recovery.

On the whole, these essays do not offer a unified theory of "opioid aesthetics." Rather, they instead argue that aesthetic experiences are essential both to understand the toll that opioids have had on communities throughout the United States and to developing immediate and long-term strategies for recovery. As long as policy makers blame opioid users for their struggles or build arguments around statistics, it is possible to recast people with opioid use disorder as dehumanized problems. Aesthetic experiences challenge that dehumanization, as aesthetic engagement can be intensely personal. Put simply, how can "problems" understand beauty? This volume, then, is an effort to intervene in the opioid crisis by offering critical analysis and new models for creativity-oriented recovery practices. And perhaps even more importantly, we hope that those readers who have a personal experience with opioid addiction will read these case studies and know that they are seen and that they matter.

NOTES

1. For the reader's sake, I will use the term *opioid* to treat both opioids and opiates unless a clearer distinction is necessary.

    The most comprehensive effort to map the emergence and expansion of the opioid epidemic in the United States was conducted by NORC at the University of Chicago and the US Department of Agriculture in "Drug Overdose Deaths in the United States," NORC, accessed December 14, 2019, https://opioidmisusetool.norc.org/. A detailed mapping of the opioid epidemic in Appalachia was published by NORC at the University of Chicago and the Appalachian Regional Commission in "Drug Overdose Deaths in Appalachia," NORC, accessed December 14, 2019, https://overdosemappingtool.norc.org/. See also James S. Goodwin, Yong-Fang Kuo, and David Brown, "Association of Chronic Opioid Use with Presidential Voting Patterns in US Counties in 2016," *JAMA Network Open* 1, no. 2 (2018): e180450, doi:10.1001/jamanetworkopen.2018.0450.

2.   Rob Stein, "Life Expectancy Drops Again as Opioid Deaths Surge in U.S.," *Shots: Health News*, NPR, December 21, 2017, https://www.npr.org/sections/health-shots/2017 /12/21/572080314/life-expectancy-drops-again-as-opioid-deaths-surge-in-u-s; Lenny Bernstein, "U.S. Lifespan Declines Again, a Dismal Trend Not Seen since World War I," *Washington Post*, November 29, 2018, https://www.washingtonpost.com/national /health-science/us-life-expectancy-declines-again-a-dismal-trend-not-seen-since-world -war-i/2018/11/28/ae58bc8c-f28c-11e8-bc79-68604ed88993_story.html.

3.   Tara Gomes et al., "The Burden of Opioid-Related Mortality in the United States," *JAMA Network Open* 1, no. 2 (June 2018): e180217, doi:10.1001/jamanetworkopen.2018.0217; Keith Humphreys, "Opioid Epidemic Is Deadlier than the Vietnam War in '68, Study Says," *Washington Post*, June 7, 2018, https://www.washingtonpost.com/news/wonk/wp/2018 /06/07/the-opioid-epidemic-is-deadlier-than-the-vietnam-war-study-says/. See also Sue Ella Kobak, "Oxycontin Flood in the Coalfields: 'Searching for Higher Ground,' " in *Transforming Places: Lessons from Appalachia*, eds. Stephen L. Fisher and Barbara Ellen Smith (Urbana: University of Illinois Press, 2012), 198–209.

      In general, statistics of overall misuse of opioids are both difficult to ascertain and notably unreliable. See, for instance, Joseph Palamar, "How Many Americans Misuse Opioids? Why Scientists Still Aren't Sure," *Daily Yonder*, October 18, 2018, https://www .dailyyonder.com/many-americans-really-misuse-opioids-scientists-still-arent-sure /2018/10/18/28088/; Joseph J. Palamar, Jenni A. Shearston, and Charles M. Cleland, "Discordant Reporting of Nonmedical Opioid Use in a Nationally Representative Sample of US High School Seniors," *American Journal of Drug and Alcohol Abuse* 42, no. 5 (2016): 530–38, https://doi.org/10.1080/00952990.2016.1178269.

4.   Lorna Collier, "Young Victims of the Opioid Crisis," *Monitor on Psychology* 49, no. 1 (January 2018): 18, https://www.apa.org/monitor/2018/01/opioid-crisis; Bryant Furlow, "Neonatal Opioid Withdrawal in the USA," *The Lancet Child and Adolescent Health* 2, no. 9 (July 18, 2018): 629–30, https://doi.org/10.1016/S2352-4642(18)30237-2; Wendy Welch, *Fall or Fly: The Strangely Hopeful Story of Foster Care and Adoption in Appalachia* (Athens: Ohio University Press, 2018).

5.   US Department of Health and Human Services, Substance Abuse and Health Services Administration, Center for Excellence for Infant and Early Childhood Mental Health Consultation, "Approaches to Supporting Families Affected by Opioid Use," accessed September 22, 2019, https://www.samhsa.gov/sites/default/files/programs_campaigns /IECMHC/approaches-supporting-families-affected-opioids.pdf.

6.   Elaine McMillion Sheldon, dir., *Heroin(e)* (Elkview, WV: Center for Investigative Reporting and Requisite Media, 2017); Sheldon, dir., *Recovery Boys* (Elkview, WV: Requisite Media, 2018); Laura Macy, *Dopesick: Dealers, Doctors, and the Drug Company That Addicted America* (New York: Little, Brown, 2018).

7.   For a historical overview of global opiate and opioid use, consult Martin Booth, *Opium: A History* (New York: Thomas Dunne, 1996). The development of OxyContin and the details of Purdue Pharma's extensive marketing and education operations are detailed in a number of sources, including, most notably, Barry Meier, *Pain Killer: An Empire of Deceit*

and the Origins of America's Opioid Epidemic (New York: Rodale, 2003; revised and expanded edition, New York: Random House, 2018); John Temple, *American Pain: How a Young Felon and His Ring of Doctors Unleashed America's Deadliest Epidemic* (Guilford, CT: LP, 2015), 40–46; Sam Quinones, *Dreamland: The True Tale of America's Opiate Epidemic* (New York: Bloomsbury Press, 2015), 98–110, 127–37; Macy, *Dopesick*, 31–56; Chris McGreal, *American Overdose: The Opioid Tragedy in Three Acts* (New York: Public Affairs, 2018), 39–48.

8.   Among others, Quinones, *Dreamland*, 107–8.

9.   Temple, *American Pain*; McGreal, *American Overdose*; Macy, *Dopesick*, 42.

10.   Temple, *American Pain*, 81, 124–38, 171.

11.   Macy, *Dopesick*, 189–208.

12.   "Drilling into the DEA's Pain Pill Database," *Washington Post*, July 21, 2019, https://www
.washingtonpost.com/graphics/2019/investigations/dea-pain-pill-database/.

13.   Macy, *Dopesick*, 7–8. See also: Jennifer R. Havens, Robert Walker, and Carl G. Leukefeld,
"Prescription Opioid Use in Rural Appalachia: A Community-Based Study," *Journal of
Opioid Management* 4, no. 2 (April 2008): 63–71; Wayne Coombs, "Analysis: The
Pharmaceutical Colonization of Appalachia," *100 Days in Appalachia*, February 12, 2018,
https://www.100daysinappalachia.com/2018/02/12/analysis-pharmaceutical
-colonization-appalachia/; Harvard T. H. Chan School of Public Health, "Life in Rural
America: Experiences and Views from Rural American on Economic and Health Issues and
Life in Rural Communities," Robert Wood Johnson Foundation, Public Opinion Poll
Series, October 1, 2018, https://www.rwjf.org/en/library/research/2018/10/life-in-rural
-america.html/.

14.   For further discussion of the impacts of the opioid crisis on nonwhite communities,
consult, among others: Ronald Wyatt, "Pain and Ethnicity," *AMA Journal of Ethics* (May
2013): 449–54; Julie R. Gaither et al., "Racial Disparities in Discontinuation of
Long-Term Opioid Therapy Following Illicit Drug Use among Black and White Patients,"
Drug and Alcohol Dependence 192, no. 1 (November 2018): 371–76, https://doi.org
/10.1016/j.drugalcdep.2018.05.033; Josefina Alvarez et al., "Substance Abuse
Prevalence and Treatment among Latinos and Latinas," *Journal of Ethnicity in Substance
Abuse* 6, no. 2 (2007): 115–41, https://dx.doi.org/10.1300/J233v06n02_08; Martha
Bebinger, "Latinos Are Hit Especially Hard by the Opioid Crisis in Mass. But Why?"
CommonHealth, WBUR, May 3, 2018, https://www.wbur.org/commonhealth
/2018/05/03/latino-opioid-overdose-deaths; Albuquerque Area Southwest Tribal
Epidemiology Center, "The Opioid Crisis: Impact on Native Communities," March 2018,
https://www.aastec.net/wp-content/uploads/2018/03/AASTEC_opioids-fact-sheet
_17x11_pages-1.pdf; US Department of Health and Human Services, "Testimony from
Christopher M. Jones, PharmD., M.P.H. on Opioids in Indian Country: Beyond the
Crisis to Healing the Community before Committee on Indian Affairs," March 14, 2018,
https://www.hhs.gov/about/agencies/asl/testimony/2018-03/opioids-indian-country
-beyond-crisis.html; Michigan Radio, "How Tribal Leaders Are Responding to the Opioid
Crisis in Michigan's Native Communities," July 13, 2018, http://www.michiganradio
.org/post/how-tribal-leaders-are-responding-opioid-crisis-michigans-native-american
-communities; Clairmont Griffiths et al., "The Effects of Opioid Addiction on the Black
Community," *International Journal of Collaborative Research on Internal Medicine and
Public Health* 10, no. 2 (2018): 843–50.

15.   "Drilling into the DEA's Pain Pill Database." See also, Eric Eyre, "Drug Firm Poured 3M
Opioids into WV Town in Just 10 Months, Report Says," *Charleston [WV] Gazette-Mail*,
December 19, 2018, https://www.wvgazettemail.com/news/health/drug-firm-poured
-m-opioids-into-wv-town-in-just/article_d229b33b-c55a-5451-ab3f-b545476516d4
.html.

16. Macy, *Dopesick*, 57–58.
17. Quinones, *Dreamland*; Steven Melendez, "The Online Chinese Labs Feeding America Its Deadliest New Drug," *Fast Company*, September 9, 2016, https://www.fastcompany.com/3063518/carfentanil-synthetic-opioids-heroin; Anyssa Garza, "Illicitly Produced Fentanyl: A Growing Cause of Synthetic Opioid Deaths," *Pharmacy Times* August 29, 2018, https://www.pharmacytimes.com/publications/issue/2018/august2018/illegally-produced-fentanyl-a-growing-cause-of-synthetic-opioid-deaths.
18. See, for instance, The White House, Office of the Press Secretary, "FACT SHEET: Obama Administration Announces Prescription Opioid and Heroin Epidemic Awareness Week," September 19, 2016, https://obamawhitehouse.archives.gov/the-press-office/2016/09/19/fact-sheet-obama-administration-announces-prescription-opioid-and-heroin; Brianna Ehley, "Trump Declared an Opioids Emergency. Then Nothing Changed," *Politico*, January 11, 2018, https://www.politico.com/story/2018/01/11/opioids-epidemic-trump-addiction-emergency-order-335848.
19. Scott Higham et al., "Inside the Drug Industry's Plan to Defeat the DEA," *Washington Post*, September 13, 2019, https://www.washingtonpost.com/graphics/2019/investigations/drug-industry-plan-to-defeat-dea/; Katie Zezima and Colby Itkowitz, "Flailing on Fentanyl," *Washington Post*, September 20, 2019, https://www.washingtonpost.com/graphics/2019/investigations/fentanyl-epidemic-congress/.
20. Macy, *Dopesick*, 269–96.
21. The National Conference of State Legislatures noted that, as of March 2017, "at least 15 states have passed legislation regarding drug testing or screening for public assistance applicants or recipients (Alabama, Arkansas, Arizona, Florida, Georgia, Kansas, Michigan, Mississippi, Missouri, North Carolina, Oklahoma, Tennessee, Utah, West Virginia, and Wisconsin)," National Conference of State Legislatures, "Drug Testing for Welfare Recipients and Public Assistance," NCSL, March 24, 2017, http://www.ncsl.org/research/human-services/drug-testing-and-public-assistance.aspx.
22. For more background on harm reduction, consult Macy, *Dopesick*, 237–41; Harm Reduction Coalition, "Principles of Harm Reduction," Harm Reduction, accessed December 14, 2019, https://harmreduction.org/about-us/principles-of-harm-reduction/; Tessie Castillo, "Harm Reduction Strategies for the Opioid Crisis," *North Carolina Medical Journal* 79, no. 3 (May–June 2018): 192–94, https://doi.org/10.18043/ncm.79.3.192. For an overview of the debate around harm reduction, consult, among others, Kris Clarke, "The Case of a Needle Exchange Policy Debate in Fresno, California," *Critical Social Policy* 36, no. 2 (2016): 289–306, https://doi.org/10.1177/0261018315608726; A. K. Clark et al., "A Systematic Review of Community Opioid Overdose Prevention and Naloxone Distribution Programs," *Journal of Addiction Medicine* 8, no. 3 (May–June 2014): 153–63, https://doi.org/10.1097/ADM.0000000000000034; Elana Gordon, "What's the Evidence That Supervised Drug Injection Sites Save Lives?" *Shots: Health News*, NPR, September 7, 2018, https://www.npr.org/sections/health-shots/2018/09/07/645609248/whats-the-evidence-that-supervised-drug-injection-sites-save-lives.
23. Ameet Sarpatwari, Michael S. Sinha, and Aaron S. Kesselheim, "The Opioid Epidemic: Fixing a Broken Pharmaceutical Market," *Harvard Law and Policy Review* 11 (2017): 473, 475; Eric Levitz, "OxyContin Billionaire Patents New Drug for Opioid Treatment," *New York Magazine*, September 7, 2018, https://nymag.com/intelligencer/2018/09/richard-sackler-oxycontin-billionaire-patent-opioid-addiction-treatment-buprenorphine.html; Ken Alltucker, "Drug Company Raised Price of Lifesaving Opioid Overdose Antidote More than 600 Percent," *USA Today*, November 19, 2018, https://www.usatoday.com/story/news/health/2018/11/19/kaleo-opioid-overdose-antidote-naloxone-evzio-rob-portman-medicare-medicaid/2060033002/.

Additionally, a recent report indicates that life insurance companies are denying insurance to people who carry naloxone with them, even if they are carrying it to be helpful to others; see Martha Bebinger, "Nurse Denied Life Insurance Because She Carries Naloxone," *Morning Edition*, NPR, December 13, 2018, https://www.npr.org /sections/health-shots/2018/12/13/674586548/nurse-denied-life-insurance-because -she-carries-naloxone.

24. On the alignment of these structural factors, consult McGreal, *American Overdose*, 166.

25. Implicitly, I am endorsing what Eve Kosofsky Sedgwick has described as "reparative reading," in which the audience must "surrender the knowing, anxious paranoid determination that no horror, however apparently unthinkable, shall ever come to the reader *as new*." Sedgwick notes that reparative reading can open the door to hope: "Hope, often a fracturing, even a traumatic thing to experience, is among the energies by which the reparatively positioned reader tries to organize the fragments and part-objects she encounters or creates." Eve Kosofsky Sedgwick, *Touching Feeling: Affect, Pedagogy, Performativity* (Durham, NC: Duke University Press, 2003), 146. Sedgwick's work is taken up at length in my home discipline of musicology by William Cheng, *Just Vibrations: The Purpose of Sounding Good* (Ann Arbor: University of Michigan Press, 2016).

26. Steve Wildsmith, "An Intimate Cause: Overdose Survivor and Pianist Plays Awareness Concert," *The [Blount Co., TN] Daily Times*, August 20, 2018, https://www.thedailytimes .com/columns/steve_wildsmith/an-intimate-cause-overdose-survivor-and-pianist-plans -awareness-concert/article_2c62633c-a75d-5f2c-b3a8-3fd13621ee88.html.

It is also worth noting that at least one chapter of the American Federation of Musicians has drawn attention to the connections between performance injuries and opioid addiction. See, for instance, Joshua Snow, "Addiction Can Start with Painkillers," *Allegro* 116, no. 11 (November 2016): http://www.local802afm.org/allegro/articles /addiction-can-start-with-painkillers.

27. "Marshall Faculty Awarded Grant for Website Featuring Recovery Stories," *HuntingtonNews.net*, December 11, 2018, http://www.huntingtonnews.net/161076?fbc lid=IwAR3VPDu8jwewgbDVq3nw5–6WnE51ky8UmjZmTd5-xK2Viujyu_QLQeMd74g.

28. Andrew Russeth, "Nan Goldin, P.A.I.N. Group Stage Protest against Sackler Family, Purdue Pharmaceuticals in Met's Sackler Wing," *ArtNews* , March 10, 2018, https:// www.artnews.com/2018/03/10/nan-goldin-p-n-group-stage-protest-sackler-family -purdue-pharmaceuticals-mets-sackler-wing/; Joanna Walters, "Artist Nan Goldin Stages Opioid Protest in Metropolitan Museum Sackler Gallery," *The Guardian*, March 11, 2018, https://www.theguardian.com/us-news/2018/mar/10/opioids-nan-goldin -protest-metropolitan-museum-sackler-wing; Ana Finel Honigman, "Nan Goldin's P.A.I.N. Group Stages Pill-Purging Protest at Sackler Gallery in Washington, D.C.," *ArtNews*, April 26, 2018, https://www.artnews.com/2018/04/26/nan-goldins-p-n -group-stages-pill-purging-protest-sackler-gallery-washington-d-c/; Graham Ambrose, "Opioid Protest at Harvard Art Museum," *Boston Globe*, July 21, 2018, last modified July 24, 2018, https://www.bostonglobe.com/lifestyle/style/2018/07/20/opioid -protest-harvard-art-museum/6DSgcZKepMyomeaxImOjkK/story.html.

Goldin, herself in recovery from opioid use disorder, has become an outspoken critic of the pharmaceutical industry. See, for instance, Nan Goldin, untitled essay, *ArtForum* 56, no. 5 (January 2018): https://www.artforum.com/print/201808/nan-goldin-73181; "Nan Goldin Denounces Richard S. Sackler's Patent of New Drug for Opioid Treatment," News, *ArtForum*, September 14, 2018, https://www.artforum.com/news/nan-goldin -denounces-richard-s-sackler-s-patent-of-new-drug-for-opioid-treatment-76611; Kate Brown, " 'This Is Reprehensible': Nan Goldin Responds to News That Richard Sackler

Has Patented an OxyContin Addiction Drug," *ArtNet News*, September 11, 2018, https://news.artnet.com/art-world/nan-goldin-sackler-statement-purdue-1346279. PAIN's mission can be found at https://www.sacklerpain.org/mission-statement.

29. Nadeem Badshah and Joanna Walters, "National Portrait Gallery Drops £1m Grant from Sackler Family," *The Guardian*, March 19, 2019, https://www.theguardian.com/artanddesign/2019/mar/19/national-portrait-gallery-turns-down-grant-from-sackler-family-oxycontin; E. J. Dickson, "Museums Are Rejecting Donations from the Sackler Family," *Rolling Stone*, March 22, 2019, https://www.rollingstone.com/culture/culture-news/tate-art-galleries-reject-sackler-donations-opioid-crisis-811775/; Nina Golgowski, "Guggenheim Museum Rejects Future Gifts from OxyContin's Sackler Family," *Huffington Post*, March 24, 2019, https://www.huffpost.com/entry/guggenheim-museum-cuts-sackler-donations_n_5c9787fae4b01ebeef108716; Brian Clark, "How the Family behind Purdue Pharma and OxyContin Became Nonprofit Pariahs," CNBC, May 31, 2019, https://www.cnbc.com/2019/05/31/how-purdue-pharmas-sackler-family-lost-the-art-world.html.

    As this book is going to press, Purdue and the Sacklers are negotiating financial settlements with state and local governments for their role in the opioid epidemic. For recent discussions of lawsuits against the Sackler family, consult, among others, Corky Siemaszko, "New Strategy in Suing Opioid Maker Blamed for Addiction Crisis: Target the Family Who Runs It," NBC News, June 16, 2018, https://www.nbcnews.com/news/us-news/new-strategy-suing-opioid-maker-blamed-addiction-crisis-target-family-n883091; Joanna Walters, "Sackler Family Members Face Mass Litigation and Criminal Investigations over Opioids Crisis," *The Guardian*, November 19, 2018, https://www.theguardian.com/us-news/2018/nov/19/sackler-family-members-face-mass-litigation-criminal-investigations-over-opioids-crisis; Barry Meier, "Sacklers Directed Efforts to Mislead Public about OxyContin, Court Filing Claims," *New York Times*, January 15, 2019, https://www.nytimes.com/2019/01/15/health/sacklers-purdue-oxycontin-opioids.html; Danny Hakim, Roni Caryn Rabin, and William K. Rashbaum, "Lawsuits Lay Bare Sackler Family's Role in Opioid Crisis," *New York Times*, April 1, 2019, https://www.nytimes.com/2019/04/01/health/sacklers-oxycontin-lawsuits.html; Jan Hoffman, "Sacklers Would Give Up Ownership of Purdue Pharma under Settlement Proposal," *New York Times*, August 27, 2019, https://www.nytimes.com/2019/08/27/health/sacklers-purdue-pharma-opioid-settlement.html; German Lopez, "The Maker of OxyContin Will Reportedly Pay Billions to Settle Opioid Epidemic Lawsuits," *Vox*, September 11, 2019, https://www.vox.com/policy-and-politics/2019/9/11/20861226/purdue-oxycontin-settlement-opioid-epidemic; Anya van Wagtendonk, "The Makers of OxyContin May Have Tried to Hide $1 Billion in Assets," *Vox*, September 14, 2019, https://www.vox.com/policy-and-politics/2019/9/14/20865918/sackler-family-1-billion-wire-transfers-new-york-letitia-james-oxycontin-opioid-epidemic; Jan Hoffman, "Purdue Pharma Warns that Sackler Family May Walk from Opioid Deal," *New York Times*, September 19, 2019, https://www.nytimes.com/2019/09/19/health/purdue-sackler-opioid-settlement.html; Andrew Joseph, "Purdue Pharma Filed for Bankruptcy. What Does It Mean for Lawsuits against the Opioid Manufacturer?" STAT, September 16, 2019, https://www.statnews.com/2019/09/16/if-purdue-pharma-declares-bankruptcy-what-would-it-mean-for-lawsuits-against-the-opioid-manufacturer/.

30. Susan Dunne, "Gallery Owner Arrested after Dropping Sculpture of Giant Drug Spoon at Purdue Pharma," *Hartford [CT] Courant*, June 26, 2018, https://www.courant.com/news/connecticut/hc-news-stamford-opioids-spoon-sculpture-0623-story.html; Colin Moynihan, "Large-Scale Art Protest outside OxyContin Maker Ends in Arrest," *New York Times*, June 22, 2018, https://www.nytimes.com/2018/06/22/arts/design/art-protest

-arrest-at-oxycontin-maker.html; "The Honor Tour," The Opioid Spoon Project, accessed September 22, 2019, http://www.theopioidspoonproject.com/the-honor-tour/.

31. Art Van Zee, "The Promotion and Marketing of OxyContin: Commercial Triumph, Public Health Tragedy," *American Journal of Public Health* 99, no. 2 (February 2009): 222; Quinones, *American Pain*, 134.

32. Jan Pytalski, "White House Takes On Opioids on Its Own Turf—The Mass Media," *100 Days in Appalachia*, June 8, 2018, https://www.100daysinappalachia.com/2018/06/08 /anti-opioid-campaign.

PART 1

ON THE OUTSIDE LOOKING IN

THE OPIOID CRISIS FROM WITHOUT

"Something Too Pure / Is Killing Us": Opioid-Addiction Porn, Endurance, and the Neoliberal Appropriation of Resilience

Jordan Lovejoy

In the first issue of the environmental humanities journal *Resilience*, journal coeditor Stephanie LeMenager interviews desert studies and subculture scholar Dick Hebdige to discuss how his work explores environmental resilience, which LeMenager defines as "adapting and thriving over time."[1] At the end of the interview, LeMenager asks Hebdige whether he ever uses the word *sustainability*, which she indicates "has become a pet term of politicians, developers, university administrators," a buzzword employed by neoliberal institutions to suggest an investment in the environment and the future. Although Hebdige no longer uses the term, he does employ others: "What I like about the word 'resilience' is that, while it posits the ability of systems to survive and bounce back from traumatic stress, it also contains the idea of 'recoil,' hence 'recoiling from' (i.e., it retains a residual connotation of alarm and revulsion at the fact we've let things get into this state in the first place.)." Hebdige further explains:

> I think my keyword has to be "crisis" (though admittedly it's hardly aspirational). It concentrates the focus within the state of emergency (in all the senses of that term), while leaving the question of outcomes— hence the possibility of recovery or radical transformation—open. Nobody knows with certainty at any moment, in any particular set of circumstances, what's going to happen next, so the bouncing back part

can't be guaranteed. I'm uneasy ascribing any permanent and essential qualities—even a quality like "resilience" with its implication of survival in the last instance—to humanity or the planet we're part of. What I like about "crisis" is that it calls us back to what is happening now, i.e., to everything that, one way or another, as human beings—individually and en masse—we're responsible for.[2]

In this chapter, I am also more interested in words like *crisis* and *endurance* than *resilience*, though I, too, recognize the usefulness and hopefulness that accompany resilience as a concept of survival. Unfortunately, as I will argue, the term—much like *sustainability*—has been co-opted by political and neoliberal institutions to draw our focus more toward the individual end product—the survival—than the ongoing, messy, critical, and quotidian effects many of us haven't survived or are still enduring. Survival—whether environmental, cultural, or chemical—is our new romantic, and resilience, our ability to overcome, takes center stage, shifting our focus away from all the endurance it takes to finally reach the reward of being labeled resilient.

By focusing on the current and ongoing opioid epidemic in the United States, this chapter first explores the term *resilience* and how neoliberal systems have appropriated it to fit their own ends. I then argue for a shift back to the middle, to a critical focus on what people must first *endure* to finally be celebrated as resilient. I then turn to two cultural productions that deal with the aesthetics of the opioid crisis as it is seen in West Virginia: Sean Dunne's documentary-like film *Oxyana* (2013) and Isabelle Shepherd's poem "Backtalking a Guy Who Tries to Get Your Number by Saying *You're Not What I Expected Out of a West Virginian, Not a Redneck at All*" (2018). Through these works I explore how the romanticization of resilience has contributed to poverty porn—or its contemporary sister, opioid-addiction porn—as well as what a shift toward endurance might look like in our everyday experiences. This shift, I hope, will help us question, observe, and possibly alter the very systems that make resilience necessary, the very systems that aim to capitalize on the aesthetic dimensions of our crises without highlighting why such massive injustices come to exist in the first place.

RESILIENCE, NEOLIBERAL APPROPRIATION, AND ENDURANCE

In the editor's column for the first issue of *Resilience* mentioned above, coeditors Stephanie LeMenager and Stephanie Foote argue that the term *resilience* has a "focus on precarity and the limits of our ability to predict and insure against the future[, which] oddly protects it from all emergency, insofar as resilience theory, when it has been applied from ecology to society, promises that unforeseeable systemic disruptions are natural and survivable, if not by everyone then by some ones—some who will perhaps even thrive, opportunistically, on the tail end of the others' disaster."[3] An opportunistic thriving on someone else's disaster or even death is perhaps what being labeled resilient allows. You've made it, either through your own disaster or through witnessing someone else's; your survival is highlighted while your struggle is relegated to the past. Such de-emphasizing also highlights individual outcomes over communal issues that continue to occur, like the opioid epidemic. As I will explore further below, individual over communal gain is a major player in the neoliberal appropriation of resilience.

Ethnomusicologist Jeff Todd Titon defines resilience as "a system's capacity to recover and maintain its integrity, identity, and continuity when subjected to forces of disturbance and change," explaining further that "resilience recognizes that perturbation, disturbance, and flux are constant characteristics of any complex system."[4] "Disturbance," according to folklorist Dorothy Noyes, "is inevitable," which makes sense environmentally and culturally but is more questionable when large numbers of life are disturbed—and lost—to a substance purposely made, prescribed, and shared by fellow humans.[5] In pointing to the neoliberal co-optation of the concept of resilience, Noyes notes, "Social policy and corporate governance seek to make us resilient." "In other words," Noyes says, "we are on our own—and the creek is gonna rise. . . . The public idiom of resilience evinces a loss of societal confidence in the modern progress narrative. Its rise indexes the decline of institutional willingness to assume responsibility for the collective wellbeing. We might call it abdication."[6]

In "Compromised Concepts in Rising Waters: Making the Folk Resilient," Noyes critiques the concept of resilience as a reactionary, not preventative, tool of neoliberalism—continuing the cycle that causes the need for resilience in the first place. For Noyes, a word like *resilience* is what she calls a "slogan-concept": "an abstraction that seems to validate concrete realities, the name of a purportedly eternal idea used to launch a time-specific project, a tent providing shelter to actors coming from all directions."[7] According to Noyes, slogan-concepts do quite a bit of work: (1) "They simulate analytical power"; (2) attract attention to the decorative while deflecting attention from the embarrassing; (3) "propose solutions for problems that have not been examined"; (4) "offer a direction that enables movement" and advancement of a larger project; (5) "discipline the behavior of marginalized actors by reconstructing all alternatives as a negative Other to themselves"; and (6) "attract marchers" or advocates.[8] Slogan-concepts are often employed as tools "for mobilizing (or immobilizing) the marginal"[9] and "for retaining power."[10]

To understand how slogan-concepts like resilience might thrive as tools of neoliberalism, we must first examine how neoliberalism functions, especially in the United States, where the opioid epidemic takes hold. According to Manfred B. Steger and Ravi K. Roy, neoliberalism is manifested in three ways: as an ideology focused on "global trade and financial markets, worldwide flows of goods, services, and labour, transnational corporations, offshore financial centres, and so on"; as a mode of governance "rooted in entrepreneurial values such as competitiveness, self-interest, and decentralization" that "celebrates individual empowerment and the devolution of central state power to smaller localized units"; and as a policy package of DLP, "(1) **d**eregulation (of the economy); (2) **l**iberalization (of trade and industry); and (3) **p**rivatization (of state-owned enterprises)."[11] We might view the pharmaceutical industry that has helped foster opioid addiction in the United States as a particularly neoliberal agent.

In *The Addiction Solution: Treating Our Dependence on Opioids and Other Drugs*, Lloyd I. Sederer notes two interconnected events that help us understand the rise of the current opioid epidemic in the US as well as how the pharmaceutical industry is connected to that rise: "Purdue Pharmaceuticals, the maker of OxyContin, drew upon scientifically flimsy evidence to declare that the use of its branded opioid carried essentially no risk of addiction," and "the American Pain Society [decided] to call pain the fifth vital sign, joining blood pressure, pulse, respiration, and temperature as the essential measurements doctors need to perform upon seeing every patient."[12] Beth Macy, journalist and author of *Dopesick: Dealers, Doctors, and the Drug Company That Addicted America*, notes how this new focus on health surveys and ratings caused a shift from seeing people as patients to seeing people as consumers, where "doctors and hospitals alike competed to see who could engender the highest scores, incentivizing nurses and doctors to treat pain liberally or risk losing reimbursements" while Purdue Pharmaceuticals' reps "fanned out to evangelize to doctors and dentists in all fifty states with this message: Prescribing OxyContin for pain was the moral, responsible, and compassionate thing to do—and not just for dying people with stage-four cancer but also for folks with moderate back injuries, wisdom-tooth surgery, bronchitis, and temporomandibular joint disorder, or TMJ."[13] We can see, then, the workings of neoliberalism through the intertwined histories of the rise of drug use—especially opioids and OxyContin—in the United States and the branding, marketing, and distribution of drugs like OxyContin by the pharmaceutical industry to its consumers. We see goods (OxyContin) and services (prescribing, marketing, and distributing of OxyContin) flow through self-regulating markets that encourage competition (among doctors and prescribers) and self-interest (financial gain) while benefiting from lax regulations and low government intervention, as suggested by the ongoing epidemic and continuation of prescribing practices despite thousands of opioid overdose deaths each year.[14]

If we are so resilient, it appears we are also enduring a lot of death, destruction, pain, and loss along the way. Noyes concludes "Compromised Concepts in Rising Waters: Making the Folk Resilient" with a quote the Louisiana Justice Institute posted around New Orleans after the devastation of Hurricane Katrina in 2005: "Stop calling me RESILIENT[.] Because every time you say, 'Oh, they're resilient,' that means you can do something else to me. I am not resilient."[15] Perhaps, by shifting our focus back to the endurance of people living through trauma, death, and disaster like that caused by the opioid epidemic, we can also better focus our attention on the messy, ongoing crisis that—although some celebrated individuals have resiled[16] through—people living with the opioid epidemic are still very much enduring. By shifting our focus to the group instead of the individual, we might also remove some of the systemic power of neoliberal agents to co-opt slogan-concepts like resilience to distract us from a public health problem we might not so easily recoil and recover from. The following section explores how the opioid epidemic is artistically represented to think about individual resilience and an empathetic gaze versus group endurance and actively noticing how the epidemic is intertwined in the everyday lives of those directly and indirectly affected by the crisis.

OPIOID-ADDICTION PORN, EMPATHY, AND EVERYDAY ENDURANCE

Williamson, West Virginia, has a population of around 3,200 people, yet from 2006 to 2016 "nearly 21 million prescription painkillers [were] shipped to [two pharmacies in the] tiny town" in Mingo County; if divided evenly among the town's residents, that is "more than 6,500 pills per person."[17] An investigation into the country's opioid epidemic by the House Energy and Commerce Committee revealed that two drug distribution companies, H. D. Smith and Miami-Luken, were also responsible for "extensive shipments" of opioids "to pharmacies elsewhere in West Virginia, including Beckley, Kermit, Mount Gay-Shamrock and Oceana."[18] According to the US Centers for Disease Control and Prevention (CDC), West Virginia has the highest rate of deaths from drug overdoses in the United States,[19] and as Beth Macy notes in *Dopesick*, "Though the opioid epidemic would go on to spare no segment of America," Appalachian towns like those in West Virginia were "among the first places where the malaise of opioid pills hit the nation in the mid-1990s, ensnaring coal miners, loggers, furniture makers, and their kids."[20]

Around an hour's drive from Williamson, one of the towns mentioned in the House report, Oceana (in southern West Virginia's Wyoming County), is the subject of Brooklyn-based filmmaker Sean Dunne's 2013 documentary-like feature *Oxyana*.[21] The film opens with a short scene of a man describing the pain of losing family, presumably to drug-related death. This scene is followed by over two minutes of scenery shots from a moving vehicle accompanied by deep music arguably meant to evoke the dark and sad seriousness of the town's situation: becoming "the epicenter of the OxyContin epidemic, earning the nickname Oxyana."[22] The two minutes of moving scenery take us on a tour of the town as we might experience it throughout a typical day. The morning begins with foggy mountains and a camper in the woods; as we drive along the winding road—which, according to critic Marlow Stern, resembles a drive one might take in a horror film like *The Shining*—we meet coal trucks, vehicles leaving Oceana, coal mining machinery, dirty and unkept homes and trailers, run-down local businesses, and a baptism in a river.[23] In the light of day, we see few people, but as night falls (indicated by the dramatic illumination of a buzzing street light) and darkness (both literal and figurative) descends, the residents of the town emerge and move within the shadows, illuminated by the neon signs of corporate chains like McDonald's, 7-Eleven, and Family Dollar shown in figure 1.1. In figure 1.2, under the light of a Family Dollar sign, a man uses a payphone, and the scene concludes with the man walking past a dusty storefront into the darkness of the night shown in figure 1.3.

If this description of the film's opening seems dramatic, it's because the opening *is* dramatic, an over-the-top depiction hinting that the sleepy town only comes alive in the shadows of night when the residents partake in equally shadowy actions and behaviors. Throughout the seventy-eight-minute film, we see four of these two- to three-minute moving scenes accompanied by eerie music and images like figure 1.4 with graveyards, industrial coal machinery, lush landscapes, and corporate signage along the winding road. The film ends with one of these musical scenes that highlight the faces of the twenty or so white Wyoming County residents the film travels with. These are the faces of people—whether personally, directly, or indirectly—touched by the opioid epidemic; these are the faces of *Oxyana*. The final face we see is that of a newborn baby.

Oxyana has been heavily critiqued as exploiting stereotypes about Appalachia and exceptionalizing the region, allowing viewers to see opioid-epidemic issues as occurring over there in that problematic place full of problematic people instead of all over the United States, often touching us in everyday occurrences. Appalachian studies scholar and anthropologist Mary Anglin argues that the film is an "illustration of how a particular iconography

Figs. 1.1–1.3. Sean Dunne, dir., *Oxyana*, 2013, 1:00:18; 2:47; 2:55.

Fig. 1.4. Sean Dunne, dir., *Oxyana*, 2013, 30:49.

of Appalachia—the lush imagery of densely forested mountains juxtaposed with footage of buildings in disrepair and trash littering yards, the roadside, everywhere—has been employed to depict the deeply flawed lives (and psycho-social makeup?) of the region's inhabitants."[24] Anthropologist and public health expert Lesly-Marie Buer furthers Anglin's critique: "By making Oceana and Appalachia appear exceptional, prescription drug misuse is 'othered' as something that happens among 'hillbillies' and the structures of power that continue to propagate misuse are left in the shadows."[25]

The film excludes any scientific data or numbers collected about the opioid epidemic, which is perhaps why reviews of the film make generalizations about the town, such as "Oceana has been dubbed the unofficial OxyContin capital of the world, with the majority of its residents addicted to the phar-maceutical drug."[26] Film critic and IndieWire writer Maggie Lange notes the "conscious choice to keep the documentary devoid of statistics, or graphs, or narration, or labels."[27] Dunne notes that this absence was a deliberate choice, remarking that "this is to give these people a voice . . . there are no experts in this film" and that "from the beginning we wanted to make something that was immersive as opposed to informative, a portrait as opposed to a social action-type documentary."[28] The portrait, though, unfortunately leaves out "the associations between misuse and pharmaceutical companies' aggressive marketing strategies and health inequalities," which Buer argues "results in a documentary that makes Oceana and drug use in the area appear exceptional. Appalachia is framed as separate from rather than part of the United States."[29] Further, Dunne's comments patronize the people in the film by suggesting the personal narratives and traumas they share don't make them experts of their own experiences.

Dunne does attempt to create an empathetic view toward the people affected by the opioid epidemic, but, as folklorist Amy Shuman notes, "Empathy can [also] produce alienation."[30] Drawing on such trauma theory scholars as Cathy Caruth, Shuman points out that "trauma victims require witnesses, rather than empathy."[31] Dunne's film does evoke witnessing by allowing some people to share their stories of trauma and survival and depicting what survivors and their families must endure. However, a work "designed to create empathy and to move the emotions of the reader rather than satisfy the teller whose experiences are told" also leads toward preservation of "a distance between those who understand and those who experience trauma."[32] For Shuman, empathy "depends on separation and is defined as a relationship that offers distance as a means of gaining perspectives on lives other than our own."[33] She ultimately claims that empathy thus "can lead to uncritical promotion of the appropriation of others' narratives for the good of the privileged appropriator and without regard for the cost to those whose narratives are used."[34] This is the danger of a film like *Oxyana*: "The appropriations are vulnerable in particular to two challenges: the criticism that in speaking on behalf of others the privileged group is further silencing an oppressed group; and the charge of voyeurism, that personal stories of personal suffering are used to satisfy privileged readers' desires to reassure themselves that they are better off than others."[35]

Oxyana's depiction of Oceana not only creates an empathetic portrayal that makes us feel momentarily sad for those "poor people in West Virginia," but it also draws upon poverty porn to create what we might call an opioid-addiction porn that only happens in exceptionally bad places like Oceana. Poverty porn, according to sociologist Tracey Jensen, aims "to transform precarity into a moral failure, worklessness into laziness and social immobility and disconnection into an individual failure to strive and aspire" while positioning "the lives of the poor as a moral site for scrutiny, something to be peered at, dissected and assessed."[36] Jensen furthers that, through presenting "the 'others' on the screen as dysfunctional in their choices and behavior," consumers of poverty porn are "compelled to understand social insecurity . . . as a problem of self-discipline, resilience and responsibility, rather than as a consequence of the extensions and excesses of neoliberalism." If resilience highlights—particularly an individual's—ability to survive disturbance, then films like *Oxyana*, despite highlighting what certain folks must endure because of the opioid epidemic, further feed into neoliberalism's co-optation of resilience as a slogan-concept. Only this time, the resilient person is the one who witnesses a problem and is able to escape it, especially when that problem exists in the faraway hills of Appalachia.[37] Just as Noyes notes the ways that neoliberalism has co-opted resilience, neoliberalism also benefits from poverty and opioid-addiction porn, allowing viewers to feel momentary sadness for those affected without having to act or think beyond an individual's resilience (and our own) despite the wider systemic issues they continue to endure. Noyes might, again, call this abdication.

Yet somewhere between the empathetic person's uncritical passivity as they consume opioid-addiction porn and our tendency as academics and advocates to celebrate resilience despite such continuing trauma are those on-the-ground lives of people *enduring* everything our neoliberal system throws at them. And somewhere between *Oxyana* and on-the-ground work being done to survive this epidemic is a poem—a creative representation—about complicated, complex life in West Virginia. Isabelle Shepherd's 2018 poem "Backtalking a Guy Who Tries to Get Your Number by Saying *You're Not What I Expected Out of a West Virginian, Not a Redneck at All*"[38] takes us on a sometimes beautiful, sometimes challenging, sometimes contradictory journey of what being a West Virginian means. Shepherd's poem is also an example of what enduring the opioid epidemic looks like, of seeing the larger connections and entanglements that all feed into the mouth of a crisis that's swallowing us up and only spitting some of us—chewed up and soaked to the bone—back out to recoil and resile from what our people are going through.

The fifth line of the poem begins to highlight the contradictory love affair West Virginians often have with the systemic issues in the state:

It means to lose
cell service in the middle of an important conversation.

It means to lose cell service at the exact moment you'd like
to be done talking. It means

to leave West Virginia. It means to try to come back. Getting directions
to a bonfire, someone says, *You'll smell it, but you won't see it.*

It means it's part of an infrastructure problem. (5–11)

The poem continues to highlight some of the further complex contradictions of life in Appalachia. Hating the extractive industries that cause fatal diseases like black lung while loving the people who love those industries and live with fatal diseases because of them. Feeling guilty for leaving and feeling proud for living. Embracing the ugly and obscene. Feeling left behind and ignored by the rest of the country and feeling pride for setting the country on the right track of union, labor, and women's rights, strikes, rebellions, and dedication. Always knowing "it's part of an infrastructure problem" (11) and that "a man with an enterprise / is far more dangerous than a man with a gun" (59–60). The poem emphasizes the everyday endurances of a group the rest of the country exceptionalizes as flawed, drug-addicted, and morally bankrupt, products of their own actions despite the careful strategies of larger power systems to financially exploit pain.

What sets Shepherd's poem apart from representations like Dunne's documentary is that the poem provides insight into how resilience is a part of endurance, how the individual is part of the group, and how larger systems and deadly epidemics are entangled in seemingly unexpected yet quotidian moments that we interact with in our daily lives. Why would a poem titled for a failed and insulting romantic encounter that took place outside of West Virginia also discuss indirect interactions with the opioid epidemic? Because the epidemic has become so commonplace not only in West Virginia and Appalachia but also in the whole of the United States that its traces linger in simple moments that reveal complex realities:

And you out there, you who put the mountain dew in our hands,
you legalized opiates and made my people rats to see how long it would
>   take

for us to die, or to kill or to grow
tumors in the places where our kidneys once lived.

To write a poem about West Virginia is to remember

my grandmother's voice and forget her secrets. It means going off
to college, and when you come home, you get stoned and drive through
>   town

with all the others that return on weekends
because you know here, your degree isn't good, so you all order munchies

from the Mountaineer Mart window because it's late
and it's gotten robbed so many times

they have to slide your chips and pepperoni rolls through a metal door.

It means you never want to believe the robbings are for pills,
oxies, but know they are. Something too pure

is killing us, they're bringing it in from up north. (63–77)

Even the act of buying a late-night pepperoni roll has been altered through the opioid epidemic, and these moments reveal how the epidemic weaves through our encounters in ways we can't ignore. How do we reckon with that realization? For Shepherd, that reckoning comes from not only highlighting the effects of the opioid epidemic but also the causes and systems that benefit from its continuation. The direct and indirect effects on the group outweigh the romanticized resilience of the individual and expose how enduring the epidemic is manifested in everyday actions that connect the West Virginian to those up north, the person living with addiction to the CEO of a pharmaceutical company, and the resilient to those still long enduring.

CONCLUSION: SHIFTING OUR FOCUS

In the 2012 article "Legends of Hurricane Katrina: The Right to Be Wrong, Survivor-to-Survivor Storytelling, and Healing," folklorist Carl Lindahl draws attention to certain interpretive viewpoints brought to the legends and stories told by survivors of Hurricane Katrina in 2005. One viewpoint often called upon by the media when viewing stories of survival is just world theory, which suggests a survivor is guilty of causing her own suffering, and another is the David effect, "through which blame migrates down the social scale and affixes itself to the poorest and most powerless."[39] To break these cycles of victim blaming that often accompany natural and social disasters (much like the opioid epidemic), Lindahl helped to establish the Surviving Katrina and Rita in Houston (SKRH) project to train and financially compensate survivors in interviewing other survivors to attempt healing and witnessing of trauma through storytelling. SKRH worked to "counter such psychic destruction in the wake of physical devastation" by helping "survivors secure the means to get their stories back, and share their stories with fellow survivors, in a deframed context, on their own terms."[40] Indeed, it is exactly this type of sharing, community organizing, and storytelling that can help build witness to the enduring effects of the trauma caused by the opioid epidemic in the United States. To close this chapter, I'd like to highlight how shifting our focus from individual resilience to group endurance can also draw attention to the vast amount of work people are continuously doing to help their fellow humans endure the crisis of the opioid epidemic. Often, this work not only benefits those currently living with addiction but also those who experience the effects of addiction rippling out to the larger community.

In "Coping with the Enduring Unpredictability of Opioid Addiction: An Investigation of a Novel Family-Focused Peer-Support Organization", Kelly, Fallah-Sohy, Cristello, and Bergman note, "While the vast majority of efforts has been focused on helping the opioid addicted individuals themselves, it has long been recognized that parents and other family members suffer greatly also from the grave and enduring unpredictability associated with having a relative with an opioid use disorder," which "has necessitated the rise of new organizations designed to provide face to face and online advice and peer-based social support to aid affected family members."[41] The authors mainly focus on the Massachusetts-based Learn to Cope (learn2cope.org), "a non-profit support network that offers education, resources, and peer support" that now has chapters in various states and "an online 'forum' which caters to approximately 7000 additional participants nationally."[42] Kelly, Fallah-Sohy, Cristello, and Bergman also found that "participants are primarily mothers of opioid addicted adult male children" who also "appear to be of White race, quite well educated . . . and with average household incomes at roughly twice the national average."[43] These results further suggest that the neoliberal urge to individualize and exceptionalize the opioid epidemic as only affecting poor, uneducated, rural hillbillies is quite a disservice to the larger populations of people who directly and indirectly encounter the crisis.

More regional groups are also working to not only assist people locally but also to assist those with more unique challenges to accessing recovery. In Wyoming County, West Virginia, the home of *Oxyana*'s subject, Oceana, another recovery and healing group has formed "to help those suffering from alcohol and drugs abuse."[44] Recovery in Wyoming County is a twelve-step program led by "licensed recovery coach and peer support specialist" Craig Rhodes, a former and recovering addict himself.[45] Rhodes was inspired to create the program because he had trouble finding "a support group for recovering addicts" in Wyoming County after "months in an intense drug recovery program."[46] The group meets regularly in locations across Wyoming County, and it recently joined forces with domestic violence resource groups to better address the " 'marriage between the addiction and the violence' " that can

sometimes accompany it.[47] This type of teaming up is a further acknowledge-
ment of how the opioid epidemic is endured not only by people living with
addiction and those in recovery but also by those with direct and indirect
ties to the crisis. Domestic violence survivor Brandi Massey, for example, was
threatened, kidnapped, and held at gunpoint by her boyfriend whose "drug
addiction fueled his erratic behavior."[48] Massey is excited for the meetings to
open to a wider audience: "You need somebody there to let you know that it's
okay, that you're going to start over, that you are going to make it through
everything . . . Because you're going to go through things. You're going to go
through anxiety, the depression. You're going to go through a lot and wonder
'why you,' more or less."[49]

As these groups and the work to assist in recovery and healing suggest, storytelling, witnessing, and a collective effort to live in the ongoing, messy, and
everyday effects of the opioid epidemic are some ways we just might survive
and even recoil back from such a devastating crisis and human-fueled disturbance that claims over one hundred lives each day.[50] The appropriation of the
term *resilience* by neoliberal agents romanticizes the individual over the group,
the result over the process, and the survival of few over the struggle of many.
If we want to resile our way through such a crisis, if we want to truly celebrate
our resilience, we must first focus on the work—however messy, hard, and
constant—many of us continue to endure every day. Resilience suggests an
overcoming, a finished product that survived the disturbance.

As of now, though, we are not quite resilient. We are still enduring.[51]

NOTES

1. Stephanie LeMenager and Dick Hebdige, "High and Dry: On Deserts and Crisis: Interview with Dick Hebdige," *Resilience: A Journal of the Environmental Humanities* 1, no. 1 (2014): http://rave.ohiolink.edu/ejournals/article/320667064.
2. LeMenager and Hebdige, "High and Dry," *Resilience: A Journal of the Environmental Humanities* 1, no. 1 (2014): para. 43, http://rave.ohiolink.edu/ejournals/article/320667064.
3. Stephanie LeMenager and Stephanie Foote, "Editor's Column," *Resilience: A Journal of the Environmental Humanities* 1, no. 1 (2014): n.p., http://rave.ohiolink.edu/ejournals/article/320667064.
4. Jeff Todd Titon, "Sustainability, Resilience, and Adaptive Management for Applied Ethnomusicology," in *The Oxford Handbook of Applied Ethnomusicology*, eds. Svanibor Pettan and Jeff Todd Titon (New York: Oxford University Press, 2015), 2, 38.
5. Dorothy Noyes, "Compromised Concepts in Rising Waters: Making the Folk Resilient," in *Humble Theory: Folklore's Grasp on Social Life* (Bloomington: Indiana University Press, 2016), 418.
6. Noyes, *Humble Theory*, 420.
7. Noyes, *Humble Theory*, 412.
8. Noyes, *Humble Theory*, 413–14.
9. Noyes, *Humble Theory*, 412.

10. Noyes, *Humble Theory*, 419.
11. Manfred B. Steger and Ravi K. Roy, *Neoliberalism: A Very Short Introduction* (New York: Oxford University Press, 2010), 12–14.
12. Lloyd I. Sederer, *The Addiction Solution: Treating Our Dependence on Opioids and Other Drugs* (New York: Scribner, 2018), 183–84.
13. Beth Macy, *Dopesick: Dealers, Doctors, and the Drug Company That Addicted America* (New York: Little, Brown, 2018), 32–33.
14. "Drug Overdose Deaths," Centers for Disease Control and Prevention, US Department of Health and Human Services, last modified June 27, 2019, https://www.cdc.gov/drugoverdose/data/statedeaths.html; "Opioid Overdose Crisis," National Institute on Drug Abuse, last modified January 2019, https://www.drugabuse.gov/drugs-abuse/opioids/opioid-overdose-crisis.
15. Noyes, *Humble Theory*, 432.
16. I use "resiled" here intentionally. Although I acknowledge that survival is associated with resilience, this adjective has been co-opted as a slogan concept, highlighting the end product of survival—attracting attention to the niceties of something, as Noyes would say—while distracting our focus from the process of endurance that makes someone resilient. Using a verb like "resiled" recognizes that process of endurance and emphasizes the movement of experiencing and enduring through something like the opioid epidemic.
17. Lindsey Bever, "A Town of 3,200 Was Flooded with Nearly 21 Million Pain Pills as Addiction Crisis Worsened, Lawmakers Say," *Washington Post*, January 31, 2018.
18. Bever, "A Town of 3,200 Was Flooded," *Washington Post*.
19. "Drug Overdose Deaths," Centers for Disease Control and Prevention.
20. Macy, *Dopesick*, 22.
21. Sean Dunne, dir., *Oxyana* (Cadillac Hash, 2013).
22. "About," Oxyana, accessed December 13, 2019, http://www.oxyana.com/about.html.
23. Marlow Stern, " 'Oxyana' Documentary, at Tribeca, Exposes the OxyContin Epidemic," Daily Beast, April 23, 2013, updated July 11, 2017, https://www.thedailybeast.com/oxyana-documentary-at-tribeca-exposes-the-oxycontin-epidemic.
24. Mary Anglin, "Framing Appalachia: A New Drug in an Old Story," *Journal of Appalachian Studies* 22, no. 1 (2016): 140–41.
25. Leslie-Marie Buer, "Oxyana," *Journal of Appalachian Studies* 20, no. 1 (2014): 90.
26. Stern, " 'Oxyana' Documentary."
27. Maggie Lange, "Tribeca: Breakout Director Sean Dunne Talks 'Oxyana' and a Portrait of a Town's Addiction," IndieWire, April 23, 2013, https://www.indiewire.com/2013/04/tribeca-breakout-director-sean-dunne-talks-oxyana-and-a-portrait-of-a-towns-addiction-198310/.
28. Lange, "Tribeca: Breakout Director Sean Dunne Talks 'Oxyana.' "
29. Buer, "Oxyana," 90.
30. Amy Shuman, *Other People's Stories: Entitlement Claims and the Critique of Empathy* (Urbana: University of Illinois Press, 2005), 144.
31. Shuman, *Other People's Stories*, 145.
32. Shuman, *Other People's Stories*, 145.
33. Shuman, *Other People's Stories*, 148.
34. Shuman, *Other People's Stories*, 148.
35. Shuman, *Other People's Stories*, 141–42.
36. Tracey Jensen, "Welfare Commonsense, Poverty Porn, and Doxosophy," *Sociological Research Online* 19, no. 3 (2014): 1–7, https://doi.org/10.5153/sro.3441.
37. For further reading on Appalachia as a distant or separate place see Allen Batteau's *The Invention of Appalachia* (Tucson: University of Arizona Press, 1990).
38. Isabelle Shepherd, "Backtalking a Guy Who Tries to Get Your Number by Saying *You're Not*

What I Expected Out of a West Virginian, Not a Redneck at All," *Powder Keg Magazine*, no. 12 (2018): n.p., https://www.powderkegmagazine.com/keegan-lester-isabelle-shepherd.

39. Carl Lindahl, "Legends of Hurricane Katrina: The Right to Be Wrong, Survivor-to-Survivor Storytelling, and Healing," *Journal of American Folklore* 125, no. 496 (2012): 139–76.

40. Lindahl, "Legends of Hurricane Katrina," 171.

41. John F. Kelly, Nilo Fallah-Sohy, Julie Cristello, and Brandon Bergman, "Coping with the Enduring Unpredictability of Opioid Addiction: An Investigation of a Novel Family-Focused Peer-Support Organization," *Journal of Substance Abuse Treatment* 77 (2017): 193–194.

42. Kelly, Fallah-Sohy, Cristello, and Bergman, "Coping with the Enduring Unpredictability of Opioid Addiction," 194.

43. Kelly, Fallah-Sohy, Cristello, and Bergman, "Coping with the Enduring Unpredictability of Opioid Addiction," 199.

44. "About," *Recovery in Wyoming County*, Facebook, accessed December 15, 2019, https://www.facebook.com/pg/craigr/about/.

45. Mary Catherine Brooks, " 'Recovery in Wyoming County' Moves into Oceana," *The [Beckley, WV] Register-Herald* , November 17, 2017.

46. Brooks, "Recovery in Wyoming County."

47. David Horak, "Recovery of Wyoming County, Resource Groups Unite to Provide Aid for Drug, Domestic Abuse Victims," Nexstar Media Group, Inc., November 9, 2018, https://www.wvnstv.com/news/west-virginia-news/wyoming-county/recovery-of-wyoming-county-resource-groups-unite-to-provide-aid-for-drug-domestic-abuse-victims/.

48. Horak, "Recovery of Wyoming County."

49. Horak, "Recovery of Wyoming County."

50. Wyoming County, West Virginia, is now home to several recovery and support programs including Wyoming County Peer Recovery Connections and Wyoming County Recovery Network.

51. Special thanks to Dr. Maurice Stevens of the Ohio State University, who first introduced me to the intersection of endurance and trauma.

CHAPTER 2

"Snort Pills on My Head": The Visual Rhetoric of Addiction, Abjection, and White Trash in *The Wild and Wonderful Whites of West Virginia*

Christopher Garland

Released in 2009, director Julien Nitzberg's feature-length documentary *The Wild and Wonderful Whites of West Virginia* (*TWWWWV*) was hailed as an "outlaw celebration" of the White family's willingness to "fuss and fight and party."[1] The White family first gained national attention through a short PBS documentary titled *Dancing Outlaw* (1991), which told the story of Jesco White, a West Virginia-born mountain dancer who inherited and practiced a particular style from his father, Donald "D. Ray" White, the family patriarch who fathered thirteen children before being shot dead by a nonfamily member during a fight.[2] However, this was not the first time that the family had caught the attention of documentary filmmakers: preceding *Dancing Outlaw* was the 1987 film *Talking Feet: Solo Southern Dance—Flatfoot, Buck and Tap*, directed by noted folklorist Mike Seeger, which profiled D. Ray. Released two years after his death, the film added to the family's regional notoriety. Taking *Dancing Outlaw* as a jumping off point—Nitzberg was a producer on that project—*TWWWWV* charts a year in the life of the White family. However, rather than extending the examination of Jesco, D. Ray, their dancing, and the violence and criminality that marked their lives, *TWWWWV* depicts what writer and film festival programmer Marc Walkow calls "the broad panoply of working class, rural Americana": the visual representation of "parking lot drug deals, home tattooing, unsafe gun handling, multiple visits to jail and rehab,

Fig. 2.1. Mamie White speaks directly to the camera. (From Julien Nitzberg, dir., *The Wild and Wonderful Whites of West Virginia*, 2009, reproduced in Bunnie Ears blog, December 3, 2011, https://bunnieears.wordpress.com/tag/the-wild-and-wonderful-whites-of-west-virginia/.)

courtroom appearances, trailer park antics, plenty of Confederate flags, and enough onscreen meth, pot and cocaine use for the viewer to practically get a contact high."[3]

As longtime residents of Boone County, the White family's bad reputation with the local establishment (a local evangelist, the district attorney, police officers) is revealed throughout the film via piece-to-camera interviews that detail their various antisocial and criminal activities. And while Jesco and Hank Williams III, a friend of the family and member of another iconic "Southern Rebel" clan, are the film's celebrity subjects—and feature prominently in the film's widely circulated trailer—*TWWWWV* concentrates on the female members of the family, specifically the journey of Kirk (D. Ray's granddaughter) from drug-addicted new mother to her admission into a drug addiction rehabilitation clinic, as well as Mamie (Jesco's sister) ascension to family matriarch after the death of her mother, the long-suffering Bertie Mae (D. Ray's wife)..

Through a close reading of the film's visual language, I argue that the film is constructed to mimic what A. O. Scott, in addressing other films, calls "the standard indie-film arc of abjection and redemption."[4] I will also address visual rhetoric and the documentary genre and then suggest that, despite its limitations, *TWWWWV* is an important documentary as it captures a specific moment at the beginning of the recent marked increase in synthetic opioid abuse and deaths from overdose. Furthermore, the Kirk subplot shows how the state's support (rather than incarceration) of one of the documentary's main subjects foreshadows changes in public policy as the epidemic worsened throughout the nation. Finally, this essay will put the representations of addiction, abjection, and white trash in *TWWWWV* into dialogue with visual representations in documentary and feature film of blackness and black abjection during the crack epidemic—an important synthesis that will highlight the cinematic treatment of those on the margins of society.

ABJECTION, WHITE TRASH, AND OPIOIDS ON SCREEN

To be clear, this extended engagement with the film is not an attempt to reclassify it as a "serious" documentary that fails to address and represent the aforementioned opioid crisis in a meaningful and comprehensive manner. Nor am I specifically concerned in this essay with how the film steers away from the cultural practices that gave the family notoriety in the first place: namely, D. Ray's creation of a particular style of dance and subsequent contribution to the rich history of West Virginia and its people. What I am interested in is the moment and space that *TWWWWV* captures in the relatively short but tragic recent history of the opioid epidemic—specifically, the illegal distribution and abuse of prescription painkillers in the contemporary United States. Whether through shots of family members snorting crushed-up oxycodone pills off a dirty toilet or rattling a pill bottle and calling the sound the local "mating call," the visual rhetoric of *TWWWWV* is steeped in abjection..

Produced by *Jackass* creators Johnny Knoxville and Jeff Tremaine through their Dickhouse Productions, *TWWWWV*'s visual language incorporates a blend of handheld shots, high-speed editing, and depiction of dangerous behaviors that call to mind the punk rock ethos and visual execution of the *Jackass* style (to be discussed further below). Here, the abject takes center stage; bodily fluids, consumption of dangerous substances, self-harm, and near-death experiences are displayed up close and in high definition to cause audiences to have visceral reactions that disgust and repel. Explicitly, *TWWWWV* trades in the kind of visual rhetoric that posits the drug-using white trash, "exploiting several intertwined [white] bourgeois anxieties, namely binaries of cleanliness and filth, attractiveness and ugliness, productive and unproductive labor—inclusion and exclusion."[5] The White family represents a whiteness apart, solidifying bourgeois white identity in contrast to an unhinged white proletariat. Moreover, in *TWWWWV*, the Whites are represented as the ultimate rural

Fig. 2.2. White family member with oxycodone pills. (From Julien Nitzberg, dir., *The Wild and Wonderful Whites of West Virginia*, 2009, reproduced in nopatpatgoku, Imgur, January 28, 2015, https://imgur.com/gallery/p9n8FWV.)

other, cast off from the American ideal of a law-abiding, sanitary, and orderly life. At the same time, due to the manner in which opioid addiction has moved from the margins of American life and barged into the homes of the country's middle and upper classes, the "corporeal reality"—to employ Julia Kristeva's term—of the porous barrier between the middle and upper classes and the financial and cultural other (namely, poor rural whites) became increasingly tangible.[6] Opioids were part of the dissolution; as the epidemic spread throughout the country, the castoffs became increasingly less distant.

Although a number of reviews mentioned the presence of prescription pill abuse and opioid addiction in *TWWWWV*, the majority of writing about the film chose to focus on the White clan's mythology: notably, the cult fame that came through the mountain dancing of family patriarch D. Ray and his son Jesco; their seemingly uncountable interactions with law enforcement and directly related predilection for interpersonal violence; the appearance and music of outlaw country hero Hank Williams III, a.k.a. Hank III; the family's willingness to allow the filmmakers access to all parts of their lives (from hospital rooms to intimate family gatherings to prison visitation tables); and the exotic nature of the West Virginia "holler" as backdrop to family drama. In short, critical reactions to the film frequently praised it as an insight into an "outlaw" family that embodied some version of freedom from contemporary

Fig. 2.3. Jesco White partying with family members. (From Julien Nitzberg, dir., *The Wild and Wonderful Whites of West Virginia*, 2009, reproduced in Grande Dame blog, December 20, 2012, https://www.grandedame.co.uk/2012/12/20/the-wild-wonderful-whites/.)

society's constraints. But in the film's diegesis, the Whites are linked by visual cues to a contemporary notion of so-called extreme "white trash" behavior: shooting guns outside of a trailer; wearing and displaying the Confederate flag; threatening violence to outsiders; fighting with one another; and maintaining suspicion of and resistance to any government intervention, unless it comes in the way of welfare, which allows them to continue in a lifestyle that is directly connected to an intergenerational transmission of poverty, ill health, and drug and alcohol addiction.

Admittedly, the term *white trash* is nebulous, shifting in meaning to various degrees according to specific contexts. Sometimes it has a clear synonym; other times it's a direct translation.[7] As outlined in Nancy Isenberg's *White Trash: The 400-Year History of Class in America*, the idiom was not born in the United States as a descriptor of the poor whites of the American South. Rather, the etymology is both longer and much more global. Essentially, it was born out of Britain's imperial project, in which poor whites from the metropole were moved around the world to build the various colonies, protectorates, dominions, mandates, and territories of the British Empire. As Isenberg notes, "After settlement, colonial outposts exploited their unfree laborers (indentured servants, slaves, and children) and saw such classes as human waste."[8] The history of white trash is intertwined with labels: "Long before they were today's 'trailer trash' and 'rednecks,'" Isenberg writes, "they were called 'lubbers' and 'rubbish' and 'clay-eaters' and 'crackers'—and that's just scratching the surface."[9] However, perhaps more important than the fact that there has been a terminology for poor whites throughout anglophone Europe's global expansion and "settlement" of the so-called New World is how this language shaped the idea of this particular class.

While the White family are certainly part of this historical continuum that stretches back into the early stages of the British imperial project, in the contemporary United States the term *white trash* is much more complex than an invective aimed at a certain node in the larger network of American class and race. In *Not Quite White: White Trash and the Boundaries of Whiteness*, Matt Wray asks us to look closely at the two words that make up the term. *White*, Wray argues, calls to mind cleanliness, purity, and the sacred. By conjoining

Fig. 2.4. Jesco White's tattoo depicting Elvis Presley and Charles Manson. (From Julien Nitzberg, dir., *The Wild and Wonderful Whites of West Virginia*, 2009, reproduced in Reel Reviews, http://reelreviews.com/tims-movie-challenge/the-ild-and-wonderful-whites-of-west-virginia-movie-review.)

it with a word so antithetical at a physical and metaphorical level, the term "names a kind of disturbing liminality: a monstrous, transgressive identity of mutually violating boundary terms, a dangerous threshold state of being neither one nor the other. It brings together into a single ontological category that which must be kept apart in order to establish a meaningful and symbolic order. . . . *White trash* names a people whose very existence seems to threaten the symbolic and social order."[10] But, for Wray, the threat posed by white trash goes beyond an existential threat to social order. There are material effects: the term can "evoke strong emotions of contempt, anger, and disgust. This is no ordinary slur."[11] Making the connection with abjection and its push and pull of attraction and repulsion, the Whites are posited as another kind of white: a comforting notion for (white) American audiences, in which Americans like the White family are a repository for fear about class slippage.

Despite the large amount of shots, sequences, and scenes that focus on opioid abuse and criminal behavior, which place the White family as occupying a "disturbing liminality" of social norms, the film was often read, at best, as some sort of ode to "the true rebels of the South"—to use Hank III's words—and, at worst, some kind of docu-comedy about a family in the American South who engage in "trailer park antics" (from a recent description of the film).[12] However, the film lacks any larger contextualization, and, in this way, plays into stereotypes about poor rural white Southerners as a people apart: not only from whites who occupy a different socioeconomic status but from the ideal American imagined community. The White family is positioned as the *über*-white trash: inevitably prone to violence; caught in an inescapable cycle of poverty; and, most of all, tied to a place and history from which they cannot escape.

VISUAL RHETORIC, THE DOCUMENTARY GENRE, AND *TWWWWV*

If the analysis of how texts persuade is the main component of rhetoric, then it would follow that documentary film (where the construction of argument is central to many texts in that genre) is an ideal candidate for rhetorical analysis. This is especially pertinent considering what documentary film scholar Bill Nichols describes as modern film theory's examination of film as systems of signs (images); in this paradigm, there has been "assumed a certain transparency between sign and referent (reality)."[13] Although Nichols admits that there have been filmmakers and critics who have transcended this particular view, there are central questions Nichols posed in his seminal 1978 essay that still hold: "What happens, however, if we refuse to trust the image's transparency, if we refuse to take on faith this apparent re-presentation of reality itself?"[14] When applying these questions to documentary film, I contend that we are engaging in a rhetorical analysis of the film. How is the filmmaker using particular rhetorical appeals (say, for example, the logos of facts and figures)? Can we trust the validity of the facts and figures included in a film? Nichols asserts that the critical scrutiny that should be applied to the relationship between sign and referent in fictional feature films is also applicable to documentary film. In David Bordwell and Kristin Thompson's canonical work of film studies, *Film Art*, the authors assert that a "documentary film purports to present factual information about the world outside the film. . . . What justifies our belief that a film is a documentary? For one thing, a documentary typically comes labeled as such. The label leads us to assume that the persons, places, and events exist and the information presented about them is trustworthy."[15] For Bordwell and Thompson, facts and labeling appear to be primary elements in establishing what is and what isn't a documentary. But whose facts? And to what ends do those facts serve?

In regards to the rhetorical choices made by the *TWWWWV*'s filmmakers, for Hank Williams III, one of the documentary's most significant participants and a popular musician whose output ranges from punk rock to country, the selection of facts and subsequent rhetorical appeals that were employed by the filmmakers to connect with the film's audience too often focused on the aforementioned behavior. The film's rhetoric, according to Williams, shifted far from the reason the family initially caught the attention of the "outside" world (namely, the White men's contribution to a specific art form) and instead zeroed in on the Whites as "redneck hillbillies" who are a purely "dope dealing, pill snorting, felonious outlaw brood."[16] Williams was clear about his assessment of the film's persuasive appeals:

> I really don't support that movie man. . . . They promoted more the dark side: the addiction, the bad stuff. They didn't really promote the creative side of the Whites. And this is no disrespect to Jesco and the family at all. It's more of *the people that made it should* have concentrated a little bit more on the creativity, and the good vibes that the White family bring to the table. Yeah, we all have problems with addiction, and stuff like that, but they made that a little too dark for me. I've only seen a couple of clips of it, just enough to rub me raw.[17]

While Williams features prominently throughout the documentary, the specter of his infamous country outlaw family also looms large over the film. By virtue of his last name and his own cult following as a punk/country impresario, Hank III is no less a "hillbilly icon" than Jesco; in fact, Williams's ethos is formulated through his direct lineage to country royalty. But the "dark side" of addiction and the representation of white trash in popular culture is also a marker of the Williams family's prominence. Hank III's father, Hank Jr., penned "O.D.'d in Denver," a song that includes the refrain, "But I O.D.'d in Denver, and I just can't remember her name." Hank Jr.'s willingness to disclose such raw subject matter through song is reminiscent of the candor displayed by the White family, who, like Williams, attached addiction to their public personas. Rather than writing and recording a song to be released on a record, played live, and broadcast on radio, the White family divulge their various demons in piece-to-camera testimonials. As with the Whites, substance abuse is part of the Williams family lore, reaching back to Hank III's grandfather's death. Born and raised in Alabama in entrenched white poverty, Hank Williams led a life marred by drug and alcohol addiction, which ultimately ended his iconoclastic musical career when, at age twenty-nine, he was found dead in the back of a car in Oak Hill, West Virginia (coincidentally, a hundred or so miles away from Boone County).[18] Whether or not his grandson knows that part of his grandfather's biography is not revealed in the film, but, if so, it might reveal his investment in a region of the world that revered his father as a seminal part of their rural white culture.

The scion of a family whose legacy is a Southern tapestry of staggering addiction and equally impressive musical achievement, Hank III appears in the first shot of the film—a shot that embodies the way that prescription drugs

Fig. 2.5. Jesco dances while Hank Williams III sings and plays the guitar. (From Julien Nitzberg, dir., *The Wild and Wonderful Whites of West Virginia*, 2009, reproduced in Lauren Wissot, "Interview: Julien Nitzberg on *The Wild and Wonderful Whites of West Virginia*," *Slant Magazine*, June 21, 2010, https://www.slantmagazine.com/film/interview-julien-nitzberg/.)

are a visual subtext that runs throughout the film—where he stands in front of a sign that says "prescriptions." In a few prominent segments later in the film, Williams—who himself comes from a family rich in American music significance, being the son and grandson of country music legends Hank Williams and Hank Williams Jr.—talks about the White family's musical history, his relationship with Jesco, and the significance of D. Ray White's contribution to American mountain dance and Southern culture as a whole. Most significantly, we see the connection between the earlier representation of the White clan and this more contemporary version in a scene that is shot outside of Williams's cabin near Nashville, Tennessee. In the scene, Williams is seated on a chair in the foreground of the camera's frame while Jesco stands on a picnic table behind him, his large figure taking up a significant portion of the frame. While Williams strums rapidly on an acoustic guitar and performs a song, "PFF" (also known as "Punch, Fuck, Fight"), Jesco dances along. For about forty-five seconds, the scene alternates between wide shots and close-ups of Williams, White, and the cabin; following in his (excuse the pun) footsteps, Jesco demonstrates the particular style of dance first recorded and circulated for a wider American audience through the 1987 PBS special *Talking Feet: Solo Southern Dance—Flatfoot, Buck and Tap* that starred his father. This scene takes on greater weight considering the fact that, not only does it capture the seemingly distant moment of Jesco's own notoriety and time as a primary focus of a documentary, it is a callback to the documentary films that led to the production of *TWWWWV*.

However, by including what Williams calls the "dark side: the addiction, the bad stuff," one could argue that the film is a response to a particular social exigency: the coming zenith of the opioid crisis and the affect that it has at the micro (the White family) and the macro (Boone County and West Virginia as a whole). This is the duality of the film. It can be read as an exploitative, stylized extension of the *Jackass* empire to now include the cliché "outlaw family" who occupy a liminal space in the milieu of the early twenty-first-century United States, but it also serves as a record of a moment in the history of the opioid epidemic in which addiction and abjection was something we could project on to a specific other: the white trash of the poorest rural and semirural spaces in the United States.

This amplification of otherness extends to the film's paratexts. For example, my first encounter with *TWWWWV* came by way of seeing a short synopsis of the film, accompanied by an image of its promotional poster. Even now, having seen the film a number of times, the poster sits prominently in my memory, perhaps because I looked closely at it before reading the synopsis.

The central image is what appears to be a young woman's naked upper back with the title of the documentary "tattooed" across her back. From the letters, which are in a standard tattoo shop-available font, there are red streams of "blood." In the background of the poster there is a bearded man facing the woman, his face blurred and shadowed. The composition and content have the feel of a horror movie, something one might see for a film in the horror or thriller genre—evoking a certain kind of pathos (trepidation) in the audience. At the top of the poster are the words that enticed me to find out more about this film: "from the creators of *Jackass*." In the YouTube era, a television show like *Jackass*—which consisted of short segments featuring often-dangerous stunts (say, for instance, flipping a motorized cart and landing on one's head in a potentially fatal accident) or slapstick pranks (a young man wearing nothing but a skimpy "G-string" and approaching strangers while performing a faux-Chippendale-style dance routine)—might be joining a crowded market of video of extreme behavior, but in the early 2000s, *Jackass* was an incredibly popular culture juggernaut.

In terms of its visual language, *Jackass* consisted of shots, sequences, and scenes of young men behaving badly: sneaking onto a golf course with an air horn that they would blow when middle-class white men were teeing off; snorting lines of wasabi at a Japanese restaurant; hanging out the top of a speeding jeep while getting a tattoo; placing a number of anacondas in a children's ball pit. The *Jackass* cast reveled in a punk-rock, white-trash ethos, embodied most strongly by their intrepid leader, the (aptly) self-named Southerner, Johnny Knoxville. The rapid editing, risk-taking behavior, and featuring of a cast of different characters is a trope we see repeated in the *TWWWWV* and its essential paratext, the film's trailer, which, as of January 2019, had close to 1.4 million views on YouTube. The trailer foregrounds drug use, first showing a medium close-up of Mamie and Jesco sharing smoke from an unidentified substance and then the following shot of Mamie snorting powder off of a decorative plate. From a 2019 worldview in which drug abuse in rural communities has received a great deal of attention, the depiction of drug use in the film is jarring. However, when the film was released in 2009, the overwhelming nature of the next wave of the epidemic and its effects on the nation's fabric was not necessarily apparent. But, when employing the relational thinking that is enabled by looking back at a film from previous years from the vantage point of the present, some scenes hold a particular poignancy. When the viewer is first introduced to Kirk, we learn of her numerous drug charges. But, as the film sets up shortly after, Kirk is not an outlier in the family: drug dealing is featured in the opening sequences of the film with the matriarch of the family, Bertie

Mae White, stating, in a very prescient moment, that "(prescription) drugs are going to take over the world." Shortly after, there is a sequence that demonstrates the incredible access that the filmmakers had to the White family.

Of all the moments in *TWWWWV* that show the extent to which drug use is part of the film's visual rhetoric, the hospital room scene might be the most pertinent. Kirk is in bed, shortly after giving birth. She is clearly upset but has her cousin by her side, ostensibly providing comfort as a supportive family member. However, a couple of shots later, Kirk and her cousin start snorting a powdery substance from the bedside table—if the other drugs of choice for various family members are any indication, it's a prescription painkiller or anxiety pill. In the next sequence, Kirk breaks down again: her newborn is being taken from her by "the state." In terms of representing the White family as the abject subject of the film, this scene is not the film's only low point. Shortly after, as a family member tattoos a family friend, he shows his shaky hands to the camera. "That's what happens when you're on Xanax," he deadpans. The action returns to Kirk, where she is popping pills in the back of the van on the way to federal prison.

By framing Kirk's pre-rehab bender as a girl's night out, *TWWWWV* posits addiction as comic relief. But, at the same time—and this speaks to the duality of interpretation possible with this documentary—her eventual entry into a rehab clinic, successful completion of the program, and reunification with her children is more than what A. O. Scott calls the aforementioned "standard indie-film arc of abjection and redemption." Kirk is not a fictional character, and by focusing on her in the second half of the documentary, *TWWWWV* shows a real-world example of state-sponsored assistance for an opioid addict helping to bring a family back together and offering the possibility of long-term sobriety. Moreover, the kairos (timeliness) of the film in terms of showing Kirk's journey needs to be considered. On the micro level, opioid addiction is treated as less problematic—and, in general, receives less direct attention—than the White family's other ills. For example, one particular subplot concerning Brandon (grandson of D. Ray and Bertie) and his attempted murder of his uncle Billy Hastings (boyfriend of Mamie) in a drug-fueled intrafamily feud is given a more thorough examination and explanation than the other forms of drug use that we see throughout the film. (Brandon is ultimately convicted and sentenced to fifty years in prison.) Instead, addiction and drug use is a family mantra in *TWWWWV*—mimicking such antidrug visual representations as the long-running A&E network television show *Intervention* or the various documentaries that deal with specific moments and places of the epidemic, such

Fig. 2.6. Kirk White speaks directly to the camera. (From Julien Nitzberg, dir., *The Wild and Wonderful Whites of West Virginia*, 2009, reproduced in *Asylum Attendant* blog, January 6, 2014, https://asylumattendant.wordpress.com/2014/01/06/the-wild-and-wonderful-whites-of-west-virginia/.)

as *One Nation, Overdosed* (2017), *Heroin(e)* (2017), *Heroin, Cape Cod* (2015), *Chasing the Dragon: The Life of an Opiate Addict* (2016), and *Warning: This Drug May Kill You* (2017). In one of the recurring piece-to-camera interviews with Mamie White, one of the filmmakers asks her what she wants to see happen at her funeral; she responds that she wants the attendees to "smoke pot" and "snort pills on [her] head." Some of the critical responses to the film demonstrate a clear fetishization of rural poverty and its adjacent social ills. In his review of the film for the *Los Angeles Times*, Gary Goldstein shows some of this worldview in his opening salvo. "Move over Osbournes, hit the road Kardashians," Goldstein writes, "there's a new dysfunctional, reality TV-ready family in town: a lawless bunch of self-described 'just right down dirty white good old people hillbillies' [who are] the stars of the nutty, oddly involving documentary."[19]

In this comparison to two of the most famous and successful reality shows—the early 2000s hit *The Osbournes* and *Keeping Up with the Kardashians*, a show that has itself spawned several hit spinoffs—Goldstein (consciously or not) brings up the issue of genre but not of class or socioeconomic status; the gulf between the Whites and the Osbournes or Kardashians is fairly obvious.

Later in the short review, Goldstein refers to the Whites as living in "chaotic, impoverished glory"—his description calls to mind the language used in other "outsiders'" poverty pornography rhetoric. The spectacle of those living on the margins—caught up in the "inherent cycle of poverty" (a phrase that's deeply ingrained in the popular discourse apropos the gaping disparity between the richest and poorest in this country)—has a long history in Appalachia. "If we constructed a mythology for Appalachia, one of the most powerful and fickle world-makers in our pantheon would be the stranger with a camera," writes Elizabeth Catte in "Passive, Poor and White? What People Keep Getting Wrong about Appalachia." A resident of the region and historian of its representation on the national stage, Catte asserts that the outsider's gaze and camera have been a constant in Appalachia: "Ever present throughout our history, the stranger appears in the region not to capture reality but contradictions."[20]

The most famous examples of the visual rhetoric of white poverty in West Virginia come in the form of photographs—a massive archive of miners covered in coal dust, shacks in ruinous condition with trash in front of them, and children emaciated (in the 1960s) or obese (in the 2000s). The repository of West Virginia as superlatively other, however, also includes the photographs of John F. Kennedy's tour through West Virginia during his 1960 campaign (which is a notable bookend to the more widely known footage of then attorney general Robert Kennedy's visit to Appalachian Kentucky in 1968). Apart from that specific moment of the white Appalachian other, in the words of AnnLouise Keating, " 'whiteness' has functioned as a pseudo-universal category that hides its specific values, epistemology, and other attributes under the guise of a nonracialized supposedly colorless, 'human nature.' "[21] In texts and representations like *TWWWWV*, this notion of the whiteness as a "pseudo-universal category" is disrupted. As with the aforementioned reviews of the film, the White family are viewed as the epitome of a "redneck brood" in a documentary filled with rampant white trash "fun," exemplified by what one critic describes as the "husband-slashing Kirk White snorting lines of crushed prescription pills in a hospital room mere moments after putting her newborn daughter to sleep."[22] The visual rhetoric of scenes like this contribute to the documentary's lore, wherein the Whites embody the most exaggerated stereotypes of American white trash: threatening violence against kin and outsiders alike; guzzling Mountain Dew; getting offensive tattoos (at the end of the film, Jesco adorns his body with depictions of both Elvis Presley and Charles Manson); and coping with legal troubles, health issues, unemployment, and general family friction by devouring drugs and alcohol.

TRANSCULTURAL REPRESENTATIONS OF ADDICTION
AND VISUAL CULTURE AS PATCHWORK

While I have kept close to *TWWWWV* and the framing of the White family as both über-white trash and romanticized social outlaws through the filmmakers' documentation of their "bad behavior," there is a precedent for this kind of visual rhetoric in recent representations of drug abuse: specifically, the urban crack epidemic of the 1980s and 1990s and the representation of African Americans in this context. Although a full exploration of the representation of race, class, and drug abuse is beyond the scope of this essay, I would be remiss to not mention the comparison between the crack epidemic and the opioid epidemic. Jennifer Egan, writing about the intersection of race, poverty, and the depiction of drug epidemics, states that we are in the midst of "a cultural overreaction reminiscent of the 'crack baby' hysteria," which significantly "overstated the negative effects cocaine would have on the children of pregnant women who smoked it."[23] This played out in a particular portrayal of a certain class and race of people, whose place in society was shaped by stereotypes that extended from the news media into the popular visual culture of film and television. But when comparing the popular representation of African American mothers who were crack addicts in the last two decades of the twentieth century and white mothers in the first two decades of the twenty-first century, " 'Crack moms' were nearly always represented as African American, adding racism to the mix of distortions at play in that perceived crisis. Race has worked the opposite way in our current epidemic—indeed, the perception of our opioid crisis as an *epidemic*, rather than a racial pathology, owes much to the fact that white Americans have been hard hit."[24] The crack mom/user was an oft-used archetype in the American hood film genre of the 1980s and 1990s, where, as Barbara Mennel argues, "stories of violence among urban Blacks associated with drugs and gang warfare and are set in decaying urban locales made to represent such problems as policing, drugs, gentrification; lack of jobs, resources, and education; incarceration and gang warfare."[25] In some of these visual representations, including *Training Day* (2001), *New Jack City* (1991), and *Menace II Society* (1993), particular black characters on the margins of America are not read as set apart from black culture writ large (as is the case with the Whites as white trash); rather, as Egan suggests, they are posited as *the* black experience in urban America, where drug abuse and criminality are part of the aforementioned "racial pathology."

In the years since the release of *TWWWWV*, representations of the opioid epidemic have become increasingly prevalent, being produced and circulated across various media platforms. While covering the breadth of just the contemporary documentary films in that very large repository of representation is far beyond what I can do here, I am interested in acknowledging this text as a fragment of a greater whole. W. J. T. Mitchell's theorizing about the production, circulation, and meaning of images is a particularly useful framework for this endeavor. Specifically, Mitchell's suggestion at the end of *Picture Theory: Essays on Verbal and Visual Representation* provides a theoretical paradigm about how to connect, for example, *TWWWWV* to the imagery employed in other depictions of the opioid epidemic. Mitchell writes, "But suppose we thought of representation, not as a homogenous field or grid of relationships governed by a single principle, but as a multidimensional and heterogenous terrain, a collage or patchwork quilt assembled over time out of fragments?"[26] Employing the idea of the visual text as part of a "patchwork or collage" will enable a teasing out of connections, differences, and specific contexts within these representations of the opioid crisis. Despite the singular focus of *TWWWWV* on one family in one part of one state at one particular moment, we know that the opioid epidemic is a sprawling network, connecting seemingly disparate social, economic, and political nodes. Putting these representations in conversation is an important extension of our critical engagement with this moment of crisis, allowing us to take in the magnitude of the opioid crisis and consider the necessary and significant responses that need to be taken.

Like trying to precisely measure the horrific, wide-ranging effects of the opioid epidemic through recent time and space, the ultimate impact of these kinds of representations is hard to pinpoint. In the course of writing this essay, I was asked by colleagues what I was currently working on. I would describe the documentary as succinctly as possible, trying not to fall into the very kind of stereotypes I've critiqued here. The majority of people I spoke to about this documentary hadn't heard of it (let alone seen it), but that was less disheartening than it may sound. In the course of writing of this essay, I came to realize one clear point: *The Wild and Wonderful Whites of West Virginia* is a significant documentary because it serves as record of a moment in time when the opioid epidemic seemingly belonged to the liminal Others—for those Americans for whom, just like the White family, Horatio Alger's "rags to riches" American narrative was more than incredibly distant. In fact, it was an alien concept, disproved in practical terms by generation after generation before them, where the mines maintained but chipped away at families, killing slowly by way of black lung and workplace accidents and finally the all-encompassing poverty that accompanied that industry's own demise. Since that time, the epidemic has seeped out from the stereotype of "trailer trash" and into the plush rooms of America's middle- and upper-middle-class homes. As with the other texts critiqued in this collection, *TWWWWV* belongs to the epistemology of a national crisis and tragedy that we must recognize if we are ever to reckon with its past and, just as importantly, its future.

NOTES

1. A. O. Scott, "From a Clan That Lives by Its Own Rules, a Tale for the Movies," *New York Times*, May 4, 2010, https://www.nytimes.com/2010/05/05/movies/05wild.html.
2. Jesco was also shot during the altercation.
3. Marc Walkow, "It's Hard to Be a White in West Virginia: Rebellion, Addiction and Rural America in 'The Wild and Wonderful Whites of West Virginia,' " Tribeca Shortlist, January 30, 2017, https://outtake.tribecashortlist.com/its-hard-to-be-a-white-in-west -virginia-b2bb9b8573ce.
4. A. O. Scott, "Moonlight: Is This the Year's Best Movie?" *New York Times*, October 20, 2016, https://www.nytimes.com/2016/10/21/movies/moonlight-review.html.
5. Travis Linnemann and Tyler Wall, "This Is Your Face on Meth: The Punitive Spectacle of White Trash in the Rural War on Drugs," *Theoretical Criminology* 1, (2013): 1–20.
6. John Fletcher and Andrew Benjamin, *Abjection, Melancholia, and Love: The Work of Julia Kristeva* (New York: Routledge, 1990), 93.
7. One of the characteristics of this particular invective is its universality. In South Africa, the *rooinek*, "redneck" in Afrikaans, were the largely Dutch (with some German and French influence) farmers who arrived in the southernmost parts of the continent in the 1600s.
8. Nancy Eisenberg, *White Trash: The 400-Year Untold History of Class in America* (New York: Viking, 2016), 1–2.
9. Eisenberg, *White Trash*, 2.
10. Matt Wray, *Not Quite White: White Trash and the Boundaries of Whiteness* (Durham, NC: Duke University Press, 2006), 2.
11. Wray, *Not Quite White*, 2.
12. Walkow, "It's Hard to Be a White in West Virginia."
13. Bill Nichols, "Fred Wiseman's Documentaries: Theory and Structure," *Film Quarterly* 31, no. 3 (1978): 15–28.
14. Nichols, "Fred Wiseman's Documentaries," 15.
15. David Bordwell and Kristin Thompson, *Film Art: An Introduction* (New York: McGraw-Hill, 2010), 110.
16. Bill Gibron, " 'The Wild and Wonderful Whites of West Virginia': This Is the Real America," Pop Matters, November 7, 2010, https://www.popmatters.com/1333214-the -wild-and-wonderful-whites-of-west-virginia-this-is-the-real-amer-2496114544.html.
17. "Hank III Disses New White Family Movie," Saving Country Music, July 26, 2010, https://www.savingcountrymusic.com/hank-iii-disses-new-white-family-movie/. Emphasis added.
18. In 2010, Hank Williams was posthumously awarded by the Pulitzer Prize jury a special citation "for his craftsmanship as a writer."
19. Gary Goldstein, "Movie Review: The Wild and Wonderful Whites of West Virginia," *Los Angeles Times*, June 24, 2010, https://www.latimes.com/archives/la-xpm-2010-jun-24 -la-wild-whites-west-story-story.html.
20. Elizabeth Catte, "Passive, Poor and White? What the Media Keeps Getting Wrong about Appalachia," *Belt Magazine*, February 8, 2018, https://beltmag.com/passive-poor-and -white.

21. AnnLouise Keating, "Interrogating 'Whiteness,' (De)Constructing 'Race,' " *College English* 57, no. 8 (1995): 904.
22. Nick Schager, "Review: *The Wild and Wonderful Whites of West Virginia*," *Slant*, May 3, 2009, https://www.slantmagazine.com/film/the-wild-and-wonderful-whites-of-west-virginia/.
23. Jennifer Egan, "Children of the Opioid Epidemic," *New York Times Magazine*, May 9, 2018, https://www.nytimes.com/2018/05/09/magazine/children-of-the-opioid-epidemic.html.
24. Egan, "Children of the Opioid Epidemic."
25. Barbara Mennel, *Cities and Cinema* (New York: Routledge, 2008), 156.
26. W. J. T. Mitchell, *Picture Theory: Essays on Verbal and Visual Representation* (Chicago: University of Chicago Press, 1994), 419.

CHAPTER 3

The Pill: Aesthetics, Addiction, and Gender in Jennifer Weiner's *All Fall Down*

Ashleigh Hardin

An addiction narrative is always in danger of undermining itself. It must not glamorize addiction, but it cannot be boring. A gritty tale can be accused of pessimism and inertia, but a euphoric narrative may be trite, preachy, or unrealistic. Though addiction narratives have been a staple of American literature since the nineteenth century, the twenty-first century confronts us with both moral and aesthetic dilemmas: from the national debates over authenticity and verisimilitude in James Frey's *A Million Little Pieces* (2003) to the highly stylized (but vaguely homophobic) depiction of sex addiction in Steve McQueen's *Shame* (2011) to the unethical and potentially dangerous consequences of asking addicts to "perform" addiction on reality TV shows like *Intervention* (2005–present). As new addiction narratives have proliferated over the last twenty years, deaths from opioid addiction have increased substantially. According to the Center for Disease Control, an American dies of an opioid overdose every eleven minutes.[1] Americans are now more likely to die from opioids than from automobile accidents.[2] Whether our narratives are compelling or clichéd, the death toll rises unabated. Examining a popular literary representation of opioid addiction, Jennifer Weiner's 2014 novel *All Fall Down*, brings to light the aesthetic and moral difficulties of representing the crisis.

To do so, it is useful to distinguish among different kinds of narratives about drug use. First, not every story of drug use or abuse is an addiction narrative; a story that focuses briefly on limited use, whether pleasurable or painful, of an addicting substance but does not explore repetition of the behavior or long-term consequences might be best termed an experimentation narrative, rather than an addiction narrative. Second, among addiction narratives, we may further distinguish by using Robyn Warhol's criteria of "euphoria" and "dysphoria."[3] A dysphoric addiction narrative ends in the protagonist's death, imprisonment, or other negative consequence; a euphoric addiction narrative sees the protagonist recover or at least take the first hopeful steps to do so. Women's stories of addiction, both fictional and real, may also be distinguished from men's, what often constitute the mainstream, literary addiction narrative. As Nancy Campbell notes, women's addiction was first perceived as a private, hidden problem.[4] Men's addiction was a topic of late eighteenth- and early nineteenth-century literary and popular texts; by the mid-twentieth century, the enormously influential Alcoholics Anonymous movement would produce a canon of addiction texts directed primarily at white male middle-class audiences. In *Inventing the Addict: Drugs, Race, and Sexuality in Nineteenth-Century British and American Literature*, Susan Zieger explores how addiction narratives, which "began as an exceptional story of white, middle-class self-making gone awry," gradually incorporated women.[5] In part, women became protagonists of addiction narratives when, during the nineteenth century, white women became subjects "who have much to lose—socially, financially, and psychologically."[6] Similarly, a woman's race and socioeconomic status inflect both the "privateness" of her story and the narratives available to her. In twentieth-century depictions of women's addiction, Campbell argues, "White women who use illegal drugs are also figured as 'cleaner' than women of color who do so. . . . Women of color who use drugs are depicted as the nonproductive inhabitants of chaos, decay, and squalor."[7] While nonwhite men of lower socioeconomic status are frequently criminalized for addiction (rather than subject to the therapeutic treatment often offered to their more privileged counterparts), they are not responsible for "reproducing" addiction (or culture more broadly) in the same way that female addicts are.

Although women's addiction narratives may typically rest outside the mainstream, female iatrogenic morphine addicts, women whose addictions began when their physicians legally prescribed hypodermic morphine for pain relief, were among the first to gain recognition by the medical community as "addicts."[8] In a sense, women not unlike Jennifer Weiner's typical "chick-lit" protagonists were the subjects of the inaugural opioid crisis. Thus despite the relative invisibility of female opiate addicts, David Courtwright notes that in the nineteenth century "the majority of [opium and morphine] addicts were women."[9] Women, especially those addicted in the course of treatment by a physician, remained the majority of opiate addicts until the early twentieth century, when the medical establishment began policing itself, limiting its "liberal use of opium and morphine."[10] Even among noniatrogenic opiate addicts, addicts whose use did not originate with a doctor's prescription, women were a significant part of the population, as taboos against women using alcohol to blunt their pain and anxieties did not apply to opiates.[11] Courtwright explains that opiates may have "suited the purposes of frustrated women whose aspirations had been blocked by male-dominated society."[12] However, women did not remain the majority of opiate addicts, nor did the therapeutic addict continue as the most prevalent or pressing type. Increasingly, the "nonmedical addict emerged as the dominant type," and this addict was predominantly male and marginalized by his class, race, and ethnicity.[13]

It is important to point out that, while women declined as a major contributor to opiate addiction in the twentieth century, they remained especially susceptible to iatrogenic addictions to other medicines. Courtwright notes that women were prescribed tranquilizers such as Valium and Librium at rates of two or three to one and that, "by the 1970s, one American woman in five over the age of 18 was taking tranquilizers for at least part of the year."[14] Also by the 1970s, drug enforcement policy had changed radically, and the government and medical establishments were far more focused on interdiction of illicit substances than the harms caused by overprescription of licit ones. Though female iatrogenic addicts, especially white upper-class ones like those depicted in Jacqueline Susann's *Valley of the Dolls* (1967), were not criminalized in the same ways that their male nontherapeutic counterparts were, the abiding existence of what Courtwright calls the "Mary Tyrone-style addict," a secretive, scarcely functioning female opiate user, suggests a continued inability to recognize and properly treat female pain, to intervene in nonpharmacological ways in women's lives, and to address addiction as a women's issue as well.[15]

Weiner's novel *All Fall Down* was published in 2014, shortly after the beginning of what the Center for Disease Control identifies as the "third wave" of opioid deaths.[16] It tells the story of Allison Weiss, an upper-class working mother who finds herself beset by financial, emotional, and social pressures. Formerly a graphic designer at a newspaper, Allison was pressured by her husband, Dave (a writer at the same newspaper), to quit her job and become a homemaker when he received a large advance on a book. Allison writes a blog about her life in her spare time for an audience of friends and family, but just as Dave's book deal falls through, one of Allison's posts goes viral, leading to a lucrative position as a writer for a women's blog called Ladiesroom.com. In her new role as the primary breadwinner for her family, she is overworked and the victim of her husband's resentment; however, the stay-at-home mother fantasy he forced upon her (complete with exurban McMansion he bought without telling her) does not fulfill her either. She lacks emotional fulfillment in most of her other relationships as well: she is the present parent for her "sensitive" daughter, Ellie, the active caretaker for her father, who suffers from Alzheimer's, and the long-suffering daughter of her absentee and alcoholic mother. Like many addicts, Allison's opioid addiction is iatrogenic; she began with a Vicodin prescription for a gym injury but progresses to stealing pills from her father and the medicine cabinet at Ellie's playmate's home and buying pills on the "dark web" in large quantities. She attempts to drive while intoxicated and is stopped by one of Ellie's teachers, who shares with Allison that her niece became hooked when painkillers were prescribed following a C-section and subsequently died of an overdose. This moral "rock bottom" does not lead Allison to rehab, but rather the debilitating physical effects of a withdrawal triggered by suboxone lead her to accept placement in an inpatient rehab facility.

Allison's use of opioids begins not solely with the doctor who prescribes Vicodin but also with the external pressure on women to maintain unrealistic standards of beauty. Allison exercises not because she enjoys it but because she worries about the rest of the world "bear[ing] witness to precisely how many chins [she] actually [has]."[17] She touches her body, feeling her "spread[ing]" hips and "the jiggly flesh" of her stomach.[18] She worries not only about the scrutiny she might face from her other mom-friends but also the anonymous critics of her blog posts who will take issue with her appearance, her feminist slant on the issues, or both. In the toxic milieu of anonymous online forums, Allison's less-than-ideal body both deserves punishment (as a physical manifestation of feminism) and is itself a punishment. Comments like *"I'd hit that . . . with a brick"* and *"This is why the terrorists hate us"* appear not on one of Allison's blog entries but on a newspaper's story on the website she writes for. Though she rationalizes that she isn't "real" to the commenters, just "a picture, a thing: Feminism, or Women Today,"[19] she must also confront the notion that her husband, Dave, is reading the comments as well, "watching the world consider his wife and find her wanting."[20] Allison's fears cannot remain confined to the internet. An email alert from her husband's computer shows he's exchanging flirty messages with a female colleague, and her mother calls to let her know she saw the comments and reassured her own friends that "probably not many people read it . . . Dave's the real writer, and you just do it for fun."[21] The reader is encouraged to see both Allison's injury and her resulting iatrogenic opioid addiction as operating in a matrix of familial, social, and physical pressures.

These pressures also align with concerns of aesthetic quality. The criticisms of Allison's body are rooted in unrealistic notions of feminine beauty. Her work as a writer is undermined (at least in part) because it is commercial (i.e., it earns her money) and because her roots are not in the printed word but the ephemeral image. The aesthetic critiques Allison faces mirror those of Weiner herself as a best-selling novelist with a devoted fan following. Weiner's publication of *All Fall Down* coincided with an increase in her advocacy for other women writers, particularly those writing in popular genres. Weiner has chafed at the label "chick lit," telling one interviewer that it "minimizes the work that women writers do and the lives women lead," adding that it allowed reviewers to "act like there's nothing substantive going on in these books."[22] She has also noted the hollowness of the label, predicated as it often is on "straight-up packaging and perception": "If your book has a cover that's just typography and color, it's literature, but if there's a female body part, it's chick lit. If you're smiling in your (color) photo, it's chick lit. If you're smirking, or giving a stern, thin-lipped stare in your black-and-white picture . . . then it's literature."[23] Despite their commercial success, Weiner's novels were long ignored by the critical literary establishment, though the *New York Times* ran a review of her in 2016 and the *New Yorker* published an in-depth profile in 2014. In addition to advocating for more serious consideration of her own work, Weiner has spoken for writers labeled "chick lit" or "mid cult" and encouraged other women writers not to state their own literary merits by negating the work of women writers of popular fiction.

For Weiner, the differences between popular and literary fiction, and the presumed supremacy of the literary over the popular, are based on gender differences rather than questions of taste. While the *New Yorker* rationalizes the lack of critical attention Weiner has received by explaining that "literary criticism, at its best, seeks to elucidate the complex, not to catalogue the familiar," Anne Helen Petersen's profile of Weiner in *Too Fat, Too Slutty, Too Loud: The Rise and Reign of the Unruly Woman* underlines the material basis of women's fiction.[24] For Petersen, the topic of aesthetics cannot be removed from the other functions writing serves for women, as "women's relation to writing has long been shaped by different forces: for many, if not most, part of the joy of writing was how its profits enable, and continued to enable, women to determine their own destiny—untethered to a man."[25] Addiction narratives have similar dual roles; whether or not a particular story of addiction and/or recovery is engaging or aesthetically pleasing, the telling of the story may give the addicted person some relief, some new agency, the ability to determine their own destiny. This is particularly true for women, whose addiction stories are often eclipsed by men's in mainstream and literary discourse.

However, *All Fall Down* will likely not be remembered among Weiner's best novels by any measure. In a scathing review for *NPR Books*, Annalisa Quinn terms the book a disappointment and claims Weiner only avoids glamorizing drug use through "clumsiness."[26] Quinn distances herself from critiques on the basis of genre by noting that all fiction, even the literary kind, operates within generic frameworks. Nonetheless, "*All Fall Down* is not mediocre because of its predictable ending or middle-aged white lady focus, [but] because it does not test its confines. . . . It doesn't even make you smile."[27] Even more positive reviews, such as Patty Rhule's in *USA Today*, provide tepid praise. Rhule suggests the book itself is addictive (precisely the opposite of Quinn's critique) but argues "it's not until the last 25 pages that we meet a character worthy of a reader's time: a post-rehab Allison."[28] The most positive review in a major publication I could locate is Hillary Busis's write-up for *Entertainment Weekly*. She praises the novel's "well-drawn characters . . . lively prose, and sharp sense of humor" but also advises readers that the novel is a fairly predictable "after-school-special-for-grown-ups" tale.[29] In all of the reviews, while Weiner's novel is considered in the context of her oeuvre, there are other, often unstated criteria against which *All Fall Down* is judged. These criteria, I argue, come from ideas about what an addiction narrative should provide for a reader. Quinn suggests what these criteria might entail by explaining "for an addiction book to be successful, there's a sense in which the readers need to be addicted, too. Weiner doesn't have the vocabulary or emotional reach to make us fall along with Allison."[30] How exactly a writer's vocabulary creates an "addictive" reading experience is left unexplained, but the notion that reading can (or should) be "addicting" is as old as Romanticism and durable enough to inflect the critical discourse surrounding the genre-defying *Infinite Jest* (1996). While Quinn's invocation of "emotional reach" is somewhat clearer, there is no explanation of why, because it is a book *about* addiction, the reading experience must not only represent but replicate the experience of addiction.

Nonetheless, the published reviews do not diverge much from the consensus apparent in the reviews of everyday readers. Though many ardent fans of Weiner's work enjoyed *All Fall Down*, a number of her Amazon reviews come from regular Weiner readers who rank the novel as her worst. Their criticisms of the novel fall along a few familiar lines. First and foremost, several mention finding the characters, especially Allison and her daughter Ellie, unsympathetic and unlikeable. One reviewer laments, "I wasn't able to connect with any of the characters, which is something I am normally able to do with her books."[31] Another rates the book highly but calls it "really good crap[, a]lthough you may want to punch out the main character for her stupidity, her self-involvement."

The reviewer goes on to suggest that Allison's drug use is unrealistic, another common topos of the reviews.[32] Using personal experience, even if it amounts only to taking a single pill after dental surgery, reviewers extrapolate to conclude that Allison could not have used as heavily as she does before she enters rehab.[33] Another review explains that she felt Weiner "didn't understand addiction," feels that Allison's withdrawal was not difficult enough and she did not face realistic consequences for stealing money or drugs.[34] However, this comment reveals the duality of the opioid crisis: Allison's race and class privilege allow her to evade consequences that plague people of color and people of lower socioeconomic status. In other words, what is realistic for the white female iatrogenic addict may not be realistic at all for the person of color addicted nontherapeutically to illicit substances. As with the published reviews, the Amazon reviews suggest a set of competing, perhaps contradictory criteria that combine the conventions of the chick-lit genre with a variety of ideas, derived from popular culture and personal experience, about how addiction should be depicted.

These three themes in the fan criticism of *All Fall Down*—the unlikability of Allison, the slow progression or predictability of the plot, and the lack of verisimilitude in the depiction of addiction—as well as the sometimes implicit suggestion that an addiction story should perform social commentary of some kind, deserve closer inspection. In my reading of the novel below, I examine the issues that critics have noted and draw attention to other problematic aspects of the novel's characterization of addicts and addiction. In doing so, I do not mean to suggest a purely "objective" reading of the text that corrects the perceptions of reviewers professional and otherwise. Instead, I aim to reveal the ways in which the impossibility of fully reconciling some of these criticisms exposes deep divisions in our cultural understandings of the addict and addiction during the opioid crisis.

Allison's "likeability" or relatability as a character is difficult to gauge, but her development can be analyzed by comparing her trajectory as an addict to the classic model of addiction narrative provided and proliferated by Alcoholics Anonymous. Robyn Warhol and Helena Micchie identified the standard narrative of AA as including a period of active addiction (sometimes called the "drunkologue"), the climax of hitting "rock bottom," and the recovery.[35] The narrative was established in the stories recounted in the organization's "Big Book" and spread through stories told by alcoholics and other addicts at AA and NA meetings everywhere. The narrative is so common that it is frequently seen in popular culture representations of addiction as well, from the best-selling addiction memoir to the "very special episode" of a sitcom to classic films like *The Lost Weekend* (1945) or *The Man with the Golden Arm* (1955). Allison's development as a character, I argue, is a negotiation between this familiar trajectory and Weiner's attempts to update it for her readers in the midst of the opioid crisis. Allison does spend the first two-thirds of the novel taking pills in typical drunkologue fashion, but the genesis of her addiction is a bit murky. As noted above, her recent prescriptions stem from an injury sustained working out. However, Allison, trying to remember past happiness with Dave, also questions whether she "had still been taking the post-C-section Percocet."[36] The novel begins with Allison in the midst of her addiction, her eyes drawn to a quiz in a magazine entitled "Has Your Drinking or Drug Use Become a Problem?"[37] Her character develops not from unaddicted to addicted but from ignorance to recognition. The novel fashions a new narrative of addiction in which the drunkologue is less about the exhilaration of inebriety and more about the difficulty of self-knowledge and self-care in the midst of active addiction.

Within the novel itself, there are criticisms of Allison's narrative set against the backdrop of a rehabilitation clinic where she encounters fellow addicts whose stories seem both familiar (in that they meet her expectations for what a "junkie" experiences) and foreign (in that she repeatedly defines herself in contrast to them). Allison vacillates between thinking "pills were how everyone got started, and that when you couldn't afford or find the pills anymore, you moved on to heroin" and insisting she is "not like these women. [She] didn't have any DUIs that needed to be expunged, a judged hadn't ordered [her] to stay, and [she] hadn't flunked a drug test at work. . . . All [she'd] ever done was swallow a few too many pills."[38] Additionally, Allison notes that other women her age in the rehab facility long for the same comforts of home that she does, including "books where every single story did not involve an identical arc of despair and recovery . . . movies that did not involve some C-list actor in the grip of either DTs or a divine revelation."[39] Despite their differences (and Allison's denial of their similarities), the women who are living with addiction do not derive comfort from or identify with the depictions of addiction they see in the books and movies they are allowed in the facility. However, the younger women also criticize Allison when she shares her personal story of addiction. One woman explains, "It's like you're telling your story, only it sounds like it happened to someone else," prompting another to add, "You don't sound sad. . . . You just sound, like, okay, this happened, then that happened, and then I started taking Percocet, and then I started taking Oxy."[40] If the sensationalistic addiction narrative of the made-for-TV movie is too familiar, Allison's detached and seemingly emotionless story leaves her listeners unmoved. This critique anticipates the reactions of readers who found the character undeveloped and the novel more difficult to sink into than Weiner's other work. However, Allison's difficult persona is the product of an addiction narrative that is unlike the familiar ones Weiner criticizes. Hers is a story not of fall and redemption but of recognition and healing.

Similarly, complaints about the plot's slow progression are also illuminated by contrasting the novel's structure with the traditional structure of addiction narratives. The three-part structure of the classical AA addiction narrative builds in little time for relapse and unsuccessful attempts to quit; the drunkologue takes up a large portion of the plot, and the climax of "hitting bottom" and the resolution of recovery are underemphasized. Weiner's novel spends more than a quarter of its pages with Allison in rehab, approaching epiphanies about her drug use and then backing away into denial. Before she enters rehab, the chronological progression of the drunkologue is upset by frequent digressions into her past—childhood memories, her early relationship with Dave, the beginning of her blogging career. When Allison experiences moments of insight that progress the plot, these moments frequently echo events that have already taken place. For instance, when Allison escapes rehab and nearly relapses at Ellie's friend's parents' home, she experiences her "turning point" and contrasts it with her fellow addicts, noting that despite the fact that it didn't involve "sticking a needle in [her] arm . . . [she] *finally made it all the way down*."[41] The turning point is similar, however, to the story Mrs. Dale tells her of her own niece's death. Just as Ellie stands in the hallway promising to be quiet if Allison needs to nap, Mrs. Dale's niece is found by her own young daughter after overdosing: "she went to sleep and she didn't wake up."[42] This moment is again echoed by the repressed memories that come to the surface when Allison has therapy with her mother. Recalling the drunk-driving accident that broke Allison's arm brings more memories of her childhood to the surface, including having to whisper to friends to be quiet because "mom sleeps late."[43] The repetition of the mother-daughter scenes strings together three parallel stories of addiction, one in which the addict dies, one in which the addict goes on using, and one which is Allison's, which ends hopefully but uncertainly. Describing herself as "not married, exactly, but not un-married," Allison waits for Aubrey, a young friend from rehab who has recently relapsed and lost custody of her child, to join her at a meeting.[44] The novel ends with Allison waiting, between marriage and divorce, between active addiction and recovery, negotiating the gaps between the platitudes of AA literature and self-help and the realities of her new life.

These are gaps that Allison also tries to fill in with popular culture and entertainment. Bored with the activities and reading material at rehab, she and the other inmates create addiction and rehab-centric parody versions of showtunes. Though Allison uses the subsequent talent show as her opportunity to escape, it is also apparent that she finds traditional narratives not only boring but insufficient because they do not speak to the experiences of women. Prior to rehab, sitting in her first AA meeting, she is unable to identify with the alcoholics speaking in part because of the sexist nature of some of their comments. A man who steps up to receive his thirty-day chip is applauded when he states, "My parole officer says if I stay clean for ninety and pass all my piss tests, that bitch has gotta let me see my kid."[45] After listening to another young man tell his drunkologue, she slips out the door and chooses to bake cookies for Ellie instead, performing the role of "regular stay-at-home mom" so that she can differentiate herself from other addicts.[46] In rehab, she takes issue with a counselor named Darnton, who mocks and shouts at the women in the group, insisting they are selfish. Allison objects, explaining that her problem is not a lack of self-control or a surfeit of self-interestedness but that she "was trying to do too much for other people."[47] She counters his objections by pointing out that she did more than her share of the family's responsibilities, prompting him to return to the Big Book and read a significant passage, glaring at her: "The alcoholic is an extreme example of self-will run riot, though he usually doesn't think so."[48] Allison objects again, not because she does not identify as an alcoholic, but because of the pronoun "he."[49] In Allison's resistance, there is the "denial" expected of the active addict in the classic AA narrative, but she also espouses the feminist critiques of the AA model that have endured for decades. By the end of the novel, Allison incorporates AA slogans into her life, but she also reads a copy of *A Woman's Guide to the Twelve Steps* rather than the Big Book alone.[50]

Nonetheless, by any intersectional standard, Allison's feminism falls far short. From the beginning of the book until the end of her time at rehab, Allison's observations are infused by class and thinly veiled race prejudices. She contrasts the mothers from "Society Hill" with "the moms from Section 8 housing" at her pediatrician.[51] She regales her prospective employer, Sarah Lai, with the "Me so horny" joke that made her fall in love with Dave.[52] Before appearing on a panel to defend an inebriated teenage girl with a vibrator in her purse against accusations that she was complicit in her own sexual assault, Allison asks the make-up artist not to make her look "slutty."[53] She uses the language of her husband's "frat buddy Dan" to describe the women at her first AA meeting as looking like "they'd been ridden hard and put away wet."[54] She dismisses her fellow inmates at rehab as a string of "Brittanys" and "Ashleys" and asks to be sent somewhere the population is "more like [her]."[55] These kinds of observations are mostly absent from the final portion of the novel, when Allison is in recovery, but certainly Allison's overriding snobbery is a reason many readers and reviewers found her unlikeable. Quinn argues "the book's least tolerable attribute is its unkindness toward the various low-rent [addicts] who populate Allison's rehab and whose addictions are of a less polite strain."[56] However, it is unclear whether this is the book's attitude or merely the transitory attitude of a deeply flawed protagonist who increasingly aligns herself with the young women she initially disdains. Weiner's novel does little to bring attention to the stories of marginalized victims of the opioid crisis: people of color, people living in poverty, people already institutionalized by the criminal justice system. Instead, it insists on the distinctions between the "sick" white female addict and the "criminal" junkie, not as a truth of the opioid crisis, but as a barrier to individual and collective recovery.

It is fair to question whether stories like Allison's need to be told, whether they accomplish anything of political or cultural significance at this moment. I argue that, despite its focus on white middle-aged upper-class opiate addiction, *All Fall Down* deserves consideration because it exposes and exploits gendered assumptions about addiction narratives and addicts themselves. Tammy L. Anderson has noted that discourse surrounding female substance abusers has overwhelmingly focused on women as victims and on "their failure to perform female roles."[57] Early research into women's addiction suggested, according to Nancy Campbell, "addiction would not be a 'woman's issue' if all women behaved like white, middle-class, heterosexual married mothers."[58] Weiner's novel does not allow its unlikeable protagonist to be seen as a victim; even in her active addiction, she fulfills her roles as wife, mother, and primary breadwinner for the family. Allison Weiss is instead a refutation of the notion that conforming to the standards of femininity and motherhood for the twenty-first century will protect one from addiction, the "parallel universe [running] alongside the normal world."[59] Neither the generic conventions of Weiner's "chick lit" nor the classic structure of the AA recovery narrative provide suitable aesthetic criteria for evaluating the novel in the context of the opioid crisis. If the novel strikes readers as foreign, alienating, or even boring, it expresses the duality of an epidemic that is pervasive, banal, familiar, and devastating.

NOTES

1. "Understanding the Epidemic," Centers for Disease Control and Prevention, US Department of Health and Human Services, last modified December 19, 2018, https://www.cdc.gov/drugoverdose/epidemic/index.html.

2.   Ian Stewart, "Report: Americans Are Now More Likely to Die of an Opioid Overdose than on the Road," NPR, January 14, 2019, https://www.npr.org/2019/01/14/684695273 /report-americans-are-now-more-likely-to-die-of-an-opioid-overdose-than-on-the-ro.

3.   Robyn R. Warhol, "The Rhetoric of Addiction: From Victorian Novels to AA," in *High Anxieties: Cultural Studies in Addiction*, ed. Janet Farrell Brodie and Marc Redfield (Berkeley: University of California Press, 2002), 99–101.

4.   Nancy D. Campbell, *Using Women: Gender, Drug Policy, and Social Justice* (New York: Routledge, 2000), 29.

5.   Susan Zieger, *Inventing the Addict: Drugs, Race, and Sexuality in Nineteenth-Century British and American Literature* (Amherst: University of Massachusetts Press, 2008), 10.

6.   Zieger, *Inventing the Addict*, 22.

7.   Campbell, *Using Women*, 3.

8.   Zieger, *Inventing the Addict*, 23.

9.   David T. Courtwright, *Dark Paradise: A History of Opiate Addiction in America* (Cambridge, MA: Harvard University Press, 2001), 36.

10. Courtwright, *Dark Paradise*, 42.

11. Courtwright, *Dark Paradise*, 59.

12. Courtwright, *Dark Paradise*, 59.

13. Courtwright, *Dark Paradise*, 123.

14. Courtwright, *Dark Paradise*, 147.

15. Courtwright, *Dark Paradise*, 147.

16. "Understanding the Epidemic," Centers for Disease Control and Prevention.

17. Jennifer Weiner, *All Fall Down* (New York: Washington Square Press, 2014), 36.

18. Weiner, *All Fall Down*, 36.

19. Weiner, *All Fall Down*, 61–62.

20. Weiner, *All Fall Down*, 65.

21. Weiner, *All Fall Down*, 65.

22. Tracy Cochran, "All Grown Up," *Publisher's Weekly*, September 13, 2004, 53.

23. Jennifer Weiner, "Having the Best-Selling Cake and Eating the Review Too: An Interview with Jennifer Weiner," interview by Jia Tolentino, *The Hairpin*, June 18, 2014, https:// www.thehairpin.com/2014/06/having-the-best-selling-cake-and-eating-the-review-too -an-interview-with-jennifer-weiner/#.61sdayevf.

24. Rebecca Mead, "Written Off: Jennifer Weiner's Quest for Literary Respect," *New Yorker*, January 13, 2014, https://www.newyorker.com/magazine/2014/01/13/written-off.

25. Anne Helen Petersen, *Too Fat, Too Slutty, Too Loud: The Rise and Reign of the Unruly Woman* (New York: Penguin Random House, 2017), 205.

26. Annalisa Quinn, "Weiner Takes a Tumble with 'All Fall Down,' " *NPR Books*, NPR, June 18, 2014, https://www.npr.org/2014/06/18/320748879/weiner-takes-a-tumble-with -all-fall-down.

27. Quinn, "Weiner Takes a Tumble with 'All Fall Down.' "

28. Patty Rhule, " 'All Fall Down' Is Addictive, for Better or Worse," *USA Today*, June 16, 2014, https://www.usatoday.com/story/life/books/2014/06/16/all-fall-down-a -novel/10246425/.

29. Hillary Busis, "All Fall Down," *Entertainment Weekly*, July 2, 2014, https://ew.com /article/2014/07/02/all-fall-down/.

30. Quinn, "Weiner Takes a Tumble with 'All Fall Down.' "

31. Leo86, "A fun read, but a little disappointing," Amazon customer review, July 1, 2014, https://www.amazon.com/gp/customer-reviews/R3JPU96JFHE1YS/ref=cm_cr_getr_d _rvw_ttl.

32. Alanw56, "This is really good crap. Although you may want to punch out . . ." Amazon customer review, July 5, 2014, https://www.amazon.com/gp/customer-reviews /R3KV80NLWM5SGZ/ref=cm_cr_getr_d_rvw_ttl.

33. StoryAddict, "Another hit from Jennifer Weiner," Amazon customer review, March 2, 2017, https://www.amazon.com/gp/customer-reviews/R38KJX1TWSRE80/ref=cm_cr_getr_d_rvw_ttl.

34. Amazon Customer, "Not my Favorite . . . Spoiler Alert," Amazon customer review, September 10, 2014, https://www.amazon.com/gp/customer-reviews/R3HLCQERRXYOIN/ref=cm_cr_getr_d_rvw_ttl.

35. Robyn R. Warhol and Helena Micchie, "Twelve-Step Teleology: Narratives of Recovery/Recovery as Narrative," in *Getting a Life: Everyday Uses of Autobiography*, ed. Sidonie Smith and Julia Watson (Minneapolis: University of Minnesota Press, 1996), 327.

36. Weiner, *All Fall Down*, 98.

37. Weiner, *All Fall Down*, 3.

38. Weiner, *All Fall Down*, 244–45.

39. Weiner, *All Fall Down*, 305.

40. Weiner, *All Fall Down*, 330.

41. Weiner, *All Fall Down*, 348–49.

42. Weiner, *All Fall Down*, 191.

43. Weiner, *All Fall Down*, 316.

44. Weiner, *All Fall Down*, 375.

45. Weiner, *All Fall Down*, 199.

46. Weiner, *All Fall Down*, 201.

47. Weiner, *All Fall Down*, 249.

48. Weiner, *All Fall Down*, 250.

49. Weiner, *All Fall Down*, 250.

50. Weiner, *All Fall Down*, 372.

51. Weiner, *All Fall Down*, 5.

52. Weiner, *All Fall Down*, 58.

53. Weiner, *All Fall Down*, 144.

54. Weiner, *All Fall Down*, 196.

55. Weiner, *All Fall Down*, 255.

56. Quinn, "Weiner Takes a Tumble with 'All Fall Down.' "

57. Tammy L. Anderson, *Neither Villain nor Victim: Empowerment and Agency among Women Substance Abusers* (New Jersey: Rutgers University Press, 2008), 1.

58. Campbell, *Using Women*, 24.

59. Weiner, *All Fall Down*, 229.

CHAPTER 4

Prince, Tom Petty, and Pain: Projections of Authenticity in Popular Music

Leigh H. Edwards

Prince's tragic death in April 2016 from an accidental fentanyl overdose trig-gered an outpouring of affective response from his fans and from audiences worldwide. Memorials sprang up in his honor, ranging from buildings, like the Eiffel Tower and the New Orleans Super Dome lit up in purple, to tribute concerts and fan gatherings, all expressing powerful grief for the dearly be-loved musician. It was the most high profile of several musician deaths from fentanyl overdoses around that time that sparked further public discussion of the opioid crisis, including the deaths of Tom Petty in October 2017 and the young rapper Lil Peep in November 2017.[1] The fact that two such prominent musicians as Prince and Petty in particular died due to fentanyl was a devel-opment that garnered press attention at the time, although in very different ways that speak to the stereotypes surrounding the ongoing opioid crisis in the US. Their tragic deaths occasion a consideration of how the larger epi-demic is being portrayed in the media. Prince was depicted in some media cov-erage as a tortured genius who hid his secret addiction and somehow needed saving from himself and his excesses, while Tom Petty was portrayed as a rational actor who made the choice that his physical pain warranted opioid treatment, which he only took in order to complete his tour and to fulfill his responsibilities to others.

The very different rhetoric in media accounts of their deaths demonstrates problematic stereotypes about race and class that are evident in depictions of the epidemic. Their deaths also force a reevaluation of their star personas, because the fact that they became part of the epidemic can reframe cultural understandings of their work and careers. Both cases reveal different specific rhetorics of authenticity around what would have caused opioid addiction. Those differing rhetorics illuminate Prince's and Petty's very different star personae, contexts, and constructions of authenticity in their own careers and popular music genres.

Their deaths reflected specific trends in the opioid epidemic at that time, particularly the rise of fentanyl, a drug fifty to one hundred times more powerful than morphine.[2] Surpassing heroin as the leading cause of overdose deaths, fentanyl is thirty to fifty times stronger than heroin, and fentanyl overdose deaths spiked higher by 30 percent between July 2016 and September 2017.[3] The National Institute on Drug Abuse, in research for the National Institutes of Health, found that, in 2016, synthetic opioids, primarily illegal fentanyl, outpaced prescription opioids to become the most common cause of drug overdose deaths in the US. That year, 64,070 Americans died from drug overdoses, and 66 percent of those deaths involved opioid compounds. Of that number, almost 50 percent (19,413) of the drug-related deaths were due to synthetic opioids, up from 14 percent (3,007) in 2010. In overdose deaths, many involved multiple drugs; of the 42,249 overdose deaths involving opioids in 2016, 45.9 percent involved synthetic opioids.[4] The NIH has detailed ongoing governmental efforts to address the opioid crisis, such as changing pain management practices, promoting the accessibility of overdose-reversing drugs such as Narcan, and increasing access to treatment and recovery services.[5]

Prince and Petty give another face to the crisis because their deaths from fentanyl are instances of well-known cultural leaders tragically lost to the epidemic, but it is also significant that both were musicians. Both sought pain management treatment because of hip injuries suffered in the context of years of touring and wear and tear on their bodies. Since at least 2005, Prince had been in need of double hip replacement surgery due to decades of acrobatic strain on his body, specifically his taxing dance routines performed in high-heeled shoes, featuring jumps from risers. Petty, meanwhile, was suffering from what turned into a broken hip but was trying to complete his fortieth-anniversary tour with his band, the Heartbreakers. Both struggled with pain and were prescribed opioids. In keeping with the opioid crisis trends, Prince had overdosed previously and had been revived with Narcan. When both Prince and Petty eventually died from a fentanyl overdose, the fentanyl was found in combination with other drugs in their systems. Investigators concluded that Prince was not aware he was taking counterfeit Vicodin that was laced with fentanyl. Petty overdosed on fentanyl—he had been prescribed fentanyl patches but also had two other derivatives of the drug in his system.[6]

The fact that Prince and Petty were framed differently in media coverage of their deaths also reflects larger trends in racial stereotyping around drug epidemics in the US. NIH studies have shown that there is racial bias and stereotyping involved in both treatment and press coverage of the opioid crisis, such that black users are treated as addicts while white users are treated as victims.[7] At the same time, black patients have been undertreated for pain management because of a longer-running stereotype and racial bias; specifically, the media associated earlier drug epidemics with black users in a way that perpetuated problematic stereotypes, as in the 1980s crack cocaine epidemic that lasted through the early 1990s. Nonwhite patients were prescribed opioids at half the rate of white patients. After a first wave of opioid use in the 1990s and a second wave in 2010, the most recent deadly wave of opioid use in the period since 2013 has been defined by increased access and use of high-concentration synthetic opioids, specifically illegally manufactured fentanyl. In US opioid overdoses in 2016, the rate of Caucasians who died was 79 percent, as compared to 10 percent for the nonwhite minorities. Additionally, the media coverage of opioid addiction and deaths problematically depicts white users as victims with rational reasons for choosing pain treatment, while nonwhite users are portrayed as addicts with a moral failing. The first wave of opioid use in the 1990s also came with a rural white working-class stereotype in part due to big pharmaceutical marketing practices like Purdue Pharmaceuticals targeting specific rural and suburban providers with oxycodone hydrochloride, later coined "hillbilly heroin" due to the rural association.[8]

Although the Prince and Petty cases dispel an earlier stereotype about the opioid crisis being solely a working-class epidemic, the media coverage of their deaths shows the persistence of racial stereotypes. While rural Southern white working-class victims might have been one early stereotype of the epidemic, Petty, who has always been identified with Southern regional cultures, speaks to a different white victim profile that challenges an older stereotype. Meanwhile, press coverage of Prince tended to describe him as a genius with a secret, hidden addiction, which was framed as a hypocritical moral failing because it went against his stated Jehovah's Witness beliefs and the frequent antidrug message of his lyrics. Prince was depicted as someone who needed saving from himself and from an excessive lifestyle. Even while he was being cloaked in the rhetoric of famous genius, he was still portrayed as a secret addict, thus the coverage of his death fit the ongoing stereotype of black users being portrayed as addicts.

PRINCE'S STAR IMAGE

The media coverage of Prince's death focused on a "hidden addiction," suggesting that his opioid use was a secret "moral failing" that made him all too human in a way that contrasted with the long-running star image he had cultivated for himself as someone with a larger-than-life mystique. Ironically, the star image Prince developed for himself rejected racial stereotyping, but media portrayals of him in death have taken on the racial stereotyping of the opioid crisis discourse. Media coverage of his death could impact his projected star image because models of stardom in the US have traditionally depended on a rhetoric of extraordinary versus ordinary that must remain in balance. Prince's tabloid-covered death from a fentanyl overdose meant that the ordinary side of the star binary came to dominate discourse around his death.

Theorist Richard Dyer argues that, in the classic Hollywood film star model, a star appears to be an exceptional person who becomes famous for some quality or talent, thereby serving as an exemplar of individualism in a capitalist society. Because the star achieved fame due to talent and merit, audiences are encouraged to believe that they can also succeed in a capitalist society through hard work. Thus, according to Dyer, stars appear to resolve the contradictions of unequal power hierarchies in capitalism and modernity.[9] Theorist John Ellis similarly argues that stars must balance the extraordinary (an exceptional talent that makes them appear unreachable, glamorous, and larger-than-life) with the ordinary (relatable to audiences, seeking happiness just as audiences do) in their star image.[10] If the star seems too familiar or ordinary, they can lose the star effect. Graphic tabloid photographs of Prince were exploitative; they showed images of his dead body in front of his elevator, with stories claiming he was alone and isolated, vainly on his way to seek help, and they purported to reveal his "secret" life of opioid addiction, in a way that undermined his exceptionality and his star image.[11]

As a result of his overdose death, Prince's authenticity narrative in his stage persona and musical performances has been complicated in important ways. His projections of authenticity have historically been tied to his virtuoso musical performances and his physically demanding stage routines, while his authenticity narrative after his death has changed as he has become another symbol of a popular musician lost to the opioid epidemic. The same impressive feats that often defined Prince's distinctiveness as a live performing artist—such as when he would perform complex guitar solos while dropping into a split and bounce back up again or leap and spin off of pianos or speakers in heeled boots—are the very same performance elements that led him to suffer severe hip injuries and pain that prompted his treatment with opioids and his eventual addiction.

Over the course of his career, Prince developed ever-more-elaborate authenticity narratives, creating a media image that involved gender bending, intersectional critiques of racial stereotypes, rebellion against corporate music industry practices, a deep engagement with participatory fan culture, and a playful use of star discourse and mystification. For example, Prince infamously changed his name to his "Love Symbol #2" combination of male and female symbols in 1993 as part of his contract dispute with Warner Brothers and his critique of what he explicitly saw as racial exploitation of him. In their dispute, he argued that he should have more control over the release of his music, while Warner Brothers tried to slow down his releases, which they believed would flood the market and reduce sales. Ultimately, Prince tried to control his own distribution in various ways, launching a series of websites from which fans could order recordings directly and signing a number of one-album deals with different record labels for distribution. Prince's use of an androgynous symbol underscored his commitment to gender bending and his support for women's rights and women artists, famously epitomized most recently by his collaborations with Janelle Monáe and his work on her *Dirty Computer* (2018) album, released after his death. As part of his gender bending themes, his music video for "Insatiable" from his album *Diamonds and Pearls* (1991) had him reversing what film theorist Laura Mulvey called the "male gaze" of the camera, which frames female characters as passive sexualized objects; instead, in Prince's video, the female character turned the camera on him, and the video imagined a female gaze.[12] Likewise, Prince spoke out against racism, supported the Black Lives Matter movement, and devoted money and resources to social justice efforts for African Americans. Famously, Prince's song "Sign 'O' the Times" decried the crack cocaine and AIDS epidemics of the 1980s and the ways they were portrayed and stereotyped in the media.

Prince's authenticity narrative has always depended on his prodigious, self-taught musical talent, as he was famously listed as playing twenty-seven different instruments on his debut album, *For You* (1978), which he produced, arranged, composed, and performed himself. While he later dismissed that number as marketing hype, he was nevertheless a voluminous multi-instrumentalist. Musically, he was known as a boundary-crossing artist in terms of musical styles historically associated with racial categories due to record company marketing practices. His signature "Minneapolis Sound" blended "black" genres such as funk, soul, and disco with "white" genres such as rock, punk, and new wave, as epitomized by his most high-profile album, *Purple Rain* (1984).[13] He also worked in jazz, hip hop, contemporary R&B, guitar rock, and electronic dance music. His work in funk, alongside his virtuoso electric guitar solos, meant he was often described as the heir both to James Brown and to Jimi Hendrix, but his innovations took him past any one genre.[14] His hit songs ranged from the apocalyptic "Purple Rain" to the gender bending "If I Was Your Girlfriend" and the sexually explicit "Darling Nikki," which faced censorship and prompted Tipper Gore to found the Parents Music Resource Center and push for parental advisory warnings. The global circulation and reach of his star image are indicated by his record sales (more than 100 million records sold), his induction into the Rock and Roll Hall of Fame, his Academy Award for Best Original Song Score for his film *Purple Rain* (1984), and his eight Grammy Awards. In 2018, the ABC TV show *Black-ish* turned its hundredth episode into a Prince tribute that focused on his range of meanings for different fans, with the characters wanting to make sure younger generations would know who Prince was.

Many of the stories about Prince during his lifetime focused on his star persona as an almost god-like aura. For example, during his 2007 Super Bowl Halftime Show performance, Prince faced a downpour but danced anyway, incorporating the rainstorm into his image and mystique. A behind-the-scenes NFL documentary shows how deluged his stage set was, with slippery tiles on his large purple stage made in the shape of his Love Symbol #2.[15] Instead of cancelling his performance, Prince asked organizers "Can you make it rain more?" and used the rain in his performance of "Purple Rain," which he played while standing behind a sheet with his image projected and enlarged upon it, highlighted amidst the downpour. He and his dancers all performed in high heels, and he played live electric guitars, with organizers fearing they could fall or be injured. The show producers described being deeply impressed by how Prince was almost "god-like" as he hailed the elements to provide him with special effects. Other frequent descriptions of Prince's god-like persona likewise commented on the consistent projection of that image, as when collaborator Jimmy Jam said of Prince's star image that he "always looked like a rock star."[16]

Prince also appeared as a trickster figure who knew how to stage his own image and maintain mystery. He was famously controlling of his image, insisting on directing most of his own music videos.[17] His art director Steve Parke observed that "he definitely wanted to present an air of mystery."[18] He also knew how to draw attention to his exceptionalism by juxtaposing it with incongruous, everyday settings—and by disappearing suddenly to sustain his mystique. On *The Tonight Show*, host Jimmy Fallon and drummer and Roots bandleader Questlove, who saw Prince as a role model, recounted how Prince once called Fallon to come play ping-pong at a bar late at night. As Prince beat Fallon, he hit a shot and suddenly disappeared on purpose, leaving a befuddled

Fallon looking for him. When Questlove was arriving at the bar, Prince was already being driven away, and he rolled down his window to tell Questlove to "holler at your boy" when he saw him and to tease Fallon for losing the match.[19] Prince reveled in incongruity and fed his mystique through these disappearances. Likewise, comedian Tracy Morgan recounted visiting with his idol, and one Morgan story illustrates Prince's style of vanishing: "I hosted the Billboard Music Awards three years ago and Prince headlined. I didn't get to talk to him because he disappeared: 'Where did Prince go?' 'He disappeared!' He *was* mystique."[20]

The circulation of infamous Prince stories, as indicated by numerous compilations of them, is a cottage industry unto itself and is one measure of how successful his star image was and how creatively he enacted it in various settings.[21] Many stories focus on his outlandishness, part of his play with his own star image: Prince had assistants call other musicians multiple times to say Prince was about to call; he would put people on hold ten times or keep them up all night talking; or he would defy scheduling and rebel against time expectations by staying up for days making music and asking for things at all hours of the night.[22] Dave Chappelle included on his comedy show a sketch parody, entitled "True Hollywood Story: Prince" (2004), about the time Prince stayed up all night and played basketball in full Prince stage regalia and made pancakes for his guests for breakfast, based on a Charlie Murphy retelling. Prince was amused and included the image of Chappelle as Prince as the cover for the release of his song "Breakfast Can Wait" (2013), entertained that some casual fans did not know the difference between that Chappelle picture and the real Prince. Chappelle later admitted admiringly that Prince had thus successfully outmaneuvered him in that parody war.[23]

Such play with his own image is also evident in Prince's guest role on the FOX television sitcom *New Girl*, where he appeared as himself in a post-Super Bowl episode (2014) and played up the eccentricity of his own image. The characters visit him in his Los Angeles mansion, where he performs a concert and advises the female protagonist on how she could fix her relationship with her boyfriend. When the characters are shocked to see him, Prince calmly intones: "I'm Prince. So what seems to be the problem." As their jaws drop, he says: "Oh, how rude of me, I haven't given you enough time to freak out yet. You may do so now."[24] The characters promptly freak out, and one screams and faints. In one scene, Prince sits between the two characters on a bench, culling comedy from the awkwardness of him being there. Showrunner Liz Meriwether, surprised that Prince was a fan of the show and asked to appear on it, later recounted how Prince amplified the incongruity of his star image. In one scene, for instance, he suggested using a flashlight to illuminate his face suddenly and to emphasize the strangeness of him being there.[25] Meriwether notes that he also had one of the Kardashians thrown out; one had agreed to appear in the party scene, but Prince objected because that reality TV family did not fit his preferred media image. Prince thus played with his star image via the juxtaposition of him in a romcom genre, but he also guarded it. Other stories depict the incongruity of his star image as he maintained it even in everyday settings; former staff describe him always wearing his high heels and even playing hide-and-seek in them.[26]

In contrast, media coverage of Prince's death portrayed it as a tragedy that could have been prevented, framing him as an iconic musical genius who hid his addiction in order to protect his carefully nurtured image as an almost mythical figure, particularly as a Jehovah's Witness (since 2001) who publicly eschewed drugs and alcohol. Media accounts focused on the addiction specialists who were rushing in to save him and arrived too late and the attempted intervention of friends who were trying to "save him from himself."[27] A week earlier, Prince's plane had made an emergency landing in Moline, Illinois, when he was flying back to Minneapolis from concerts in Atlanta on April 14. He had taken Percocet and was found unresponsive on the plane. After being given Narcan, he was revived on the airport tarmac and taken to the hospital, where he then checked himself out against medical advice. At the time, Prince tweeted "I am #transformed."[28] The addiction specialist Dr. Howard Kornfeld had been called to treat Prince and was scheduled to travel from California. Kornfeld sent his son, Andrew, ahead with a supply of buprenorphine, used to treat opioid dependence. The son arrived at Paisley Park the morning of April 21 only to find Prince dead; he was the person who called 911 to report that Prince had died, apparently approximately six hours earlier, from a drug overdose. Prurient tabloid coverage retraced Prince's steps in the days leading up to his death, circulating earlier pictures of him going to see a doctor in town and going to Walgreens to get more prescription opioids under someone else's name. Tabloid stories ended with photographs of his dead body in his Paisley Park mansion, alone in front of the elevator, isolated and bereft, professional help finding him only just too late.[29] The death investigation revealed a supply of illegal fentanyl stashed around his home, but it did not result in any criminal convictions because it did not uncover how he got the pills.[30]

Instead of reinforcing his star image of genius shrouded in secrecy, the media coverage of Prince's synthetic opioid overdose has recontextualized him, framing him as an all-too-human artist who suffered and became addicted because of his art. The tenor of the coverage is that the addiction secret now revealed is the skeleton key that will unlock all of his mysteries. Entertainment media at the time reported that Prince had a history of using prescription Percocet and speculated that he might have thought he was getting extra illegal Percocet when instead he was being given fentanyl, a switch that often happens in the illegal drug market because fentanyl is cheaper, but the far more powerful drug has caused a number of overdose deaths.[31] Media coverage of his hip injuries and treatment has lacked clarity. Some stories claimed he had hip problems for more than thirty years due to injuries he suffered during the *Purple Rain* tour, while others insisted that he was in need of hip replacement surgery for both hips by 2005.[32] Some argue he never got the surgery and was prescribed Percocet in 2009 for the pain, while others aver that he did have a hip replacement procedure in 2010 that resulted in him using a cane afterwards and that had him using opioids in recovery.[33] Some outlets also falsely argued that he had avoided surgery due to a refusal to have blood transfusions as a Jehovah's Witness.[34] The fact that Prince was not forthcoming about his condition and treatment is only in keeping with his practice of mystification regarding his own star persona. However, after his death, his opioid addiction has become the one key explanatory narrative, with tabloids implying that much of his secretive behavior can be explained by that hidden addiction.

Media accounts continue to describe him as a genius full of "mystery" now revealed as addiction.[35] One typical press article describes his death as a "cry for help," saying: "Prince summoned a drug counselor the day before his tragic, lonely death. Now, his addiction comes to light."[36] Another account focused on how Prince was "shrouded in secrecy," and after his death, the "world is learning just how much he was concealing," including not only what the story claims was a secret addiction to Percocet for hip pain since 2009 but also his lack of a will that the article claims was due to a supposed paranoia about signing legal papers and his vault of unreleased music worth purportedly as much as $1 billion.[37] The account goes on to describe Prince's "hidden pain" and how his "sudden, shocking death has left questions about his drug use." Other media outlets reported that the toxicology reports showed "exceedingly high" concentrations of fentanyl in his system.[38] TMZ reported that "Prince's death scene was riddled with pills strewn around his home."[39] Media accounts continue to focus on how "the strict proponent of clean living" was able to "conceal his opioid addiction."[40]

Ultimately, the investigation into his death has created a new sensationalized narrative in the popular press about his hidden opioid addiction, a story line filled with stereotypes that Prince himself critiqued and clearly tried to avoid during his lifetime. Only now has another layer of a Prince authenticity narrative emerged, one that involves his efforts to keep private his medical pain, opioid treatment, and struggles to keep performing in that context. His efforts to deal with that cycle of pain and opioid abuse also affected his specific performances of authenticity, as when he started using a cane but framed it as a fashion statement or presented his final concerts and tour, the Piano & a Microphone Tour, as a more pared-down, authentic model of performance through which he was seated playing the piano, not letting on that he needed to sit because of his health. His own authenticity narrative, particularly as it related to his religious beliefs, led him to keep private his use of painkillers and even to preach against it. Posthumously, Prince has become an artist irrevocably identified with the opioid crisis, and that crisis is the engine behind how his authenticity narratives have become more complex and how they resonate now.

TOM PETTY AND HEARTBREAK

In the press, Prince's authenticity narrative became that of a secret addiction revealed. In contrast, the authenticity narrative around Tom Petty remained more intact in media coverage of his death, in keeping with how both narratives fell into familiar racial stereotyping around drug use and addiction. Petty was famous as a well-regarded rock musician who began releasing music in the 1970s, an artist influenced by the folk rock of Bob Dylan, with whom he later toured. Petty also founded the Traveling Wilburys supergroup with Dylan, Jeff Lynne, Roy Orbison, and George Harrison in the late 1980s. Both in albums with his band, the Heartbreakers, and in solo albums, Petty featured his rough vocal delivery that made his recordings instantly recognizable. His level of global fame can be measured by the fact that he sold more than eighty million records, played the Super Bowl Halftime Show in 2008, and was inducted into the Rock and Roll Hall of Fame. He was well known for hit songs such as "Refugee," "The Waiting," "Don't Do Me Like That," "Free Fallin'," "I Won't Back Down," and "Runnin' Down a Dream," as well as duets with Stevie Nicks, such as "Stop Draggin' My Heart Around."

Petty's projection of authenticity also involves the use of the country-rock genre in his oeuvre, which touches upon some of what Jimmie N. Rogers calls the "sincerity contract" of projections of authenticity in country music, entailing the idea of "staying true" to one's roots and not "selling out."[41] Famed hip hop producer Rick Rubin produced one of his more pared-down solo albums, *Wildflower*, in 1994, and Petty and the Heartbreakers served as the band for Johnny Cash's second American Recordings album with Rick Rubin, *Unchained* (1996) (originally to be entitled "Petty Cash"). In addition to rock, country, and

Americana roots music, Petty also worked in the blues genre, as with his album *Mojo* (2010). Born in Gainesville, Florida, Petty was identified with Southern regional cultures, as in his *Southern Accents* album (1985), even though he lived and recorded in the Los Angeles area. As anecdotal evidence, his brother and Tallahassee-based family report that Petty's public image both in Gainesville and in Tallahassee is that of a well-respected cultural leader in the area, and a park was named after him in Gainesville after his death.

Media coverage of Petty's death on October 2, 2017, focused on quotations from his family members who said that they understood why he would have chosen to use opioids for pain management because he was in so much pain and that he was just trying to fulfill his responsibilities and finish his fortieth-anniversary tour. Petty was in such pain that he used a golf cart to get around backstage. Media coverage framed his opioid use as a rational choice he made because he was suffering, and accounts were careful to specify that it was an accidental overdose, not an intentional one. As if to dispel any speculation, articles about his death quoted his family as saying Petty's death was accidental and that he had just been talking about being on "top of the world."[42] Even though Petty had earlier in his career had a heroin addiction, he was not framed in these accounts as an addict but rather as someone suffering from pain and a victim of an accidental synthetic opioid overdose. There was some initial confusion about his death because CBS reported his death prematurely, speaking to the viral fake news phenomenon and digital-era anxieties about what is real and what is fake. He died from cardiac arrest due to accidental overdose from multiple drug toxicity.

Many media outlets quoted his family's initial statement, posted first on Facebook and then on Petty's official website, and their commentary on his death was given equal billing with the coroner's report, allowing his family to help shape the rhetoric of the media coverage.[43] In their statement, his wife Dana and daughter Adria explained why he kept touring in spite of his hip injury: "Despite this painful injury he insisted on keeping his commitment to his fans and he toured for 53 dates with a fractured hip and, as he did, it worsened to a more serious injury."[44] They went on to say, "On the day he died he was informed his hip had graduated to a full-on break and it is our feeling that the pain was simply unbearable and was the cause for his over use of medication." Here, they frame his decision to take more medication as a rational result of his pain and suggest that he had delayed hip surgery out of a feeling of responsibility to others. They continued: "We knew before the report was shared with us that he was prescribed various pain medications for a multitude of issues including fentanyl patches and we feel confident that this was, as the coroner found, an unfortunate accident." Petty's widow, interviewed almost a year after his death, elaborated on why he put off the hip surgery that his doctors had advised: "He would do anything to help anyone—his bandmates, the crew, the fans—and that's why he did the last tour with a fractured hip. He was adamant. He found out a few days before the tour was gonna start—and that he had emphysema." While he was using drugs to keep him going for what he saw as his last tour, he planned on having the surgery later. Petty's widow explained: "That's why he wouldn't go to the hospital when his hip broke. He'd had it in mind it was his last tour and he owed it to his long-time crew, from decades some of them, and his fans." She also poignantly observed that he was in great spirits just before he died: "Never had he been so proud of himself, so happy, so looking forward to the future—and then he's gone."[45] Her comments capture their grief at his sudden loss as well as their careful reasoning of his intentions.

In terms of Petty's long-running authenticity construction and star image, his folk rock authenticity was tied to progressive political causes, like his participation in Farm Aid, Live Aid, and "no nukes" activism. Describing some of his motivation, he explained: "I turned anger into ambition. Any sort of injustice would outrage me. I couldn't contain myself."[46] In the Peter Bogdanovich documentary *Runnin' Down a Dream: Tom Petty and the Heartbreakers* (2007), Petty talks about being inspired by the western as a film genre and Americana, as well as by specific musicians, such as Elvis. He tells Bogdanovich: "I always liked the idea of the guitar, because cowboys played the guitar." He also describes needing to escape his abusive father and turning to rock music as a way out: "It was very clear, here's a way out of this situation that I'm in." In the documentary, Bogdanovich praises the Heartbreakers as "America's truest rock and roll band," later claiming that "Tom Petty is a particularly American story."[47] Producer Rubin, meanwhile, characterizes Petty in the documentary as a "craftsman" with great "inspiration," able to wring songs with complicated stories in a mere five minutes; Rubin recounts that Petty says it "comes through him" and that he can "channel material in a pretty strong way."

Part of Petty's construction of authenticity is as a sympathetic figure who moved across several genres, as he bridged rock, folk, blues, and country genres at various points in his career, and as someone who argued for musician rights. His engagement with Cash, country, and Americana roots music in his work with Rubin is a good example of that confluence. In addition to producing Petty's *Wildflowers* album, Rubin produced Tom Petty and the Heartbreakers albums such as their soundtrack to *She's the One* (1996) and the album *Echo* (1999). As a producer, Rubin built a reputation for capturing the essence of artists, and Cash argued that his albums with Rubin, like *Unchained*, encapsulated "the honest, unadulterated essence of Johnny Cash, whatever that is."[48] In liner notes to the later posthumous Cash release, *Unearthed*, Petty praised the idea that Rubin could reach the authenticity of musicians by paring down the production. When Cash covered Petty's "I Won't Back Down," Petty saw that as validation of him as a songwriter and found that version definitive because "it sounds like God singing my song."[49] Significantly, Petty also praised Cash for fighting through extreme pain to keep touring and ignoring the pain onstage. Petty recounted about Cash, "Well, his jaw was bothering him" when they were recording, but he "had this incredible way of walking through extreme pain." He went on to recall Cash brushing aside the pain of a knee replacement: "I was saying, 'Well, how do you deal with that?' He was on the road, and he called me from it. And he said, 'Well, I go onstage and nothing hurts.' "[50] Petty's admiration of Cash's endurance parallels Petty's own efforts to keep touring with a broken hip and extreme pain. However, Cash himself suffered drug addiction relapses due to opioid pain treatment.

Just as earlier accounts framed Petty seeking out his musical career in part as a rational way to escape his father's abuse, accounts of his death focused on his feelings of responsibility to his musical family. After his death, his family released another statement saying that they hoped his death would shed light on the opioid epidemic and help others: "As a family, we recognize this report may spark a further discussion on the opioid crisis and we feel that it is a healthy and necessary discussion and we hope in some way this report can save lives." They went on to say, "Many people who overdose begin with a legitimate injury or simply do not understand the potency and deadly nature of these medications."[51] There, they try to turn his loss into a warning that others can learn from. As the media coverage of his death follows the family's words and rationales, those stories leave Petty intact as a respected artist who was trying to serve others and frame him as someone who just fell victim to an accidental overdose because of the deceptive nature of the drugs.

There is one infamous performance that joins Petty with Prince and that showcases their different authenticity projections. For the 2004 Rock and Roll Hall of Fame induction ceremony, where Prince was inducted, Petty (a 2002 inductee) and Prince played for a tribute to George Harrison, who was inducted posthumously, in a performance of "While My Guitar Gently Weeps" that also featured Lynne, two other members of the Heartbreakers, Steve Winwood, and Harrison's son Dhani. Petty is dressed in an understated black suit with purple shirt and sunglasses, while Prince purposefully stands out with a striking bright red fedora, in a dark suit with a red shirt, replete with a leopard-print guitar strap and guitar. Producers invited Prince to play lead guitar for the song, but Lynne's guitar player, Marc Mann, kept taking the Eric Clapton solo in the rehearsal. Prince told producers that was fine, that he would just embellish the outro solo, although he did not rehearse it. At the performance itself, Petty anchored the song, singing the lead and steadily lending his straightforward delivery and raspy voice, collegially interacting with the other musicians and celebrating the music of his peers. Prince, waiting in the shadows, emerged for the final guitar part and launched into a virtuoso performance that has been lauded as one of the greatest live awards show performances of all time. He turns and plays directly to Petty, who smiles at him and encourages him. As Prince contributed an ever-more intricate three-minute guitar solo, he engaged in playful theatrics, falling backward from the stage to be caught and returned to his feet and ending by throwing his guitar into the air—leaving an aura of mystery, since the guitar appeared never to come down, as no one could remember where it went or who caught it. After Prince's death, Petty recounted how he nodded at Prince to "Go on, go on" and gave him a " 'This is going great!' kind of look. He just burned it up. You could feel the electricity of 'something really big's going down here.' "[52] Petty wistfully recalled that, just a few days before Prince's death, he had been thinking about Prince and was going to call him to see how he was but regretfully did not. He concludes: "I'm starting to think you should just act on those things all the time."[53] In that performance together, Petty the relaxed, avuncular collaborator with the rock persona joins Prince the genius virtuoso who was bursting from the stage. Not only are Petty and Prince joined together through that endlessly watched YouTube video of their memorable joint performance, they are posthumously joined together by how they both later died.

CONCLUSION

Tom Petty's performance had to navigate the challenges posed by his own pain and pain management, but the coverage of his death did not impose the same stereotypes that media portrayals of Prince's did. Petty's family has now vowed to advocate for guidelines for opioid use and to raise awareness in other musicians about the dangers of fentanyl. Journalist David Browne argues that musicians are particularly at risk because they are often in physical pain from heavy touring or from ailments like carpal tunnel syndrome, and many people do not know that they are taking counterfeit pills laced with dangerous amounts of fentanyl.[54]

Meanwhile, the evolution of Prince's authenticity narrative in his music, lyrics, stage performances, and press interviews has been more altered by the media coverage of his death from opioid overdose. While it might be tempting to see Prince's trajectory as one of before and after the public realization of his addiction, it would be more accurate to see his addiction as a key strand driving his earlier authenticity narrative, because his aesthetic output was not separate from his physical suffering and, in retrospect, his performance identity involves both at the same time. His staging of his own performances and media image involves both his aesthetic expression and the challenges posed by his pain and his pain management, as well as ongoing racial stereotypes about drug addiction.

NOTES

1. Earlier high-profile overdose deaths of musicians caused by fentanyl include Jay Bennett (Wilco guitarist), Matt Roberts (3 Doors Down guitarist), and Paul Gray (Slipknot bassist).
2. "Fentanyl," NIH National Institute on Drug Abuse, last modified February 2019, https://www.drugabuse.gov/publications/drugfacts/fentanyl.
3. David Browne, "Music's Fentanyl Crisis: Inside the Drug That Killed Prince and Tom Petty," *Rolling Stone*, June 20, 2018, https://www.rollingstone.com/music/music -features/musics-fentanyl-crisis-inside-the-drug-that-killed-prince-and-tom -petty-666019/.
4. "Fentanyl and Other Synthetic Opioids Drug Overdose Deaths," NIH National Institute on Drug Abuse, last modified May 2018, https://www.drugabuse.gov/related-topics /trends-statistics/infographics/fentanyl-other-synthetic-opioids-drug-overdose-deaths.
5. "Fentanyl and Other Synthetic Opioids," NIH National Institute on Drug Abuse.
6. Browne, "Music's Fentanyl Crisis."
7. Taylor N. Santoro and Jonathan D. Santoro, "Racial Bias in the US Opioid Epidemic: A Review of the History of Systemic Bias and Implications for Care," *Cureus* 10, no. 12 (December 2018): e3733, https://doi.org/10.7759/cureus.3733.
8. Santoro and Santoro, "Racial Bias."
9. Richard Dyer, "Four Films of Lana Turner," in *Star Texts: Image and Performance in Film and Television*, ed. Jeremy G. Butler (Detroit: Wayne State University Press, 1991), 228.
10. John Ellis, "Stars as Cinematic Phenomenon," in *Star Texts: Image and Performance in Film and Television*, ed. Jeremy G. Butler (Detroit: Wayne State University Press, 1991), 302.
11. "Prince: Cops Release Video of Death Scene . . . Pics inside His Vault," TMZ, April 19, 2018, https://www.tmz.com/2018/04/19/prince-death-scene-body-video-photos -released/; "Prince's Hidden Pain," *OK!*, May 16, 2016, 4; Maria Vultaggio, "Prince Elevator Death Scene Photos and Video Released by Police," *Newsweek*, April 20, 2018, https://www.newsweek.com/prince-death-scene-photos-pictures-video-elevator -895741; "Prince: Questions after His Death," *Us Weekly*, May 16, 2016, 46–47.
12. Laura Mulvey, "Visual Pleasure and Narrative Cinema," *Screen* 16, no. 3 (1974): 6–18.
13. Griffin M. Woodworth, "Prince," in *The Grove Dictionary of American Music*, ed. Charles Hiroshi Garrett (New York: Oxford University Press, 2013), 604–5.
14. Joe Levy, "Prince," *Rolling Stone*, May 19, 2016, 42.
15. NFL, "Prince Performs 'Purple Rain' during Downpour," YouTube, February 12, 2016, https://www.youtube.com/watch?v=7NN3gsSf-Ys.
16. Alynda Wheat, "Prince 1958–2016," *People*, May 9, 2016, 46, 48.
17. Rob Tannenbaum, "Prince's Career on Camera: Insiders Recall Late Genius' Difficult

Relationship with Music Videos," *Billboard*, April 22, 2016, https://www.billboard.com/articles/news/7341616/prince-music-videos.

18. Ekow Eshun, "How Prince Invented Himself. Over and Over," *New York Times*, November 3, 2017, https://www.nytimes.com/2017/11/03/arts/music/prince-memorabilia.html.

19. "Jimmy Fallon Pays Tribute to Prince," *The Tonight Show Starring Jimmy Fallon*, April 26, 2016.

20. Camille Dodero, "Tracy Morgan Remembers Prince," *Billboard*, May 7, 2016, http://www.billboard.com/articles/news/cover-story/7348552/tracy-morgan-remembers-prince.

21. In terms of the emerging biographical conversations about Prince after his death, Vogel, in his academic thematic biography of Prince, and Greenman, in his biographical journalistic account, record many such stories. Joseph Vogel, *This Thing Called Life: Prince, Race, Sex, Religion, and Music* (New York: Bloomsbury, 2018); Ben Greenman, *Dig If You Will the Picture: Funk, Sex, God, and Genius in the Music of Prince* (New York: Henry Holt, 2017).

22. Derrick Bryson Taylor, "Prince Once Put Alicia Keys on Hold 10 Times," *Page Six*, April 22, 2016, https://pagesix.com/2016/04/22/prince-once-put-alicia-keys-on-hold-10-times/.

23. Dave Chapelle, interview by Jimmy Fallon, *The Tonight Show Starring Jimmy Fallon*, June 14, 2014.

24. "Prince," *New Girl*, season 3, episode 14, directed by Fred Goss, aired February 2, 2014, on FOX.

25. Michael O'Connell, " 'New Girl' Creator Liz Meriwether Talks Prince, Super Bowl Pressure and Letting Zooey Sing," *Hollywood Reporter*, January 30, 2014, https://www.hollywoodreporter.com/live-feed/new-girl-creator-liz-meriwether-675315.

26. Wheat, "Prince 1958–2016," 46, 48.

27. Wheat, "Prince 1958–2016," 46, 48.

28. Wheat, "Prince 1958–2016," 46, 48.

29. Ian Drew, "A Cry for Help," *Us Weekly*, May 23, 2016, 44–48.

30. Joe Coscarelli and Sheila M. Eldred, "Prince's Overdose Death Results in No Criminal Charges," *New York Times*, April 19, 2018, https://www.nytimes.com/2018/04/19/arts/music/prince-death-investigation.html.

31. Wheat, "Prince 1958–2016," 45; Drew, "A Cry for Help," 48.

32. Levy, "Prince," 42.

33. Vogel, *This Thing*, 170.

34. Wheat, "Prince 1958–2016," 47; Ollie Gilman and Kelly McLaughlin, "The Lonely Last Hours of the Purple One," *Daily Mail*, April 22, 2016. https://www.dailymail.co.uk/news/article-3554472/Prince-s-autopsy-complete-body-set-handed-family-weeks-cause-death-known-officials-await-toxicology-results.html.

35. Wheat, "Prince 1958–2016"; Gilman and McLaughlin, "The Lonely Last Hours."

36. Drew, "A Cry for Help," 44.

37. "Prince's Hidden Pain," *OK!*, 4.

38. "Prince Unaware He Was Taking Fake Pain Pills with Fentanyl: Prosecutor," *Page Six*, April 19, 2018, https://pagesix.com/2018/04/19/prince-didnt-know-he-was-taking-counterfeit-pain-pills-containing-fentanyl-prosecutor/.

39. "Prince's Death: Search Warrants Reveal Pills Hidden Everywhere," TMZ, April 17, 2017, https://www.tmz.com/2017/04/17/prince-death-search-warrant-pills-overdose/; "Prince: Cops Release Video," TMZ.

40. Joe Coscarelli and Serge F. Kovaleski, "How Prince Concealed His Addiction: Aspirin Bottles of Opiates," *New York Times*, April 17, 2017, https://www.nytimes.com/2017/04/17/arts/music/prince-opioid-death.html.

41. Jimmie N. Rogers, *The Country Music Message: Revisited* (Fayetteville: University of Arkansas Press, 1989), 17–18.

42. Fred Schruers, "Tom Petty's Widow and Bandmates Reflect on His Unreleased Material—and What's Next," *Billboard*, September 28, 2018, https://www.billboard .com/articles/columns/rock/8477364/tom-petty-box-set-interview.

43. Kory Grow, "Tom Petty's Cause of Death: Accidental Overdose," *Rolling Stone*, January 20, 2018, https://www.rollingstone.com/music/music-news/tom-pettys-cause-of-death -accidental-overdose-202789/; Ralph Ellis, "Tom Petty Died of Accidental Drug Overdose, Coroner Says," CNN, January 21, 2018, https://www.cnn.com/2018/01/19 /health/tom-petty-cause-of-death/index.html; Daniel Arkin and Andrew Blankstein, "Tom Petty Died of Accidental Drug Overdose, Coroner and Family Say," NBC News, January 19, 2018, https://www.nbcnews.com/pop-culture/music/tom-petty-died -accidental-drug-overdose-coroner-family-say-n839381.

44. Dana Petty and Adria Petty, "A Statement from the Petty Family," Tom Petty, January 19, 2018, http://www.tompetty.com/news/statement-petty-family-1764366.

45. Schruers, "Tom Petty's Widow."

46. Jon Pareles, "Tom Petty, a Mainstay of Rock with the Heartbreakers, Dies at 66," *New York Times*, October 3, 2017, https://www.nytimes.com/2017/10/03/arts/music /tom-petty-dead.html.

47. David Carr, "Big Screen Embraces Hot Muse: Rock Stars," *New York Times*, October 10, 2007, E1.

48. Johnny Cash and Patrick Carr, *Cash: The Autobiography* (New York: HarperCollins, 1997), 346.

49. C. Eric Banister, *Johnny Cash FAQ: All That's Left to Know about the Man in Black* (Milwaukee: Backbeat Books, 2014), 295.

50. Banister, *Johnny Cash FAQ*, 288.

51. Browne, "Music's Fentanyl Crisis."

52. Finn Cohen, "The Day Prince's Guitar Wept the Loudest," *New York Times*, April 28, 2016, https://www.nytimes.com/2016/04/28/arts/music/prince-guitar-rock-hall-of -fame.html.

53. Cohen, "The Day Prince's Guitar Wept the Loudest."

54. Browne, "Music's Fentanyl Crisis."

CHAPTER 5

"Maybe If I'd Stayed": Appalachian Outmigration and Narratives of Loss in Nate May's *Dust in the Bottomland*

Travis D. Stimeling

Huntington, West Virginia, is an urban epicenter of the opioid crisis in Appalachia. Situated on the banks of the Ohio River, the city has suffered the fate of many Rust Belt communities, with job losses followed by population losses, population losses followed by neglect, and neglect followed by despair.[1] A former industrial city with a large steel mill and a state university, Huntington was also once West Virginia's largest city, boasting a population of more than 86,000 residents at its peak in the 1950 decennial census, but now maintains only 47,000 residents.[2] Although the city has attempted to develop new businesses and public pride (particularly around the development of a multiuse commercial and transportation hub, Pullman Square, and the buzz around the Matthew McConaughey film *We Are Marshall* [2006], which focused on the plane crash that killed the Marshall University football team in 1970), the city's residents have continued to struggle.[3] Opioids—as well as the opiates heroin, fentanyl, and carfentanil—are in abundant supply there as a result of overprescription and drug traffickers who can easily reach Huntington from midwestern cities, and they have left a path of destruction in their wake.[4] In August 2016, for instance, twenty-six Huntington residents overdosed in only three and a half hours from accidental overdoses after a batch of heroin laced with the powerful opioid fentanyl was unleashed in the city.[5] As a consequence of Huntington's struggles with the opioid epidemic, it has become a center of national attention. Members of the Trump administration—as well as First Lady Melania Trump—have frequently visited the city to draw attention to recovery programs there, including especially Lily's Place, a facility that provides recovery services for opioid-exposed infants.[6] And documentary filmmaker Elaine McMillion Sheldon's Oscar-nominated film *Heroin(e)* has documented the devastating impacts that the opioid crisis has exerted on families and first responders in Huntington while drawing national attention to the work of Huntington fire chief Jan Rader, who developed protocols for first responders to use the overdose-reversing drug naloxone.[7]

Huntington native Nate May's (b. 1987) musical composition *Dust in the Bottomland* (2013) situates the opioid crisis within the broader contexts of Appalachian outmigration, deindustrialization, and the expansion of the environmentally devastating practice of mountaintop removal coal mining, which dominates the coal industry in the nearby southern coalfields of West Virginia.[8] Described as a "monodrama for modern-day Appalachia," *Dust in the Bottomland* presents the experiences of a male-voiced speaker who, after several years of living in the Midwest, returns to West Virginia to be with his family following his sister Stephanie's hospitalization from a near-fatal overdose. Cast in six movements, the dramatic action unfolds over four days, during which time the audience witnesses the speaker come to terms with his absence, the reasons he felt the need to leave in the first place, and the many losses that he and his family have experienced. The work is filled with signs of loss and absence in both the text and the music, both of which May created.

In using the frame of the opioid epidemic to open a larger discussion about the environmental, economic, and human costs of extractive economies in Appalachia, May's *Dust in the Bottomland* highlights some of the complex factors that have contributed to this public health crisis. That is, evidence suggests that opioids were expressly marketed to people in the Appalachian coalfields *because* of the high incidence of workplace injury, and their common and frequent distribution made them easy targets for abuse. Moreover, as mountaintop removal sites required fewer laborers while simultaneously exerting widespread environmental damage, the few nonextractive economic opportunities that existed prior to mountaintop removal's deployment dried up, leaving people to battle the social problems that often contribute to addiction in a setting marked by easy access to addictive drugs. The environmental impacts of mountaintop removal have also contributed to high incidences of cancer in the region as particulate matter from explosions of mountain sediments, heavy metals, and chemical runoff find their way into ground and surface water. Cancer pain is commonly treated with opioids, as are the pains resulting from injury and overuse in coal mining and related labor. Mountaintop removal and opioids are, therefore, inextricably linked. For people in diaspora, though, these impacts are often unfelt or are, at a minimum, muted because of physical, social, and, often, economic distance from home. And, as fewer people populate the area, fewer people are able to bear witness to the incremental loss of their homes. Rather, they are felt as acute—and quite alienating—experiences that demand action—either a deeper retreat from Appalachia or a commitment to political action. This essay, then, explores the role that aesthetic experiences play in the experience of Appalachian outmigrants and the people they leave behind. It considers as well the ways that these experiences might contribute both to the exacerbation of systemic challenges to coalfield recovery in the wake of the opioid crisis and to the creation of new avenues for valuable, grassroots community action.

Although Nate May composed *Dust in the Bottomland*, its composition was prompted by bass Andrew Munn, a Fayetteville, West Virginia, native who had taken a break from his formal voice studies to return to the southern coalfields, where he worked as a community organizer in the fight against the expansion of mountaintop removal coal mining in the region.[9] As May recalled in a 2018 interview with me, he and Munn had "been friends in college" at the University of Michigan and corresponded periodically about their shared interests. During the winter of 2012, their correspondence turned toward potential collaboration on a song cycle focusing on the experiences of people in the West Virginia coalfields. In his reflections on the work's genesis, May noted that he had just begun to develop his compositional skills when Munn approached him: "I don't think he [Munn] really knew that I was trying to be a composer. . . . He probably just knew that I played jazz piano and worked some jazz gigs, but he still shared this vision with me, and I got really excited about it."[10] In an email from May to Munn dated February 16, 2012, for instance, May offered to "come down to your part of WV, meet some of the local people who are affected by MTR, and write the cycle, probably from an informed fictional perspective." May noted that he hoped the piece "wouldn't so much be propaganda, or protest songs, but would reveal some of the absurdity of the conditions there, as well as the beauty of it."[11] During the summer of 2012, then, May visited Munn in West Virginia's southern coalfields, where they attended the memorial service for anti-mountaintop removal activist Larry Gibson and talked with many people throughout the region. As May recalled, this travel encouraged him to explore the intersections of mountaintop removal and the opioid epidemic, focusing on the extensive environmental and cultural destruction that they wrought on the region:

The first time I went to West Virginia to do some research for this was also for Larry Gibson's . . . memorial service in Charleston. So Andrew and I were in the audience for that, and it was obviously super emotional. . . . It very much motivated me to work on this piece, sitting in that audience and seeing everyone's reactions and hearing their pleas for the work to go on.

And really the addiction side of this came because I was talking to Andrew about what other sorts of things should be folded into this narrative, and he started talking about . . . a pill problem with opioids. And then we traveled around and went to Oceana [in Wyoming County, West Virginia], and this was before that documentary *Oxyana* came out. It was just a town that I guess Andrew had heard about and had passed through. And so he brought me there, and we went to the little flower shop and talked to the owner, Bev, and got her perspective on life there and addiction and kind of the daily fabric of things. And that's when that became a really important part of the story after we realized how integral this was in the life of what would be a character in southern West Virginia.[12]

Upon returning from these travels, May set to work on *Dust in the Bottomland*, writing both the text and the music. By the following summer, the work was complete, and it received a "soft premiere" at Interlochen, where May was working at the time, and a more formal premiere at a house concert in Huntington in August 2013.[13] The piece was later performed in New York; Pittsburgh; Louisville; State College, Pennsylvania; Lewisburg and Fayetteville, West Virginia; Blacksburg, Virginia; and Rock Hill, South Carolina, and was broadcast over WMMT (Whitesburg, Kentucky), SCTV (Fayetteville, West Virginia), and WWVU (Morgantown, West Virginia).[14]

Dust in the Bottomland begins in Stephanie's flower shop, an obvious homage to Bev's flower shop in Oceana. Immediately, the speaker is confronted by the visual and auditory silence of a once-vibrant place: the daisies that had been cut and arranged had "faded to coffee stains" when the store was closed to customers; a scuff mark on the floor stands as a reminder of Stephanie's once-dynamic movements around the shop; and the absence of human activity in the space makes it possible to hear that "buzzing lights and . . . humming furnace." The subsequent monologue—accompanied by the sound of a conspicuously ticking clock—reveals the depths of this absence. Not only is Stephanie's shop silent in the wake of her overdose the day before, but the speaker's home—the physical place he grew up—no longer exists. "Home had coal underneath it," he reports, "so home is gone now. Mom, Dad, and Stephanie have new houses, but they still aren't homes yet."

That *Dust in the Bottomland* begins with such a scene of absence is not terribly surprising, as absence and loss are characteristic tropes in a great deal of expressive culture addressing the diasporic experiences of Appalachians. Since the end of World War II, Appalachians—and particularly Appalachians from West Virginia, southwestern Virginia, and eastern Kentucky—have left the mountains for urban centers in the Midwest, the Mid-Atlantic, and the North Carolina Piedmont.[15] For generations, children from the region have been taught to seek out educational opportunities so they can find high-paying work in those urban centers, an education that often challenges kids to put aside traditional folkways and dialects in order to adopt the persona of a nonspecific middle-class American. Such diasporic movements have, as is often the case in such situations, resulted in a large body of expressive culture that addresses the complicated identities of diasporic Appalachians and uses a rhetoric of longing, loss, and absence to express these anxieties. *Dust in the Bottomland* opens with the same sorts of imagery made famous in bluegrass music. The Stanley Brothers, a bluegrass group from southwestern Virginia that was immensely popular in the Appalachian diasporic communities of Ohio, among other places, discuss these themes in their 1950 recording "The Fields Have Turned Brown."[16] In this song, the speaker leaves "his old home to ramble this country" with the advice of his parents ringing in his head: " 'Son, don't go astray' was what they both told me. / 'Remember that love for God can be found.' " Unfortunately, among his travels, he finds little reason to return home until he receives a letter informing him of his parents' passing. For the speaker, "the fields have turned brown." West Virginia native Hazel Dickens, too, traces the feelings of loss and dislocation in her "West Virginia, My Home," a song that reflects her own experiences as an Appalachian migrant to the Washington, DC/Baltimore area in the 1950s; she describes: "This city life's about got the best of me. / I can't remember what I wanted to be, / what I wanted to do, what I wanted to see. / But I can sure remember where I come from."[17]

The opening movement of *Dust in the Bottomland*, as well as the monologue that links the first two movements, reveals one of the more devastating aspects of life in the Appalachian diaspora: the effects of everyone else's absence on those people who remain behind after their friends and family leave. Although, following Appadurai, modern diaspora has often been framed as a set of multidirectional communication networks, capital flows, and travel pathways, comparatively little work has been done on the impacts of diaspora on those people who lack the means or the desire to seek better circumstances elsewhere.[18] But, as the speaker articulates clearly in the first connecting monologue, Stephanie struggled to maintain structure in a physical and human geography that was constantly in flux and that was characterized by loss and alienation. He notes: "My first stop is here in the flower shop—I found a key taped inside the mailbox, where our parents used to leave it. It's a whole world she made for herself, and for that town. She built this world when she was in control—when she didn't have to act. But the move changed that. It wasn't just a move, [*sic*] it was an uprooting—memories were literally buried or blasted away. And she turned back to the thing that she could once count on to make her feel human—pills."

The piece's second movement takes place in the intensive care unit of St. Andrew's Hospital, two days after Stephanie's overdose. Marked "gentle but driving," the movement places the pianist's right and left hands in constant tension with one another, articulating their respective parts in a canon offset by only one eighth note. This canonic technique captures the emotional intensity and unrest that often surrounds a visit to a loved one—especially an estranged one—within the healing space of an intensive care unit. Rather than presenting the speaker's reflections on his experiences of this difficult moment, though, May draws the audience into the speaker's experiences of the room itself. After addressing Stephanie directly, noting "I know you wouldn't want flowers in your room. / I know you'd want to escape them here in your hospital room, / but there they are, / dozens of them," the speaker sings words he found on the cards that were sent along with the flowers they brought to the hospital. The reported speech here begins uncomfortably, capturing the rhythm of the text but setting it within the confines of a relatively monotonous melody. But, by the end of the movement, this reported speech moves more fluently between registers and begins to capture the inflections of the individual visitors who have come to report on the health of Stephanie's dog and the burned-up clutch in her car and to pray for her physical and spiritual well-being.

This growing comfort with the tones and inflections of coalfield English, I would argue, offers another example of the kinds of losses and absences experienced by diasporic Appalachians: the loss of dialect, accent, and language more generally as diasporic Appalachians interact with and integrate into their new communities. Ethnomusicologist Aaron Fox, in his ethnography of white working-class communities in Texas and Illinois, observes that the ability to mimic the voices of people in their immediate communities—as well as those of "hard country" musicians—is prized within white working-class communities. By contrast, the professional class—which we are led to believe the speaker in *Dust in the Bottomland* at least *aspires* to be part of—commonly encourages the use of a nonmarked English pronunciation and inflection, perhaps best reflected in the speech of professional national broadcasters.[19] That the speaker here takes some time to reacclimate to the speech patterns of home reflects the loss—or, at a minimum, the displacement or misplacement—of marked speech. His return to the lyrical lines of his opening observations furthermore draws attention to the performative nature of speech and his efforts to put the sounds of home out of his mouth.

The spoken interlude linking the second and third movements of *Dust in the Bottomland* clarifies the speaker's relationship to his boyhood home. The southern coalfields weren't for him, he claims, because no one really noticed the place or its residents. He frames his move to Detroit as an "escape," noting, "This is the place I escaped from, ten years ago. The place where I felt forgotten by the world. I would see Dan Rather on the TV set, and I would think about who he was looking at when he stared into the camera. Millions of Americans. But he wasn't looking at us in West Virginia. He was looking right through us." Rather than staying to fight for positive change, then, the speaker left the area in order to attain some degree of recognition, even if that recognition came from becoming part of the unmarked "American middle class."[20] Such experiences speak to the powerful effects that media narratives—and the absence or stereotyping of communities in them—can have on the lived experiences of marginalized communities. That the speaker points to Dan Rather as an arbiter of national belonging also highlights the ways that national media reinforce the marginalization of regionally and ethnically marked voices. Or, put another way, the speaker likely first learned to put Appalachian speech out of his mouth by taking in national media products that marginalize marked speech. The third movement, "Driving at Dusk," also highlights the contrast between local and national media, as the movement finds the speaker driving from the hospital to the sounds of a "radio preacher" whose fiery evangelical preaching—likely evocative of the trance-inducing chants that ethnomusicologist Jeff Todd Titon describes in *Powerhouse for God*—anoints the landscape with Pentecostal spirit.[21] As the speaker describes, "On the mountain the tongues of flame touched their lips, and they knew just what to say," here evoking the notion of speaking in tongues, a core tenet of Pentecostal belief and an apt metaphor for the code-switching that the speaker struggles to accomplish on his own. Joined by a soft and dense piano accompaniment, the anxieties of Stephanie's health crisis and the speaker's uncomfortable return after a decade away seem to fade away as the speaker is enveloped by the sounds and sights that mark the place as familiar.

Dust in the Bottomland's fourth and fifth movements—"The Old Neighborhood: Part I" and "The Old Neighborhood: Part II"—unfold on the morning of the speaker's third day in the coalfields, four days following Stephanie's overdose. The peace and wonder of the previous evening give way to the stark realities of the present, in which the sounds of explosions from nearby mountaintop removal coal mining operations fill the air.[22] The movement begins with a piano gesture that emulates blasting sounds, a sonic marker of the changing landscape. In these movements, the speaker accompanies his father to the hill overlooking the old neighborhood, where he finds signs of nature's reclamation of the human landscape along with evidence of the community's decline. Among the sites he enumerates are "lion's mane hanging from the crook of a beech tree," "an F-100 [pickup truck] filled with buckshot holes," "a limping doe with fawns that bolted when we cracked a twig," "an iron mattress frame, rusted and twisted and sunk into the clay," and "four dirt-caked dolls in chairs beneath a willow tree." But even among these signs of the human lives that once thrived there, it is the devastation of mountaintop removal coal mining that seems to alienate the speaker, as the very things he remembers about the landscape of his youth are gone. (Or, put another way, at least the busted-down truck, rotting mattress frame, and creepy dolls were somewhat familiar, unlike the newly formed landscapes caused by the explosive blasts used in mountaintop removal.) Shifting from a predominantly stepwise melody to a highly angular one, the speaker repeatedly returns to what "should have been" there: "hunks of busted rubble where there should have been walnuts. / A sediment pond where there should have been a beaver dam. / A drainage pipe where there should have been a fox den. / An eighteen-story dragline where there should have been a hunting stand. / Distorted angles where there should have been God's fingerprints. / And sky where there should have been a mountain." Following this initial litany— and the recognition that the mountain is missing—the tempo increases as the accompanying piano plays *meccanicistico*: in an extremely mechanistic manner. The speaker's voice steadily reaches higher and higher, moving the peak of the motive from Bb3 to D4 as the pace of the litany quickens and the speaker bears witness to the "reclaimed" mountaintop removal site that has supplanted his boyhood home. It is at this point, then, that we hear the speaker's rawest emotional response to absences and losses that, although dramatic and shocking to him, were experienced as chronic loss by the ones left behind.

"The Old Neighborhood: Part II," played *attacca* (connected), further underscores the speaker's dramatic experience of loss in this moment. The movement takes the form of a theme and variations, the speaker intoning a repetitive text, part meditation and part mad scene. He observes, "The things that never could have changed, / these things not even dreams could rearrange, / the everyday world I passed through in haste / has now been replaced with something deranged." Beginning quietly and slowly building in intensity over the course of six variations and a coda, "The Old Neighborhood: Part II" finds the speaker revealing the emotional trauma, the raw experiences of loss and alienation, that is expressed more stoically in the bluegrass songs of diaspora noted earlier. In the subsequent monologue, the speaker begins a search for truth and a reconciliation with his past by reflecting on his roots in the area. He recalls that he "always knew" that coal extraction would take his home, citing his discovery of coal during a childhood dig in his backyard and the obvious expansion of mining operations in the area as evidence. Accompanied by the sounds of a coal train making its way down the track, the speaker admits that he tried to keep these observations from his family and that he wanted to save his own heart from suffering the losses that were on their way. "I didn't want to break their hearts with the news," he reflects. "And I didn't want to be around when it happened." His escape to Detroit, his entrance into the Appalachian diaspora, then, was predicated on loss and absence. But, rather than allowing him to escape the pain altogether, it seems that he was simply deferring it, putting it off until a time when he would eventually return to deal with the passing of his inevitably declining family. Like the diasporic singers in the bluegrass tradition, who seem to imply that they believe they had a hand in the collapse of the world they fled, the speaker also reflects, "I wonder if it would have been different if I had been here." He also notes that he probably "could [not] have saved" Stephanie from her opioid addiction and quickly dismisses his guilt and speculations as useless. To be sure, speculative thinking about potential alternate outcomes does little to solve contemporary problems—no need to cry over spilled pills, as it were—but it is striking that the speaker's acute emotional responses to the destruction around him can be addressed in one acute fit of expression, while Stephanie's experience of chronic, if never-at-once-devastating, loss pushed her toward pills intended for the relief of chronic pain. Would the speaker have turned to pills himself if he had stayed? We don't know, but it seems at least statistically likely.

To regain his grounding, the speaker sets out at dawn to visit the cemetery "on Hodgkin Hill," where his "Papaw and Uncle Silas and Aunt Roberta" have been laid to rest. Set syllabically and, initially, in a homophonic texture with planing harmonies that parallel the vocal melody's contours, "Driving at Dawn" finds the speaker locating the "hills that swaddled" him. That his journey to the cemetery takes him to a familiar landscape, even in the midst of the environmental destruction associated with mountaintop removal coal mining, is significant. Cemeteries are generally protected from such devastation, even if mountaintop removal can encroach dangerously close to the graves themselves.

Moreover, in many parts of Appalachia, cemeteries are important sites of communal gathering and community building, particularly through the tradition of Decoration Day, in which people travel to family or community cemeteries to maintain the graves of those people who have gone before. Decoration Day is often a reason for people in the Appalachian diaspora to return home, making the cemetery a site of reunification, as well.[23] The speaker here participates in this same work, albeit on his own, taking in the encroachment of mining from his perch "on Hodgkin Hill."

Dust in the Bottomland concludes ambivalently. In an accompanied monologue, the speaker reveals that he finds no truth or wisdom among the dead, who he suggests "just let everything come and go." Stephanie remains in a coma, on the boundary between life and death, and, should she end up dead, we learn, the speaker has "found the place where they would put her" in the cemetery, a place "up high enough that the dust from the mines couldn't reach her." He hopes to plant poppies around her grave, the opiate flower accompanying her in death and evoking fairy-tale tropes of somnolent beauties taken too young. But, even as Stephanie's medical condition remains in limbo, the speaker seems to be newly awakened to the challenges his old friends and family back home have been dealing with while he put his home on pause. "Sleep is so much easier than dealing with life," he reflects. "But I think I know what . . . [it] feels like . . . [to wake] up." Perhaps this awakening will lead to a deeper commitment to the problems faced by the people in his coalfield home, perhaps even a return from Detroit to claim a new home there. Perhaps it is opening a path to greater political activism on behalf of coalfield communities. Or perhaps it will lead to little more than personal reconciliation with his reasons for leaving and greater compassion for those people who have stayed behind.

If *Dust in the Bottomland* gives us little indication of how the speaker will operationalize his newfound awareness, May's and Munn's own lives provide some clues as to how he may act. Both May and Munn have lived in West Virginia—May in the Ohio Valley industrial hub of Huntington where he grew up and Munn in Fayette County, a major center of the southern coalfields, where he moved after college. Both became deeply involved in coalfield issues following educational relocations to the Midwest. Munn returned and began a lengthy stint as a community organizer and anti-mountaintop removal activist, and May moved to Fayetteville, where he dedicated his compositional efforts to a second piece using oral histories in the Berea College archives as the basis for a work addressing the experiences of the Appalachian diaspora in Cincinnati.[24] Both May and Munn have now left Appalachia physically: May is currently completing his DMA in composition at Yale, while Munn is touring

Europe, filling operatic roles in Germany, Poland, and elsewhere.[25] Prior to moving on to these new educational and professional opportunities, though, they toured with *Dust in the Bottomland*, playing it not only in larger metropolitan settings but in house concerts and community venues throughout Appalachia, where the work was generally well-received, according to May's recollections.[26] That they returned to the communities that inspired the work speaks volumes about their commitment to reflexive and transparent work. Unlike many national journalists who come to the coalfields for easy stories about poverty, energy, and "Trump country," May and Munn put their work up for face-to-face critique and, by and large, found audiences that saw themselves in the work.

Works like *Dust in the Bottomland* tell us a great deal about the ways that people experience the opioid epidemic and about possible solutions not only to the opioid epidemic but to the many structural problems that have contributed to it. As the contributors to *Appalachian Reckoning: A Region Responds to Hillbilly Elegy* have demonstrated, there is real power simply in sharing stories that challenge prevailing assumptions of a region and of a group of people.[27] Moreover, as rhetorician Amanda Hayes has recently suggested, Appalachian rhetoric itself may allow competing narratives and interpretations to coexist rather than arguing for the dominance of a single story: "It is a rhetoric . . . that allows for both individual interpretation and humility in the face of alternatives, that can accept ambiguity and multiplicity. It is a rhetoric that seeks connection over argumentation."[28] *Dust in the Bottomland*, then, might be heard as only one story among many, the story of someone who might be easily dismissed as not Appalachian enough because of his move to the Midwest, of someone who has gotten "above his raisin'." To amplify that voice too loudly might inadvertently drown out the voices of people living at ground zero of the opioid crisis, but to squelch it would be to ignore the valuable perspectives of someone who can witness these traumas with fresh eyes. By bringing diasporic perspectives into the dialogue, *Dust in the Bottomland* raises profound questions about the resilience of people who live with loss and trauma every day and, by bringing a fresh perspective on the many factors that contribute to such losses and traumas, has the potential to inject new energy into the fight for social and environmental justice and to imagine a world in which the fate of Appalachia was not determined by the extraction industry.[29] Moreover, as performative works, *Dust in the Bottomland* and similar projects have the power to literally bring people together, placing them side by side in concert venues and encouraging dialogue between people with widely varied experiences of the opioid crisis. As we continue the generations-long process of recovery from the opioid epidemic, then, such creative work might prove to be a particularly useful tool to repair broken relationships, to rebuild trust, and to reimagine a future.

NOTES

1. The population of Huntington declined by 4.3 percent between April 2010 and July 2017 with a net loss of nearly two thousand residents (US Census Bureau, "Quick Facts: Huntington City, West Virginia; West Virginia," https://www.census.gov/quickfacts/fact/table/huntingtoncitywestvirginia,wv/PST120217#PST120217).
2. "Huntington, WV Population," World Population Review, posted 12 June 2018, http://worldpopulationreview.com/us-cities/huntington-wv-population/.
3. Pullman Square, https://pullman-square.com; Lacie Pierson, " 'We Are Marshall' Ten Years Later," The [Huntington, WV] Herald-Dispatch, December 12, 2016, https://www.herald-dispatch.com/news/marshall_university/we-are-marshall-years-later/article_fc4e2e76-97cc-5ff6-a18f-f2305300b228.html.
4. Corky Siemaszko, "Fentanyl Seized, 90 Arrested in Takedown of 3-State Drug Ring," NBC News, April 17, 2018, https://www.nbcnews.com/storyline/americas-heroin-epidemic/fentanyl-seized-90-arrested-takedown-3-state-drug-ring-n866841; Amanda Garrett, "Opioid Crisis: West Virginia Officials Say Akron Street Dealers Fueling Drug Crisis," Akron Beacon Journal, November 9, 2018, https://www.ohio.com/news/20181109/opioid-crisis-west-virginia-officials-say-akron-street-dealers-fueling-drug-crisis.
5. Andrew Joseph, "26 Overdoses in Just Hours: Inside a Community on the Front Lines of the Opioid Epidemic," STAT, August 22, 2016, https://www.statnews.com/2016/08/22/heroin-huntington-west-virginia-overdoses/.
6. See, among others: Kate Bennett and Betsy Klein, "Melania Trump Visits West Virginia Opioid Treatment Center," CNN, October 10, 2017, https://www.cnn.com/2017/10/09/politics/melania-trump-west-virginia-opioid-treatment-center-visit/index.html; Bishop Nash, "HHS Deputy Secretary Praises Huntington's Response to Opioid Epidemic," The [Huntington, WV] Herald-Dispatch, October 31, 2018, https://www.wvgazettemail.com/news/health/wv_drug_abuse/hhs-deputy-secretary-praises-huntington-s-response-to-opioid-epidemic/article_6b369d5a-c582-5219-b9a2-92cf361fb453.html.
7. Elaine McMillion Sheldon, dir., Heroin(e) (Netflix and the Center for Investigative Reporting, 2017). For more background on Chief Rader, consult Renee Montagne, " 'Heroin(e): The Women Fighting Addiction in Appalachia," Weekend Edition Sunday, NPR, March 4, 2018, https://www.npr.org/2018/03/04/589968953/heroin-e-the-women-fighting-addiction-in-appalachia; Dave Peyton, "Local Officials Bring Huntington Back from the Brink," The [Huntington, WV] Herald-Dispatch, January 9, 2019, https://www.herald-dispatch.com/opinion/dave-peyton-local-officials-bring-huntington-back-from-the-brink/article_a8f00e47-3509-5032-bc52-94b168db77ea.html. Rader also delivered a memorable TED talk on the subject, which can be found at https://www.ted.com/speakers/jan_k_rader. She was also named to the Time 100 list in 2018 (Joe Manchin, "Jan Rader," in Time, "100 Most Influential People 2018," last accessed January 14, 2019, http://time.com/collection/most-influential-people-2018/5238151/jan-rader/).
8. "About," Nate May Music, last accessed January 14, 2019, http://www.natemaymusic.com/about.
9. Munn has discussed his connection to this work in Travis D. Stimeling, Saro Lynch-Thomason, Nate May, and Andrew Munn, "Music and Coal Activism: Perspectives from the Field," Ecomusicology Review 4 (December 31, 2016): http://www.ecomusicology.info/music-and-coal-activism-perspectives-from-the-field/, republished by Ethnomusicology Review, April 14, 2016, https://ethnomusicologyreview.ucla.edu/content/music-and-coal-activism-perspectives-field.
10. Nate May, telephone interview with author, August 6, 2018.

11. Nate May, email to Andrew Munn, February 16, 2012 (used with permission).
12. May, telephone interview with author, August 6, 2018.
13. May, telephone interview with author, August 6, 2018; "Dust in the Bottomland: A Musical Monodrama for Present-Day Appalachia," Nate May, released May 11, 2014, https:// natemay.bandcamp.com/album/dust-in-the-bottomland.
14. May, email correspondence with author, December 30, 2018.
15. For more background on the Appalachian diaspora, consult, among others: William W. Philliber, Clyde B. McCoy, and Harry C. Dillingham, eds., *The Invisible Minority: Urban Appalachians* (Lexington: University Press of Kentucky, 1981); Carl E. Feather, *Mountain People in a Flat Land: A Popular History of Appalachian Migration to Northeast Ohio, 1940–1965* (Athens: Ohio University Press, 1998); Phillip J. Obermiller, Thomas E. Wagner, and E. Bruce Tucker, eds., *Appalachian Odyssey: Historical Perspectives on the Great Migration* (Westport, CT: Greenwood, 2000); Chad Berry, *Southern Migrants, Northern Exiles* (Urbana: University of Illinois Press, 2000); Roger Guy, *From Diversity to Unity: Southern and Appalachian Migrants in Uptown Chicago, 1950–1970* (Lanham, MD: Lexington Books, 2007).
16. "The Old Home" b/w "The Fields Have Turned Brown," Columbia 20667, February 13, 1950 (Gary B. Reid, *The Music of the Stanley Brothers* [Urbana: University of Illinois Press, 2015], 226).
17. Hazel Dickens with Bill C. Malone, *Working Girl Blues: The Life and Music of Hazel Dickens* (Urbana: University of Illinois Press, 2008); Tim Newby, *Bluegrass in Baltimore: The Hard Drivin' Sound and Its Legacy* (Jefferson, NC: MacFarland, 2015), 9–48.
18. Arjun Appadurai, *Modernity at Large: Cultural Dimensions of Globalization* (Minneapolis: University of Minnesota Press, 1996).
19. Aaron A. Fox, *Real Country: Music and Language in Working-Class Culture* (Durham, NC: Duke University Press, 2004), 37–38.
20. Consider, for instance, the argument put forth in Amanda E. Hayes, *The Politics of Appalachian Rhetoric* (Morgantown: West Virginia University Press, 2019).
21. Jeff Todd Titon, *Powerhouse for God: Speech, Chant, and Song in an Appalachian Baptist Church* (Austin: University of Texas Press, 1988), 257–92, esp. 271–73.
22. May notes, "I saw 'Driving at Dusk' and 'Driving at Dawn' as opportunities to let the mind wander the way mine does when I drive on rural roads in West Virginia" (May, email correspondence with author, December 30, 2018).
23. Alan Jabbour and Karen Singer Jabbour, *Decoration Day in the Mountains: Traditions of Cemetery Decoration in the Southern Appalachians* (Chapel Hill: University of North Carolina Press, 2010).
24. Nate May, *State* (2016), http://www.natemaymusic.com/state.
25. "Andrew Robert Munn, Bass," Andrew Robert Munn, accessed December 16, 2019, https:// www.andrewrobertmunn.com/; "About," Nate May Music, accessed December 16, 2019, http://www.natemaymusic.com/about.
26. May, email correspondence with author, December 30, 2018.
27. Anthony Harkins and Meredith McCarroll, eds., *Appalachian Reckoning: A Region Responds to Hillbilly Elegy* (Morgantown: West Virginia University Press, 2019).
28. Hayes, *The Politics of Appalachian Rhetoric*, 27.
29. Here, I am drawing on the work of folklorist Dorothy Noyes, who has problematized the notion of "resiliency" and suggested that we should instead focus on the factors that led to a need for resiliency. Dorothy Noyes, *Humble Theory* (Bloomington: Indiana University Press, 2016), 410–37.

PART II

IF YOU LIVED HERE

REPRESENTING THE OPIOID EPIDEMIC FROM WITHIN

CHAPTER 6

Pretty Lil Azzie

Crystal Good

Written in the spirit of the ingenious, inventive rhythmic singing and hand clapping games of the Black child....

>Pretty Lil Azzie, Auntie wrote ya a song.
>Cause the dog dun bit ya MammaDaddy gone.
>Gone. Gone. Gone too long.
>Pretty Lil Azzie Auntie wrote ya a song.
>
>Ya Paw Paw work. Ya Paw Paw pray.
>Dear Lord, she be ok.
>Be Ok. Be Ok.
>Dear Lord, she be ok.
>Pretty Lil Azzie, she be ok.
>
>Paw Paw wake ya up everyday.
>Everyday. Everyday.
>While ya MammaDaddy gone away.
>Gone. Gone. Gone away.
>Paw Paw wake ya up everyday.
>Ya MammaDaddy gone away.
>
>Your smile is light.
>Your eyes are bright.
>Social Worker say you be alright.
>Pretty Lil Azzie born fight.

Cause the dog dun bit ya MammaDaddy gone.
Gone. Gone. Gone. Gone.
MammaDaddy gone gone, another night.

Pretty Lil Azzie, ya gonna be alright.

CHAPTER 7

The Way the World Is:
From *Maggie Boylan*

Michael Henson

"That's the way the world is," the girl said. And she did not seem to like it.

"Honey, you ain't seen nothing," Maggie Boylan wanted to say. But the girl did not skip a beat.

"All I did was take her in because she was homeless and I get throwed in jail for what she done."

A late November wind rattled the windows of the lobby where they sat, side-by-side on a bench. The girl was a heavy girl—a young woman, really, but to Maggie Boylan, just a girl. She was thick in the body, weighted in the shoulders, heavy in the cheeks and around her eyes. She was pierced in several places, pierced in one nostril, pierced with a ring in her brow, pierced by an arc of studs in her ear.

"There I was," she said, "coming out the door at Walmart. I had a cart full of groceries and diapers and what not. I was fixing to feed her and her kids right along with mine, and all of a sudden, you'd of thought I was Osama Bin Laden. There goes the alarm ringing and here come the security cop and a few minutes later here come the police and there's my little kids crying and these cops want to know did I think I was smart trying to get away without paying for that purse and I'm, like, what purse?"

"And what it was, that penniless bitch I took in off the street had snuck this purse she wanted into my cart after I done checked out so she skips on ahead. She borrowed my car keys, you see, and she says, I'll go ahead and unlock the door. And she skips out like there ain't nothing going on."

"She set you up."

"She didn't have the guts to steal it herself and she figured if anybody was gonna get caught it'd be me. And she would of got away with it, except I pointed her out and they ended up taking both of us to jail. And I'm thinking, there's my little kids off to foster care, and they're crying their little hearts out. And my parents had to come up from Wilsonville to fetch my kids and bail me out."

Maggie Boylan had been nodding as the girl spoke, but she perked up her ears at the mention of the children almost gone to foster care. She was small as the girl was large, small-boned and spare of flesh with the quick, fierce eyes and sharp features of a fox. She watched the girl more closely now.

"But that's the way the world is," the girl said again. "You try to help somebody and you get stiffed."

A deputy passed through the lobby. He was a heavy man with a heavy tread and he called out, "What d'you know, Maggie?"

"I know I want to visit my old man," she called. But the deputy slung himself through the door without another word.

The girl had lit a cigarette; she blew out smoke and nodded. "That's just how they treat you," she said.

"They won't let you smoke in the building." Maggie pointed to a sign above the counter.

The girl raised a skeptical brow. "They can't do no more to me than what they done already." But she drew on her cigarette one more time, stubbed it out carefully on the rim of a trashcan, then slid it back into the pack.

"They can slap you with a fine," Maggie said. "They can write you a ticket in a heartbeat."

"Right now, I don't hardly care. They could throw me right back in that cell and I wouldn't care."

"Honey, you don't know what you're saying."

"They couldn't do me no worse than what they done already. What could they do worse than what they already done?"

Maggie held her peace.

"This is the worst that's ever happened to me," the girl said. She folded her arms, unfolded them, then placed her hands on her knees. "I ain't never been inside a jail before. Never did expect to be. But there I was. And all because I wanted to help some girl that wouldn't help herself."

She looked toward the door where the deputy had gone and folded her arms again.

"Like I say," she continued. "If it hadn't been for my parents coming up to make my bail, I probably would of lost my kids to foster care. And God only knows what would of happened to them."

"How many you got?"

"I got a boy and I got a girl. Three and two."

"Little tiny ones."

The girl's shoulders sagged as if she carried a world of care. "That's why I couldn't stand to see her homeless and all. Cause she got three, and all of them under six. Ain't even in school yet. So, I understand what it is to have kids and you want them safe and fed and all. She comes to me complaining how she's homeless and their daddy beat on her and she had to take them kids of hers and leave home. Well, big-hearted me, I had to take them in off the street.

"So, I asked her, 'Why in the world would you do something like this to somebody trying to help you out?' She says, 'Well I reckoned you're smart and you know how to talk to people and if you got caught you'd talk your way out of it because you didn't know it was there.' And I told her, 'Well, it didn't work out like that, did it?' "

Maggie had been staring at the door, but now she turned to the girl. "You want to smoke that cigarette?"

"Ma'am?"

"You still want to smoke? Let's go outside."

"I can't. I'm waiting for that bitch that put me in here."

"Come on, you can whup her ass later."

"I ain't planning to whip her ass." She stood, with a glance toward the counter. "But I do plan to give her a piece of my mind."

"You better." Maggie led the girl out onto the front steps of the courthouse. Out in the yard, a trusty pushed a pile of leaves against the wind. "You sure don't want to whup some girl's ass in the courthouse; they'll slap you in a cell inside a cell. They'll stroke you good. If you want to whip her ass, you got to go somewhere else."

"No," the girl said. She pulled out her pack and tapped out the cigarette she had stubbed out before. "I ain't a violent person. I just want her to know what I got to say."

The steps of the courthouse were cold. They cupped hands for a windbreak, lit their cigarettes, and smoked and shivered together.

"I mean," the girl said, "it just don't make sense. You pick somebody up out of the gutter and you feed their children like they was your own. You do everything it says in the Bible to do. And here I get arrested for the very first time in my life. And I don't do drugs. I don't drink. I don't do nothing. I just go to work and clean house and take care of my kids and now I probably got this on my record."

"You done?" Maggie nodded toward the cigarette.

The girl was not. Maggie had hit hers hard; she had barely stopped to breathe. She flicked the butt of it ten feet out into the yard. "Let's get out of this wind," she said.

For a second time, the girl stubbed out her cigarette. This time, she dropped it into the shrubs.

The heavy deputy was at the counter when they came back in. He glanced up from some paperwork and nodded. "You staying clean, Maggie?"

"When can I see him, Burke?"

"Tuesday. Visiting day."

"But I can't come on Tuesday."

"Can't help you, Maggie." He turned and took his papers into an inner office.

"He's the nice one," the girl said. "That other one—I ain't seen him yet today—he was mean."

"What was his name?"

"I don't know. I don't know any cops' names. Never did need to know any cops' names."

"Ain't none of them nice far as I'm concerned. Especially that one."

"At least he didn't say nothing smart, like that other one."

There was a stir in the inner office and both looked up.

"That's her," the girl said. "That's the bitch that got me arrested."

"That scrawny thing? Hell, you could whup her ass with one hand." The scrawny thing wore an oversize coat and kept losing her arms in the sleeves. She had long hair strung back behind her ears that fell down every few seconds into her eyes, so that she was in constant motion to pull back her sleeve, tuck back her hair, shift her feet, pick up a pen, sign where the deputy pointed, set down the pen, adjust her hair, and lose her arms again in her sleeves.

"Nervous little bitch, ain't she?"

"What're they doing?"

"Looks like they're fixing to let her go."

"About time. I posted her bond an hour ago."

"You done what?"

The girl shrugged.

"After everything that shifty little bitch done you?"

"Who else is gonna do it? She don't have nobody else."

"Well I'll be damned." Maggie stood, went to the counter, and called, "Burke, Tom Burke, when can I visit my old man?"

"Tuesday, Maggie. Visiting day is Tuesday."

"But I ain't got no ride for Tuesday. I got a ride today."

"There's nothing I can do about it, Maggie."

"At least let me leave him some money while I got it."

"Tuesday."

"I got twenty dollars to give him for cigarettes."

"He'll live."

"At least let me get him a can of Bugler and some papers."

The deputy shut the door.

"Fucking prick!" Maggie shouted. "Fat fuck probably shut the door so he could collect his blow job. Possum-headed punk ain't never worked the starch out of that uniform, but he can tell me Tuesday when I know damn well what day visiting day is. All he can say to me is, 'What d'you know, Maggie?' I'll tell you what I know. I know he was my old man's buddy growing up but he's too good to do me a turn even for his buddy's sake. And then he wants to know am I staying clean, as if that's any business of his."

She turned to the girl on the bench. "You want to talk about the way the world is. Well, that right there's the way the world is. Your old man is doing six months in this little rat hole jail over some bullshit and you can't even get to see him because some shit in a uniform can't do you a little favor."

"I know what you mean," the girl said.

"No, you don't know what I mean. Not till you done what I done. Not till you seen what I seen. Not till you heard them bars slam shut behind you and you know it'll be two long years before you get to hold your babies again. Then you come and tell me what the world is like."

"You're pushing your luck, Maggie," the deputy called from behind the door.

"I ain't had no luck since the day I was born."

————————

Maggie's ride back home was still at the pool hall and might be there another hour yet, or even two.

"Yes," the neighbor boy told her. "I'm going to town, but just long enough to cash my check." Then, "Half an hour," he told her when she found him at the pool hall.

Then, "Just let me finish this rack," when she came back around.

So now she stood out on the courthouse steps, shivering in her jean jacket, cursing softly.

She had a cigarette in one hand and her twenty-dollar bill balled up in the other and she smoked and shivered until she had smoked the cigarette down to a nub. The jailhouse door swung open and out came the scrawny thing and the heavy girl right behind her.

"What do you want me to do?" the scrawny thing said. "I already told you I'm sorry."

"You can tell my mom and dad why they had to drive all the way up here and bail me out."

A gust of wind snatched away the rest of their words and Maggie watched them take their argument up the street and around the corner.

That's the way the world is, Maggie thought. One damn fuss after another.

She looked across to the pool hall. Half an hour, she thought. It's been that long at least. That boy's liable to be there till closing time. What do I do till then?

The wind picked up a scatter of leaves and blew them across the yard and in the rattle of the leaves it seemed she could hear the scrawny thing and the heavy girl going at it hammer and tongs.

Not another soul was out. She reckoned there were people drinking coffee at the Square Deal Grill and people in line at the bank and one or two that stood at the drugstore counter for a prescription. But the wind had driven everyone off the streets and off the square. The trusty's rake leaned against a wall.

Leaves had gathered under the shrubs, leaves in the gutters, leaves on the windshields of the parked cars.

She looked at her sweaty, balled-up twenty and wished she would not do what she was likely now to do. She crossed the street and looked into the window of the pool hall. The neighbor boy stared at the table and slowly chalked his cue. Another broke a new rack.

So, she had time, plenty of time by the look of it. That neighbor boy would play out every dollar in his pocket before he drove her back to Wolf Creek. And then he would want to dun her for gas money, and all she had in life was that twenty.

Her hands began to tremble; she began to ache in every bone at the thought of all that dead time and the money getting hot in her hand. She knew where she could get something for her twenty, something that would ease her mind and take away the ache and blunt the hard edges of memory and the world, something that would set the world aright.

The next gust of wind pushed hard against her. The snows of December were just around the corner. She shivered at the thought and gripped her twenty hard. It was ten cold miles back to Wolf Creek. She looked toward the jailhouse where her old man sat in his cell, then through the pool hall window where the boys were racking up another game. She hesitated for another moment, then with a curse for the neighbor boy, for Deputy Burke, for the heavy young girl and the scrawny thing, she followed her twenty down the alley.

CHAPTER 8

Finding Maggie Boylan

Michael Henson

Not long ago, I was running errands in my neighborhood when I saw a former colleague who happens to live nearby. We once worked in different nooks of the same large Cincinnati social services agency, and we have a nodding, hi-how-are-you kind of acquaintance. I asked him, "What are you up to?" and he told me he worked now as a supervisor at one of the new for-profit addiction treatment centers that have popped up in the wake of the opiate epidemic.

"You ought to check it out," he said. "This opiate epidemic is a gold mine."

Gold mine seems a weirdly inappropriate way to describe an epidemic that has taken the lives of over 350,000 people, but apparently, there is still money to be made out of other people's pain.[1]

I have no interest in checking out his treatment center. Or any other. When I retired, I decided I was done with all that. After years working with individual clients, I am now much more interested in causes and conditions. I want to know what is causing all this pain, and I want to help stop it. I volunteer with a neighborhood group committed to fighting the epidemic by way of education and advocacy.

And I write.

In the years since I first became aware of OxyContin, I have written stories, essays, and even a song based on my encounters with the people caught up in the addictive horror in its wake.

I never intended to be an addictions counselor. I just wanted to write. To pay the bills and to care for my family, I knew I would have to find work. So, to help the writing along, I tried over the years to find work that would put me in contact with those whose stories I wanted most to tell, people on the margins, people whose dignity is most at risk. To explain this preference would take us far afield from the purpose of this essay, but I am aware of the risks involved in such a preference, much as James Agee, my personal literary patron saint, was aware of the moral risk in writing *Let Us Now Praise Famous Men*, that of exploiting the subjects of his study in the name of speaking for them. But I believe that the greater risk is *not* to tell these stories if a writer is capable of so doing. Thus, at various times, I have worked as a schoolteacher, factory hand, farm worker, and house painter. For fourteen years, I worked as a community organizer. And, by way of a life accident too complicated to explain in these pages, I worked for over twenty years as an addiction counselor, which is how I first met this particular neighbor who now works in his treatment gold mine.

I find my former colleague's attitude to be morally repugnant. The history of the opiate epidemic is full of morally repugnant behavior. While completing this essay, I was going back and forth between reading journalist Chris McGreal's book on the origins of the epidemic and a piece in *Mother Jones* magazine on scams in the treatment industry in which "treatment" providers prey on vulnerable addicts to collect finders' fees for addicts whom they try to keep using, knowing that if these clients stay clean, the finders' fees will dry up.[2] Perhaps the greatest irony in this whole thing is Purdue Pharma's recent bid to license a new drug to aid in treatment of the illness they did so much to cause. The readiness of people in the helping professions to profit from this catastrophe carries such a load of irony that I can barely speak of it without sputtering in rage.

But before I mount too high a horse, let me also point out that the writer, or any artist, can dig in the gold mines as well. There is not much literal gold to be had. Very few artists make even a bare living out of their art. Nearly all have to do something else to earn a living. But there are other sorts of gold—fame, awards, gratified egos, attention, burnished reputations.

I managed to strike a bit of that kind of gold with *Maggie Boylan*, my second book of OxyContin fiction.

Maggie Boylan is a collection of linked short stories that follow nine months in the life of a woman addicted to OxyContin in rural Appalachia. Maggie is angry, foulmouthed, and conniving, but I tried to portray her with an inner core of resilience and compassion. In ten stories that cover nine months of Maggie's life, we see her lie and cheat her way into the legal system, then into treatment, and, at the end, stumble into the shaky beginnings of recovery. Along the way, she encounters corruption in local politics, just a fraction of the massive web of corruption that is the genesis of this crisis.

With *Maggie Boylan*, I wanted to tell a story that described the brutal

realities of the opiate epidemic that still left the essential dignity of my characters intact. I wanted to tell a story of redemption.

I had written about addiction and its impact on community before. In fact,
I have been writing about addiction all my life, starting with my novel *Ransack*,
published back in 1980. My novella *Tommy Perdue*, released in 2013, may have
been the first published fictional account of the opiate epidemic. That book was
released by a small, independent press, a one-person operation that, in spite of
the dynamism of its publisher, was never able to get the book much attention.

But Swallow Press has a hardworking and creative promotional staff.
Among the results of their efforts are *Maggie Boylan*'s selection by the Women's
National Book Association as a 2018 Great Group Read and reviews in publications both major (*Publishers Weekly*, "harrowing, haunted, and often beautiful")
and minor (*The Observer*, from Shepherdstown, West Virginia, "compulsively
readable").[3] Samara Rafert and Jeffrey Kallett have helped connect me with
gigs in Ohio, West Virginia, Kentucky, and Tennessee to read from the book
and to speak about it in bookstores, libraries, and schools.

Inevitably, as I go to various groups to read from *Maggie* and to speak about
the opiate crisis, I am asked, How did you come up with this story? Is Maggie
based on a real person? Where did she come from?

Good question.

When OxyContin swept into Cincinnati, I was working in the neighborhood
called Lower Price Hill as a community organizer with the Urban Appalachian
Council.

Lower Price Hill is not a hill at all. It sits in the floodplain where the Mill
Creek dumps into the Ohio River. For years, Lower Price Hill was where the ef-
fluents of the factories that turned Cincinnati into an industrial powerhouse
flowed downstream. Procter and Gamble was just one of the factories sited
further up the Mill Creek Valley. Lower Price Hill, also known as Eighth and
State, developed into a mixed residential and industrial neighborhood in the
late 1800s. In the fifties and sixties, the Germans, Italians, and Irish of the
neighborhood fled to the hills as economic refugees from eastern Kentucky,
West Virginia, Tennessee, and southeast Ohio took their place. Poverty in
Cincinnati, if it is white, tends to be Appalachian, so a group of us founded the
Urban Appalachian Council in the seventies to speak for the displaced mountain people. By the year 2000, when I came to work in Lower Price Hill, there
was a history of resistance to an array of industrial polluters, which included
a barrel recycling facility and an eighty-acre sewage treatment plant operated
by Hamilton County. All this industry caused, we believed, a concentration of

childhood illnesses that included hearing defects, asthma, learning disabilities, and cancer. My job, funded by a federal grant, was to help residents confront the polluters.

It was challenging and fulfilling work. I came to the job after seventeen transformative but difficult and somewhat confining years as a substance abuse counselor, and I was happy to be in a position where I could be more creative and where I could work directly with people for social change. I continued to work as an addictions counselor with a few clients, and I continued to volunteer as clinical supervisor with a treatment center that operated out of a homeless shelter. I also began a monthly column on issues of poverty and addiction in *StreetVibes*, the local homeless newspaper. You would think addiction had nothing to do with the work of fighting pollution. But several of the members of our activist organization, the Environmental Leadership Group, struggled with addiction. Addiction affected everything we did.

And yet, I could not have predicted the tidal wave of addiction issues that was presented by OxyContin.

We were networked with other Appalachian environmental groups, so I had heard the stories. Articles had already begun to appear in places like the *New Yorker* and the *New York Times*. I saw a documentary film about the early stages of the epidemic. I also had friends across Appalachia and, in particular, in the southern Ohio community where I once taught school, who told me how the epidemic was affecting them. And so, I was aware of OxyContin's spread through Appalachia.

It didn't take long for the opioid epidemic to leap from the mountains into the city. I noticed that it got harder and harder to keep our group focused on the issues we had identified as crucial; their families were too stressed over what was happening to them from Oxy. Lower Price Hill had always been a hard-drinking, hard-drugging community. But now, people had trouble functioning. The neighborhood had seen trouble before but never prostitution on the streets. Girls walking to school were harassed by men from downtown trying to pick them up. Shoplifting and break-ins increased. We held several funerals for overdose victims. An elderly woman overdosed on the steps of the office of Santa Maria Neighborhood Services. Things went from bad to unbelievable.

So, we turned our attention to the developing drug crisis. We formed a coalition to combat the spread of prescription abuse; it still operates today. A big part of the problem was the East Indiana Treatment Center, a "treatment" facility just across the Indiana border. Clients there got minimal therapy, but for a few dollars, they could claim they were still experiencing craving to get higher doses of methadone, which they could then sell on the street.[4] The elderly grandmother who overdosed on the steps of Santa Maria had been using some of this bootleg East Indiana methadone. We pressured East Indiana to tighten up its protocols and to get serious about actually providing treatment. We held prevention groups for kids and rallies and public forums.

But when the funding for community organizing ran out, I had to go back to working in treatment. I took a job with Talbert House, the same agency I had left eight years before. This time, I worked as a clinical supervisor for a string of halfway houses for men coming out of prison. Many of the convicts I dealt with were from southeast Ohio. To a man, they had gone to prison on Oxy-related charges. I also continued my volunteer work providing clinical supervision at the homeless shelter. And I stayed in touch with friends living in southern Ohio and in other parts of Appalachia who were dealing with the spreading opiate epidemic.

It used to be that, when I told someone what I did for a living, they would often say, "Oh, that must be so hard." Often as not, I told them, "I get paid to have people tell me stories. What's hard is living the stories." In fact, the work brought me into a new relationship to story. My job consisted of listening, day after day, to story, to interpreting story.

I had already begun to write the opiate stories that led first to *Tommy Perdue*, then later, to *Maggie Boylan*.

The idea for *Tommy Perdue* came straight from local headlines. Two burglars were caught one night trying to break into a Lower Price Hill restaurant called the Paradise Café. One of them served as a lookout in the alley and was quickly arrested. The other, trying to squeeze down a vent to reach the cash register, called out, "I'm almost there," as police stood outside and laughed. Local news played the story as comedy. I saw it as a tragedy and wrote it that way in a short story. In a subsequent series of stories, I followed Tommy back in time to the story of his teenage mother, her migration to the city, and the formation of a community around him in a fictional neighborhood much like Lower Price Hill and centered on a restaurant called, of course, the Paradise Café. (What writer would throw away a name like that?)

I had a problem in writing the *Tommy* stories: how do you write about a kid whose poor choices lead to a wasted life without turning him into a monster or a freak?

It's easy to go wrong in writing about people on the margins. The first, probably most obvious, mistake is to fall into negative stereotyping. A variant of stereotyping, one that attempts to put a positive spin on events, is sentimentalizing. Yet another is to fall into what I think of as hypodermic porn, a fascination with the mechanics of tying off, finding a vein, inserting the needle, and so on, to the exclusion of the inner life of the addict being depicted. There are probably others. But I wanted, desperately, to create characters and situations that were fully rounded, that had all the bruises and blisters of reality, but which left the inherent dignity of my characters intact. Where possible, I wanted to show hope, even where there seems to be none. There wasn't much hope to be had in Tommy's story, but I believe a reader can catch a glimpse of hope in the community that survives around him.

As I started these opiate stories, first *Tommy*, then *Maggie*, one of my goals was to expose the nefarious nature of the corporate criminals responsible for this epidemic. For the deeper you study this issue, the more stunning it becomes to consider the sheer numbers of people, most of them already doing well, who were willing to make a dollar off the suffering of others less fortunate. As a substance abuse counselor, I worked with many convicted drug traffickers. I even designed and implemented an intervention group designed to help traffickers break with their drug-dealing patterns. Nearly all of these convicted dealers grew up in poverty. But the OxyContin traffickers were doctors, pharmacists, scientists, salespeople, executives, and lawyers—lots of lawyers, all of whom were making professional salaries and living comfortably. All of them jumped onto the OxyContin bandwagon.

Very few of these professionals have suffered any serious consequences. When I worked in the halfway houses for men coming out of prison, every one of the convicts from rural Ohio had gotten in trouble over OxyContin. A few doctors and nurses who helped cause their problems have seen some jail time, but most of the perpetrators still live comfortably. It infuriates me, having seen the devastation this epidemic has spread in a widening circle from individual addicts, to their families, to whole communities. I wanted to bring some of this frustration into the stories I was writing. I had hopes that these stories might expose the perfidy of the Sacklers, Purdue Pharma, and of the chain of greedsters who helped create the Maggies and the Tommys dying in their numbers.

I was able to express some of this anger in an essay with the somewhat extravagant title "The Strange Story of OxyContin: A Tale of Predictable and Utterly Preventable Catastrophe." I published the first version of this essay as one of my monthly columns in *StreetVibes*. Later, I updated and expanded the essay for *Still: The Journal*, an online magazine of Appalachian literature.[5] Yet another version of the essay ran in *The Fix*, an online magazine devoted to addiction and recovery. And finally, a version is to be included in *Not Far from*

Me: Stories of Opioids and Ohio, an anthology of writings about the epidemic from Ohio State University Press.[6] In the essay, I contrast the image of a young prostitute on the streets of Lower Price Hill with the Egyptian figures in the Sackler Wing of the Metropolitan Museum of Art in New York City, which I had visited with my daughter (and which was recently the scene of an anti-Sackler protest by a coalition of artists.)

Later, after my best friend lost his son to an opiate overdose, I wrote a song that explicitly makes the charge:

> *I could tell a hundred stories*
> *Of lives thrown into a ditch*
> *How the poor folks got the OxyContin*
> *And the rich folks just got richer.*
> *They said these drugs would help us*
> *They said these drugs would heal.*
> *But the young graves on the hillside*
> *Say those promises weren't real.*[7]

You can make that sort of charge in a song or in an essay. But not in fiction. At least, not the way I write fiction.

The characters would never let me.

In each case, whenever I was tempted to go on an editorial rant, the characters stepped in. One and all, they firmly refused to serve as my mouthpieces.

I believe that the artist best serves the community by remaining true to the demands of his or her art. As a writer of fiction, I am responsible to be true to my story, without reference to anything that intrudes into the story that does not belong. John Gardner, in his book *The Art of Fiction,* speaks of the work of fiction as a "vivid and continuous dream" and describes a host of elements that interrupt the continuity of the dream and, thereby, the implicit pact between writer and reader. "By detail, the writer achieves vividness; to make the scene continuous, he takes pains to avoid anything that might distract the reader."[8] Among these distractions would be inclusion of a political or social agenda that comes from the world of the author, not the character. To put a political or social speech into the mouth of a character, which obviously comes not from the character but from the mind of the author, is a flagrantly false element that takes us out of the story and betrays the trust of the reader.

In order to tell the truth a story is meant to tell, the writer must remain at the mercy of his or her characters. The writer may have a grand initiative. He may want to end discrimination; she may want to promote a worthy cause.

But their characters want only to have their stories told. And they want their stories told true.

The truth available in a fictional story is what is true for the characters within the bounds of the story. Anything else brought in—any authorial imposition onto the characters—is a betrayal of the responsibility of a writer of fiction to create characters who are true within themselves.

Every writer—every artist—is responsible to a certain kind of truth. A journalist is responsible to verifiable factual truth. A memoirist is responsible to the lived experience. The author of fiction would seem to have been cut free from all that, but the truth-telling of the author of fiction is just as rigorous. As a writer of fiction, I don't have a factchecker to answer to or a recorded interview to fall back on. But if what I have put down on the page rings false, then it is, in fact, false.

In both of my books on the opiate crisis, the characters made it clear that the story they wanted told was that of their personal grief, shame, and rage, and their longing for personal and collective redemption.

But how, in a cynical age, suspicious of sentimentality and puffery, does a writer create a convincing path to recovery and redemption? In *Tommy Perdue*, this was not so important an issue. *Tommy* follows a long tradition in addiction stories that we might call the Downward Spiral Into Destruction, as seen in films like *The Rose*, *The Jim Morrison Story*, or *Basquiat* or in literature, in a story like *Maggie: A Girl of the Streets*.

In *Tommy*, if there is a glimmer of hope, and I believe there is, it lies in the Paradise Café community, which has alternately cursed and coddled Tommy all his life.

But in *Maggie*, I saw a different path, one which comes out of a different tradition.

Before the Civil War, a significant new literary genre emerged: the slave narrative. These were stories of slavery told by fugitives eager to tell the world about their enslavement, escape, and rebirth as free persons. Most of these fugitives were illiterate, so many of these narratives were of the *as told to* variety, by which the fugitives described their experiences to abolitionist supporters who recast the stories into narratives acceptable to their readership. Other escaped slaves, like Frederick Douglass and Solomon Northup, were literate and could tell their stories in their own words. Either way, these stories were direct and compelling. Together with fictional accounts like *Uncle Tom's Cabin*, these were powerful voices in helping readers, mostly in the North, to see the slave as a full human and to see slavery as an evil, dehumanizing force. They helped mobilize sympathy for the slave and pointed to a day when slavery could be eliminated.

In recent years, a new narrative has emerged in response to addiction, the recovery narrative. Without minimizing the horrors of slavery, we can at least see some parallels in that the slave's story and the addict's story each tend to follow the same narrative arc. I first noticed this comparison when I reviewed *Most Unlikely to Succeed*, a self-published memoir by my friend, the activist Donald H. Whitehead. I have no way to know how many of these addiction narratives have been published in the last, say, twenty years, ever since the initiation of the War on Drugs. If we count self-published narratives or those published by small, independent presses, they may even number in the hundreds. When *The Fix* published a list of the "ten best addiction memoirs,"[9] dozens of readers chimed in with the names of books they each felt had been unfairly left off the list. (And some of these respondents had a point, noting the preponderance of white and male authors on the list.) I started to write them down but quit at twenty-one.

Some of these memoirs, like Mary Karr's *Lit* or Claude Brown's *Manchild in the Promised Land*, are classics, not just of the genre, but of Literature itself. The best of these stories are compelling *as stories*. But they also have a historic resonance: they follow the narrative arc of the slave narratives. They describe the features of compulsive subjugation to the drug; they describe the feelings of those subjugated and their desire for freedom. Then there is the break, the escape into freedom. Then, finally, they demonstrate the benefits of freedom as the formerly subjugated individuals take up new lives in recovery. Just as the nineteenth-century slave narrative helped humanize the slave and thereby helped change public attitudes toward slavery, these new liberation narratives have helped create a public understanding of the nature of addiction and of the human potential of the addict. They are helping change public attitudes and policy in a more supportive direction.

These recovery narratives have also helped introduce to the reading public the language of twelve-step recovery, which comes originally from the most historically significant book of recovery narrative, *Alcoholics Anonymous*, also known as the Big Book, the text which is the guide and original model for twelve-step recovery. In "How It Works," the fifth chapter of the Big Book, the anonymous author describes a recommended format: "Our stories disclose, in a general way, what we used to be like, what happened, and what we are like now."[10] The recovering individual uses this formulation to share his or her story with others in "lead" meetings, in discussion meetings, in written form, or one on one.

The Big Book is a testament to the healing power of story. We look to stories to entertain ourselves, of course, to distract us from our daily cares. But we also look to story to educate ourselves, to inspire, to help us imagine our best or better selves. The Big Book can be described as a manual, or how-to, and is full of philosophical rumination. But at its core is story. "Bill's Story," the saga of Bill Wilson, one of AA's cofounders, anchors the text. The second half of the book, the part which has been periodically updated to represent an increasingly diverse population within the fellowship, is entirely made up of stories. Most meetings of AA and the other twelve-step fellowships, are devoted to story-telling. Members are encouraged not to preach to newcomers but to tell their stories. These stories help "the still-suffering alcoholic" imagine a new life, to see the path to that new life, and help him or her connect to a supportive community. In reading these stories, the addict realizes he or she is not alone. He sees a path; she is encouraged to partake of the narrator's "experience, strength, and hope." The newcomer is encouraged to take on the narrator's courage, ingenuity, and determination to engage in a liberatory journey of his or her own.

But does this guide the writer of fiction?

A memoirist and a writer of fiction have to use many of the same skills. We each have to create compelling and discrete scenes, believable dialogue, and a plot line that keeps a reader turning the page. But, while I admire the work of my memoirist colleagues, I have never felt a call to tell my own story nearly as strong as my desire to tell the stories I have been gifted from those around me.

The writer of fiction has freedoms—and restrictions—that are distinct from those of the memoirist. The freedoms are obvious. The memoirist is stuck with characters who really existed and incidents that really happened whereas, god-like, I am able to create characters and places and incidents out of nowhere. As a writer of fiction, I can just make it all up. This is liberating but also terrifying in equal measure. In writing the stories that made up *Tommy Perdue* and *Maggie Boylan*, I started in each instance from incidents I knew to be true, either by direct observation, testimony of clients or friends, or from my reading. I could adjust these facts to suit the needs of my story. In *Tommy Perdue*, for example, I put homes across the street from the restaurant that had been torn down long before the time of my story. I made no attempt to people the café with actual proprietors and patrons. I just made up the population that I felt I needed to tell the story.

But there is at least one area in which I am more confined than the memoirist. While the memoirist can insert his or her own views on political, social, or philosophical issues into the narrative, as much as possible, I have to leave my own agenda behind.

I wanted to write narratives that humanized my subjects, that told hard truths but left their essential dignities intact. And I wanted to show that healing, if healing is possible, takes place within a community, a potentially regenerative amalgam of flawed but essentially compassionate human beings.

And I wanted—badly—to excoriate the greedy bastards who caused the whole thing.

As you read the journalistic accounts of the genesis of the opioid epidemic, you read a tale of aggressive promoters and passive guardians that combine into a pervasive web of corruption. Within this web, you will find corporate CEOs, physicians, state and federal regulators, pharmacists, lawyers, many lawyers, and law enforcement officials in varying combinations of cowardice, arrogance, and pure, unadulterated greed. In general, the higher the individual is on the social scale, the more culpable they were in victimizing (and blaming) a population made vulnerable by economic dislocation, a culture of disempowerment, and pervasive patterns of work-related injury. The heroes of this story are, one and all, at the lower end of the social scale—a small-town doctor, a small-town cop, a nurse in a rust-belt city, a few reporters—battling the titans of law, commerce, and science. There was a part of me that wanted to expose all that in a book like *The Jungle*, *The Gilded Age*, or *Germinal*.

But that work has been done by journalists like Sam Quinones, Beth Macy, and Chris McGreal. And it's never been what I do anyway. There is just one story I have been trying to tell my whole life, that of the retention of dignity by those for whom it would seem life has stripped all dignity away. My strength, if I bring any strength at all to this situation, has always been to tell the story as it is lived by the people who might otherwise be no more than statistics—so many overdosed, so many jailed, so many suffering the losses on the side streets, in trailer parks, or up isolated hollers.

I left the Sackler-level villains out of my story and concentrated on the story I had at hand.

I had at least a couple models for the structure of *Maggie Boylan*. Sherwood Anderson's *Winesburg Ohio* and Denis Johnson's *Jesus' Son* both used the novel-in-stories format. Johnson's book was the first I have seen that successfully used twelve-step culture as a setting for a story. It's a book that takes a central character from the depths of addictive chaos, into treatment, and through the first struggling days of recovery. The first chapter is nightmarish and haunted. It is also frequently anthologized, which goes to show that there is still a prejudice for the valorization and romanticizing of using behavior, something I wanted to avoid in my work. In the twelve-step lead, the speaker will sometimes spend an inordinate amount of time talking about the adventures before recovery in what is known as a "drunkalogue." But the Big Book speaks of "our adventures before and after," a phrase that makes it clear that there is at least as much adventure in recovery as there was in the sloppy, destructive, and self-destructive days of using. Anyone really in recovery knows that the real adventure is in recovery.

I also had the Big Book's suggested narrative arc. It's formulaic. It's simple. It's repeatable. It has the force of tradition behind it. It flies in the face of post-modern preference for the disjointed and multifaceted.

I listened, and I observed—in my office, on street corners, in the living rooms of friends in double-wide trailers, in twelve-step meetings in church basements or AA clubhouses. The title story, "Maggie Boylan," began with a gust of wind booming down a mountain highway. I wanted to capture that wind and, somehow, I constructed a story around it. In other cases, I took stories I have been told and expanded on them. Maggie's encounter with local corruption came from my reading. The mass killing that is at the center of the final story had its beginnings in news reports of a similar killing—still unsolved—in Pike County, Ohio.

Why do I think I have the right to tell such a story? What gives me the right to that little bit of artistic gold?

Here's what I think: If, in your life, you have experienced pain (and who has not experienced pain?) and you are willing to put that experience toward an understanding of the pain of another, to the exclusion of your own ego, then I believe you can tell any story you choose, as long as you have paid attention. If it is truly impossible to make that imaginative leap, then there really is no hope for any of us to understand one another or to empathize with one another. But I refuse to believe this. Literature, and its allied arts, is the place with the greatest capacity for helping us make this connection.

This is the connection I hoped to make in *Maggie Boylan*.

So where did Maggie come from? She came from Lower Price Hill, and she came from West Virginia. She came from east Kentucky and from small towns along the Ohio River. She came from stories told around kitchen tables, and she came from the pages of the *New Yorker*. She came from certain individuals I knew, and she came from the inner folds of my imagination.

There is not just one Maggie Boylan; there are thousands.

NOTES

1.   "From 1999–2017, almost 400,000 people died from an overdose involving any opioid, including prescription and illicit opioids" ("Understanding the Epidemic," Centers for Disease Control and Prevention, US Department of Health and Human Services, last

modified December 19, 2018, https://www.cdc.gov/drugoverdose/epidemic/index
.html).

2.   Chris McGreal, *American Overdose: The Opioid Tragedy in Three Acts* (New York: Hachette,
     2018); Julia Lurie, "Mom, When They Look at Me, They See Dollar Signs," *Mother Jones*,
     March/April 2019, https://www.motherjones.com/crime-justice/2019/02/opioid
     -epidemic-rehab-recruiters/.

3.   Review of *Maggie Boylan*, *Publishers Weekly*, May 7, 2018, https://www.publishersweekly
     .com/978-0-8040-1202-7; Gonzalo Baeza, "One of the Best Appalachian Short Story
     Collections in Years," *The Observer*, June 2018, https://wearetheobserver.com/wp-content
     /uploads/2018/06/1806_Observer.pdf.

4.   Methadone is an effective adjunct to treatment when administered properly. However,
     taking an amount greater than needed to control cravings can lead to intoxication and
     even overdose. See "Vital Signs," Centers for Disease Control and Prevention, last
     modified July 3, 2012, https://www.cdc.gov/vitalsigns/methadoneoverdoses/.

5.   Michael Henson, "The Strange Story of OxyContin: A Tale of Predictable and Utterly
     Preventable Catastrophe," *Still* 24 (Summer 2017): http://www.stilljournal.net
     /michael-henson-cnf2017.php.

6.   Henson, "The Strange Story of OxyContin."

7.   Michael Henson, "Willy Was a Strong Man," unpublished song.

8.   John Gardner, *The Art of Fiction* (New York: Knopf, 1983), 32.

9.   Sam Lansky, "The 10 Best Addiction Memoirs," *The Fix*, August 23, 2011, https://www
     .thefix.com/content/10-best-addiction-memoirs.

10. Bill W., *Alcoholics Anonymous: The Story of How Many Thousands of Men and Women Have
     Recovered from Alcoholism* (New York: Alcoholics Anonymous World Services, 1976), 58.

CHAPTER 9

You Talkin' about Me? Turning the Blood of Appalachia's Opioid Epidemic into Ink

Jacqueline Yahn

"Deaths of despair" is a term that quickly became associated with the opioid epidemic's stronghold in places throughout Appalachia and rural America. The descriptor gained momentum after the release of Anne Case and Angus Deaton's work on the rising mortality and morbidity of white non-Hispanic Americans from 1999 to 2013.[1] The link is frequently made for three reasons. First, Case and Deaton define deaths of despair as deaths due to drug overdoses, suicide, and alcohol-related diseases. Second, the timeframe of their work coincides with the rise of the opioid epidemic.[2] Third, as journalists and researchers traced the epidemic back to the communities where it began, they saw notable examples of despondency that they believed to be the result of economic decline and associated social welfare issues.[3]

Case and Deaton's seminal research on the sudden rise of white mortality made a murder suspect out of hopelessness. It inspired additional research on links between despair and opioid addiction in Appalachia and rural America with examples including Shannon Monnat's article "Deaths of Despair and Support for Trump in the 2016 Election" and the Appalachian Regional Commission's sanctioned report "Appalachian Diseases of Despair."[4] At the same time, Sam Quinones's book *Dreamland* introduced the possible association to the broader public by inking such lines as "That it [the opioid epidemic] began in voiceless parts of the country—in Appalachia and rural America—helped keep it quiet at first."[5] The mass prescriptions of OxyContin, the prescription painkiller widely accepted as the catalyst for the opioid epidemic, came to the market in the latter half of the 1990s, and investigative journalists trace the epidemic's beginnings back to Appalachia.[6] Yet, as Beth Macy explains in *Dopesick*, the epidemic did not remain place-bound but instead gained momentum and spread to the suburbs, morphing into a nationwide problem.[7]

The opioid epidemic's suburban sprawl complicates the indictment of despair. Whereas researchers and journalists point to economic hardship as a reason for Appalachians to despair and engage in the taking and selling of opioids as an alternative, they admit they are less sure how to explain the drug's appeal in more economically stable communities.[8] Similarly, Case and Deaton have retreated on their indictment of despair, noting in their most recent research that they are less sure that despair alone could explain the opioid epidemic's stronghold in places throughout Appalachia and rural America.[9] Instead, they have joined other academics to suggest the culprit's genesis is associated with what they call "cumulative" disadvantages that build in these places overtime, including displacement of the white working class, the environmental degradation that follows natural resource exploitation, and the economic decline of much of rural America.[10]

In this essay, I further push the issue, suggesting that simplifying the story of opioid epidemic's grasp upon Appalachia as one of despair infantilizes those enmeshed in the crisis. I point out that creative classes of "voiceless" Appalachians are finding the words to challenge this single story of the opioid epidemic. I begin by briefly discussing the long history of pinning despair as the root cause of Appalachia's most pressing issues. The essay moves forward with an overview of social scientists insistence, despite conflicting research and evidence, that Appalachia's opioid epidemic is driven by despair, which serves as a preface to the heart of this essay: the analysis of two native Appalachian's fictional works that feature plotlines situated within the region's opioid epidemic, *Maggie Boylan* by Michael Henson and *Weedeater* by Robert Gipe.[11] I point out that, through the art form of fiction, Henson and Gipe offer a more intense look at the myriad of complications that have sprung from the opioid epidemic. For this reason, their works should be read alongside the reports of esteemed researchers and journalists, as they hold the potential to equip interested parties with more relevant knowledge to form viable research questions, drive public policy, and inform community outreach. As Chimamanda Ngozi Adichie, the great combatant of the single story, remarks, "Stories can break the dignity of a people, but stories can also repair that broken dignity. . . . When we reject the single story, when we realize that there is never a single story about any place, we regain a kind of paradise."[12]

"YOU TALKIN' ABOUT ME?": THE SINGLE STORY OF DESPAIR IN APPALACHIA

Single stories of Appalachia's despair inspired the region's political inception.[13] As Elizabeth Catte argues in *What You Are Getting Wrong about Appalachia*, when so-called authority figures such as politicians, researchers, and reporters characterize the region and its inhabitants as being in a perpetual state of despair, they promote spurious claims that Appalachia's issues are a result of moral failings while justifying disadvantageous government and corporate interventions.[14] Decades of state-led schemes enacted under this assumption are supposedly designed to improve the human condition in Appalachia, but, more frequently, they complicate it.[15] A prominent example in Appalachia is the current fracking boom, which is promoted under the guise it will be an economic boon for the region, while the known environmental hazards are dismissed as a necessary secondary consequence.[16]

Posturing about deaths of despair in Appalachia is not confined to the academy, nor has it dissipated with time. J. D. Vance's treatise *Hillbilly Elegy: A Memoir of a Family and Culture in Crisis* provides a relevant example as it revives and rebrands the culture of poverty narrative.[17] Vance's work was widely acclaimed for pointing to the moral failings of Appalachia's people as the reason for their despondent responses to larger political and social forces, such as supporting Donald Trump's presidential bid and falling prey to the addictive qualities of opioids such as OxyContin.[18] Vance has managed to parlay the success of his memoir into a platform for pontificating about the opioid epidemic and serving as a self-appointed spokesperson for the greater Appalachian region.[19] The legitimacy of Vance's promotion to spokesperson of the Appalachian regions has been vehemently opposed by respected Appalachian voices in the collective work *Appalachian Reckoning*.[20]

Vance's misstep is not in suggesting Appalachia has troubles, nor are Case and Deaton wrong to surmise that economics has a hand in the complications associated with the opioid epidemic. The issue is that such work has led journalists and researchers to uniformly characterize Appalachia—a region spanning from Mississippi to New York—as if it is enmeshed in a singular plight of despair that explains the opioid epidemic. As Ronald Eller explains in *Uneven Ground: Appalachia since 1945*, a multitude of places throughout the greater Appalachian region have experienced long bouts of economic decline, environmental degradation, outmigration, and troubling social welfare issues.[21] Yet, what concerns Appalachian scholars as we read assumptions that the opioid epidemic can be explained as one of despair or learn of Vance resuscitating the "culture of poverty" narrative is that both simplify the opioid crisis by too casually placing blame on the deficiencies and vulnerabilities of the culture entrenched in the crisis. Moreover, the association between despair and opioid abuse is flawed; Christopher Ruhm's statistical analysis concluded that, by including controls for confounding factors, the connection between economic decline and the rise in opioid use is weak, almost nonexistent.[22] Ruhm suggests it may be much more likely that it is the drug environment, rather than the economic environment, that gave rise to the epidemic.[23]

THE DISEMPOWERMENT OF THE OPIOID EPIDEMIC'S SINGLE STORY

The stigma attached to the opioid epidemic supports popular commentaries on how despairing people in places such as Appalachia and parts of rural America opt out of the American Dream because of their moral failings and penchant to engage in criminal activities.[24] Curiously, this stigma persists despite the opioid epidemic's swift crossover into multiple geographic landscapes—rural, suburban, and urban. In fact, the descriptions of opioid-related deaths are found to vary across these populations.[25] In the case of the Appalachian people, associating the opioid epidemic as a mere response to despair is a troubling precedent that may have a nefarious influence. It offers those with the power to direct funding, legal inquiries, and policy solutions a reason to hesitate. Furthermore, it abdicates pharmaceutical companies, medical professionals, and government agencies from the role they played in the epidemic's genesis.

This single story of the opioid epidemic is ahistorical. Barry Meier, the *New York Times* reporter who did some of the first serious reporting on the epidemic, explains that—before opioid use morphed into an epidemic now associated with illicit activities such as drug dealing, heroin use, child neglect and abandonment, and homicide—opioids were remarketed as a medical marvel.[26] And it was one readily promoted by business people in the corporate boardrooms of Purdue Pharma, where a campaign was conceived to market the company's newest opioid OxyContin as the right fit for such a revolutionary pain management approach.[27]

Despite Meier's careful reporting on the origins of the epidemic, the deaths of despair narrative remains a best seller, proliferated by social scientists whose work on the epidemic is widely cited. C. Wright Mills was emphatic that social scientists must recognize the intersection of history and biography in the dilemmas they study.[28]

Yet the moniker "deaths of despair" and its application—mainly to rural white working-class areas—indicates social scientists skidded to a halt just shy of the intersection of history and biography in their work on the opioid epidemic. While they recognize crucial aspects of Appalachia's history such as the toll of economic downturns, and they acknowledge the change in the drug environment, they repeatedly insinuate that Appalachia's people possess characteristics that make them more prone to medicating despair.[29] This is paradoxical, given that it does not explain why opioids swiftly made their way to the suburbs and proved to be equally destructive. Research is almost nonexistent on why economic recovery and prosperity outside of Appalachia is not enough to stop opioid addiction. One telling example of the inconsistent interpretation is a study mining the headlines of the popular press. Researchers Julie Netherland and Helena Hanson learned that journalists take a distinctly different tone in popular press coverage of suburban deaths from opioid and heroin overdoses in comparison to the same type of deaths in urban areas by depicting deaths of suburban whites as a tragedy rather than a moral failing.[30]

What social scientists seem reluctant to include in their descriptions of places where they believe inhabitants are likely to despair is how a number of US public policies and a plethora of corporate strategizing has repeatedly left these places throughout Appalachia on what Eller dubs "uneven ground" since the end of World War II.[31] The influence of Case and Deaton's seminal work on the concept of deaths of despair proves Mills point, as it has been widely cited, particularly in work published by the Appalachian Regional Commission and Sharon Monnat, which has influenced political and journalistic interpretations of the epidemic.[32]

The influence of the opioid epidemic in Appalachia is not due to despair inherited through a genetic bloodline. Instead, the opioid epidemic is eerily similar to the mountaintop removal, oil and gas exploration, logging, and outmigration that have plagued the region. Each is a capitalist scheme developed to monetize the region's resources. The extraction of natural resources and human capital found their way to Appalachia because the resources were readily available. In the case of OxyContin, it first became widely available in pockets of the region because Purdue's database identified potential prescribers with a host of medical patients battling chronic pain. Also similar to natural resource exploitation and outmigration, opioids were championed by a corporation as a solution to people's problems. Natural resource exploitation is pitched as economic boon, while opioids are recommended as the panacea to chronic pain inflicted by job-related injuries, life-threatening diseases, and other forms of chronic pain.

As Chris McGreal wryly chronicles in *American Overdose*, the exploitive nature of Purdue's opioid campaigns has kept sections of Appalachia firmly in the opioid epidemic's grip for more than two decades.[33] The outbreak of overdoses now extends beyond prescription opioids, with heroin and synthetic opioids regularly found in the bloodstream of overdose victims.[34] Sections of Appalachia chart some of the highest death tolls in the nation, and in these areas, first responders, lawmakers, social welfare agencies, and the general public report they are struggling to respond to the magnitude of the epidemic.[35] In the midst of this crisis, "deaths of despair" remains a favored misnomer.[36] After all, Appalachia's inability to withdraw from the addiction proves social scientists correct, right? Is it not obvious that opioids and spin-off drugs induce anesthesia, numbing the pain not of just the body but of economic and social hardships? Dee Davis, a venerated rural journalist, also balks at this claim, telling McGreal the argument is pompous and flawed: "It's easy to put a template over it and say these people are full of despair. 'What is their hope? Who are they?' But it is a business decision to introduce these drugs to this community. It was somebody figuring out how to have a good quarter and a better year. They made some choices. They decided which people are valuable and which ones are expendable."[37]

READING AGAINST THE GRAIN

Building upon Davis's point, I contend that it becomes harder to attribute the epidemic solely to despair when we are confronted by the stories of the people who live within its midst every day. In their fiction, Robert Gipe and Michael Henson challenge the idea that opioids effectively numb the pain of a people, whether economic or personal. Instead, the stories they tell position readers to flinch in anguish, frustration, or sorrow at several events in the plotlines. As Gipe explains in regard to his own work: "I also write books to try and catch what it's like when a whole bunch of things go wrong at once for readers for whom not so many things have gone wrong."[38] Both authors make it nearly impossible to be a bystander who is no longer aware of what it is like to live through "so many things gone wrong." Henson's Maggie Boylan, the addled junkie, and Gipe's Dawn Jewell, the outspoken critic of her own family, both talk directly to readers at points in the narratives. The characters capture the opioid epidemic, not from the vantage point of a journalist reporting a story or a researcher collecting and interpreting data, but rather as a person living the experience.

Maggie Boylan

Michael Henson, author of *Maggie Boylan*, spent his life working as an addiction counselor, so he has a keen awareness of the opioid epidemic's origin story.[39] Yet in his fiction, Henson offers no answers. In *Maggie Boylan*, he provides a narrative for us to analyze rather than an analysis. The distinction is crucial. Henson suggests the work of an artist is "[not to] come up with solutions, an artist comes up with questions."[40]

Maggie Boylan, the protagonist of Henson's story collection, is "straight as a bullet, foul mouthed, death-head-looking, Oxy-addled, [and] thieving."[41] The ten stories in the novel coalesce to form a plotline throughout which readers are positioned to be rubberneckers, learning about Maggie mostly from others, while occasionally getting a glimpse into her thoughts. Through Maggie's conflicts and interactions with fellow citizens, law enforcement, fellow addicts, addiction clinic personnel, and drug dealers, readers become embedded in the experience of living among people who have been afflicted by the opioid epidemic. One such example occurs in the opening story of the novel when Maggie cajoles James Carpenter, a disgraced former local policeman, into giving her a ride into town. During the experience, Carpenter silently reflects on Maggie's addiction and on the broader crisis unfolding:

> OxyContin was a terrible thing. It could turn a good man into a thief, a good woman into a prostitute. It could make a farm go to seed; a house to go to foreclosure. Three days after his wife died, he caught a man in his kitchen at three in the morning. You're too late he would have told the man if he didn't run. Her cousin had stolen the pills from her bedside before she was even cold.[42]

When Maggie speaks, though, we become familiar, if only for a moment, with the experience of being the addict. Yet, if we dare to think we are living vicariously through her addiction, she reminds us:

> No, you don't know what I mean. Not till you done what I done. Not till you seen what I seen. Not till you heard them bars slam shut behind you and you know it'll be two long years before you get to hold your babies again. Then you come and tell me what the world is like.[43]

In the stories leading to the culminating "Pillhead Hill," readers learn the hill is home to Maggie Boylan and the place where her neighbor is peddling drugs to locals.[44] One night, during a party on the hill, a shootout ends in a massacre of many of the town's well-known dealers and users. The death toll includes a known associate of Maggie's named Shelia.[45] Shelia's complicated friendship with Maggie includes shared addiction but also her testifying against Maggie in court, which led to their estrangement. Still, in the culminating scene of the novel Maggie finds herself at the hospital racked by the grief of Shelia's death, perhaps because she is reported to be the one who introduced Shelia to drugs.[46]

Opioids promote anesthesia, or a medically induced immunity to pain. In his work, Henson forces readers to sit in the middle of that pain, with no relief in sight. Henson does not imagine a way to undo the epidemic, nor does he seek justice by countering the empirical works on "deaths of despair." As Henson explains: "I had hoped to expose the nefariousness of the corporate structures that brought this crisis to us, but the story wouldn't allow for that. . . . The characters just wanted to tell their stories; they didn't want to deal with all that political stuff."[47] Therefore, the novel ends in a manner that forces readers to live in the reality his characters are living: that the opioid epidemic will not cease because of prosecutions, new laws, or emerging empirical research. Communicating this sentiment is Shelia's mother, who, as she joins together her daughter's mourners, tells them that "She lost her daughter long before she had lost her that night. . . . Do not argue, she said. Do not blame. All we have is one another and this is not a time to argue or blame. Nothing in this world will last, she said. Nothing in this world will ever be right."[48]

Weedeater

Robert Gipe lives, teaches, writes, and directs in Harlan County, Kentucky. As Beth Macy points out, if you are looking for narratives that give voice to the people J. D. Vance renders mute with his elegy, Gipe's fiction deserves your attention.[49] *Weedeater* is the second of Gipe's two illustrated novels about Dawn Jewell, a character born into an eastern Kentucky family entangled in the region's decades-long economic and environmental decline. Dawn comes to age during the contentious battles over mountaintop removal and enters adulthood during the first years of the opioid epidemic. Throughout her analysis of Dawn, Amy Tipton suggests the power of this fictional character is that she is never intended to be a transferable culture symbol.[50] In Dawn, readers find an antidote to the single story of Appalachia.

Like Henson, Gipe skillfully engages in what Henson calls "the work of the artist."[51] He, too, asks questions that focus on what it is like to be part of the proletariat suffering through an epidemic sponsored by corporations and supported by the government. As Dawn Jewell describes the experience:

> Keith Kelly was the first one any of us knew to OD on Oxy. That's what caused him to wreck. That was six years ago. By the time Momma died, seemed like there were people overdosing every week. And it didn't

seem like it would ever end. One day they were normal people—some of them nice, some of the mean, some of them funny, some of them quiet—and the next day they was zombies or acting wild, acting so different to whatever they had been before. It would be like you hadn't ever met them, and then the day after that they was dead. And you were left sitting there missing a person you could barely remember.[52]

Dawn stands in juxtaposition to Maggie Boylan. Although she is surrounded by the opioid crisis and loses a number of family members to overdose deaths, Dawn is not an addict. For this reason, Dawn offers insight into the lives of people with opioid use disorder that can only be gained from living with the experience. When she flashes back to the beginning of her mother Tricia's addiction, Dawn reminds us that, where academics might see despair as forming under the pressure of more grandiose cumulative disadvantages (e.g., economic downturns), a more localized set of troubles may be traced back to the first pill popped or needle inserted. As Dawn remembers it, "mothers always know best, except when their husbands die in coal mine accidents and they grieve themselves down a pill bottle and get in trouble with the law . . . and then them not even care cause they're so far gone."[53]

Annie Woodford suggests what makes Dawn Jewell's character powerful is that she occasionally breaks the fourth wall of fiction, speaking directly to readers.[54] This occurs in one of the most poignant moments of *Weedeater* when Dawn pauses to remark on the penultimate conflict of her mother Tricia's life. Dawn's uncle Hubert makes a last attempt to save her from her addiction while Tricia viciously fights off her family's affection and concern. In this moment, Dawn relents in a mix of frustration and exhaustion: "I wanted to put her [Tricia] down, like they do a mad dog. I just wanted her over."[55]

Dee Davis's point regarding the inaccuracies that arise by explaining the mortalities resulting from the opioid epidemic as deaths of despair is captured in Dawn's loss of faith in her mother and throughout the chapter "Already Dead." In this chapter, a number of people die from overdoses: Tricia (Dawn's mother), Evie (Dawn's former best friend), and Albert (Dawn's brother). Since each person plays an intimate role in Dawn's life, readers are privy to the conflicts leading up to their deaths. This forces readers to question what Gipe explains as the difference between most things going right in your life as opposed to "a whole bunch of things going wrong."[56] What Gipe hopes the reader will learn is deceptively simple: "It's easier when fewer things go wrong in your life to think you're smarter or better than the people who are always in the soup. But you're not. You're just luckier."[57]

TURNING BLOOD INTO INK

To paraphrase T. S. Elliot, Henson and Gipe write literature that turns the blood of the opioid epidemic into ink, challenging the single story of an epidemic rooted in despair. In *Maggie Boylan* and *Weedeater*, the characters are talking to stakeholders throughout the United States. The question Henson and Gipe leave readers to answer is: Will we merely reshelf the book, or will we turn the blood of the epidemic into action? The novels challenge readers to revise their understandings of Appalachia and the opioid epidemic in two vitally important ways. First, they testify to the fact that people living in the midst of the opioid epidemic are not voiceless but are, instead, seldom heard. Second, and perhaps even more importantly, they make it clear that deaths from opioid use are avoidable. As Henson writes in the "Strange Story of OxyContin," "None of this needed to happen. It would not have happened if greed had not over-ruled common sense. But greed almost always does."[58] The Sackler family, the owners of Purdue Pharma, not only profited from the sale of OxyContin, but they used their earnings to endear themselves as philanthropists throughout the Western world.[59] In stark contrast, the people of Appalachia, Purdue Pharma's targeted consumers, are depicted as a lower class of whites, afflicted by poverty and therefore prone to illicit actions like the fictional Keith Kelly and Tricia Jewell.[60] As Nancy Isenberg observes, ideas about the moral depravity of a lower class of whites has a four-hundred-year history in the United States, predating the founding of the nation.[61] She finds that throughout this history the evidence is clear that it behooves the elite—including corporate giants like the Sacker family—to maintain power by promoting widespread ideology that people's failure to overcome the obstacles before them (such as opioid addiction) is a result of ineptitude.[62] Isenberg suggests that there is an alternate explanation: the option of success is actually restricted from a significant faction of the American citizenry by the same elite who proselytize about lack of gumption.[63]

In their fiction, Henson and Gipe, like Isenberg, push back at the idea of failed whiteness and a class-based predisposition to despair. Gipe explains: "I try to write stories that help people identify with and love people with too-complicated lives. I don't want anybody feeling sorry for them. I want people to see what it's like, and realize maybe hard-luck people are actually pretty smart and creative and have a lot of grit and are a lot of fun to root for, whether you are one of them or not."[64]

A close reading of Henson and Gipe should result in a second look around the region. In doing so, readers will find real-life examples of the region's denizens combating the single story of Appalachia's opioid epidemic. Examples abound: Dr. Art Van Zee was one of the first medical professionals to push back against the overprescribing of opioids in the region, and he vehemently challenges the narrative that Appalachians were just more prone to abusing the pharmaceutical because they were a people living in despair. Instead, he tirelessly tracked the movement of pharmaceutical companies to the region, uncovering profiteering motives while persistently working with all levels of government to curb the enthusiasm leading to opioids' widespread use in pain management.[65] In the Northern Panhandle of West Virginia, Lisa Allen, owner of the Ziegenfelder Company, was awarded the Good Samaritan Award for her long-term commitment to compassionate hiring practices, which is a purposeful practice that gives recovering addicts and applicants with criminal records a viable option for employment, when many other companies will not consider their applications.[66] A final example is the recent edited collection *Not Far from Me: Stories of Opioids and Ohio*, throughout which editors Daniel Skinner and Berkeley Franz take on the important work of bringing the responses of Ohioans—addicts, teachers, healthcare workers, coaches—living with the state's opioid epidemic.[67]

When Appalachia's opioid overdoses are characterized as deaths of despair, stakeholders such as policy makers, educators, law enforcement, journalists, and researchers are left with a sense that the situation is so dire that no hope exists. Worse, it assumes that those living in the midst of the epidemic lack the resourcefulness to take any steps towards reclaiming their communities or personal welfare. But when Roxy Todd of West Virginia Public Radio asked Gipe if Dawn Jewell was hopeless, he replied, "I think, to answer your question, she must have hope, or she'd have already been incinerated by this life of hers."[68] Dawn Jewell's hope is not fictional—it lives in the persistence of Dr. Art Van Zee, it breathes from the pages of *Not Far from Me,* and it is realized on the payroll of the Ziegenfelder Company of Wheeling, West Virginia.

NOTES

1. Bill Bishop, "Everyone Knows Rural Americans Are Overdosing on 'Despair,' Right?" *The Daily Yonder*, January 22, 2018, https://www.dailyyonder.com/rethinking-rural-drug-epidemic/2018/01/22/23387.

2. Anne Case and Angus Deaton, "Rising Morbidity and Mortality in Midlife among White Non-Hispanic Americans in the 21st Century," *Proceedings from the National Academy of Sciences* 120, no. 49 (2015): 15081.

3. Bill Bishop, "Everyone Knows Rural Americans Are Overdosing on 'Despair,' Right?"

4. Shannon M. Monnat, "Deaths of Despair and Support for Trump in the 2016 Presidential Election," Penn State Department of Agriculture, Economics, Sociology, and Education, Research Brief, December 4, 2016: https://aese.psu.edu/directory/smm67/Election16.pdf; Michael Meit, Megan Heffernan, Erin Tanenbaum, and Topher Hoffmann, "Appalachian Diseases of Despair," The Walsh Center for Rural Health

Analysis, NORC at the University of Chicago, August 2017, https://www.arc.gov/assets/research_reports/AppalachianDiseasesofDespairAugust2017.pdf.

5. Sam Quinones, *Dreamland* (New York: Bloomsbury Press, 2015), 289–90.

6. Richard D. deShazo, McKenzie Johnson, Ike Eriator, and Kathryn Rodenmeyer, "Backstories on the U.S. Opioid Epidemic. Good Intentions Gone Bad, an Industry Gone Rogue, and Watch Dogs Gone to Sleep," *The American Journal of Medicine* 131, no. 6 (2018): 595.

   For examples of such journalism, consult Beth Macy, *Dopesick: Dealers, Doctors, and the Drug Company That Addicted America* (New York: Little Brown, 2018); Chris McGreal, *American Overdose: The Opioid Tragedy in Three Acts* (New York: Hachette, 2018); Quinones, *Dreamland*.

7. Macy, *Dopesick*, 103–88.

8. Monnat, "Deaths of Despair and Support for Trump in the 2016 Presidential Election," 5; Margaret Talbot, "The Addicts Next Door," *New Yorker*, June 5, 2017; Quinones, *Dreamland*, 273–77.

9. Anne Case and Angus Deaton, "Mortality and Morbidity in the 21st Century," *Brookings Papers on Economic Activity* (Spring 2017): https://www.brookings.edu/bpea-articles/mortality-and-morbidity-in-the-21st-century/.

10. Case and Deaton, "Mortality and Morbidity," 429–39.

11. Michael Henson, *Maggie Boylan* (Athens, OH: Swallow Press, 2018); Robert Gipe, *Weedeater* (Athens, OH: Swallow Press, 2018).

12. Chimamanda Ngozi Adichie, "The Danger of the Single Story," TEDGlobal, filmed July 2009, Oxford, UK, 18:34, https://www.ted.com/talks/chimamanda_adichie_the_danger_of_a_single_story.

13. Allen W. Batteau, *The Invention of Appalachia* (Tucson: University of Arizona Press, 1990).

14. Elizabeth Catte, *What You Are Getting Wrong about Appalachia* (Cleveland, OH: Belt Publishing, 2018), 19–35.

15. Catte, *What You Are Getting Wrong about Appalachia,* 121–27.

16. Jacqueline Yahn, "Frackonomics," in *Appalachia Revisited,* ed. Rebecca Fletcher and William Schumann (Lexington: University Press of Kentucky, 2016), 144–46.

17. J. D. Vance, *Hillbilly Elegy: A Memoir of a Family and Culture in Crisis* (New York: HarperCollins, 2016).

18. Joshua Rothman, "The Lives of Poor White People," *New Yorker*, September 12, 2016, https://www.newyorker.com/culture/cultural-comment/the-lives-of-poor-white-people.

19. Barrie Barber, "J. D. Vance Returns Home to Focus on Jobs, Drug Crisis," *Dayton Daily News*, August 25, 2017, https://www.daytondailynews.com/news/vance-returns-home-focus-jobs-drug-crisis/IQlG2kRIQZZhnodRgNHa7M/.

20. Anthony Harkins and Meredith McCarroll, eds., *Appalachian Reckoning: A Region Responds to Hillbilly Elegy* (Morgantown: West Virginia University Press, 2019).

21. Ronald Eller, *Uneven Ground: Appalachia since 1945* (Lexington: University Press of Kentucky, 2008).

22. Christopher J. Ruhm, "Deaths of Despair or Drug Problems?" National Bureau of Economic Research, Working Paper No. 24188, 2018, 42–43.

23. Ruhm, "Deaths of Despair or Drug Problems?," 43.

24. Daniel Z. Buchman, Pamela Leece, and Aaron Orkin, "The Epidemic as a Stigma: The Bioethics of Opioids," *The Journal of Law, Medicine and Ethics* 45 (2017): 611.

25. Julie Netherland and Helena B. Hanson, "The War on Drugs That Wasn't," *Culture, Medicine, and Psychiatry* 40 (2016): 664–86.

26. Barry Meier, *Pain Killer: An Empire of Deceit and the Origin of America's Opioid Epidemic* (New York: Random House, 2018).

27. Nalini Vadivelu, Alice M. Kai, Vijay Kodumudi, Julie Sramcik, and Alan D. Kaye, "The

Opioid Crisis: A Comprehensive Overview," *Current Pain and Headache Reports* 22, no. 3 (23 February 2018): 2.2–3.

28. C. Wright Mills, *The Sociological Imagination* (Oxford, UK: Oxford University Press, 1959), 143–64.

29. See, e.g., Sharon Monnat, "The Contributions of Socioeconomic and Opioid Supply Factors to Geographic Variation in U.S. Drug Mortality Rates," Institute for New Economic Thinking, Working Paper No. 74, 2019, 31.

30. Netherland and Hanson, "The War on Drugs That Wasn't," 670–81.

31. Eller, *Uneven Ground*, 9–52.

32. US Congress, House of Representatives, Subcommittee on Economic Development, Public Buildings, and Emergency Management of the Committee on Transportation and Infrastructure, *The Opioid Epidemic in Appalachia: Addressing Hurdles to Economic Development in the Region*, 115th Cong., 1st sess., 2017, 2; Sam Quinones, "Donald Trump and Opiates in America," *Dreamland . . . A Reporter's Blog*, November 21, 2016, http://samquinones.com/reporters-blog/2016/11/21/donald-trump-opiates-america/.

33. McGreal, *American Overdose*, 99–227.

34. McGreal, *American Overdose*, 99–227.

35. Meit et al., "Appalachian Diseases," 4; Talbot, "The Addicts Next Door."

36. McGreal, *American Overdose*, 110–13.

37. McGreal, *American Overdose*, 112–13.

38. Robert Gipe, "In the Place I Live: Welcome to Rural Kentucky and 'Weedeater,'" *BookPage*, March 19, 2018, https://bookpage.com/behind-the-book/22490-place-i-live-welcome-to-rural-kentucky-weedeater#.XHyWK62ZPUo.

39. Michael Henson, "The Strange Story of OxyContin: A Tale of Predictable and Utterly Preventable Catastrophe," *Still* 24 (Summer 2017): http://www.stilljournal.net/michael-henson-cnf2017.php.

40. Brian Baker, "Cincinnati Author and Former Addiction Counselor Examines Lives Caught in an Appalachian Crisis," *City Beat*, April 3, 2018, https://www.citybeat.com/arts-culture/article/20999204/examining-lives-caught-in-an-appalachian-crisis.

41. Henson, *Maggie Boylan*, 1.

42. Henson, *Maggie Boylan*, 7.

43. Henson, *Maggie Boylan*, 29.

44. Henson, *Maggie Boylan*, 71–87.

45. Henson, *Maggie Boylan*, 114–51.

46. Henson, *Maggie Boylan*, 150–51.

47. Baker, "Cincinnati Author and Former Addiction Counselor Examines Lives Caught in an Appalachian Crisis."

48. Henson, *Maggie Boylan*, 151.

49. Beth Macy, "The Mountains Aren't Empty," *Oxford American*, September 2018, https://www.oxfordamerican.org/item/1564-the-mountains-aren-t-empty.

50. Amy Tipton Cortner, "The Recalcitrant Redemption of Dawn Jewell," *Appalachian Journal* 43, no. 1–2 (2016): 86–90.

51. Baker, "Cincinnati Author and Former Addiction Counselor Examines Lives Caught in an Appalachian Crisis."

52. Gipe, *Weedeater*, 170.

53. Gipe, *Weedeater*, 105.

54. Annie Woodford, "Untelling: *Trampoline* as a Text of Bliss," *Journal of Appalachian Studies* 24, no. 2 (2018): 220.

55. Gipe, *Weedeater*, 157.

56. Gipe, "In the Place I Live."

57. Gipe, "In the Place I Live."

58. Henson, "The Strange Story of OxyContin."

59. Henson, "The Strange Story of OxyContin."
60. McGreal, *American Overdose,* 110–13.
61. Nancy Isenberg, *White Trash: The 400-Year Untold History of Class in America* (New York: Viking, 2016).
62. Isenberg, *White Trash,* 1–16.
63. Isenberg, *White Trash,* 310–22.
64. Gipe, "In the Place I Live."
65. Meier, *Pain Killer,* 3–18.
66. Nick Musgrave, "Zieggy Tribe Honored at YSS Good Samaritan Dinner," *Weelunk,* August 19, 2018, https://weelunk.com/zieggy-tribe-honored-at-yss-good-samaritan-dinner/.
67. Daniel Skinner and Berkeley Franz, eds., *Not Far from Me: Stories of Opioids and Ohio* (Columbus: Ohio State University Press, 2019).
68. Roxy Todd, "Appalachian Writer Robert Gipe Talks about Crisis and Hope in His Second Novel 'Weedeater,' " West Virginia Public Broadcasting, August 1, 2018, http://www.wvpublic.org/post/appalachian-writer-robert-gipe-talks-about-crisis-hope-his-second-novel-weedeater#stream/0.

CHAPTER 10

Remediating the Opioid Crisis in Museums

Ethan Sharp

Because of the depth and vastness of the opioid crisis, there are many opportunities for artists and museum curators to engage the crisis in their work and programs, and in 2018 and 2019, several artists and curators provided a foundation for the ongoing exploration of the dimensions of the opioid crisis in museums. One of the best known "art actions" in response to the opioid crisis was photographer Nan Goldin's series of protests in several major art museums, including the Metropolitan Museum of Art and the Solomon R. Guggenheim Museum in New York City.[1] The protests targeted Purdue Pharma, the company that developed and marketed OxyContin, and the Sackler family, the owners of Purdue Pharma, and ultimately led both the Met and the Guggenheim to affirm in 2019 that they would no longer accept funds from the Sacklers. In addition, in 2018, the Taubman Museum of Art in Roanoke, Virginia, staged an exhibition of photographer Josh Meltzer's portraits of activists, mothers, and other people on the frontlines of the opioid epidemic in southwest Virginia—several of the photographs also appeared in journalist Beth Macy's best-selling book *Dopesick: Dealers, Doctors, and the Drug Company That Addicted America*—and the McClung Museum of Natural History and Culture on the University of Tennessee campus in Knoxville presented an exhibition on the varying uses and interpretations of opioids and four other psychoactive drugs throughout history. Public programs providing space for storytelling and dialogue were important features of exhibitions at both the Taubman and McClung.

Nan Goldin's protests, the Taubman exhibition, and the McClung exhibition emerged entirely independently; to my knowledge, there was no coordination or communication among the main participants. They are, however, linked by a shared sense of the opioid crisis as a phenomenon that museums must address. In this chapter, I briefly examine each of these three events. For the series of protests, I refer to images and information provided via social media and online news sources. For the Taubman exhibition, I draw on my personal observations of the exhibition and the opening public programs, and for the McClung exhibition, I draw on personal observations of the exhibition, communication with the exhibition's cocurator, and video recordings of public programs. The chapter is concerned primarily with the ways in which the representational techniques and goals of the three events converge and the ways in which all three events both invited and forestalled reflection on the causes and consequences of the opioid epidemic. As a museum employee and a researcher committed to critical museum studies, I explore some questions that increasing numbers of museum employees and their audiences are confronting: such as, What are the benefits and disadvantages for museums in responding to and educating the public about the opioid crisis? How can museums develop programs and exhibitions about opioids, opioid use disorder (OUD), and recovery advocacy that are engaging and respectful while also opening spaces for critical inquiry and difficult dialogues?

My point of departure is to question the circulation of the term *crisis* as a way of framing the opioid epidemic. The anthropologist Janet Roitman has written that to call an event or confluence of events a crisis is to create a "blind spot," or a distinction that makes certain things visible and others invisible.[2] To invoke the term *crisis*, according to Roitman, is to regulate narrative construction, to allow certain questions to be asked while others are foreclosed. I focus here on how events in museums have engaged the opioid crisis critically, creatively, and strategically to reveal the broad impacts of the epidemic on society, grassroots activism in response to the epidemic, and the degree to which pharmaceutical industries and healthcare industries, in general, are responsible for the epidemic. I also address the fact that efforts to construct or reconstruct narratives about the opioid crisis in museums have participated in maintaining blind spots, foreclosing a fundamental questioning of the political and economic systems that museums and healthcare industries depend upon and reinforce.

The basic argument for this chapter is that museum representations of the opioid crisis are transformative yet well established in conventional museum practice. Efforts to engage and represent the opioid crisis are consistent with a trajectory within museums toward offering an ever-greater variety of exhibitions and public programs, pursuing partnerships with an ever-wider range of donors, sponsors, educators, artists, journalists, and activists, engaging controversy, and incorporating more voices and interests in public discourse. Goldin's protests (followed weeks later by the Met and the Guggenheim meeting some of her demands), the Taubman exhibition, and the McClung exhibition all reflect museums' commitments to providing opportunities for revealing personal experiences and advancing solutions to social problems. At the same time, museum engagements with the opioid crisis adhere to well-established display practices of sparking and responding to curiosity, of revealing what is overlooked, hidden, or mysterious within a controlled environment with an intention of producing more vigilant and engaged publics, and inviting recognition of and reinforcing shared values. These display practices repurpose things, discourse, and ideas related to the opioid crisis to facilitate visual and aural encounters that refocus attention and generate narratives of discovery, healing, and renewals of trust.

I use the term *remediation* to refer to the practices of repurposing and re-framing elements of the opioid crisis for displays and storytelling in museum settings.[3] Anthropologists Clémentine Deliss and Frédéric Keck, clarifying Paul Rabinow's approach to remediation in museums, point out that remediation involves two steps, the diagnosis of a problem and addressing the problem through a change of medium. They write that this change of medium will use technologies in new ways and "also might mean that the way visitors, museum workers, and observers interact is given a creative form, one of experimenta-tion that enriches experiences . . . so that return and revisiting is encouraged."[4] Goldin's protests and the Taubman and McClung exhibitions converge on the diagnosis that the problem of media concerning the opioid crisis is that greater attention and new perspectives on the crisis are needed. They also converge on a strategy of addressing the problem by taking overlooked materials and stories and presenting them in easily readable, largely conventional formats within the museums' emerging spaces and networks.

TRANSFORMATIONS IN MUSEUMS

Museums in the US and around the world have continued to grow in size and increase in number as new museums specializing in ever-more specific subjects and topics are opened, including museums concerned with drugs and addiction, like the Hall of Opium Museum in Thailand and the Museum of Addictions in Mexico. Administrators and curators of large, well-estab-lished museums that maintain commitments to be comprehensive in their approaches to a discipline or field, expand their audiences, and ensure that their audience are increasingly diverse must develop and host a wide variety of new, relevant, and marketable exhibitions and public programs; promote exhibitions and programs through multiple channels; and periodically renovate and expand their facilities.[5] For all of this, museums in the US must reach ambitious fundraising goals by forging partnerships with sponsors and donors with considerable financial resources and, in turn, naming programs, museum spaces, and entire museums for sponsors and donors.

For museums with regional and statewide audiences, healthcare organizations are often reliable sponsors of programs, and, for museums with national audiences, the Sackler family and other families and foundations with ties to major pharmaceutical companies have provided substantial donations. In the 1970s, the three Sackler brothers who helped to develop the pharmaceutical industry into one of the largest industries in the United States and are best known today for their affiliation with Purdue Pharma—made one of their first major donations to the Metropolitan Museum of Art for the construction of the Sackler Wing, which houses the ancient Egyptian Temple of Dendur, one of the museum's biggest attractions. Since then, members of the Sackler family have contributed to many other museums, including the Smithsonian Institution and the Harvard Art Museums. Their contribution to the Guggenheim Museum in New York City funded the creation of the museum's Sackler Center for Art Education.

For several decades now, both museum scholars and practitioners have been producing publications that report on how museums are changing and suggest how museums should change, but these publications have often failed to explore the degrees to which transformations in museums are dependent on the extraordinary financial advantages and generosity of a small percentage of the population and thereby intertwined with neoliberal political and economic structures and policies, including profit-generating health care in the US. In an influential article originally published in 1971, the museum administrator Duncan Cameron wrote about changes in museums and proposed that museums were both "temples" and "forums." As temples, museums enshrine public values and a widely accepted view of reality, and as forums, they provide "opportunities for the artists and the critics of society . . . to confront established values and institutions."[6] For readers who are not already steeped in museum-related work, Thomas's vision may seem unsustainable because temples and forums have contradictory purposes, but there is substantial evidence that something very much like this vision has been key to the growth of museums around the world, as these two distinct purposes ensure that museums have broad support as welcoming and dynamic sites and arbiters of shared knowledge and values. This vision remains in many ways consistent with the "museum idea" promoted during the museum boom in the late nineteenth century, in which the museum was imagined to be a dynamic site that could support education, sanitation, and social reform for an evolving citizenry.[7]

Indeed, instead of avoiding controversies about their roles, many museums have creatively and productively engaged controversies as "hybrid" institutions.[8] Museums have been able to thrive at the intersection of the "social imaginary" of "dominant power structures" and a commitment to "inclusion of hidden and difficult histories, as well as all facets of contemporary national life."[9] They have emerged as hubs of information and resource flows that reach across various sectors of society—connecting the elite, academics, artists, critics, and many other groups and institutions—and become meeting points for diverse audiences where revelations and inclusion can occur in mostly safe environments. As typically small or medium-sized institutions, museums can advance the economic development goals of various and competing groups; they can be prestigious assets for cities promoting tourism and a regional identity and for universities seeking to achieve international recognition for their research, training, and outreach.

Like museums, healthcare industries have occupied hybrid spaces and productively engaged controversies and crises. In the 1990s, as many journalists have reported, healthcare industries accepted, without serious consideration of its implications, the claim that pain was woefully undertreated.[10] This dramatic shift in the industries' approach to pain coincided with a growth in pain management specializations as well as the prescription of OxyContin and other opioids for outpatient, long-term treatment of chronic pain, generating tremendous profits for Purdue Pharma. The overprescription of OxyContin and other opioids in turn contributed to high rates of OUD and overdoses.[11] Healthcare industries, including pharmaceutical companies, have responded to the opioid crisis by producing new drugs for counteracting overdoses and treating addiction and implementing and expanding new treatment modalities.

The ongoing reconfigurations of pain and OUD treatment have had an impact on the lives of millions of people, but how the opioid crisis originated and the responses of healthcare professionals are still not well known. It remains important, therefore, to uncover and retrace some threads in the narrative about the opioid crisis, and museums can play valuable roles in this effort through their evolving partnerships with healthcare industries. They can expose problems within the healthcare industries in effective ways, drawing together visual displays, storytelling, performances, architecture, digital-media production, and other tools and techniques. As museum practitioners Joanna Besley and Carol Low have demonstrated in their work with people with mental illness, "When the act of telling has been constrained . . . bringing into the light of day that which has hitherto been private or hidden can be of powerful therapeutic value."[12] Museums can help the public to piece together more complete narratives about the opioid crisis while also rebuilding public trust in healthcare industries and their capacity to fix the opioid crisis.

THE ART OF RESISTANCE

In an article in *Artforum* in January 2018, Nan Goldin revealed that she was a survivor of the opioid crisis.[13] She recounted that, after a doctor had prescribed OxyContin for surgery, she "got addicted overnight" and started purchasing opioids through the black market. After overdosing on fentanyl, Goldin entered treatment. With her article, she published several photographs, including a photograph of her "dope" strewn across the floor of her apartment, as well as photographs of the entrances to a dozen museums, galleries, museum wings, and other museum spaces named for the Sacklers. Goldin writes, "The Sackler family and their private company, Purdue Pharma, built their empire with the lives of hundreds of thousands. . . . They have washed their blood money in the halls of museums and universities around the world." She announced that she was starting a campaign called Prescription Addiction Intervention Now, or PAIN, to demand the Sacklers "use their fortune to fund addiction treatment and education."

Since the publication of her story, Goldin has sought to situate her story amid the stories of other survivors through carefully orchestrated protests in museums that repurpose prescriptions and prescription pill vials for spreading information about the opioid crisis and constructing a narrative that lays the blame for the crisis on the Sackler family. The protests are at once acts of rebellion that appropriate museum spaces in an effort to increase public awareness of the campaign and demands that the staff and governing bodies of museums stand in solidarity with PAIN and remove the Sackler name from their buildings. PAIN's first major protest had about one hundred participants and took place around the reflecting pool in front of the Temple of Dendur in the Sackler Wing of the Metropolitan Museum of Art. Protesters began by throwing hundreds of vials into the reflecting pool and shouting, "Fund Rehab," "Shame on Sackler," and "Sacklers lie! People die!" The vials had prescription-like labels on them; at the center of the label was "OXYCONTIN" in bright red letters, and the texts above and below read, "brought to you by the Sacklers . . . major donors of the Met." Several protesters then staged a "die-in" around the pool while other protesters continued to shout slogans. Protesters recorded the events using their smartphones and posted several recordings on

Twitter and Instagram. Then protesters cleared a space for Goldin, who stood against the backdrop of a black banner with white letters that read "SHAME ON SACKLER," and shouted a series of different short phrases. At this point, a security guard intervened, tearing down the banner and asking protesters to leave the building. As the protesters exited the building, reporters and television camera crews met them on the front steps, and protesters answered questions from the reporters.

In 2018, PAIN staged other protests at the Smithsonian Institution and the Harvard Art Museums, but the group's most coordinated action was at the Guggenheim Museum on February 9, 2019. The atrium of the Guggenheim, designed by Frank Lloyd Wright and inaugurated in 1959, is perhaps the most recognizable museum space in the US because of its appearance in several popular movies. The Guggenheim provided PAIN an opportunity for a theatrical, highly effective display of outrage against the background of the museum's atrium and iconic spiral ramp. The protest took place a few days after the Massachusetts attorney general made public new evidence that members of the Sackler family continued to push for more OxyContin sales while knowing that drug was contributing to an addiction epidemic, including emails written by Richard Sackler, former chairman and president of Purdue Pharma.

On a Saturday evening, when the Guggenheim is open late and entry is offered on a "pay as you wish" basis, several hundred supporters of PAIN filed quietly into the building and moved up the ramp that spirals the atrium and onto the ground floor. As they positioned themselves in places all along the ramp's balcony, they were able to look down on the ground floor of the atrium. While several protesters on the ground floor staged a die-in, led by Goldin, the protesters along the ramp threw into the open space of the atrium thousands of small sheets of paper, faux prescriptions, which fluttered in the air as they fell and settled on the protesters below (fig. 10.1). Some of the prescriptions included a quote by Richard Sackler from the recently released emails, which read, "The launch of OxyContin will be followed by a blizzard of prescriptions that will bury the competition. The blizzard will be so deep, dense and white." Protesters hung large red banners over the ramp's balconies reading, "400,000 DEAD," "SHAME ON SACKLER," "200 DEAD EACH DAY," and "TAKE DOWN THEIR NAME," and shouted in unison, "Sacklers lie! People die!" Again, dozens of people recorded the protest and posted videos and photographs of the blizzard of prescriptions falling in the midst of the banners and shouts condemning the Sacklers, and major news outlets, including the *New Yorker*, featured reports on the protest.[14] In my review of news reports, I found no evidence that security personnel intervened or that the Guggenheim's representatives commented

Fig. 10.1. Protesters stage a die-in under a "blizzard of prescriptions" in the Guggenheim in New York City on February 9, 2019. Photo by Ryan Hampton.

publicly on the protest, although they did announce a month later they would no longer accept donations from the Sackler family.

PAIN's actions subverted the expectations and regulations governing behavior in the museums as a means of generating broader interest in the campaign across various media channels. At the same time, PAIN elevated the importance of museums amid the opioid crisis and helped to direct and shape museums in ways that will allow them to continue to focus on the opioid crisis through exhibitions, public programs, and other initiatives. By highlighting the relationships between art museums and the Sackler family and inviting exploration of other linkages between museums and healthcare industries, the campaign not only demanded that prominent art museums reject the Sackler name but also revealed that museums generally are positioned to do something about the opioid crisis. PAIN contributed to the push for greater acceptance that museums should be sites for recovering stories and provoking dialogue about injustice and traumatic events.

Furthermore, although PAIN's actions were raucous and mocked the branding of museum spaces and museums with the names of wealthy donors, they were mostly in line with the logic of conventional remediation practices in museums. Much like installations or pop-up exhibitions, the protests were limited, orchestrated displays that creatively used museum spaces, offering intriguing clues that allow audiences to piece together a larger narrative about the opioid crisis and discover the reasons for frustration and outrage. The display remediated bits of information, texts, prescription pill vials, and prescription slips and generated a wealth of photographs and videos for circulation on the internet to be repurposed later. PAIN's actions identified deficiencies within existing representations and public awareness of the opioid crisis, both in and beyond museums, and appropriated and reframed elements of the crisis, within the museum space, to increase awareness and demand accountability and reforms.

STORIES FROM CENTRAL APPALACHIA

Beginning in 2012, journalist Beth Macy began reporting on the opioid crisis in the suburbs of Roanoke, Virginia. Over a period of years, her reporting took her to small towns like St. Charles, Virginia, and towns in the Shenandoah Valley and eventually developed into a book project. Macy invited photojournalist Josh Meltzer to photograph the people that she had met, as well as the landscapes that she had traveled through. For the 2018 launch of Macy's book *Dopesick*, one of only a handful of books that offers a comprehensive overview of the development of the opioid crisis, involving interviews with a wide variety of individuals across southwest Virginia, the Taubman Museum of Art—which occupies a ten-year-old building in downtown Roanoke that is a dramatic mix of stainless steel and glass with a roofline that emulates the peaks and valleys of the Blue Ridge Mountains—organized an exhibition featuring large versions of Meltzer's black-and-white photographs, almost all of which were also included in Macy's book. The exhibition opened in the museum's Media Lab on August 4, 2018, and ran through December 30, 2018. The exhibition's sponsor was Carilion Clinic, a major healthcare organization.

Titled *Beth Macy and Josh Meltzer: Portraits from the Frontline of the Opioid Epidemic*, the exhibition was curated by Eva Thornton, assistant curator of the

Taubman, and Beth Macy and Josh Meltzer. The exhibition blended several projects—remediating texts, stories, and photographs from the book—and it was one of the first long-running exhibitions about the opioid crisis in a museum in the Appalachian region, although it privileged urban Appalachian perspectives on the crisis. The exhibition aimed to generate respect for and a studied intimacy with the people and landscapes in the photographs, providing audiences an appreciation of the deeply personal dimensions of the crisis. As Meltzer explained for the opening of the exhibition, he made the portraits using large-format film photography because the subjects of the photographers "deserved respect, and one way that a photographer can do that is to make a very deliberate, formal, flattering portrait." At the entrance to the exhibition, visitors encountered a large close-up photograph of Sister Beth Davies, a Catholic nun and cofounder of the Addiction Education Center in Pennington Gap, Virginia, and another large photograph of Dr. Art Van Zee, a physician in St. Charles, Virginia, perched on an examining table. In the early 2000s, Sister Beth and Van Zee were some of the first activists to demand that Purdue Pharma stop recommending OxyContin for chronic pain and reformulate OxyContin to prevent abuse.

Walking through the exhibition, visitors found an additional fifteen typical wall hanging-size photographs, with small paragraphs explaining each photograph, on otherwise empty off-white walls. To appreciate the photographs, visitors had to step close to them and read the accompanying texts taken from Macy's book. Rather than exclusively focusing on people with OUD, or commemorating people who have died with OUD, the exhibition captured the weight of the opioid epidemic on the larger society—on the professionals and family members whose lives have been intertwined with the epidemic and who have worked with and supported people with OUD. It also hinted at some of the broader political and economic conditions that contributed to the spread of the epidemic. The people featured in portraits included a pharmacist; four law enforcement officers; a grandmother of a woman who was convicted for heroin distribution and is now helping to raise her great-granddaughter; three activists who promote opioid awareness, treatment, and recovery; and three mothers who lost children to overdoses. Alongside each portrait of a mother was a pocket-size photograph of the child who died. Photographs of landscapes included scenes of a closed coalfield, the Appalachian Mountains, and a street in suburban Roanoke. Meltzer explained, "I wanted to make sure that geographically we had a sense of who this epidemic affects . . . and really to say that this happens everywhere."

Perhaps the most important aspect of the exhibition was the public program that occurred in conjunction with the opening of the exhibition on August 12, 2018. Billed as a community conversation and held in the museum's auditorium while the conversation was simulcasted for an overflow crowd in an adjoining lecture hall, the public program had an audience numbering in the hundreds on a Sunday afternoon and provided opportunities for the audience to hear the stories that are woven into the book and the exhibition. At the event, Meltzer and Macy addressed the audience briefly. Macy explained that, following the advice of a former editor and friend, she had sought with the book and the exhibition not to "solve the opioid crisis" but to "expose it" and "mobilize people to care." Macy then introduced three of the people featured in her book and the exhibition and asked them to make some brief comments, beginning with Sister Beth Davies. Sister Beth offered her support for what Macy sought to achieve with her book, noting that "a lot of people to this day are still in denial [about the opioid crisis] . . . They really don't want to look at it. There's too much pain in everybody's lives when they really look at it."

Next to speak was Vinnie Dabney, a recovery counselor, and then Patricia Mehrmann, a nurse whose daughter died from OUD, offered her story and hopes for the book and exhibition. Mehrmann addressed the audience a bit longer than the other speakers, taking time to remember her daughter. She explained, "As a mother of a beautiful young woman who struggled with addiction, struggled with the love of her son, struggled for years to come out of her disease, of all the trips that I made of driving her to different physicians, driving her to different treatment programs, of trusting people in the medical community who sent her home with a new bag of tricks every time she went to a three- or four-day treatment center, another bag of pills, uh, the answer just was not there." While Mehrmann noted that there had been significant advances in OUD treatment in recent years, and expected that treatment would continue to improve, she concluded by emphasizing that the most important response to the opioid crisis was engagement and compassion, saying, "We have to be strong at the grassroots. . . . We have to reach out with love and compassion."

The Taubman exhibition and the community conversation that opened it did not provide a complete understanding of the opioid crisis; rather, they invited audiences to read Macy's book to explore the origins of the crisis and the stories of people whom the crisis has touched. Despite the exhibition's tendency to be understated in its approach to the opioid crisis, it was significant because it reinforced PAIN's and others' efforts to ensure that museums would be sites where the opioid crisis is exposed, where personal stories of courage and transformation emerged and were celebrated, and where diverse publics could participate in assessments of the crisis and advancing solutions. It also aligned the museum with some of the most vocal critics of pharmaceutical companies that produce prescription opioids and built support within the museum for the same ideas that PAIN has advanced: that pharmaceutical companies had profited enormously from the sales of prescription opioids and should be held accountable and that there should be more resources devoted to treatment and recovery support. Despite its critiques of healthcare industries, the exhibition provided a foundation for continuing to strengthen the relationships between museums and healthcare industries by demonstrating how museum projects and programs can effectively identify issues within healthcare systems and mobilize healthcare industries, in conjunction with grassroots activists, to work toward solutions.

As the exhibition at the Taubman was opening, another exhibition in the Appalachian region that addressed the opioid crisis was ending its run at the University of Tennessee's McClung Museum of Natural History and Culture, housed in a building from the late 1950s that blends in with other buildings around it on the university's campus. The exhibition *Pick Your Poison: Intoxicating Pleasures and Medical Prescriptions* ran from March 23, 2018, through August 19, 2018, and revealed the varying attitudes to and uses of alcohol, tobacco, marijuana, cocaine, and opium across history, with a section of the exhibition devoted to each drug. Although *Pick Your Poison* was not focused exclusively on the opioid crisis, I address it briefly here because of the opportunities that it provided for storytelling and dialogue through public programs and the ways in which the exhibition allowed audiences to situate the opioid crisis and possible solutions to it within broader contexts, from perspectives rooted in central Appalachia.

Pick Your Poison was produced by the McClung and cocurated by Catherine Shteynberg, assistant director and curator of the McClung, with content provided by the US National Library of Medicine (NLM) and Professor Manon Parry of the University of Amsterdam. Indeed, the exhibition had the same title as that of a traveling exhibition offered by the NLM and included some materials from the traveling exhibition, such as an advertisement for children's morphine-containing "soothing syrup" from the nineteenth century, an advertisement from the early twentieth century in which a physician endorsed smoking cigarettes, and containers from various periods in which medicines containing alcohol, marijuana, cocaine, and opiates were sold without medical or legal regulations. The exhibition also presented propaganda and other materials warning against the use of each of the drugs from various periods, including scenes from the 1936 film *Reefer Madness*, which targeted marijuana use among young adults. Shteynberg made the McClung's version of *Pick Your Poison* unique by incorporating items from the university's collections, including a large moonshine still from the museum's collections, which was placed prominently at the entrance to the exhibition, and scenes of opium dens and warnings of their dangers in magazines from the nineteenth century also from the university library's collections. Shteynberg also participated in accessioning new items for the exhibition, including a hypodermic needle with a dose of naloxone, or Narcan, a morphinan derivative used to reverse opioid overdoses (fig. 10.2). Displayed alongside texts that provided the only references to the opioid epidemic within the exhibition space, the Narcan was integrated into the exhibition's repurposing and showcasing of pharmaceuticals, advertisements, and other popular media for instructing audiences about the ongoing development and fluctuating uses of drugs across time..

In the midst of nineteenth-century advertisements for morphine-based products and condemnations of opium dens, the display of Narcan and references to the opioid epidemic were useful for highlighting how opium-derived substances continue to be used today, but they also raised questions about the relationships between previous and contemporary configurations of opioid use and how contemporary opioid use is unusual for generating widespread alarm while also being closely intertwined with medical industries and calling forth medical interpretations and responses. For audiences who were interested in exploring gaps in the exhibition and learning more about the history of drug use and the emergence of the opioid epidemic, the McClung offered two public programs. One of the public programs in the museum's auditorium included a presentation by Dr. Stephanie Vanterpool, a pain-management specialist affiliated with the University of Tennessee Medical Center, followed by a "town-hall" discussion on April 16, 2018. The program provided a format for sharing stories about the opioid crisis.

During her presentation, Vanterpool offered a story about one of her patients to illustrate the "juxtaposition of pain and addiction." She recounted that a young man, whom she called J. C., came to her clinic two years after a motorcycle accident with partial paralysis in his legs and severe back pain. On his first visit, she was encouraged to learn that he maintained a very active lifestyle and was in recovery for OUD. According to Vanterpool, "He had recently completed an inpatient stay that had allowed him to change a lot of his circumstances pre-addiction to where he felt like he was confident he'd be able to beat this addiction." Nevertheless, after several weeks, J. C. showed up for an office visit high. He had gone to a neurologist, who had prescribed him oxycodone. Vanterpool responded by warning J. C. that he could not tolerate

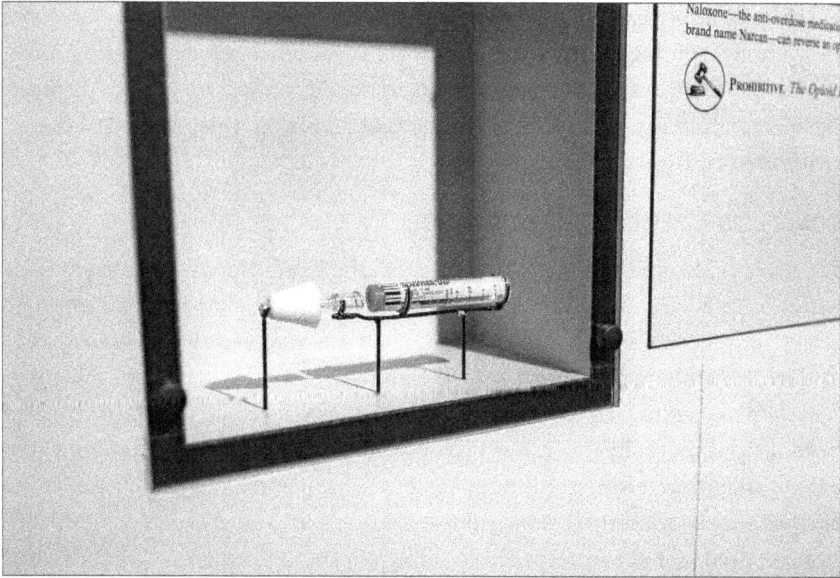

Fig. 10.2. Naloxone injection kit on display in *Pick Your Poison: Intoxicating Pleasures and Medical Prescriptions* at the McClung Museum of Natural History and Culture, University of Tennessee, 2018. Photo by Tom Schirtz.

oxycodone, but J. C. did not heed her warning. She concluded the story with, "Eventually J. C. left my practice. He found another pain clinic that prescribed him oxycodone."

For her presentation at the McClung, Vanterpool showed a panoramic photograph of the Blue Ridge Mountains during the fall and compared the opioid crisis to the Blue Ridge Parkway, hidden in the photograph amid the mountains and forests. She noted, "The opioid crisis is not a mystery but has a very distinct path that we can follow." With this comment, she echoed the voices featured in the Taubman's public program and their commitments to exposing the opioid crisis. Indeed, her comment seems to summarize more generally the approaches of the McClung and Taubman exhibitions to the opioid crisis: they contend that popular media and discourse concerning the opioid crisis have tended to present it wrongly, as a kind of mystery, and that audiences must look more deeply into the origins and development of the crisis in order to solve it. By remediating the opioid crisis, offering diagnoses of a problem and solutions to the problem that involve return and revisiting, the exhibitions drew on conventional display practices in museums, which have rarely ever been simply exposing things for public view. Rather, they have involved multimodal strategies, involving storytelling and dialogue, generating interest and curiosity, raising questions, and retracing connections across displays, performances, newsprint, televised or social media, images, texts, and the architecture of museum spaces.

CONCLUSION: REVISITING BLIND SPOTS

PAIN's protests and the Taubman and McClung exhibitions converged in their use of the museum space as both a temple and forum. The three events appealed to the museum's role as a temple to establish a shared view of the opioid crisis and reinforce shared commitments to vigilance, empathy, solidarity, and progress while appealing to the museum's role as a forum to incorporate a greater number and more diverse range of voices in public discourse. Ultimately, the events supported efforts to render museums as dynamic, indispensable institutions—hubs linking diverse groups of people and sites capable of sustaining personal and social reforms. In doing so, they relied on well-established display and storytelling practices to probe the hidden and overlooked dimensions of the opioid crisis. Their display practices adapted and deployed materials, forms, and epistemes in new ways to bring to light for museum audiences the recklessness of the pharmaceutical companies, the frustration and grief of healthcare providers, counselors, and family members of people with OUD, and a broader history of drug crises. These practices worked to reveal that the use and promotion of drugs in health care has not been wholly committed to careful applications of science but has often been haphazard, seemingly responding to the latest fad or moral panic. These revelations opened pathways for museums, healthcare industries, and recovery advocates to collaborate on engaging the broader public, reevaluating attitudes and approaches to the opioid epidemic, and advancing solutions to the epidemic.

Because museums will continue to be in demand for rebuilding trust and renewing a sense of unity, it is important to consider the practical benefits of the three events that I have highlighted here for future museum programs. PAIN's actions did not provide models that museum practitioners can realistically implement within their public programs, but they showed clearly that museums are well-positioned to communicate with a wide range of audiences about the opioid crisis. Furthermore, they called attention to a web of rallies, memorials, public art, and other public culture about the opioid crisis that can be found beyond the walls of museums that museums can engage and connect with in their programs. In contrast to PAIN's actions, the Taubman and McClung exhibitions, while they had very different scopes and purposes, provided realistic and valuable models that museum practitioners can adapt to their purposes. The exhibitions, for the most part, effectively balanced the competing goals that museums seek to achieve, as forums and temples, and helped to increase awareness of and respect for victims, survivors, and heroes of the opioid crisis. They indicated that museums can and will continue to be arenas for making sense of the opioid crisis and that artistic and museum-based actions will be vital for healing.

From a critical perspective, however, I must also point out that PAIN's actions and the Taubman and McClung exhibitions, while hinting at the possibilities of a wider range of interpretations of the opioid crisis, foreclosed further critical examinations of neoliberalism, globalization, innovations in technology, entertainment, and leisure, the connections of these large-scale developments with the opioid crisis, and the possibilities for radical solutions. PAIN's protests, for example, could have led to a consideration of the dependence of museums on a much broader array of exploitative industries and the relationships of art with power and wealth, but they insisted on narrower, though extremely important, demands, like increasing funding for treatment. Similarly, the Taubman exhibition could have yielded to a thorough exploration of economic restructurings and its connections to the opioid epidemic, as well as the psychological and cultural factors that make some individuals more susceptible to OUD, but it remained focused on the goodwill of people, including healthcare professionals, in southwest Virginia and featured regionally meaningful, small-scale responses to the opioid epidemic. The McClung exhibition provided a foundation for recognizing that prevalent attitudes to drugs have responded across history to the growth of capitalist markets, consumerism, and political and social movements, but it did not address these forces in a detailed and sustained manner and allowed ample room to believe that healthcare industries and US society over time will correct their mistakes and oversights. In sum, through their commitments to rebuilding trust in healthcare industries, and maintaining the museum's place within society as a privileged arbiter of values, PAIN's actions and the Taubman and McClung exhibitions helped to forestall the much more difficult actions, dialogues, and transformations that will be needed to reveal and address the political, economic, and other complex causes of the opioid epidemic and to prevent healthcare industries and government regulators from creating another public health crisis.

NOTES

1. One of the participants in the protests described the protests as "art actions." Andrew Russeth, "Nan Goldin, P.A.I.N. Group Stage Protest against Sackler Family, Purdue Pharmaceuticals in the Met's Sackler Wing," *ARTnews*, March 10, 2018,

http://www.artnews.com/2018/03/10/nan-goldin-p-n-group-stage-protest-sackler-family-purdue-pharmaceuticals-mets-sackler-wing/.

2. Janet Roitman, "Crisis," *Political Concepts: A Critical Lexicon*, accessed April 4, 2019, https://www.politicalconcepts.org/roitman-crisis/.

3. For another point of view on remediation, see Teri Silvio, "Remediation and Local Globalizations: How Taiwan's 'Digital Video Knights-Errant Puppetry' Writes the History of the New Media in Chinese," *Cultural Anthropology* 22, no. 2 (2007): 286. Silvio uses the term *remediation* for studies of new media that incorporate earlier forms of media to "capture the psychic and social experiences of a particular time and place." I am using the term here in a somewhat different way, to capture more conventional uses of the term, as a process of diagnosis, repair, and restoration, which involves the reconfiguration of media.

4. Clémentine Deliss and Frédéric Keck, "Remediation, and Some Problems Post-ethnographic Museums Face," *HAU: Journal of Ethnographic Inquiry* 6, no. 1 (2016): 388.

5. According to Silke Arnold-de Simine, "Museums are expected to provide a service to society by being inclusive, engaging diverse audiences, and offering opportunities for participation, often by showcasing personal stories, and portraying the effects of historical forces on the individual. But they are also expected to be innovative, respond to current issues and debates and remodel their exhibitions constantly" (Silke Arnold-de Simine, *Mediating Memory in the Museum: Trauma, Empathy, Nostalgia* [New York: Palgrave Macmillan, 2013], 9).

6. Duncan Cameron, "The Museum, a Temple or the Forum," in *Reinventing the Museum: Historical and Contemporary Perspectives on the Paradigm Shift*, ed. Gail Anderson (Lanham, MD: AltaMira Press, 2004), 69.

7. Tony Bennett, *Museums, Power, Knowledge: Selected Essays* (New York: Routledge, 2018), ch. 2.

8. Arnold-de Simine, *Mediating Memory in the Museum*, 9.

9. Kylie Message, *The Disobedient Museum: Writing at the Edge* (New York: Routledge, 2018), 94.

10. Beth Macy, *Dopesick: Dealers, Doctors, and the Drug Company That Addicted America* (New York: Little, Brown, 2018), 28.

11. See Phil Skolnick, "The Opioid Epidemic: Crisis and Solutions," *Annual Review of Pharmacology and Toxicology* 58 (2018).

12. Joanna Besley and Carol Low, "Hurting and Healing: Reflections on Representing Experiences of Mental Illness in Museums," in *Re-presenting Disability: Activism and Agency in the Museum*, ed. Richard Sandell, Jocelyn Dodd, and Rosemarie Garland-Thomson (New York: Routledge, 2010), 135.

13. Nan Goldin, "Nan Goldin," *Artforum*, January 2018, https://www.artforum.com/print/201801/nan-goldin-73181.

14. Masha Gessen, "Nan Goldin Leads a Protest at the Guggenheim," *New Yorker*, February 10, 2019, https://www.newyorker.com/news/our-columnists/nan-goldin-leads-a-protest-at-the-guggenheim-against-the-sackler-family.

CHAPTER 11

A Hole Is Not a Void: Extraction, Addiction, and Aesthetics

Jonas N. T. Becker

A tall tale is a narrative that is difficult to believe, a story with hard-to-swallow elements told as if they were truths. This form of storytelling is often associated with the Appalachian region of the United States, although it can be found in many rural areas. The underlying assumption of a tall tale is that there is something about the reality of a situation that leaves something to be desired, something to be rewritten, something better said another way. In my local community, tall tales informed everything from how people constructed their identities to relaying the details of banal daily occurrences. But beyond its role as a mode of communication, the tall tale is helpful for understanding the larger sociopolitical ecosystem of Appalachia at large, whose extraction-based economy operates at its core from truths so outlandish they are not believed by those outside and lies propagated as if they were truth to residents and workers of the region.

Growing up in a mining state taught me that what is underneath is as important as what is on the surface. Land must be understood as intersecting layers of history, institutional power, and cultural identity. In this context, extraction in Appalachia can be recognized as the result of generations of exploitive relationships between institutions, land, and people. I read the complex challenges of opioid addiction through this frame, as both symptom and repetition of extractive practices, where sustainability and community welfare are sacrificed—in this case by large drug manufacturers—for capital gain somewhere else. But sedative addiction is just one symptom of extractive late capitalism in the United States; this cycle of exploitation and consumption—whether of products, images, or painkillers—relies on sedation as both fuel and byproduct. In this context, sedation and apathy are entwined—sedation is the result of consumption and oppression, and apathy is the resulting state of being that perpetuates this cycle.

This essay will focus on two manifestations of this concept: political apathy, numbness to the issues of others; and visual apathy, the blindness to images induced by fatigue and oversaturation. Addressing what it means to look in this context, I will focus on artistic strategies and modes of looking to create new ways of understanding the complex legacy of extraction, and now sedative addiction, in Appalachia. I will illustrate this through my own projects as a visual artist working primarily in photography. I understand the camera, like land, to be encoded with layers of cultural ideology, commercially produced and constructed to support the ideas of mainstream culture.[1] In our current oversaturated image ecology, it is necessary to disrupt the function of the camera itself or the context for viewing images in order to create investment in the content of the work. My projects highlight an intersectional approach to land, drawing connections among identities, histories, and people that might otherwise remain siloed and disconnected. In something of a call and response to what some have called a zombie state, my work creates new forms of seeing and causes disparate audiences to become engaged.[2]

To address extraction in a contemporary context, it is necessary to understand its larger history that includes generations of extraction. The first European settlers to West Virginia arrived in the eastern part of the state, having been pushed out of other more fertile geographies.[3] Their existence on this land was in itself a result of precarity. Most families established self-sustainable and, at times, communal structures for creating sustenance from the land, harvesting food, raising and butchering livestock, and creating a self-sufficient system.[4] In a pattern common to the entire United States, modernization drew agrarian communities to participate in mechanized labor, receive pay, and then purchase food from commercial vendors, extending their fiscal and food dependencies outside of the familial group, reliant on both company and capital. In West Virginia, when mining began in earnest in the late 1800s, workers became separated from the value of their labor.[5] Paid in scrip, miners were forced to recycle their pay back into goods purchased at the company store, without the ability to participate in a free market. With this kind of closed-circuit relationship, workers became completely dependent, from the house they lived in, which was owned by the company, to the pay they received, which was only viable at the company store. Workers were paid based on the amount of coal mined at a rate that comprised a small fraction of the coal's market value.[6] This equation reflects on the value of both human resources and mineral resources. It also evidences extraction's true violence, not simply as a model where something is taken out of the earth, but a model where value—human, mineral, or otherwise—is taken elsewhere, leaving behind a void when depleted.

In the 1970s, mining began to mechanize as the larger underground coal seams began to be depleted. Because of both of these shifts in the industry, new ways of mining coal were invented to more efficiently mine the last deposits of mineral from smaller seams closer to the surface.[7] These new mining models were many times more destructive to both land and people, destroying and subsequently restructuring much of the topography of West Virginia.[8] With the advent of these strategies, first surface mining and then mountaintop removal, most miners lost their jobs as they were replaced by large machines.[9] These extreme and shortsighted mining practices were at their height in the early 2000s, but, by 2010, even the last seams were drying up, and mining operations began closing completely.[10] Mining corporations were evading earlier promises, declaring bankruptcy to avoid environmental standards and compensation for job-related injuries.[11] The region's role in a larger system of industry and extraction became increasingly clear: mining companies only cared

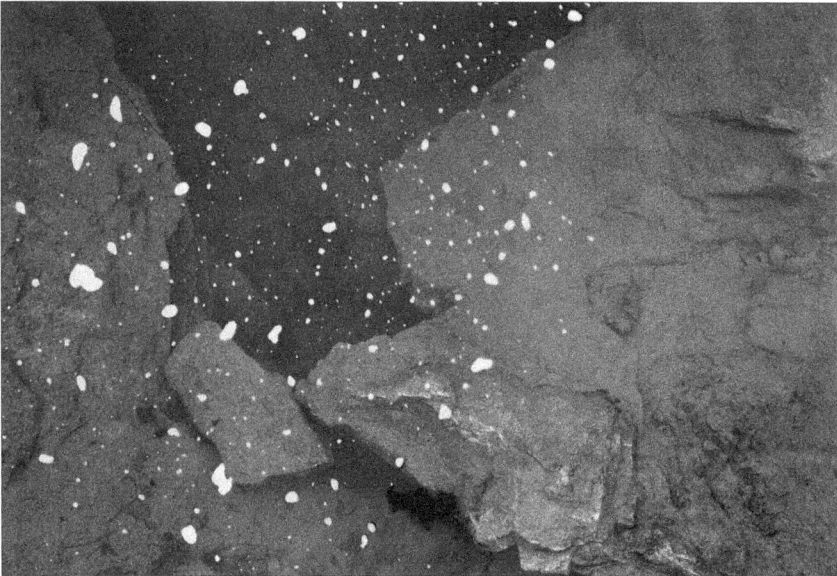

Fig. 11.1. Jonas N. T. Becker, *Thank G-d for Mississippi: Green Hole, WV* (2009), digital C-print on Fujiflex, 44 × 55 in. Courtesy of the artist.

about the end of the line, the value miners' labor and our land would have somewhere else to someone else.

Opioids entered the state as the mining industry was declining, and the rise and fall of these industries are entwined.[12] There are direct corollaries: the opioid epidemic was ushered in by the type of labor and the social conditions of a precarious, single-industry mining economy. Mining is among the most dangerous occupations in the United States, and the coalfield regions have higher than national average rates of job-related injury, unemployment, and addiction. When OxyContin entered the market in the 1990s, it was prescribed heavily for work-related injuries, falsely promised to be less addictive than previous drugs.[13] Opioids spread quickly, and their sedative effect had a significant impact on individuals and communities struggling with lack of jobs, recreation, and options for the future endemic in postindustrial regions. A testament to the causal relationship, studies of the US opiate overdose epidemic indicate that rural coal country is one of the epicenters of the drastic increase in fatal use of the drug.[14]

The opioid and mining industries can also be understood as exchangeable forms of extraction—where value is taken out leaving little in return. Mining extracts minerals from the earth and labor from workers' bodies, exporting the value of both outside the region. In similar formation, after the decline of mining, the opioid industry continues to extract profit from the unemployed and injured, following the previous generation of extraction. Both industries masked the one-directional nature of this dynamic, instead marketing their benefit to communities. Mining companies promised economic development on former mine sites, and Purdue Pharma, OxyContin's manufacturer, promoted that the drug was a safe way to get people back on their feet with slogans like "Get in the Swing with OxyContin."[15] Meanwhile, mining towns remain toxic, and newly available evidence clearly shows Purdue Pharma's intent to withhold safety information to increase the widespread growth of the drug. Addiction feeds a new generation of extraction; a booming pharmaceutical industry headquartered in Connecticut is built on income and livelihoods taken from Appalachia and the Midwest, leaving behind broken communities.[16]

I first encountered opioids in a recreational context in the late nineties, just as mountaintop removal mining was reaching its height. At the time, I was active in the electronic music scene. Ironically, one of the leveled peaks, now a meadow marred like a surface from outer space, made a great landing pad for outdoor music festivals. These festivals prospered in a way that was distinct from their urban cousins, fueled in part by a West Virginia libertarian bent—don't tread on me, and I won't tread on you—and, as a consequence, we were mostly left alone. Drugs played a huge part in the utopian aspirations of these huge parties. We all wanted to get somewhere else. The early drugs, mostly acid, ecstasy, and other psychedelics, were meant to extend the human sensory palate: see more, feel more, do more. But things shifted. Newer drugs mostly included sedatives; in 2000, the drug of choice was ketamine, a horse tranquilizer. And it was around this time that I was first offered an opioid, with the suggestion that, similar to other popular drugs at the time, I would feel euphorically sedated. This occurred to me as an odd alignment—equating sedation with pleasure. In years since, opioid painkillers have become endemic, and in addition to the popularization of sedative drugs, there has been a broader cultural shift to naturalize the pairing of sedation and pleasure. In this context, opioid use can be read as part of a larger cultural turn toward sedation.

The widespread pursuit of sedatives—whether drugs, products, or activities—and corresponding apathy have proliferated in the United States under late capitalism. Economists and sociologists point to a host of root causes including anxiety related to widening income disparity and precarious labor, individualism, and media saturation.[17] Evidence of the shift is wide-ranging. In health and wellness, the meditation, yoga, and supplement markets have experienced atypical growth—for example, an increase in the number of Americans meditating from 4 percent to 15 percent from 2012 to 2017.[18] Other prime examples include the apparel market rebranding shopping as therapeutically sedative "retail therapy" and the television industry restructuring to promote binge watching. Increased appetite for sedation is closely tied to our changing relationship to images and technology. Images have become so pervasive, intruding in all elements of both public and private life, that theorists such as Lev Manovich argue that images have transcended text to become our primary language.[19] Extending this, ubiquitous devices such as cell phones ensure ever-present points of connection to a world of visual content, enveloping us in an infinite image ecology comprised of everything from news photographs to friends' memes. Many media theorists have marveled at how, given these circumstances of being more connected to the culture and realities of others than ever before, we don't care more.[20] To the opposite effect, we care less, a phenomenon named in pop-theoretical terms like "compassion fatigue."[21] Perhaps the Situationists, an art movement in France in the 1960s, predicted this best, describing how the saturation of images would dull the masses.[22] Whether we have become lost in an image ecology and numb to content or have become physically sedated by pharmaceuticals, our current cultural moment must be understood through the operations of sedation and apathy.

This pervasive malaise has extended beyond popular culture and media to visual art. Art is often thought of as a powerful tool for questioning larger issues not visible in more commercial media. But in some ways, the contemporary art world, funded by industry tycoons and built on a similar capitalist structure to consumer luxury goods, has not escaped the larger cultural move towards sedation.[23] Over the last twenty years, art viewing has shifted dramatically to focus on large-scale fairs, where hundreds of galleries exhibit work at once. These fairs are physically exhausting—visitors clock miles in viewing the work—and visually exhausting beyond anything we have experienced. Viewing in this context must be reduced to categorical filtering by genre, as well as brand recognition for artists. Everything else fades into the larger experience of being at an art fair. In other viewing contexts, fine art is apprehended with a similar approach—the task of looking is supplanted by recognition—and our preexisting assumptions about mediums, contexts, venues, and artists provide most of our understanding of the artwork, allowing fast absorption and a quick exit. And so, fine art is not immune from the impact of visual fatigue and sedation.

Though images have become part of the problem, perhaps in recognizing this, artists still have the capacity to refocus us. The evidence is compelling. Art has historically been at the edge, the avant-garde, capable of capturing a zeitgeist, even one of mass apathy, and somehow reframing our moment,

Fig. 11.2. Expo Chicago, 2019. Photo by Jonas N. T. Becker.

leaving us with questions. For example, postwar movements such as Dada and Surrealism highlighted the impact of mass trauma on a still-forming genera-tion.[24] Political cartoons, poking fun via allegory, said things that the other pages of the newspaper were not able to. Perhaps visual culture, particularly art, still has the capacity to create reactions antithetical to apathy, instead en-couraging criticality and raising awareness. In our current context, is it pos-sible to turn pervasive image saturation on its head to create moments of connection? In the specific geographies and culture of Appalachia, framed by generations of extractive economies, can visual work create new links between the people and resources extracted and consumers? Extraction has prolifer-ated widespread apathy—the condition of living and the condition of looking, perhaps aesthetic work can be a medium to resituate, if not to outright jolt, viewers from sedation to concern, from new normal to new questions.

In my art practice, I use visual work to examine these questions. My proj-ects make visible the layers of identity, culture, and politics that intersect in landscape. In addressing these layers in my images, I see a parallel between the ways that photography and landscape have often been misrecognized as neutral, only seen for their surface. In a context of both political and visual fatigue, it is necessary to disrupt the way the camera makes meaning; my proj-ects call attention to the surface of the image, disrupt consumptive and ex-ploitative models of viewing, and instead create connections between viewers and socioeconomic issues. Embracing an intersectional approach to land, my work seeds the ground for criticality and concern by connecting interrelated histories of oppression and reconfiguring new ways of seeing.

My most recent work, *Better or Equal Use*, visibly binds generations of extrac-tive practices in Appalachia, from mining to incarceration and consumerism, and connects urban art audiences to the economic and social systems at the other end of their light switch. The series of photographs of former mining sites printed using coal dust began when I first visited Federal Correctional Institution McDowell, built on the former Belcher Mountain. Driving down the prison's driveway, we cut markedly through the former walls of a mountain, the scars in the topography evident. The road ended at the prison, where this isolated hole with high walls on all sides became a perfect geography for incarceration. There, I was struck with the realization that the extraction of mining was not a singular event. Instead, what I was looking at was an insatiable cycle, one that had started with the extraction of coal and that has continued through the extraction of labor and value in other ways, such that I could not see the end of it.

Each of the redevelopments that I visited—prisons, golf courses, shopping

Fig. 11.3. Jonas N. T. Becker, *Better or Equal Use: Belcher Mountain* (2019), ground coal, gelatin, paper, 20 × 24 in. Courtesy of the artist.

malls—were ushered in under the Surface Mining Control and Reclamation Act of 1977 (SMCRA).[25] The act mandates that, after mining, a company must restore "the original contour of the land" or redevelop the site for an "equal or better economic or public use."[26] From an optimistic perspective, it is possible to view this legal doctrine as an attempt to put a stopper in the unidirectional flow of extraction. And certainly, this legislation provides more specific standards than those that exist in many parts of the world. But at its core is a flaw: the idea that replacing one form of capitalist extraction with another can fill the gap left by the first. Strip malls provide local employment, but the labor terms of big-box chains are designed to extract as much value as possible to company headquarters, paying as little as the market will bear (minimum wage in the vacuum left by mining) and evading benefit premiums through part-time employment.[27] These developments, instead of stopping the flow, perpetuate oppressive labor dynamics and consumerism, replicating previous extractive models.

Better or Equal Use animates this moment of recognition of the deep ties that bind these histories of extraction. The project is a series of photographs; each image depicts one redevelopment rendered in coal collected from its site.

Fig. 11.4. Research photograph of former mining site redeveloped as a strip mall in Louisa, Kentucky. Photo by Jonas N. T. Becker.

Fig. 11.5. Coal sample from Pickering Knob Business Park. Photo by Jonas N. T. Becker.

The photographs are printed through an invented process that uses coal dust as pigment, based on a historic carbon printing process. This process, valued in the early 1900s for its tonal qualities to depict both untouched nature and industrial innovation, references photography's longstanding romanticization of both landscape and industry.[28] In *Better or Equal Use*, the photographs represent the redevelopment through its image, while they also represent the mine that preceded it through the physical trace of coal. The prints *depict* the site and are also *made of* the site, connecting form and material to highlight the continued cycle. The redevelopments replace one system of extraction, a mine, with another, a prison or mall.

SMCRA does provide an alternative course of action to redevelopment. In lieu of finding a better or equal use, a mining company may choose to rebuild the mountain to match its original facade. Through this equation, Congress makes a rare foray into aesthetics, suggesting that something that *looks* the same *is* the same. According to this act, a human-made mountain built with rock and filled with toxins is an equivalent substitute for the previous biodiverse mountain created by the movement of tectonic plates. The act is built on a mimetic misrecognition common to the photograph: when we see a photograph of a prison, we say, "This is a prison." We mistake the photograph for an unmediated representation of reality. To resist this misrecognition, the images in *Better or Equal Use* make their surfaces apparent, uneven and dimensional, obviously constructed of black dust. The surfaces point to the photographs' construction and draw viewers' attention to their own act of looking, their own process of making meaning out of what they see. The images say that how things *look* and how they *are* are not the same. Instead, asking viewers to consider the layers of history and representation informs a practice of active looking in lieu of apathy or passive spectatorship.

Often, the detachment induced by images and social issues has a direct relationship to scale: sedation by overwhelm. It is hard to understand a set of politics whose numeric representation goes beyond anything that we have a relationship to in our own lives. An artist I know once spent days tallying over two million marks in the pages of a journal after realizing that she did not know what it meant to have such a large number of people incarcerated in the United States. The scale of such statistics makes them difficult to understand, overwhelming to consider, and as a result, often paralyzing.

My photography series *Thank G-d for Mississippi* is a direct response to this kind of sedation by overwhelm, focusing on the individual effects of these larger socioeconomic conditions and resituating the viewer's act of looking to a one-on-one exchange. In this project, I returned to the most common sites

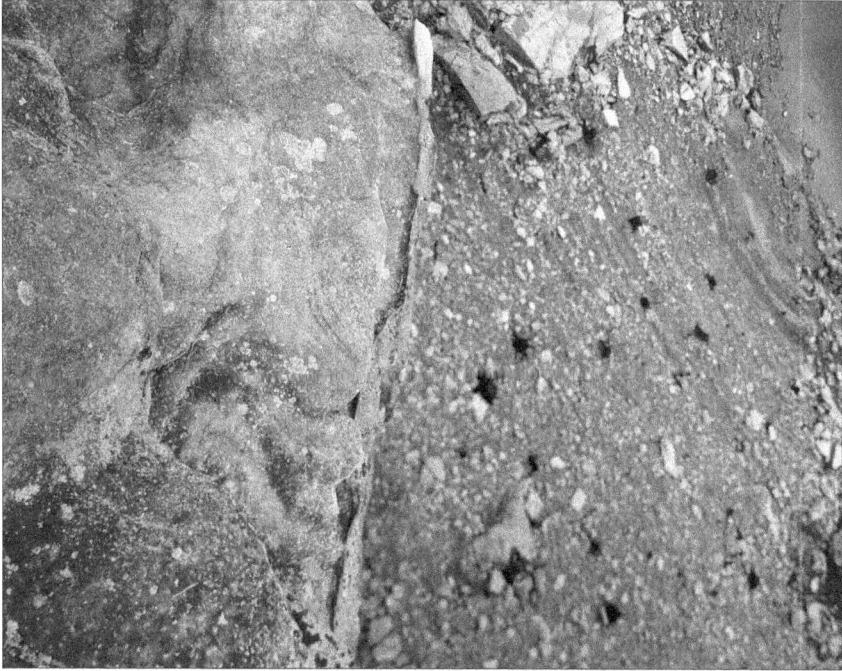

Fig. 11.6. Jonas N. T. Becker, *Thank G-d for Mississippi: Summersville Lake Possibly on Whippoorwill Cliffs, WV* (2009), digital C-print on Fujiflex, 44 × 55 in. Courtesy of the artist.

of fatal jumps in West Virginia. To photograph these sites, I constructed a boom to extend my camera twelve feet out over each ledge, capturing a view you could only see after having decided to jump. The photographs demand that the viewer leave their position of safety and distance in order to embody the gaze of the other.

Thank G-d for Mississippi, the series title, references annual state rankings on socioeconomic conditions. It is a phrase I grew up hearing that roughly means "it could be worse" and references the commonplace occurrence that West Virginia would fall low in the rankings—but Mississippi would be lower.[29] The work arose from my experience of the ways that these conditions translate into individual lives in nuanced and complicated ways. My mother worked as a social worker for the state of West Virginia, through which I witnessed how one socioeconomic condition may actually be a symptom of another—for example, how family employment and substance abuse may impact a child's education. Tagging along on my father's weekly drives around

Fig. 11.7. Jonas N. T. Becker, *Thank G-d for Mississippi: Bull Run, WV Also Called Blue Hole* (2009), digital C-print on Fujiflex, 44 × 55 in. Courtesy of the artist.

the state as an extension agent for West Virginia University, I further came to see the ways these conditions are experienced differently across race, class, and gender.[30] These experiences of the nuanced personal realities of living within larger socioeconomic conditions drew me to the sites I photographed in *Thank G-d for Mississippi*, identified by local and state records as the most common locations of fatal falls. While often understood as suicides, the reality of these deaths is in fact much more complicated; many were related to high-risk behavior or accidental slips while under the influence. This simple misconstruction, the flattening of these deaths to suicide, exemplifies the inadequacy of abstract social language to accurately reflect and honor the experiences of the people whose lives they describe. In returning to these sites of individual trauma, the project attempts to resituate large abstract modes of understanding the complicated layers of class, race, and economics within individual decision making.

Photographers and other artists frequently explore larger social issues through their work but often through portraiture and documentary formats that replicate extractive models. In the most egregious examples, such images exploit the experiences and circumstances of others, reduce them to symbolic expressions of suffering, and distribute them for mass consumption through the Associated Press or frame them to be viewed as objects of otherness on museum walls.[31] As with massive statistics, these images are consumed from a distance, the complex experiences of others reduced to an archetype. Within this framework, I understand the history of photography in Appalachia, where these types of images have historically followed the same lines already cut by the extraction of coal. In the 1930s, FSA photographers traveled through Appalachia to find families living in the most extreme poverty and distributed images that helped create the hyperbolized Appalachian image. This continued during the War on Poverty in the 1960s, 1970s, and 1980s, this time in vivid color. And most recently, during the 2016 presidential election, documentarians brought back the horror-movie-inspired image of the rural other, often depicted in barbaric social formation, mouths agape in protest, as if to suggest their otherness and inhumanity.[32] Regardless of political views, it is important to understand how image mining continues to function in Appalachia, following a long history. This extractive model of documentary photography not only takes the value of identity elsewhere, leaving little or nothing in exchange, but it also creates a dynamic of urban viewership in which the experiences of others are reduced, simplified, and consumed or passed over when the week's news is thrown out.

My series *Thank G-d for Mississippi* upends this relationship between subject and viewer. While my work focuses on similar socioeconomic issues with an arguably similar intent to reach distant, unfamiliar audiences, there is a crucial difference in my approach. The images use the camera to directly place the viewer inside the perspective of the other. In constructing the image, instead of shooting the view I could see safely from behind a guardrail, I photographed a view one could only achieve after having jumped, straight down. When looking at the photographs, the viewer is positioned as if they too have already committed to jumping. The images replace the relationship between detached viewer and simplified other with one that collapses the distance between us and them. This disruptive perspective has another function; it inverts the normative upright vantage point from which we view images, established when a baby learns to walk, making it difficult to determine up from down, foreground from background. By disrupting the act of looking, these images interrupt the indifference of passive spectatorship to encourage a deeper consideration of the experiences they embody.

Fig. 11.8. Jonas N. T. Becker, *Thank G-d for Mississippi: Birch Run, WV* (2009), digital C-print on Fujiflex, 44 × 55 in. Courtesy of the artist.

In the context of *Better or Equal Use* and *Thank G-d for Mississippi*, photography can be seen as a medium that can break its own rules, pushing the viewer from passive to active looking. In *Better or Equal Use*, the work calls our attention to the mimetic quality of photography, highlighting that what is pictured is not the same as what is. In *Thank G-d for Mississippi*, the shift in perspective to embody that of the subject forces the viewer to inhabit the position of the other rather than consume their image. A pivotal professional moment early in my career demonstrated to me the potential social and political impact of this way of working in photography. I was working with an art dealer who was identifying potential acquisitions for a wealthy Southern mega-chain. She presented *Thank G-d for Mississippi* as part of the proposed acquisitions. The family was ecstatic—I can imagine that in many ways the luscious landscapes, rocks, and rivers felt like home to them—and expressed interest in acquiring a portion of the series. As the deal was negotiated, they inquired more about the background of the work, and after learning the details of the work's premise, the deal fell apart. For me, this moment highlighted precisely the success of the work: that in depicting poor socioeconomic conditions through landscape images, the work operated like a Trojan horse of sorts. Masquerading in this way, the work's aesthetic qualities collide with its political content to create a productive moment of misrecognition; the process destabilizes the viewer's assumptions in order to generate a more layered examination of both form and content.

This experience made me reconsider the importance of repurposing specific contexts of reception toward political ends, particularly in an oversaturated image ecology and, by extension, an oversaturated art ecology. Each context of visual communication carries its own language and structure of meaning, whether advertising, news media, or documentary. News media are produced under the promise of objectivity. Advertising is designed to prompt purchase. Popular media like YouTube claim to present DIY expressions of users' authentic selves. Visual content is interpreted through the assumptions, histories, and expectations of the specific context it is presented within. In recuperating these forms, artists can perform the aesthetics or structure of commercial media, inserting artistic concepts within more mainstream frameworks. But these masquerades are never seamless; there is misalignment between what you expect to see and what you actually encounter. The misrecognition prompts reconsideration and, in the process, creates space for new meaning.[33]

My ongoing series of work, *Mountain is a Mountain*, embodies this intermodal approach, creating works that perform elements of fine art, popular culture, and commercial media through their aesthetics. The premise of the project connects two sites, a little Switzerland in Appalachia and the Swiss Alps, as a way to consider issues of value and environment. The first work in the series is an interactive installation called *Please Enjoy* . . . . The work, originally installed in Switzerland, is comprised of two mini refrigerators containing bottles of clear liquid. A sign above the installation reads, "please enjoy a drink fresh from the mountains." The installation's provocation centers on the dramatically different mountain economies referenced by the project. In Switzerland, water running off mountain cirques is bottled and sold for a high price, whereas in West Virginia, you would be better off drinking moonshine than mountain water.[34] Extending this comparison, a video in the series, *Holographic Mountain*, uses the language of corporate design innovation to suggest that, on sites where Appalachian Mountains have been leveled by mountaintop removal mining, we should project holographic Swiss peaks in their place. The script for the video, narrated by two detached corporate voices, is based on George W. Bush's speech-writing techniques, which included trademarks like the double

Fig. 11.9. Jonas N. T. Becker, *Mountain is a Mountain: Holographic Mountain* (2017), single-channel HD video with sound, 2:45 minutes, looping, dimensions variable. Courtesy of the artist.

negative, euphemisms such as the War on Terror, and gross exotifications of culture.[35] Situating its rhetoric in this context, the video slips in and out of propaganda, design proposal, and artwork..

In exhibiting these works, I have created installations that further blur the context for art viewing, composing the works within the architecture of commercial and corporate venues. This recontextualization allows viewers to reconsider the content of each installation through the connotations of commercial spaces and prompts them to question what is perceived as real versus artistic fabrication. In the Miami installation *Please Enjoy a Drink Fresh from the Mountains*, I converted a mall storefront into a corporate office, replete with boardroom table and water coolers, blending with the architecture of the mall. However, in the installation, *Holographic Mountain* was projected on the wall like a consultant's pitch while the floor slowly flooded with water. The film and flooding present an odd intrusion in the otherwise familiar commercial scene. Their outlandish, yet conceivable, proposals (holographic Alps and flooding Miami) draw links between corporate America, consumerism, and environmental destruction. More recently at a Los Angeles art fair, the video appeared on an iPad atop a podium-like sculpture accompanied by rows of water bottles labeled with abstract pictures of mountains. Formally referencing the aesthetics of a trade show, the work acts as a totem to the commercial expos normally

Fig. 11.10. Jonas N. T. Becker, *Please Enjoy a Drink Fresh from the Mountains* (Exterior view, Mana Contemporary at 777 International Mall, Miami, Florida) (2018), single-channel HD video with sound (projected), 3:00, water, water pump, office furniture, water tanks, sculpture in basement below, dimensions variable. Courtesy of the artist.

housed in the same convention centers as art fairs. Unlike the paintings hung neatly on the high walls of each gallery's booth in order to disguise the space as a luxury experience, this work ruptures the facade and points to the relationship between the art market and other forms of consumerism. Both the Miami and Los Angeles installations destabilize the architecture of art consumption, instead borrowing the frame of corporate structures to create connections between consumption, art, and the environment.

The context and medium of visual communication often determine whether we trust the source or believe the message. In expanding *Mountain is a Mountain*, I am creating new elements of the series that include community engagement, social practice, and documentary forms. In working in these formats, I am invoking each one's relationship to authenticity and truth. Over the next few years, I will be working with community organizations in West Virginia and Kentucky to create performances and other site-specific interventions on sites of former mines. I will document the brainstorming and creation of these works alongside participants. The documentation will be exhibited with *Holographic Mountain*, placing the community-generated proposals for reclaiming mine sites alongside my own artistic fabrications. Installing these elements together complicates the relationship between documentary and fiction, making the familiar seem strange and the improbable seem possible..

In working across many modes of creating visual knowledge, the works in *Mountain is a Mountain* directly oppose the fatigue of looking. Overwhelmed by the excess of images, we understand most of what we take away from art through what we already know about its context. We don't see; we recognize. Much of the preexisting information that frames our viewpoint is created through institutions that reinforce cultural ideology. Art in a museum is assumed to be historically important and vetted. Paintings in a thrift store are understood as decorative and sentimental. *Mountain is a Mountain* disrupts these assumptions about context and medium. Each work in the series breaks the rules for the media format in which it masquerades, performing and failing at sculpture, public engagement, performance, and advertising. But in the failures, the works rupture the kind of hermeneutic echo that each of these mediums rely on to produce seamless meaning: *Please Enjoy* . . . is at once an austere sculpture and participatory work made to be touched and consumed. The *Holographic Mountain* video embodies the format of a design proposal but instead suggests a provocative fantasy that highlights the problematics of large, international design projects. The impact is a subtle alienation. We are at once familiar and unsure. The works in the series defamiliarize us from what we think we know. Instead, we see anew. Loosened from the histories we are taught, we create relationships and interpretations independent of institutional ideology.

Sometimes, when we change what we see, we change who we are and what we think. José Esteban Muñoz describes in his theory of disidentification a process of scrambling, exaggerating, and repurposing dominant cultural representations, not only to expose their seams, but also to create the possibility of new, more radical reconstructions.[36] In considering disidentification in the context of land and politics, art can remix the normative representational tropes and beliefs inscribed in specific geographies, such as Appalachia: reimagining traditional photographic forms, such as documentary, landscape, and historic carbon printing, as well as situating images outside of art contexts in corporate spaces or commercial media. Through these reconfigured forms, we can imagine reexamining how land is valued or taken advantage of and complicating narratives around poverty and addiction that are associated with the region. Above all, in breaking out of the repetitive molds, reconstructed forms and

Fig. 11.11. Jonas N. T. Becker, *Mountain is a Mountain: Please Enjoy* . . . (Installation view, Saas Fee, Switzerland) (2017), two Electrolux mini refrigerators, clear bottles with "moonshine" and "water" labels, clear liquid, sign, 72 × 26 × 72 in. Courtesy of the artist.

content not only break through endemic visual and political apathy but provide pathways for creating new meaning. The possibilities of working in this way are encapsulated in responses to my recent work, *Holographic Mountain*. In contrast to my social media posts about regional issues—particularly among urban art audiences—the film's hyperboles and remixed content broke through visual fatigue and political apathy to provoke a reconstitution of beliefs about Appalachia. Often, in response to *Holographic Mountain,* people would ask me if it was true. This question confirmed the strategy I had executed—creating a reality so jolting it demands questioning its truth and plausibility; but its likeness to things we know makes us in turn question everything.

The extraction of mineral resources in Appalachia left a hole that made way for the opioid crisis, both by creating community structures cantilevered precariously, supported by a single-industry economy, and also by demanding dangerous physical labor, often resulting in injury and requiring pain management. Opioids offered to suppress both the physical pain and emotional unrest of communities and individuals struggling to cope with an evacuated industry. Parallel to this visible social violence, an extractive model of looking has a similar injustice, one in which the movement of the image is one-directional. We consume images en masse but rarely consider their context and implications, dulled by an oversaturated image ecology. But artists and other visual producers can disrupt this, reconfiguring new ways of seeing and connecting viewers to socioeconomic issues to cause disparate audiences to become engaged. Addressing what it means to look in the context of the sedative opioid epidemic, aesthetic production can break cycles of apathy to incite larger social and political change.

NOTES

1. Vilém Flusser, *Towards a Philosophy of Photography*, trans. Anthony Mathews (London: Reaktion Books, 2000).
2. Marshall McLuhan, *Understanding Media: The Extensions of Man* (New York: Signet Books, 1964), 63.
3. "German Settlers in the Appalachians," *Digital Heritage* (blog), October 8, 2012, https://digitalheritage.org/2012/10/german-settlers-in-the-appalachians/.
4. "Agriculture," *e-WV: West Virginia Encyclopedia*, accessed February 12, 2019, https://www.wvencyclopedia.org/articles/166.
5. "History of West Virginia Mineral Industries: Coal," West Virginia Geological and Economic Survey, last modified June 20, 2017, http://www.wvgs.wvnet.edu/www/geology/geoldvco.htm.
6. "West Virginia's Mine Wars," West Virginia Archives and History, accessed February 13, 2019, http://www.wvculture.org/history/archives/minewars.html.

7.   Syd S. Peng, "Mountaintop Removal Controversy Slows West Virginia Coal Mining," *Mining Engineering* 52, no. 9 (2000): 53.

8.   Jedediah Purdy, "The Violent Remaking of Appalachia," *The Atlantic*, March 21, 2016, https://www.theatlantic.com/technology/archive/2016/03/the-violent-remaking-of -appalachia/474603/.

9.   James R. Green, review of *What's a Coal Miner to Do? The Mechanization of Coal Mining*, by Keith Dix, *The Business History Review* 65, no. 1 (Spring 1991): 183–85.

10. The Federal Energy Information Agency has studied and quantified this decline in the coal industry; this report found the largest decline occurring in Appalachia, where the market value of the largest mining companies declined from $34 billion in 2011 to $150 million in 2016 (Purdy, "The Violent Remaking of Appalachia").

11. "Court Rules Coal Companies Must Pay into Pension Fund," *Washington Post*, July 26, 1992, A24.

12. In West Virginia in the 1950s, coal employment was nearly six times what it is now ("Labor Market Information: Economic Indicators," *WorkForce West Virginia*, accessed February 13, 2019, http://lmi.workforcewv.org/).

13. "History of the Opioid Epidemic," Poison Control: National Capital Poison Center, accessed February 14, 2019, https://www.poison.org/articles/opioid-epidemic -history-and-prescribing-patterns-182.

14. Matthew Bloch and Haeyoun Park, "How the Epidemic of Drug Abuse Deaths Rippled across America," *New York Times*, January 9, 2016, https://www.nytimes.com /interactive/2016/01/07/us/drug-overdose-deaths-in-the-us.html.

15. Art Van Zee "The Promotion and Marketing of Oxycontin: Commercial Triumph, Public Health Tragedy," *American Journal of Public Health* 99, no. 2 (2009): 221–7, https://doi .org/10.2105/AJPH.2007.131714.

16. "Purdue Pharma Locations and Operations," Purdue Pharma, https://www.purduepharma .com/about/locations-operations/.

17. Douglas Kellner, *Media Culture: Cultural Studies, Identity and Politics between the Modern and Post-modern* (New York: Routledge, 1995), 237; "Fatigued by the News? Experts Suggest How to Adjust Your Media Diet," *New York Times*, February 1, 2017, https:// www.nytimes.com/2017/02/01/us/news-media-social-media-information-overload .html; Steven Poole, *"The Inner Level* review: How More Equal Societies Reduce Stress and Improve Wellbeing," *The Guardian*, June 20, 2018, https://www.theguardian.com /books/2018/jun/20/the-inner-level-review.

18. Tainya C. Clarke et al., "The Use of Yoga, Mediation, and Chiropractors among U.S. Adults 18 and Older," National Center for Health Statistics, NCHS Data Brief, No. 325, November 2018, https://www.cdc.gov/nchs/data/databriefs/db325-h.pdf.

19. Lev Manovich, *Instagram and Contemporary Image* (online publication, 2017), 115, http://manovich.net/content/04-projects/151-instagram-and-contemporary-image /instagram_book_manovich_2017.pdf.

20. Ralph Schroeder, *Social Theory after the Internet: Media, Technology, and Globalization* (London: UCL Press, 2018), 84.

21. Elisa Gabbert, "Is Compassion Fatigue Inevitable in an Age of 24-Hour News?" *The Guardian*, August 2, 2018, https://www.theguardian.com/news/2018/aug/02/is -compassion-fatigue-inevitable-in-an-age-of-24-hour-news. Gabbert applies the theory of compassion fatigue from Charles R. Figley, ed., *Compassion Fatigue: Coping with Secondary Traumatic Stress Disorder in Those Who Treat the Traumatized* (New York: Routledge, 1995).

22. Guy Debord, *Society of the Spectacle* (Kalamazoo: Black and Red, 2002).

23. Anna Louie Sussman, "The Industries That Drive the Art Market," *Artsy*, August 22, 2017, https://www.artsy.net/article/artsy-editorial-industries-drive-art-market.

24. Paul Trachtman, "A Brief History of Dada," *Smithsonian Magazine*, May 2006, https://www.smithsonianmag.com/arts-culture/dada-115169154/.
25. "Surface Mining Control and Reclamation Act," *Digest of Federal Resource Laws of Interest to the U.S. Fish and Wildlife Service*, accessed February 14, 2019, https://www.fws.gov/laws/lawsdigest/surfmin.html.
26. "Surface Mining Control and Reclamation Act," 76, 83.
27. For example, the labor practices uncovered by Barbara Ehrenreich in *Nickel and Dimed: On (Not) Getting By in America* (New York: Picador, 2011).
28. Sandy King and John Lockhart, "A Brief History of Carbon Printing," Alternative Photography, accessed February 14, 2019, https://www.alternativephotography.com/a-brief-history-of-carbon-printing/.
29. "Thank God for Mississippi," Wikipedia, last modified December 1, 2019, https://en.wikipedia.org/wiki/Thank_God_for_Mississippi; "Mississippi State Rankings," *U.S. News and World Report*, accessed February 14, 2019, https://www.usnews.com/news/best-states/mississippi.
30. "Extension Service County Offices," West Virginia Extension Service, accessed February 14, 2019, https://extension.wvu.edu/offices.
31. Susan Sontag, *Regarding the Pain of Others* (New York: Picador, 2003).
32. David Bell, "Anti-Idyll: Rural Horror," in *Contested Countryside Cultures: Otherness, Marginalization, and Rurality*, eds. Paul Cloke and Jo Little (London: Routledge, 1997), 91–104.
33. See, for example, Viktor Shklovsky's formulation of defamiliarization in his 1917 article "Art as Technique" (Viktor Shklovsky, "Art as Technique," *Russian Formalist Criticism: Four Essays*, trans. and ed. Lee Lemon and Marion Reis [Lincoln, Nebraska, 1965], 5–22).
34. "Water Quality Reports," *West Virginia: American Water*, accessed February 14, 2019, https://amwater.com/wvaw/water-quality/water-quality-reports.
35. Debra Merskin, "Making Enemies in George W. Bush's Post-9/11 Speeches," *Peace Review* 17 (October 2005): 373–81.
36. José Esteban Muñoz, *Disidentifications: Queers of Color and the Performance of Politics* (Minneapolis: University of Minnesota Press, 1999).

CHAPTER 12

Narrative Engagement with the Opioid Epidemic: From Personal Story to Personal Reflection

Amanda M. Caleb and Susan McDonald

In a 2016 Kaiser Family Foundation poll, 68 percent of respondents blamed opioid users for their addiction, yet 62 percent of these same respondents claimed that reducing social stigma about addiction would effectively address the opioid epidemic.[1] Notably, and implied in this survey data, "substance use disorders are more highly stigmatized than other health conditions."[2] Much of this stigmatization stems from the language we use to discuss the crisis, which reflects societal attitudes, assumptions about users, and efficacy of treatment plans.[3] Recently, changes in the literature on addiction have abandoned the descriptor "abuser" in favor of "substance use disorder." The former, a pejorative description of the individual, stigmatizes the individual and "reduces quality of care"; the latter is a medical assessment of the condition, not the person.[4]

Shifting from criminalization to medicalization is destigmatizing, which is essential for those seeking help in dealing with this epidemic. Reducing stigma includes education, contact, and advocacy. Studies have suggested that meaningful interaction with members of an out-group can enhance empathy; however, such interactions risk voyeurism or sentimentalism, particularly if the interaction is inauthentic or artificial.[5] Society's addiction narrative can also be changed through symbolic interactionism, which can be used to alter the dominant addiction discourse from a cold, statistical report to an individual and evocative narrative.

This chapter discusses how a symbolic interactionist perspective depicting the lives of persons who died as a result of an opioid epidemic engaged a university community as an innovative way of understanding the opioid epidemic. Displayed at Misericordia University's student center, the Pennsylvania Recovery Organization Alliance's Our Lives Matter quilt shares the stories of those who have lost their lives to opioid addiction. Viewers of the quilt were invited to write and post their reflections to the project. This interactive process connected the Misericordia community to the lives of people with a substance use disorder in a humanizing and destigmatizing way.

Communities that are affected by the opioid epidemic need a narrative that reflects their populations' personal experiences. Connecting these experiences through artistic expression gives meaning to all the lives impacted by this epidemic by focusing on the individual and not the drug. Both the quilt and the written responses speak to a creative way of engaging with the opioid epidemic and offer a partial solution to ending it through the use of written engagement that reduces social stigma and moves the conversation away from a moral failing of addiction to advocacy for social obligation of care and compassion.

CONFRONTING STIGMA: OUR LIVES MATTER QUILT AT MISERICORDIA UNIVERSITY

On a near daily basis, national headlines address the opioid crisis, revealing another staggering statistic about lost lives or another attempt at curbing the epidemic that has yet to prove significant results. Despite decades of research on addiction, the opioid crisis has proven particularly difficult to curb: one issue is the neglect of the impact on communities of color.[6] Another issue is an oversimplification of policy changes, particularly a reliance on a single-policy approach.[7] The greatest challenge to ending the opioid crisis is how we understand the cause of the problem itself: while news media often target doctors who overprescribe or pharmaceutical marketing that encourages such over overprescribing, the source of the epidemic is more complicated and involves moving away from only considering external sources and to focus more on the individuals using opioids. Considering the socioeconomic factors that contribute to opioid use—including the impact of national economic shifts, such as the 2008 financial crisis, and employment associated with poor communities, such as manufacturing jobs—is a starting point to better understand the individuals affected by the opioid crisis and to develop a better solution to ending the epidemic.[8] The socioeconomic factors are only one part of the picture: we need to see those with substance use disorder as individuals and reflect upon how a number of individual factors impact their opioid abuse.

The opioid epidemic is very much a part of our community in northeast Pennsylvania. We see the impact in near weekly news reports and social media postings. The prevalence of opioid overdoses in our area drew national attention in 2017 when an NBC News report cited "137 fatal drug overdoses [in 2016]—more than half of them the result of heroin laced with fentanyl—in a county of just 318,000 people. That death rate is four times higher than New York City."[9] The sheer number of drug overdoses has risen each subsequent month since this report. One particularly cold headline in January 2019 read "Luzerne Country overdose deaths break another record"—in 2018, it was 156 deaths, and again over half were from opioids.[10] The magnitude of the opioid problem makes it almost impossible to comprehend the devastation for families and friends. Everyone in this area has been affected in some way by this epidemic. This ongoing devastation requires new ways of addressing drug addiction, including prevention and education, naloxone, and medication-assisted treatment. "We're not going to police ourselves out of this," County Coroner William Lisman said in 2017. "This is more of a social statement. We have to change people's minds about drugs. Until we change that, I don't see this coming to an end."[11]

The statement about changing people's minds resonated with us, and we began to think about the stigma that surrounds addition. The enormity of this epidemic requires a change in basic assumptions in people's perception of addiction. The opioid epidemic has been addressed actively on our small university campus in northeast Pennsylvania since 2015, when Dr. Susan McDonald (who began her career as a certified addictions counselor) engaged the university community to think more critically about an issue that was not just national but local. These public outreach programs, which also supported our addictions counseling minor, have included panel discussions, educational events, and political speeches on legislative activities, yet we discerned that these events had not gone far enough to break down the stigma surrounding addiction. Our intent was to reach students, faculty, and staff in a more humanizing and inclusive manner that would extend beyond what had been previously done and to adopt a model that would actively work to reduce stigma.

A number of conversations in the social work department led to a decision to apply the symbolic interactionist theory, developed by Herbert Blumer, as the primary theory in creating new educational programming.[12] This theory continues to be widely used and respected in the ongoing debate about how addiction is viewed as a crime or a disease. Additionally, Lindesmith's fieldwork on addiction (1935–1937) holds true today, focusing on the fear of withdrawal rather than a moral failing. This debate continues with society's view of substance addiction as a criminal offense rather than a medical disorder. Symbolic interactionism provides ways to challenge how the dominant discourse depicts addiction as criminal behavior. Changing minds in our community using symbolic representation of those who died from overdoses was a step in separating the addiction from the person.

Changing minds requires understanding how the individual and society are interconnected and interrelated. Sociologist Charles Horton Cooley (1864–1929) was first to explore how society and the individual are "twin-born." Cooley introduced the concept of the "looking glass self" to explain how individuals develop a sense of self in the development of identity and in relation to how we perceive others' view of us.[13] If society holds a pejorative view of addiction, that view is internalized by individuals with a substance use disorder. Understanding the interconnection and interrelation of society and individual in the context of symbolic interactionism laid the framework for our project.

With this structure in mind, we reached out to Pennsylvania Recovery Organization Alliance (PRO-A), a nonprofit organization that has been proactive in changing the opioid epidemic narrative by employing creative means to honor lives lost to a stigmatized, misunderstood, and feared disease by giving voice to a marginalized community. PRO-A constructed a quilt project memorializing lives lost to addiction created by family members and friends alike. They decided to name the quilt project Our Lives Matter, using the same concepts used in the creation of the AIDS quilt, which gave voice to those who died and helped to reduce stigma regarding AIDS.[14] The AIDS quilt raised awareness about individuals with AIDS and shifted the rhetoric from *them* to *us*; the Our Lives Matter quilt seeks to do the same by sharing the stories of individuals who are more than just their addiction and remain part of our community.

The Our Lives Matter quilt employs social justice in the inherent dignity and worth of all people; similar to the AIDS quilt, the Our Lives Matter quilt depicts another dispirited story of the United States. Both projects are part of a larger history of quilting, a history that is both personal and political. Quilts have been used to tell stories, symbolically giving meaning and messages; quilts are also a symbol of family and community, telling of their heritage and people. Largely seen as women's work, quilting has enabled women to record their family histories and to do so as a communal act with other women; moreover, quilts are often passed down to daughters, thereby continuing the story of women and their families. Politically, quilts have been used to fund wars, as in the case of Southern women selling quilts to support the Confederacy, or to help stop injustices, as in the case of Northern women using quilts to create a map of safe passage for slaves as part of the Underground Railroad.[15] The

Fig. 12.1. Dr. Susan McDonald (*center*) with Misericordia faculty, staff, and students and a representative from Pro-A in front of the Our Lives Matter quilt.

history of quilting, then, is not just one of women's work but also of women's roles in recording stories and contributing to political action—a history that is steeped in feminism and moving women from the domestic to the public sphere. While the panels for the AIDS and Our Lives Matter quilts were not created exclusively by women, they are part of this larger women's history that is steeped in political action and communal responsibility.

Both quilt projects are examples of "counter-memorials," which serve as physical symbols of remembrance that seek to alter the narrative about addiction and AIDS.[16] The panels in the Our Lives Matter quilt tell the stories of lives before addiction: pictures of graduations, family photos, beloved pets, and symbols of vibrant lives beckon to viewers and memorialize individuals. This reframing rewrites the story of addiction by depicting personal stories, separating the person from the addiction. The pejorative symbols of addiction—the syringe, the junkie, and the criminal—have served as the dominant symbols telling stories of addiction; the Our Lives Matter quilt offers a humanizing counternarrative. The Our Lives Matter quilt's symbols tell stories of lives that mattered. Professionals, mothers, fathers, sisters, brothers, sons, daughter, friends, and neighbors connected viewers to these lives. Viewer interactions with the personal stories have the potential to connect and destigmatize.

The Our Lives Matter quilt project was exactly what we were seeking to encourage—an interactive activity that would create a new way to understand this epidemic from people who lost loved ones to the disease of addiction in a forum that respected and honored their stories and could help destigmatize those with a substance use disorder. After a few discussions with the PRO-A team, we decided to "air the quilt" in the lobby of our student center. The student lobby is a very public place that all members of the university walk though in the course of their daily university life. Displaying the quilt in this public space allowed for interaction with people viewing the quilt, interaction with the quilt narratives, and interaction through introspection. The size of the quilt was 12.5 feet by 12.5 feet, and the individual panels were 3 feet by 6 feet, representing the size of a human grave. This subtle symbolic message gave us reason to pause: this was more than an educational endeavor about the opioid epidemic. The beginning and planning of this project brought people together in conversations that would not have otherwise occurred on this small university setting, including the student support and utilities staff who weighed in on organization and how the quilt display would elicit a wide range of reactions and reflections. The conversations evolved from planning to sharing stories of who they knew lost a loved one. It became clear that this project was interactive in all phases with all involved, and these early conversations were echoed by the community who later viewed the quilt. The display gave our university an opportunity to bear witness to the human cost of addiction and to engage with and shape that new meaning as a community.

SYMBOLIC INTERACTIONISM AND WRITTEN ENGAGEMENTS WITH ADDICTION

One unique aspect of this project—as compared to something like the AIDS quilt—is that we asked viewers to actively engage with the Our Lives Matter quilt by writing a reflection on notecards on how the quilt has affected them, which we then posted next to the quilt. The space between the quilt and the notecards was deliberately designed to keep people engaged in the process of viewing, in the act of sharing, reading, and listening to stories, and in the creation of written reflections that were physically added to the space occupied by the quilt. Writing reflections on the notecards created additional openings that generated new meanings and understanding; the responses allowed for metareflection, creating space in which people could respond to both the quilt

Fig. 12.2. Announcement for Our Lives Matter quilt display.

itself and other reflections about it and building a sense of community and shared experience as a consequence.

The use of written responses further developed our symbolic interactional approach, whereby viewers moved through the three core principles, meaning (what people assign to an entity), language (how people assign meaning and understand the meaning of others), and thought (the interpretation of meaning).[17] Thus, we were interested in how the reflections spoke to these three premises in their reaction to the Our Lives Matter quilt. The responses were of three types: bullet-pointed or brief comments about the project and the writer's response to it, a direct conversation with an individual on the quilt or who made the quilt square, and advocacy imperatives. Although not prompted in this direction, these last two categories of response align with the stigma-reduction approaches of contact and advocacy, respectively.[18]

The first category of responses, the bullet-pointed/brief comments, was the largest type of response and accounted for 40.6 percent of the total responses. These notecards contained mostly single-word responses focusing on both what the responder saw and what they felt. The most repeated words were "sad," "heartbreaking," "emotional," and "devastating," which were almost always combined on the same notecards. These single-word responses revealed the raw and unprocessed response to the quilt; in other words, they signaled a connection between the viewer and the quilt—the individual's broken heart coupled with the sadness of the story they interpret—but did not move beyond an emotional tie. The ordering of the bullet responses revealed how individuals processed their responses; if included, "sad" was the first word provided, followed by "heartbreaking" as either the second or third term. The meaning assigned here is one of sympathy (sad for another) and empathy (feeling the pain of another), which is a first step toward changing the public mindset about opioid addiction. The use of the word "heartbreaking" is particularly encouraging, as it indicates an emotional and implied physical response to pain family and friends have suffered in losing a loved one. "Devastating" indicates the impact of addiction, whether on the family or on society, and speaks to a deep impression on the viewer's experience with the quilt.

Although these shorter responses may seem less developed because of their brevity and heavy reliance on emotion, they demonstrate a first step toward wanting to change the addiction narrative through their recognition of the human experience and the connection between individuals. One bulleted response illustrates this point in its progression of words: "sad. empathetic. compassion. awareness." Moreover, they demonstrate the effect of contact via symbolism and narrative to help shape perspectives on opioid addiction. The responses were all personal engagements with the quilt, and the individual stories are suggestive of genuine and empathetic connections. A note on the AIDS quilt read: "Perhaps this is because the particular, not the universal, is what connects us as humans."[19] In other words, the individuality of each lost life is a means of connecting one-to-one with the viewer.

The second category, those that engaged in direct conversation with the quilt and/or families and friends, was the smallest response group at 21.9 percent. These responses ranged from more common phrases, such as "prayers to you and your family," to very personal engagement, such as "I never met you, but I feel the pain of not having you here." This last response is worth noting, as it both acknowledges connectivity and absence and links the viewer to the act of grieving. The public act of grieving via the quilt panels allows for the community to be part of the grieving process for a death that is largely stigmatized by public opinion.[20] The direct address allows for the creation of dialogue that does not close down understandings of opioid addiction but instead encourages more conversation, more discussion, and ultimately more action. The movement toward action is evident in the direct address notecards that indicate the need to offer help to others, moving from the direct address to the quilt to a broader direct address to society. Thus, we can see this direct address as demonstrating the power of contact or what we might term indirect or symbolic contact by way of the quilt instead of the individual or family directly. The use of contact to destigmatize mental health is well documented; there is less research on indirect or symbolic contact in general—with the exception of work on the AIDS quilt—and nothing specifically on addiction. Our preliminary work suggests there is a positive effect at least in how people communicate connectivity, and therefore community, through language, which will then translate to changing views about opioid addiction.

The final category of responses, that of advocacy imperatives, made up 37.5 percent of the reflections and included broader calls for prevention and specific calls to destigmatize addiction. On the surface, these responses appear simultaneously personal and impersonal. There are responses to the quilt, but they do not speak directly to it or with the same empathetic tone as other responses; rather, they focus on opioid addiction in a way that recognizes the loss as epidemic. However, they also represent a more developed response to the Our Lives Matter quilt in that they move beyond the immediacy of the response to advocacy and futurity. In nearly half of these reflections, this call for advocacy is done through either directly recognizing and rejecting the stigma of addiction or speaking to how the quilt humanizes addiction, which implies the need to destigmatize addiction. In these responses, the addressee is not the families and individuals represented in the quilt, nor the writer, but rather society as a whole. One notecard ends with, "have an open mind and kind heart. Listen." This card in particular emphasizes the need for meaningful and empathetic engagement and for shifting the public narrative of opioid addiction.

The other responses in this third category focus directly on prevention, either through asking about how these deaths could have been prevented (a turn toward the past that has implications for the future) or a call for measures to prevent future deaths. One notable response is one that used both sides of the notecard with one side reading "empathy prevention" and the other side reading "prevention = empathy." The use of antimetabole may not have been deliberate; still, it offers a profound response that questions our perceptions of prevention (Does empathy create prevention? Or does prevention create empathy?) and draws a clear connection between empathy and prevention. Because the two phrases were written on two different sides, we had to make a decision as to which side to display, which required us to engage in further dialogue about empathy and prevention; now we were part of the dialogue in making a placement decision. As an act of advocacy, this and the other responses in this third category engaged the broader community through a sense of solidarity and shared responsibility to reject the stigma of addiction.[21]

One final note about the reflections that defy these categorizations: 25 percent of responses included a drawing to accompany the written response. These drawings were of hearts, broken hearts, sad faces, and flowers and occurred most often with the direct address responses. The use of images offers another symbol in the dialogue about opioid addiction, one that focuses on pain, shared suffering, and hope. This last interpretation holds up when we considered that the whole hearts appeared on cards that noted the need for compassion or advocated for change.

CONCLUDING THOUGHTS

The telling and retelling of stories followed by written reflections was an enriching experience for the Misericordia community. The epidemic has touched the lives of most viewers, and this connection with each other and the quilt gave rich context for reflection. Displaying the Our Lives Matter quilt and asking viewers to actively engage with it encouraged community. Here, many voices could speak individual stories and feelings with a united purpose of challenging the impersonal and inaccurate narrative about opioid addiction. While more research needs to be done regarding the long-term impact of public engagement with the Our Lives Matter quilt, we imagine that such studies would reveal results that echo and reaffirm what we saw in the written responses from the Misericordia community and what has been documented in the research about the AIDS quilt: public engagement with personal grief and celebration of life is an effective and meaningful way to challenge dominate narratives about stigmatized groups and conditions and humanize headline stories.[22] The act of remembering, the act of grieving, and the act of advocating are intimately tied to the visual and reflective experience of the Our Lives Matter quilt, offering a different avenue to pursue in humanizing the opioid epidemic.

NOTES

1. Bianca DiJulio, Bryan Wu, and Mollyann Brodie, "Survey of Long-Term Prescription Painkiller Users and Their Household Members," *Washington Post* and Kaiser Family Foundation report, December 9, 2016, http://files.kff.org/attachment/Survey-of-Long -Term-Prescription-Painkiller-Users-and-Their-Household-Members.
2. James D. Livingston et al., "The Effectiveness of Interventions for Reducing Stigma Related to Substance Use Disorders: A Systematic Review," *Addiction* 107, no. 1 (January 2011): 40, https://doi.org/10.1111/j.1360-0443.2011.03601.x.
3. Daniel Z. Buchman, Pamela Leece, and Aaron Orkin, "The Epidemic as Stigma: The Bioethics of Opioids," *The Journal of Law, Medicine, and Ethics* 45, no. 4 (January 2018): 607–20, https://doi.org/10.1177/1073110517750600.
4. Colleen Walsh, "Revising the Language of Addiction," *Harvard Gazette*, September 1, 2017, https://news.harvard.edu/gazette/story/2017/08/revising-the-language-of -addiction/.

5. Thomas F. Pettigrew and Linda R. Tropp, *When Groups Meet: The Dynamics of Intergroup Contact* (New York: Psychology Press, 2011), 1–27; Alicia H. Nordstrom, "The Voices Project: Reducing White Students' Racism in Introduction to Psychology," *Teaching of Psychology* 42, no. 1 (January 2015): 43–50, https://doi.org/10.1177/009862831456 2524.

6. Abdullah Shihipar, "The Opioid Crisis Isn't White," *New York Times*, February 26, 2019, https://www.nytimes.com/2019/02/26/opinion/opioid-crisis-drug-users.html.

7. Allison L. Pitt, Keith Humphreys, and Margaret L. Brandeau, "Modeling Health Benefits and Harms of Public Policy Responses to the US Opioid Epidemics," *American Journal of Public Health* 108, no. 10 (October 2018): 1399, https://doi.org/10.2105/AJPH.2018 .304590.

8. Nabarun Dasgupta, Leo Beletsky, and Daniel Ciccarone, "Opioid Crisis: No Easy Fix to Its Social and Economic Determinants," *American Journal of Public Health* 108, no. 2 (February 2018): 182–86, https://doi.org/10.2105/AJPH.2017.304187.

9. Corky Siemaszko, "Wilkes-Barre Faces Heroin Scourge Turning It into 'the Most Unhappy Place in America,'" *NBC News*, January 9, 2017, https://www.nbcnews.com /news/us-news/wilkes-barre-faces-heroin-scourge-turning-it-most-unhappy-place -n699541.

10. Jennifer Learn-Andes, "Luzerne County Overdose Deaths Break Another Record," *Times Leader*, January 3, 2019, https://www.timesleader.com/news/729174/luzerne-county -overdose-deaths-break-another-record.

11. Bill O'Boyle, "NBC News Report Looks at 'Deadly Math' of Opioid Crisis in Luzerne County," January 9, 2017, https://timesleader.com/news/623884/nbc-news-report -look-at-deadly-math-of-opiod-crisis-in-luzerne-county.

12. David Keys, "Myth-Making and Opiate Abuse: An Early Symbolic Interactionist Theory of Addiction in the Fieldwork of Alfred Lindesmith and Its Opposition," *Contemporary Justice Review* 11, no. 2 (June 2008): 177–86, https://doi.org/10.1080/102825807016 77428.

13. Caroline Winterer, "A Happy Medium: The Sociology of Charles Horton Cooley," *Journal of the History of Behavioral Sciences* 30 (January 1994): 19–27.

14. Christopher Stephen Knaus and Erica Weintraub Austin, "The AIDS Memorial Quilt as Preventative Education: A Developmental Analysis of the Quilt," *AIDS Education and Prevention* 1, no. 6 (December 1999): 525–40.

15. Elizabeth Higgs and Polly F. Radosh, "Quilts: Moral Economies and Matrilineages," *Journal of Family History* 38, no. 1 (December 2012): 57–58, https://doi.org/10.1177 /0363199012470063.

16. Jennifer Power, "Rites of Belonging: Grief, Memorial, and Social Action," *Health Sociology Review* 18, no. 3 (October 2009): 266, https://doi.org/10.5172/hesr.2009.18 .3.260.

17. Hebert Blumer, *Symbolic Interactionism: Perspective and Method* (Berkeley: University of California Press, 1969), 2–6.

18. National Academies of Sciences, Engineering, and Medicine, *Ending Discrimination against People with Mental and Substance Abuse Disorders: The Evidence for Stigma Change* (Washington, DC: The National Academies Press, 2011), chapter 2, https://www.ncbi .nlm.nih.gov/books/NBK384923/.

19. Kevin Michael Deluca, Christine Harold, and Kenneth Rufo, "Q.U.I.L.T.: A Patchwork of Reflections," *Rhetoric and Public Affairs* 10, no. 4 (Winter 2007): 639, https://doi.org/10 .1353/rap.2008.0029.

20. Power, "Rites of Belonging," 261, 265.

21. National Academies of Sciences, Engineering, and Medicine, *Ending Discrimination*, ch. 2.

22. Powers, "Rites of Belonging," 268–69.

CHAPTER 13

Recovering from Addiction in *Sobriety*: Narrating Disability/ Mental Illness through the Medium of Comic Art

Tatiana Prorokova-Konrad

(RE-)DEFINING ADDICTION THROUGH A DISABILITY STUDIES PERSPECTIVE

Addiction to alcohol and/or drugs is a condition that is hard to define. Some are convinced that it is just a manifestation of one's weakness, while others consider it a serious illness. The American Psychological Association's *Diagnostic and Statistical Manual of Mental Disorders* (*DSM-5*), in turn, has published extensively on addiction "disorder," thus offering an even more provocative definition of addiction, claiming that it is, in principle, a mental illness and, hence, equating addiction to disability.[1] Daniel D. Maurer and Spencer Amundson's graphic novel *Sobriety* (2014), I argue, offers a similar understanding of addiction. Through its focus on the twelve-step program—first "created by the founders of Alcoholic Anonymous to establish guidelines for the best way to overcome an addiction to alcohol" and later adopted by "other addiction support groups"—and the main characters' personal experiences with addiction, the chapter aims to uncover new perspectives that viewing addiction as a form of disability/mental impairment, or on the contrary, refusing to do so, opens regarding addiction.[2]

Addiction has been widely treated in a number of cultural texts since the end of the nineteenth century, including in literature and film. Sir Arthur Conan Doyle's Sherlock Holmes consumes cocaine in *The Sign of Four* (1890), presumably to keep his brain active while there is no mystery case for the detective to solve. In *The Shining* (1977), Stephen King shows the dangers of alcoholism through the character of Jack Torrance, for this addiction, in combination with other mystic events, transforms Jack into an obsessed maniac coveting to murder his family. In well-known cinematic explorations of addiction such as Lisa Cholodenko's *High Art* (1998) and Darren Aronofsky's *Requiem for a Dream* (2000), the viewer witnesses the scarily surreal world of heroin addicts. Danny Boyle's *Trainspotting* (1995), in turn, reveals the brutality of withdrawal. Addiction and its sociocultural, political, and economic complexities have generated a massive cultural response. Addiction has been also scrutinized through the medium of comics and graphic novels. While the images of alcohol and pills can be found in a number of superhero comics—including (Iron Man) Tony Stark's alcoholism in *The Invincible Iron Man* (2008–2012) and the drug use of Peter Parker's friend Harry Osborn and Harry's father Norman Osborn (better known as Green Goblin) in *The Spectacular Spider-Man* (1968–)—*Sobriety* is one of the few *autobiographic* accounts of addiction. On both visual and narrative levels, there is a distinct difference between superhero comics and the kind of comic art that focuses more on autobiographic accounts; consequently, the treatment of addiction in the two varies. In autobiographic comics, the author's function "as an agent of self-representation, a figure, textual to be sure but seemingly substantial, who can claim 'I was there' or 'I am here' " is largely intensified due to his/her visual presence.[3] This is evidently an advantage of graphic texts that focus on such a complex and controversial issue as addiction, for they arguably have a greater potential to reach the hearts and minds of readers with or without addiction. In addition, although superhero comics tend to stigmatize various human health issues by presenting them as the causes of superpowers or contributors to villainy, autobiographic graphic narratives can provide a more realistic portrayal of these problems. This chapter thus considers addiction as a form of mental illness and a subject matter of cultural production through the filter of the medical humanities and comics studies.

Stressing the dangers of addiction, *Sobriety* begins a discussion about the tragedy of addiction, the difficulties of the healing process, and the joys of being sober again. Maurer and Amundson reveal the complexities of addiction and recovery, treating them not just on an individual level but within the context of various power structures, institutions, and societal practices. Moreover, the graphic novel can be seen as a useful medical intervention due to its effectiveness in laying out the twelve steps. Discussing the steps in detail as well as various concerns that might emerge regarding them through the voices of the main characters, *Sobriety* is a handy source that can be passed around to people with addictions who might not be willing to read the traditional Alcoholics/ Narcotics/Overeaters Anonymous materials. This chapter thus examines addiction as a political, cultural, and medical issue as represented in *Sobriety* and considers the power of comics to communicate issues relating to mental illness and disability. I explore how Maurer and Amundson use what they describe as "the magic of comics" to portray recovery as an accessible and achievable process.[4] This "magic of comics" manifests itself through various types of freedom, including the freedom to *imagine* as well as to easily move in *space* and *time*, that *Sobriety* employs.

In my analysis of *Sobriety*, I treat drug and alcohol addiction (the two types of addiction that the graphic novel focuses on) as a form of disability. I argue that the novel's approach to addiction as a(n) (mental) illness helps imagine addiction as a complex medical condition that, despite its power over individuals, is curable. Yet defining addiction as disability entails a number of questions regarding the status of addiction as such and its place in our cultural, medical, and political environments. Pekka Sulkunen claims:

> Although it appears that the notion of addiction is increasingly applied in popular consciousness, there is no universally accepted understanding of what it means. The dominant view with many different modulations is that addictions are symptom of weak will. This has been interpreted as a reflection of the modern ethos of social control where individuals are expected to exercise invisible surveillance of themselves and others, in the manner of Jeremy Bentham's Panopticon, and to use their own willpower to constrain their desires. This would also explain why it seems to be so easy to extend the idea of addiction to almost any form of harmful repetitive behaviour.[5]

Interpreting addiction as a weakness is the major danger in understanding the problem, and it has already largely contributed to the collective mistreatment of addiction as such. Additionally, the following questions emerge: How does one define addiction to something, judging by the consumption of certain products? How much does one need to consume to be called an addict? What effects should such consumption produce on one's body to allow one to classify consumption as addiction? There are, undoubtedly, numerous products that one can consume; these products can also influence individuals differently. I view addiction as a process that is triggered by consumption of certain products or substances in quantities that harm one's life, causing physical and psychological transformations in oneself, and influencing one's life in such a way that an individual does not seem to any longer fit various social, cultural, political, and economic parameters regulated by society. The deterioration of one's health that leads to certain illnesses and impairments as well as the process of social exclusion that individuals with addictions might experience are defined in this essay as forms of medical and social disability, in accordance with the American Psychiatric Association's treatment of addiction as a "disorder" in the fifth edition of *The Diagnostic and Statistical Manual of Mental Health Disorders (DSM-5)*.[6]

Disability studies scholars are, however, rather careful in defining addiction as a form of disability. Focusing on addiction to food, Sander L. Gilman asks: "Is obesity a mental illness that is the result of an addictive personality in which food is the addiction? Does the addiction indicate a lack of will? Is it physical dependency, as in heroin addiction? Is the addiction a genetically programmed 'error' in the human body that expresses itself in psychological desire for food or in the inability to know when one is no longer hungry?"[7] Gilman's work thus raises the problem of weakness versus genetics in causing and sustaining various types of addiction. Georgina Kleege, in turn, ponders the following problem: "Are such conditions as shyness, addiction, and depression legitimate disabilities? This debate can fuel a reactionary backlash in which it is argued that since everyone has a trait that can be perceived as a disability in certain contexts, we are all disabled, and therefore no measures to accommodate anyone need to be taken."[8] Such an approach indeed can be dangerous as it, first, risks undermining the action and attention that people with disabilities demand to feel medically well and socially included, and, second, it neglects to acknowledge that people respond to different genetic predispositions and environmental stimuli in different ways. Disability manifests itself through a physical or psychological impairment and the restrictions that one might experience as a result of that impairment.

Discussing the issues of illness/disease and exclusion, Susan Merrill Squier and Diana Price Herndl provide similar explanations of how the two are related to disability. Considering "the medical and social models" of disability, Squier argues that, medically, "a disability may be either congenial or acquired, but it requires treatment by healthcare professionals until it has been ameliorated or cured," whereas, from a social perspective, "a person's impairment (whatever its etiology) becomes a disability only if and when the social environment fails to accommodate it. This extends from mores that stigmatize people with disabilities to built environments that restrict access by people with disabilities."[9] In turn, Price Herndl claims that "the definition of disability used in disability studies focuses not on the body but on the social." The scholar distinguishes between the concepts of disability and disease, arguing that disability is "something one encounters when dealing with other people or with physical spaces that are inaccessible," whereas disease "is almost always understood as located in the body itself."[10] I agree with both scholars and, therefore, in my discussion of *Sobriety*, I treat addiction as a form of mental *illness* that, in its prolonged effect on one's body, mind, and capacity for everyday activities, sometimes leads to *disability*.

In so doing, though, I acknowledge Price Herndl's observation that "most people in disability community do not want to be considered ill, and most people who are ill don't want to be considered disabled."[11] Although people who are addicted to various substances might not want to be considered disabled (indeed, many do not even view themselves as ill), professionals can identify and communicate the health problems that people with addiction have and explain the ways that these problems might lead to medical and social disabilities. At the same time, explaining to the sober majority that people with addictions are *disabled* people might help change the general attitude toward addicts. Scholars accentuate the largely negative view on people with addiction as well as those who have mental impairments, which results in "stigma and discrimination." For example, "many Americans are unwilling to have a person with mental illness or substance abuse as a work colleague or neighbor, and more than half of Americans believe that persons with schizophrenia, alcohol addiction, and drug addiction are likely to be violent toward others."[12] The issues that become evident from this are the societal rejection of people with mental impairments and downgrading of addiction as something that is even "worse" than a mental illness. Explaining that addiction is a form of mental illness that can lead to disability might help the sober majority reimagine addiction as not something degrading, disgraceful, and life-threatening (importantly, not only to the addict him/herself but also to the ones who surround this person) but rather as a condition that demands certain actions, including medical treatment, assistance, guidance, and social acceptance, both from professionals and nonaddicts. For, indeed, scholars claim in unison that the aggression and rejection that come from nonaddicts toward people with addiction are still there. According to Emma E. McGinty et al., "stigma toward persons with mental illness and substance abuse in the US has remained constant—or by some measures increased—over past decades."[13] Colleen L. Barry et al. note that "research has revealed pervasive and persistent negative attitudes among Americans toward persons with mental illness," yet "Americans hold significantly more negative attitudes toward persons with drug addiction than toward those with mental illness."[14] (Re)defining addiction as a form of disability that potentially causes social disability and might lead to the emergence of other physical and/or mental impairments is essential for understanding and treatment of addiction.

GRAPHIC NOVELS AND ADDICTION

Sobriety is not the first graphic autobiography to deal with addiction, but it is a rare example. When it comes to a cultural portrayal and interpretation of addiction, one usually thinks about more traditional media, like novel and film. Mark C. J. Stoddart, for example, argues that "many people's understanding of drug users and drug trafficking has been shaped by both the factual accounts of news media, as well as the fictional accounts of film or television."[15] Cultural production has indeed largely shaped the image of addiction. Yet comics and graphic novels are another significant medium through which one can learn about and teach addiction. As Nimrod Tal and I have already argued elsewhere, comics and graphic novels "explore phenomena in ways that other media cannot."[16] It is crucial that "the evolution of American autobiographical comics over the past decades has been increasingly accompanied by a strong trend toward subject matters of illness, disability, or more generally any physical or psychological traits perceived as deviations from the norm."[17] And although I do not share the understanding of a binary division into "normal" and "abnormal" when it comes to illness and disability as they are tackled in comics and graphic novels, I think that the focus on physical and psychological impairment and disability as such reveals the changing status of disability from mute and invisible to audible and visible as well as foregrounds the potential of comics and graphic novels to deal with such an intricate and sensitive issue in unique and profound ways. Looking at comics more broadly, one certainly notices how terribly and unjustly disability is treated in many titles, for numerous villains manifest various impairments, which are (ab)used to intensify their evil nature and thus dehumanize them. Narratives that explicitly tackle issues like illness/disease, impairment, and disability discuss these problems rather literally; yet figurative meanings and perceptions of disability, including the process of dehumanization—on both visual and verbal levels—still frequently come into place, as is also the case with *Sobriety*.

To understand why addiction, among other illnesses, is now powerfully represented through the medium of comics and graphic novels, one needs to examine the medium's specific expressive capabilities. Hillary L. Chute observes that even "after the rise and reign of photography, . . . people yet understand pen and paper to be among the best instruments of witness."[18] And although Chute's primary interest is in "how comics expresses history," her analysis of the medium is helpful here, as she considers comics to be a "drawn form" and accentuates its "spatial grammar of gutters, grids, and panels suggestive of architecture." Moreover, Chute argues that, "through its spatial syntax, comics offers opportunities to place pressure on traditional notions of chronology, linearity, and causality—as well as on the idea that 'history' can ever be a closed discourse, or a simply progressive one." She concludes that comics is "a source of cultural, aesthetic, and political significance."[19] In the introduction to *Cultures of War in Graphic Novels: Violence, Trauma, and Memory*, Tal and I argue that "the visual-verbal peculiarity of graphic novels is conjoint: the verbal is not reduced to the text, and the visual is not merely about the image."[20] We thus see the power of comics and graphic novels in their two components—the visual and the verbal—that are equally important to constructing a meaning. William Murray contends that "the marrying of these two media [the visual and the written] allows for new and engaging ways of transmitting stories, and in graphic novels the visual and written components often work to create competing and contradictory narratives that complicate and challenge familiar stories."[21] In turn, Chute argues, "Pitting visual and verbal discourses against each other, comics calls attention to their virtues and to their friction, highlighting the issue of what counts as evidence."[22] And while these discussions attempt to recognize the significance of comics and graphic novels as a medium through which to document and discuss history, the characteristics of the medium that turn the narratives into sources of evidence allow me to argue that comics and graphic novels have a powerful potential to deal with the questions of disability, impairment, and addiction.

Ian Williams calls graphic narratives about illnesses "the intellectual, emotional and manual act of somatic self-expression."[23] The verbal part in the comics and graphic novels about addiction is significant in narrating the ways in which communication with/about addicts shapes, first, addicted people's perception of themselves, their situation, and possible ways out, as well as, second, the perception of nonaddicts about addicts. The conversation that is very precise and selected turns into a powerful instrument to verbalize addiction. In turn, the visual helps recreate the events that led to addiction and picture the process of addiction as well as its effects and results. Both the visual and the verbal are important tools to use on the way to rehabilitation. Although discussing art in general, and not specifically the art of comics and graphic novels (about illnesses), Ruth M. Parker et al. argue: "Most would agree that art communicates, but few actually turn to the arts to listen for messages that inform us about who we are. Fewer still are those who would even think to engage art for supporting health, promoting healing, and alleviating suffering."[24] Graphic novels about addiction and recovery come out in some of the best ways against substance use and for the necessity of medical treatment for addicts. As Parker et al. suggest, "The arts do not teach the audience *how* to be present to their different expressive forms; they simply teach us *to be present* as we listen carefully to what that form of art communicates. Art can serve as a vehicle for compassion or as a locus of communication that crosses time and cultures."[25] In that respect, comics and graphic novels about addiction can be helpful to both people with and without addiction to understand the problem of addiction from inside out, be compassionate to those who acquire this harmful habit, and view it as, indeed, a form of illness rather than weakness or a source of temporary pleasure.

Through their portrayals of substance use and addiction, comics and graphic novels have provided rather distinct interpretations of the matter. Stoddart argues that

> comic books reproduced a dominant discourse of negative drug use, which focused primarily on hard drugs such as heroin and cocaine. Discourses of pleasurable or revelatory drug use existed only at the margins of comic book drug narratives. Furthermore, most comic book drug narratives set up a dichotomy between victimized drug users and predatory drug dealers. Drug users were depicted as victims who may be saved rather than criminalized. At the same time, drug dealers were constructed as villains who were subjected to the justifiable violence of comic book heroes. The comic book construction of drug users and drug dealers was also marked by gendered, racialized, and class-based patterns of representation. Finally, comic books privileged a model of vigilante justice, where ritualized violence was the dominant form of punishment for drug dealers. In this fictive world, the police, courts, and prisons were only of marginal relevance. Discourses of drug use that focused on managed use, decriminalization, or legalization—rather than criminalization—were rendered invisible.[26]

Comics, in their own way, thus contribute to the sustaining of an image of addiction as a process that is criminal, humiliating, dangerous, and that grants the participants only a one-way ticket. Noteworthy, too, the recent advent of graphic medicine that brings together writers, artists, healthcare workers, and (prospective) patients is socially, politically, and culturally symbolic, for it triggers and, in a sense, reflects the shift in the societal consciousness regarding ex-/inclusion of people who have health issues as well as recognizes the potency of graphic texts to display and help solve or ease these problems.[27] Although the negative images of substance use prevail in graphic narratives, there are also those that engage in a more complex dialogue with addiction, attempting to understand the mechanisms behind it and find ways out. One such text is *Sobriety*.

THE "MAGIC" OF *SOBRIETY*

Sobriety: A Graphic Novel focuses on the stories of five twelve-step group members who are trying to overcome their addictions and experiencing different difficulties on the way. Larry is an ex-alcoholic who became addicted shortly after graduating from high school, but he now seems to "live a life of **sobriety and freedom**."[28] Debby is a single mother of two who is on her "third treatment for benzos and alcohol."[29] Matt's "poison of choice is **crystal meth**."[30] Hannah is an eighteen-year-old who used to "**lift pain meds** from [her] parents' friends."[31] Finally, Alex had "bad withdrawals from opiates and coming off x," but he has, by now, had "six months of drug-free time."[32]

The graphic novel opens with images of the author himself—Daniel D. Maurer—who introduces himself to the reader: "Hi. My name is **Dan**. I'm an **alcoholic and an addict**. I am also in recovery. I'm **sober, just for today**."[33] Dan appears only several times in the novel to remind us about "the **magic** of comics," which, in his words, is "relevant to sobriety too."[34] This is so "because in sobriety we begin to recover our creativity and imaginations again! With openness and courage. . . It's about **life—recovering** a new life that has yet to be discovered."[35] Dan continues: "So we're going to show you a world that is really different from what you've **become used to**, and the **magic** of comics will allow you to see this in a different way than you might have seen it in the past!"[36] Dan, therefore, resorts to the medium of graphic novel because of its unique way of dealing with such a sensitive and controversial issue as addiction. He uses the graphic novel's major advantage over other media: namely, that "graphic narratives rely on representing things in a way that is predicated on our cognition of how we make sense of our known world. In this respect, the visual elements in a graphic narrative are like objects on stage: they are animated with potential signification, adopting meanings beyond what they may simply represent in the everyday world."[37] The narration in *Sobriety* frequently alters the location and jumps in time and space, making the reader realize that, just like in graphic novels, *everything* is possible, so *recovery* from addiction is an achievable goal. "The drawings that make up the story are not at all dependent on being real objects in real space and real time to establish the story; rather, the images are compiled in the reader's mind, and inferences are drawn from the similarities and differences between the available visual forms and how that information correlates to real experience."[38] Moreover, as is already clear from the selected quotations above, the graphic novel frequently employs the bold font—a creative choice that takes advantage of the graphic novel's visual power to help the author accentuate various factors that contribute to addiction, provoke its maintenance, help people recover from it, and characterize sobriety.

Negotiating addiction and recovery from it through the flexibility and unlimited potential of graphic representation, the reader is immersed in the world of magic through which the process of healing is explored. In this respect, "comics proposes an ethics of looking and reading intent on defamiliarizing standard or received images."[39] *Sobriety* rejects the rhetoric of impossibility and opens up a new trajectory in viewing addiction as a phenomenon one can fight and overcome. Magic is not synonymous with impracticability or unrealizability, however, but is a tool through which the author demonstrates that, despite widespread belief that recovery is a myth and that addiction will lead to (slow) death, recovery and sobriety are possible.

The graphic novel starts not with the term *addiction* (although the reader does find out that Dan is an addict) but rather with a definition of *sobriety*. Dan says, "As we addicts know, **sobriety** isn't just about puttin' a **cork in the bottle** or **stayin' away from drugs. Sobriety** is more than the definition we find in the **dictionary**. It's a **new lifestyle** that we embrace. It gives us **a real existence**. It's wholly different from what we experience in our addiction."[40] Foregrounding sobriety at the very beginning of narration, the author attempts to draw the reader's attention to the *result*, not the *process* itself—recovery—and not even the *type* of addiction that one might have. Only after having accentuated the positive outcome, Dan invites the reader "to **join** us!" on the way to recovery.[41]

The graphic novel's treatment of addiction is rather straightforward. Although *Sobriety* focuses on five different stories and, as a result, five different interpretations of what addiction is, how one becomes an addict, how one learns to accept the truth about addiction, and what *exactly* this truth is, the narrative presents addiction as a force that takes possession of one's body and mind, transforming both in such a way that neither of them belongs to the individual any longer. For example, Larry says, "You see, that was my problem: I could not stop, but I couldn't go on."[42] Alex's experience is somewhat similar: "Gradually, though, [while in rehab] I began to notice just how **unmanageable** my life had become. It was a carousel (what do you Americans call it? A **merry-go-round**?). I couldn't ever get off. I was always chasing. Always wanting. Always trying to get somewhere I never would, because I was **going in circles**!"[43] Matt tells us how he "did **whatever** [he] could to score **merca** to pawn off." He goes on to say, "I did things for people. Things I don't wanna remember. I muled bags for **the real bad guys** south o' the border—guys you don't **dare** fuck with. In it all, I smoked it up. When I broke my pipe, I went to the hospital bathrooms and broke into the needle containers and slammed my stash. I was getting pretty bad."[44] Debby confesses: "I honestly don't remember all that much. Taking my meds and drinking on top of them put everything in a blur. . . a haze."[45] Finally Hannah shares the following: "It gets to the point where you're willing to go **to any length** to get to a place where there isn't the pain. It's not about getting high anymore—it's about just **stopping the pain**."[46] From the experiences of all five characters, the reader realizes that consuming alcohol and drugs turns into a *vital* (no matter how paradoxical this is) necessity for addicts, for it is the substance that controls their bodies and minds, and not vice versa.

Through a discussion about control, *Sobriety* moves to the problem of illness and disability. It first does so introducing the term *normal*. For example, Larry says, "Any **normal** person seeing my life would respond the same as Linda [Larry's girlfriend] had"—and Linda's response was, "Your **life**—it's **insane**!"[47] Debby explains her starting to drink to calm herself down, thus dealing with stress, as follows: "That's what I did every night. I thought I was normal. Isn't that what people do?"[48] It is crucial that Linda calls Larry's life "insane," as that description automatically classifies Larry's problem as an impairment. Through the issue of normalcy and the space of normality, however, the graphic novel does not necessarily explore addiction as a form of deviation and abnormality (the terms that bear negative meaning and insist on exclusion). Instead, addiction is an illness that transforms a person's usual condition and their regular environment into something entirely different, from which one can recover with the assistance of professionals, relatives, and friends.

The important discussion regarding what addiction is takes place toward the end of the novel among all five characters. Larry calls addiction a "**disease**," to which Hannah disagrees, saying, "**Diseases** are heart disease or cancer or the stomach flu. They are things that just happen to people. It's not their **fault**." To that Larry responds: "Did you ever **intend** on **ruining your life** and ending up in treatment for drug and alcohol addiction? . . . I'm not speaking to your **culpability**. . . or the **consequences** of your actions. I'm asking whether or not you **planned** on **ending up here** when you started to **drink** and **drug**."[49] Yet Alex intervenes: "I don't call it a **disease**. To me, it's an **induced mental illness**. . . . It means that alcoholism and addiction are just like a **mental illness**. It's the brain you're **born with** and you've **added chemicals** to it. That's what 'turns your brain on.' Essentially, it makes you **crazy**. It's an **illness** of the mind."[50] And while the conversation is full of confusing and offensive terminology, like "disease" and "crazy," it accurately sets the tone of how *Sobriety* perceives addiction. While it might be hard to verbalize that, the graphic novel leaves the reader with the idea that addiction is a mental illness that transforms an individual. Because addiction is a mental impairment/disability, in order to cure it one needs to seek the help of professionals. Addiction should not be treated as something shameful, for "**shame** is what makes addiction so **deadly**"[51]; addiction is an impairment that can provoke further impairments, and it should be viewed as a medical condition rather than one's desire. It is because of this that societal understanding and inclusion are the key steps on the way to recovery.

Although the graphic novel seems to take some time to *verbalize* the definition of addiction, it brilliantly *illustrates* the concept in multiple images. Portraying how the characters were consuming various substances, *Sobriety* includes images that depict either only the drug itself or unrecognizable characters consuming substances. For example, Larry designates the moment in his life when he started to drink by referring to the "innocent" can of beer, offered to him after a hard day at work (see p. 23). The small can is contrasted to a large bottle of a harder drink that Larry's dad used to consume (see p. 24). The juxtaposition serves to intensify how harmless beer looked to Larry at that time as well as to provoke mute shock and confusion in both the characters and the reader who realize that drinking beer can, indeed, turn one into an alcoholic. As Larry's alcoholism progresses, the reader views the images that explicitly reflect the man's preference in drinks, for he now rejects beer and consumes harder drinks instead (see p. 31). Debby's drinking is portrayed in a similar manner. And although there are images in the graphic novel that depict the woman with a bottle in her hand, there are also the ones that, without contextualization, cannot be understood as illustrating *Debby's* addiction (see p. 91).

All these images have a very peculiar focus on the substances that the characters are addicted to. Readers could hardly correlate the images with Larry or Debby without an indication of who the speaker is. This detachment from the characters is further represented in the images of consumption, which are framed as the acts of an individual: fingers holding a syringe that injects fluids (fig. 13.1) and a full arm pouring a generous alcoholic drink into a glass, the hand with a death grip on the bottle—an effort to visually depict the control that drink has over the characters' situations, as well as the impact of the tremors, as can be understood via the multiple curvy lines along the arm and the bottle (fig. 13.2). Only with the narrative framing does one understand that the hand holding a bottle in both cases belongs to Larry or that the fingers holding a syringe are those of Hannah; taken out of context, these images are depersonalized and made more universal.

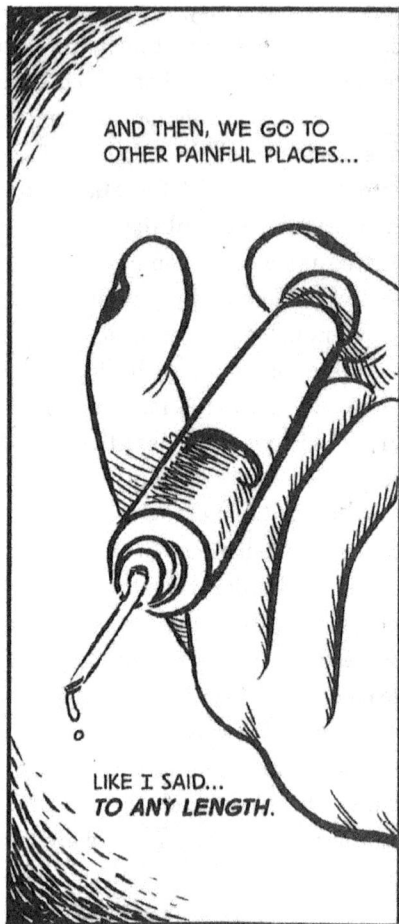

Fig. 13.1. Fingers holding a syringe.
(Daniel D. Maurer and Spencer Amundson,
Sobriety, 2014, p. 122.)

Similarly, images that seem to depict a specific person are sometimes drawn in such a way that the characters are unrecognizable. In figure 13.3, for example, the reader sees Debby during one of the moments when addiction takes full control over her body and mind. The image of Debby is, however, made unrecognizable through the distorted facial features, including her mouth and eyes. In figure 13.4, one can observe Hannah consuming meds, yet the reader can see only her hand, lips, nose, and partially her chin and cheeks; the upper part of Hannah's face is not depicted at all, which makes the woman unrecognizable. It is through the distortion or omission of the characters' eyes in both images that the graphic novel achieves the effect of depersonalization, suggesting that literally *anybody* could be in place of these characters.

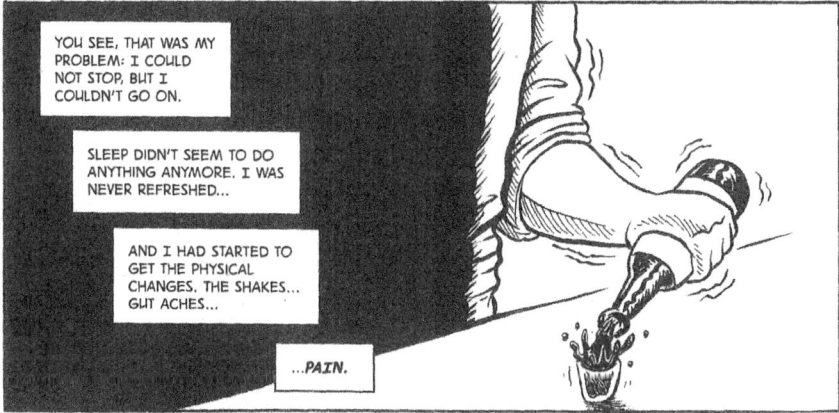

Fig. 13.2. The character's full arm is exposed; the hand holds a bottle of alcohol that is being poured into a glass. (Daniel D. Maurer and Spencer Amundson, *Sobriety*, 2014, p. 46.)

Fig. 13.3 (*above left*). Addiction takes full control over Debby. (Daniel D. Maurer and Spencer Amundson, *Sobriety*, 2014, p. 95.)

Fig. 13.4 (*above right*). Hannah consuming meds. (Daniel D. Maurer and Spencer Amundson, *Sobriety*, 2014, p. 121.)

An even more ambiguous image appears toward the end of the novel, when Hannah and Larry argue whether addiction is a disease or not. In figure 13.5, the reader can view a de-gendered figure of a human, holding a bottle of alcohol fully upside down and greedily pouring the liquid into a glass, staring with avidity at it (importantly, this effect is achieved despite the face not even being fully drawn). One can hardly state whether this is Larry or Hannah, as both were spotted with a bottle earlier; that the text included in the image belongs both to Hannah (upper right corner) and Larry (lower right corner) does not help the reader identify the figure either.

Fig. 13.5. An unidentifiable addict. (Daniel D. Maurer and Spencer Amundson, *Sobriety*, 2014, p. 140.)

It is through images like these that *Sobriety* insists that addiction is an illness that can strike anyone, regardless of gender, class, or race. Presenting unidentifiable characters, the graphic novel foregrounds the ubiquity of addiction, as well as invites the reader to imagine addiction as an illness, instead of simplifying it to a manifestation of a mere weakness of *specific* individuals. Through such images, *Sobriety* also comments on the problem of social exclusion: when people become addicts they turn into *nobodies* and are rejected by the sober majority. The process of dehumanization is, indeed, powerful here. All this helps the graphic novel imagine addiction as a form of disability—mental but also social and cultural.

CONCLUSION

Stories such as the one(s) narrated in *Sobriety* are helpful in the construction of a cultural understanding of addiction. The graphic novel reimagines addiction not as a negative habit but as a more complex medical, cultural, social, and political process that numerous individuals throughout the world suffer from. Along with its cultural value, *Sobriety* clearly has a very prominent practical value. It teaches the reader—whether he or she is an addict or not—what addiction is as well as how difficult yet *doable* recovery is. Distinguishing illness narratives as a specific genre, scholars argue:

> Recently, a distinctive sub-genre of graphic stories that we call graphic pathographies—illness narratives in graphic form—has emerged to fill a niche for patients and doctors. These graphic pathographies can be helpful to patients wanting to learn more about their illness and find a community of similarly affected people. Graphic pathographies also provide doctors with new insights into the personal experience of illness (especially regarding concerns patients might not mention in a clinical setting) and misconceptions about disease and treatment that could affect compliance and prognosis.[52]

The mission of these texts is recognized: "graphic stories have an important role in patient care, medical education, and the social critique of the medical profession."[53] The meditation upon images as represented in *Sobriety*, as well as in other comics and graphic novels that touch upon the issues of addiction, illness, and disability, is significant because it helps one consider or tackle various problems that pertain to the medical, social, political, and cultural spheres of our lives: "The consideration of visual depictions of disease in painting and photography is a worthwhile exercise with which to explore cultural ideas surrounding illness and healthcare."[54]

Finally, *Sobriety* is a graphic novel that contributes to reshaping societal imagination regarding addiction and recovery from it. Williams argues:

> Images do not just "mirror" the world; they help build it. The proliferation of image based media has also ensured that iconographic representations of health, illness, and disease have become increasingly important in Western societies. These representations help construct the illness stereotypes that influence the way in which a condition is viewed by others as well as the patient's experience of the condition. The self-picturing of suffering is a relatively new phenomenon that

expanded in the twentieth century due to the availability of suitable media, such as photography. In constructing new visual styles of suffering and illness, therefore, the authors of graphic pathographies might be subtly altering the discourse of health and the social mediation of illness outside of the clinic.[55]

The chief task of *Sobriety* is, undoubtedly, to demonstrate to people with various forms of addiction that there is a way out; yet its other significant sociopolitical contribution is an attempt to influence the minds of nonaddicts, showing how complex addiction is and how important society's support and care for (former) addicts is in the process of healing, adapting, and starting a new life. Understanding that addiction is an illness rather than a weakness can entirely change the medical, social, and cultural treatment of people with this problem.

NOTES

1. Jon E. Grant and Samuel R. Chamberlain, "Expanding the Definition of Addiction: DSM-5 vs. ICD-11," *CNS Spectrums* 21, no. 4 (2016): 300–3, https://www.ncbi.nlm.nih .gov/pmc/articles/PMC5328289/.
2. "12-Step Programs," AddictionCenter, accessed November 28, 2018, https://www .addictioncenter.com/treatment/12-step-programs/.
3. Leigh Gilmore, *The Limits of Autobiography: Trauma and Testimony* (Ithaca, NY: Cornell University Press, 2001), 9.
4. Daniel D. Maurer and Spencer Amundson, *Sobriety: A Graphic Novel* (Center City, MN: Hazelden, 2014), 5.
5. Pekka Sulkunen, "Images of Addiction: Representations of Addictions in Films," *Addiction Research and Theory* 15, no. 6 (2007): 544.
6. Grant and Chamberlain, "Expanding the Definition of Addiction."
7. Sander L. Gilman, "Defining Disability: The Case of Obesity," *PMLA* 120, no. 2 (2005): 515.
8. Georgina Kleege, "Reflections on Writing and Teaching Disability Autobiography," *PMLA* 120, no. 2 (2005): 610.
9. Susan Merrill Squier, "The Uses of Graphic Medicine for Engaged Scholarship," in *Graphic Medicine Manifesto*, MK Czerwiec et al. (University Park: Penn State University Press, 2015), 49.
10. Diana Price Herndl, "Disease versus Disability: The Medical Humanities and Disability Studies," *PMLA* 120, no. 2 (2005): 593.
11. Herndl, "Disease versus Disability."
12. Emma E. McGinty et al., "Portraying Mental Illness and Drug Addiction as Treatable Health Conditions: Effects of a Randomized Experiment on Stigma and Discrimination," *Social Science and Medicine* 126 (2015): 73.
13. McGinty et al., "Portraying Mental Illness and Drug Addiction as Treatable Health Conditions."
14. Colleen L. Barry et al., "Stigma, Discrimination, Treatment Effectiveness, and Policy: Public Views about Drug Addiction and Mental Illness," *Psychiatric Services* 65, no. 10 (2014): 1269–70.
15. Mark C. J. Stoddart, " 'They Say It'll Kill Me . . . but They Won't Say When!': Drug

Narratives in Comic Books," *Journal of Criminal Justice and Popular Culture* 13, no. 2 (2006): 66.

16. Tatiana Prorokova and Nimrod Tal, "Introduction," in *Cultures of War in Graphic Novels: Violence, Trauma, and Memory*, ed. Tatiana Prorokova and Nimrod Tal (New Brunswick, NJ: Rutgers University Press, 2018), 9.

17. Christina Maria Koch, " 'When You Have No Voice, You Don't Exist'?: Envisioning Disability in David Small's *Stitches*," in *Disability in Comic Books and Graphic Narratives*, ed. Chris Foss, Jonathan W. Gray, and Zach Whalen (New York: Palgrave Macmillan, 2016), 29.

18. Hillary L. Chute, *Disaster Drawn: Visual Witness, Comics, and Documentary Form* (Cambridge, MA: Belknap Press of Harvard University Press, 2016), 2.

19. Chute, *Disaster Drawn*, 4.

20. Prorokova and Tal, "Introduction," 8.

21. William Murray, "Reimagining Terror in the Graphic Novel: Kyle Baker's *Nat Turner* and the Cultural Imagination," *CEA Critic* 77, no. 3 (2015): 320.

22. Chute, *Disaster Drawn*, 7.

23. Ian Williams, "Graphic Medicine: The Portrayal of Illness in Underground and Autobiographical Comics," in *Medicine, Health and the Arts: Approaches to the Medical Humanities*, ed. Victoria Bates, Alan Bleakley, and Sam Goodman (London: Routledge, 2014), 74.

24. Ruth M. Parker et al., "Communicating through the Arts: Lessons for Medicine and Public Health," *Journal of Health Communication: International Perspectives* 18, no. 2 (2013): 140.

25. Parker et al., "Communicating through the Arts," 142 (italics in original).

26. Stoddart, "Drug Narratives," 66–67.

27. cf. MK Czerwiec et al., *Graphic Medicine Manifesto* (University Park: Penn State University Press, 2015).

28. Maurer and Amundson, *Sobriety*, 10 (bold type in original).

29. Maurer and Amundson, *Sobriety*, 11.

30. Maurer and Amundson, *Sobriety*, 12 (bold type in original).

31. Maurer and Amundson, *Sobriety*, 13 (bold type in original).

32. Maurer and Amundson, *Sobriety*, 14.

33. Maurer and Amundson, *Sobriety*, 4 (bold type in original).

34. Maurer and Amundson, *Sobriety*, 5 (bold type in original).

35. Maurer and Amundson, *Sobriety*, 5–6 (bold type in original).

36. Maurer and Amundson, *Sobriety*, 7 (bold type in original).

37. Robert S. Petersen, *Comics, Manga, and Graphic Novels: A History of Graphic Narratives* (Santa Barbara, CA: Praeger, 2011), xvii.

38. Petersen, *Comics, Manga, and Graphic Novels*, xvii.

39. Chute, *Disaster Drawn*, 31.

40. Maurer and Amundson, *Sobriety*, 9 (bold type in original).

41. Maurer and Amundson, *Sobriety*, 9 (bold type in original).

42. Maurer and Amundson, *Sobriety*, 46.

43. Maurer and Amundson, *Sobriety*, 66 (bold type in original).

44. Maurer and Amundson, *Sobriety*, 82 (bold type in original).

45. Maurer and Amundson, *Sobriety*, 95.

46. Maurer and Amundson, *Sobriety*, 122 (bold type in original).

47. Maurer and Amundson, *Sobriety*, 47 (bold type in original).

48. Maurer and Amundson, *Sobriety*, 91.

49. Maurer and Amundson, *Sobriety*, 140 (bold type in original).

50. Maurer and Amundson, *Sobriety*, 141 (bold type in original).

51. Maurer and Amundson, *Sobriety*, 142 (bold type in original).

52. Michael J. Green and Kimberly R. Myers, "Graphic Medicine: Use of Comics in Medical Education and Patient Care," *BMJ* 340 (2010): 574, https://www.bmj.com/content/340/bmj.c863.
53. Green and Myers, "Graphic Medicine," 574.
54. Ian Williams, "Comics and the Iconography of Illness," in *Graphic Medicine Manifesto*, MK Czerwiec et al. (University Park: Penn State University Press, 2015), 117.
55. Williams, "Comics and Iconography of Illness," 118.

CHAPTER 14

"Hey, Let's Have a Very Good Time": The Opioid Aesthetics of Post-Verbal Rap

Austin T. Richey

"FUCK A DOUBLE CUP I WANNA FEEL IT FASTER"

On December 31, 2017, an Instagram post thrust Atlanta-based rapper Young Thug into the national debate surrounding opioid abuse. Shared via thugger-thugger1, the rapper's personal social media avatar, the post gave Instagram users a glimpse at life behind the scenes: taken from a first-person point of view, the image featured Young Thug's left arm laying on a bed, surrounded by tour wardrobe, and hooked to a rather suspicious, purple-tinted IV drip.[1] Followers immediately identified this solution as Actavis, a cough syrup with promethazine and codeine.

This prescription opioid has been used recreationally within the hip-hop community for decades and is the active ingredient in Young Thug's favorite recreational drug: lean.[2] Lean is a concoction of cough syrup, a light soda like Sprite, and hard candy like Jolly Ranchers added for flavor. The mix is served over ice in a double stack of white Styrofoam cups, which itself has become an icon for the drug. As the drink is sipped over the course of an evening, the user can achieve a euphoric, disembodied high through the combination of large dosages of the opioid codeine and the antihistamine promethazine. While lean may be part and parcel of contemporary hip-hop culture, Young Thug's approach took opioid abuse to new and excessive heights. To avoid any ambiguity in his intentions, Young Thug wrote across the image in bold white letters: "Fuck a double cup I wanna feel it faster."[3]

This graphic example of prescription drug abuse is an extension of Young Thug's artistic brand, one that features extreme drug use. In 2013, the rapper broke into mainstream hip-hop consciousness with his hit single "Stoner," an ode to excessive cannabis smoking. While the song's lyrics play on familiar rap tropes, Young Thug's unique vocal delivery characterizes his artistic agency, and, as I show, the opioid aesthetics of his music: his high-registered voice swings from pointillist rapping to vocalise, often shifting through multiple timbres while presenting lyrics in rhythmically angular phrasings. This melodic style is complemented by a distinct approach that heavily inflects particular words while mumbling through others, a tactic that has been described by journalists and linguists as "post-verbal."[4] Post-verbal performance describes an approach to language that emphasizes the sonic and emotive qualities of a vocalist's utterances in combination with or *over* the lyrics themselves. Further, the concept of "post-verbal" critiques presumed constructions of what a "proper" voice is—namely, well-trained, identifiably gendered, and free of technological mediation.

While "Stoner" brought him to the forefront of the rap world, Young Thug has been clear about his penchant for opioids, particularly lean. This proclivity comes out in songs such as "Drinking Lean is Amazing," "Two Cups Stuffed," and "OD." Beyond the lyrical content of his music and visuals that showcase the extravagancies of his drug use, Young Thug's post-verbal rapping can be heard as symptomatic of the euphoric highs and dysarthria (i.e., slurred speech) of opioid abuse. Critical inquiries of the lyrical content and lifestyles of rappers who promote prescription drug abuse have proliferated, yet I extend this into sound studies by arguing that both the orality and aurality of contemporary hip hop—trap music and "mumble" rap—reflect a particular sonic opioid aesthetic.[5]

In this essay I ask, How do we *hear* the effects of the US opioid epidemic in the performance and production of trap music and mumble rap? I begin by situating this post-verbal aesthetic within sound studies discourse to reveal sonic elements that signify beyond lyrics themselves. Following this, I discuss the physical effects of opioid abuse and parallel these symptoms with the performance of mumble rappers and the use of studio technologies; through their artistic choices they simultaneously construct an embodied opioid aesthetic while also emphasizing the disembodied feelings caused by the drugs. I apply this sensorial approach to contemporary hip hop via three case studies, featuring some of the biggest names in the genre: Young Thug, Future, and Lil Uzi Vert. Through my reading of vocal performance and technological interventions of the music studio, I suggest that these contemporary hip-hop styles signify mental health issues, addiction, and anhedonia within the black American community.

EMBODIMENT IN "MUMBLE" RAP

Trap is a hip-hop genre that has emerged directly from drug culture; its name is derived from the "trap house," a space, often abandoned, used by drug dealers to buy, produce, and distribute drugs.[6] Further, the "trap" references a depressed socioeconomic situation that necessitates alternative, illegal economies that participants get caught up in. Instrumental trap music is marked by booming, syncopated Roland TR-808 pitched bass drums, subdivided hi-hats, and relatively sparse, monophonic, and often minor-mode melodies provided by digital synthesizers. Trap music is frequently composed around 150 bpm, yet characteristically, these tracks are designed to feel much slower through the syncopation of the 808 basses, which give the track a half-time feeling. The quick sixteenth- and thirty-second-note bursts of the hi-hats create tension with the slow-moving bass, and through this rhythmic bookending, instrumental trap music provides expansive sonic room for rappers to perform within.

However, the rapping style that has developed alongside the trap sound regularly eschews the importance of lyricism in earlier rap styles and, instead, presents a melodious and affected aesthetic that obscures the lyrics themselves.[7] Sidestepping decipherability has caused this style to be pejoratively labeled "mumble" rap; through elided phrasing, slurred delivery, and an emphasis on digital studio tools such as Auto-Tune, delay, and chorus effects, the rapper plays with orality and aurality. This style often follows particular flows, or rhythmic delivery, which have become synonymous with mumble rap, such as the "Migos" flow, which relies on repeating triplet rhythms. Through these regular rhythmic forms, rappers have a frame to write lyrics within, and this standardization of rhythm gives rise to more emotive and sensorial approaches to vocalization. The performance becomes less about *what* is said and instead *how* it is said.

The resultant "mumbling" has been critiqued by lyrical rappers. In the intro to Los Angeles rapper Hopsin's 2015 parody track "No Words," he claims, "these fools ain't spittin' no type of dope shit. . . they're not even saying words anymore. . . I know for a fact nobody knows what the fuck these dudes be saying."[8] Other rappers are less critical and understand that this style departs from other rap flows. Pittsburgh rapper Wiz Khalifa is considered the originator of the term *mumble rap*, which he discussed during a 2016 interview with Hot 97 DJ Ebro. "We call it mumble rap," said Khalifa. "It ain't no disrespect to the lil homies, they don't want to rap. It's cool for now, it's going to evolve. Those artists, if they want to stay around, they'll figure out the next thing to do. But right now, that's what's poppin'."[9] Clearly, even supportive artists view this style as a passing trend.

When placed in context of opioid abuse, the mumbling of contemporary rappers takes on new significance. Are we hearing the sedative effects of lean or other prescription-strength painkillers like Xanax or Percocet? Are these rappers performing addiction? While conventional music analysis cannot capture the nuances of post-verbal performance, a sound studies approach can explore the space between orality, what is said, and aurality, what is heard. In the process, we recognize emergent sociocultural elements that inspire artistic choices in both the recording booth and in the mix.

My exploration of the opioid aesthetics of mumble rap builds from Nina Sun Eidsheim's recent work, *Sensing Sound: Singing and Listening as Vibrational Practice* (2015) and *The Race of Sound: Listening, Timbre, and Vocality in African American Music* (2019). With these texts, Eidsheim develops a sensorial approach to studies of the voice. In *Sensing Sound,* she focuses on the phenomenological aspects of sonic production, particularly embodiment in both the vocalists' performance and the audiences' listening, while in *The Race of Sound,* Eidsheim focuses on the listener's responses to the *acousmatic question,* that is, Who am I listening to? This question is a problematic one; by not *seeing* the performer themselves, the listener is forced to construct a set of assumptions about the vocalist, including stereotypes based on race, gender, and ability. Eidsheim offers three correctives that show us that listening is a process of sociocultural mediation: "Voice is not singular; it is collective . . . Voice is not innate; it is cultural . . . Voice's source is not the singer; it is the listener."[10]

These correctives provide new trajectories for sound studies, ones that tease out mediations between performers and listeners. Post-verbal sound studies show us that the sonic event is not solely about the vocalizer but how their words are heard, interpreted, and embodied by listeners. Elements such as timbre, inflection, and intonation give more emphasis to the "grain of the voice," which for semiotician Roland Barthes is "when the voice is in a double posture, a double production: of language and of music."[11] As the listener perceives and interprets a vocal performance, this doubling is made even more complicated and becomes a feedback loop, in which the singer and the listener are engaged in mediating one another.

Eidsheim's work on the sonic aspects of race in music suggests a reading of singing and listening that focuses on the "physical and sensory properties of singers' and listeners' bodies," with an emphasis on the bodies of black vocalists.[12] This sensorial approach, according to Eidsheim, "does not offer a stable explanation of what sound or music is. Instead each such account unveils a composite manifestation of our understanding of sound at a given moment in time and space."[13] Through the opioid aesthetics of mumble rappers, we may hear their sonic experimentation as a thick event, one that simultaneously performs aesthetics of addiction while bringing attention to the symptoms of opioid abuse.

This tactic of anti-mediation is a hallmark of Henry Louis Gates Jr.'s "signifyin(g)," a theoretical framework for understanding the rhetorical play of black American expressive culture.[14] Signifyin(g) explores the gap between what is said and what is implied and often uses an indirect or anti-mediation approach to achieve its ends. Music scholar Samuel Floyd argues that signifyin(g) is indelibly connected to black American music and, similar to the rhetorical play of signifyin(g) language, the "calls, cries, holler, riffs, licks, [and] overlapping antiphony" of black American music are elemental sonic tropes that can be engaged to understand musical ideas that are difficult to describe through formal analysis.[15] Floyd points to the spiritual as a source for signifyin(g) elements such as "call-and-response devices; . . . blue notes, bent thirds, and elisions; hums, moans, grunts, vocables, and other rhythmic-oral declamations, interjections, and punctuations; . . . constant repetition of rhythmic and melodic figures and phrases; . . . [and] timbral distortions of various kinds," elements heard in the opioid aesthetics of mumble rappers.[16] Signifyin(g) amplifies the intimacy of the "grain of the voice" and teases out the power dynamics of sonic mediation by listening closely to the black American experience.

Signifyin(g) allows us to unpack the embodied vocal performance of mumble rappers and the use of schizophonic studio techniques—that is, a sound's separation from its source and re-presentation in a separate context.[17] Through a sensorial approach, the artist's creative choices become signifiers of addiction and mental health issues. Rappers perform the physical aspects of opioid use, using relaxed oral muscles to play with timbre and rhythm, as well as the mental aspects, such as feelings of euphoria and creative liberation from linguistic norms. This takes rhetorical wordplay to a new level by doubling meaning through inflection.

The rappers' performance is augmented in real time by studio engineers, who use technologies such as Auto-Tune, delay, and chorus to alter and disembody the voice. These live studio effects provide another layer of signifyin(g) inflection for the rapper to manipulate their ideas around. Finally, the listener takes this information and, as Eidsheim argues, makes meaning and constructs the vocalist via sonic signifiers. Through their acousmatic manufacturing, the listener embodies properties that parallel the side effects of opioid use: sedation, disembodiment, and a hazy euphoria. And in the process of vocalizing, studio processing, and mediating between sound source and receiver, we may hear the *acousmatic question* as an aesthetic loop where the vocalist in part influences the listeners' understanding of their individuality (for both vocalist and listener).

PERFORMING OPIOID AESTHETICS

High-strength opioids such as codeine, oxycodone, and hydrocodone are prescription pain relievers that activate opioid receptors in the brain, "blocking" pain by reducing the transference of pain messages to the brain. Due to their euphoric effects, opioids are often misused by taking them in large quantities, without a prescription, and in dangerous ways, such as Young Thug's intravenous approach.[18] Side effects of this abuse include euphoria, dissociation from one's body, slurred speech, and sedation. When high levels of opioids are mixed with other drugs such as alcohol, the mix can cause serious physical problems. In 2012, rapper Lil Wayne was hospitalized for seizures; while these issues were allegedly caused by dehydration, Lil Wayne is a noted lean abuser, and following this incident he went on record to discuss quitting lean and the withdrawals that came with it: "It ain't that easy—feels like death in your stomach when you stop doing that shit. You gotta learn how to stop, you gotta go through detox."[19]

High dosages and repeated abuse of lean can be fatal. Codeine is a respiratory depressant, promethazine is a central nervous system depressant, and excess use can cause the user to stop breathing. Since the 1990s, there have been several high-profile deaths in the hip-hop community *directly* tied to opioid abuse: influential lean-aesthetician DJ Screw in 2000, rapper Pimp C in 2007, producer ASAP Yams in 2015, and rappers Fredo Santana and Mac Miller in 2018.

One of the most audible effects of opioid abuse is dysarthria, a speech disorder caused by weaknesses of the facial muscles. According to the American Speech-Language-Hearing Association, dysarthria is characterized by: "mumbled" speech that can be hard to understand; slow speech as well as rapid fire, clumsy, and choppy delivery; difficulty maintaining a constant volume; and a particularly nasal quality to the voice.[20]

These same qualities may be heard within the vocal aesthetics of mumble rap. "[Addiction is] rough," Mac Miller told *Vibe* in 2015, "my music was getting to the point where you couldn't even understand what I was saying on records anymore. I was just, like, mumbling."[21] The vocalizing of other rappers like Young Thug has been unpacked by fans, critics, and scholars alike; through their interpretations of linguistic, semantic, and rhetoric play, we are given a glimpse into the multiple responses rappers' acousmatic performance elicits. "I love when people ask me what I'm saying," Young Thug said in an interview, "even though I ain't gonna tell them. I'll let them listen ten more years before I tell them."[22]

However, I am not suggesting a direct causal relationship between the opioid aesthetics of mumble rap and the abuse of opioids. Via signifyin(g), opioid aesthetics become an anti-essentialist, anti-mediated approach to discussing larger sociocultural issues. For example, rapper Future represents himself simultaneously as drug producer, drug dealer, and drug user—signifyin(g) the circularity of trap life. In his discussion of Detroit rapper Eminem, socio-musicologist Simon Frith describes the "disturbed and disaffected" lyrics of the rapper as part of an artistic performance and suggests that "to articulate a sensibility musically is not to endorse it."[23]

At the same time, primary sources indicate that the effects of prescription and manufactured drugs *have* had an impact on his musical performances. In an interview with Hot 97 DJ Peter Rosenberg, Future describes his 2011 hit "Tony Montana," which features the rapper singing the name of the *Scarface* protagonist in a muted and heavily sedated fashion, as emerging from a late-night, drug-influenced session: "I remember being so fuckin' high on this song, I couldn't even open my mouth," said Future. "When I listened back to it the next day, I was like man, what the fuck is this? But I loved it. Like, that shit sound raw, though."[24]

Scholars have noted an uptick in performative rap that takes on embodied roles. For example, while noting that the excessive use of recreational drugs is not new to hip hop, Calvin John Smiley argues that a lyrical shift from third-person to first-person accounts of drug use—from dealers, such as The Notorious B.I.G.'s and Jay-Z's boasts about slinging crack, to artists like Lil Wayne, Future, and Young Thug detailing their personal use of drugs—signifies a move to "addict" rap.[25] Alex Porco extends this performative lens by discussing the vocal performance of rappers whose bodies have undergone some physical strains: "Rappers Fat Joe, Raekwon, Guru, and Coolio . . . have voices distinguished by aspirated timbre connected to chronic asthmatic conditions. . . . Ghostface Killah and Phife Dawg . . . suffer from diabetes: their dietary restrictions alter the body's processes. . . . Grillz—designer gold teeth—change the physical make-up of the mouth cavity and its resonance, as the vocal iconicities of Ol' Dirty Bastard and Lil' Wayne indicate."[26] Porco argues that "disability is a desirable vocal practice in hip-hop," but quickly adds, "only to the extent that it doesn't eventually result in total vocal failure or death."[27] While opioid aesthetics can reflect creative signifyin(g) practices, we are well aware that the actual abuse of these drugs can prove fatal.

"CHOPPED AND SCREWED": THE EARLY SOUND OF LEAN IN HIP HOP

Lean aesthetics have been closely tied to technology since the 1990s, when Houston producer DJ Screw popularized the sonic sedation of lean through the "chopped and screwed" technique. In this process, DJ Screw created a woozy, elongated vocal and instrumental track by slowing the speed of the turntables, situating the "screwed" tracks around 60 bpm. This slow tempo was further effected through "chopping": playing two identical tracks on different turntables allowed DJ Screw to move between each, creating a delayed effect where the vocals and rhythms of one turntable were echoed by the other. It is in this syrup-soaked state that DJ Screw asks the audience, "Who knows the feeling, how it feels to lean? It's cough syrup or Barr promethazine."[28]

DJ Screw claimed that the aesthetics of this music were not connected opioids but instead the high from cannabis. In a 1995 interview with *Rap Pages Magazine*, Screw says the style emerged "in the crib mixing, you know, getting high. When you smoke weed, you really don't be doing a whole lot of ripping and running. I started messing with the pitch adjusters . . . and slowed it all the way down. I thought it sounded better like that."[29] Yet his lyrics and lifestyle heavily revolved around drinking lean, and in 2000, the producer died of a drug overdose in his Houston recording studio at the age of twenty-nine.

Soon after DJ Screw's death, lean usage would hit "epidemic proportions" in the mid-2000s.[30] A new wave of Southern artists pushed the regional culture to national standing, fueled in part by artists such as UGK and Three 6 Mafia. The two groups came together for the 2000 single "Sippin' on Some Syrup," which made it to Billboard charts and was a staple of hip-hop radio play. The music and vocal performance of these Southern artists did little to embody the feelings of opioid use, like the "chopped and screwed" style, but instead relied on boastful lyrics to describe their opioid use. Three 6 Mafia's Juicy J raps about the sedative effects of cough syrup that contains acetaminophen, stating, "NyQuil will slow me down, something that keep me easy. . . . Talking like, what's up, fool? Vocal cords sounding lame . . . I feel like I'm gonna fucking faint."[31] UGK's Pimp C's lyrics list multiple cough syrups, bragging that "I got the red promethazine, thick orange, and yellow tuss. Hydrocodone on the hands-free phone . . . I'm choking on that doja sweet and sipping on that sizzurp."[32] Seven years after the release of "Sippin' on Some Syrup," Pimp C died due to an overdose of codeine via lean consumption.[33]

In 2008, rapper Lil Wayne released the song "Me and My Drank," a love letter to the lean culture that he was immersed in growing up in the South. At the time the rapper was going through serious medical issues, which was later revealed to be influenced by codeine abuse.[34] In response to media outlets critiquing him for the public abuse of lean, Lil Wayne raps, "It feel like the whole world against me ever since the death of Pimp C."[35] Even his friends, family, and fans were concerned about him, but his response shrugs off their worries and turns instead to lean as both a coping mechanism and an emblem of the Southern culture he embodies. "My homeboys say I should slow down a little, but that shit I'm on make me slow down a lot. . . . I buy a bottled pop, drop some syrup in it. Get out my Waffle House, I live in Wayne's World, represent our South."[36] The track ends with Lil Wayne namechecking the late originators of lean culture: "Rest in peace Big Moe, rest in peace Pimp C. And fuck what they say, Mr. DJ Screw, I'mma do this for you."[37]

Throughout the track, the lyrics of Lil Wayne's toasting and boasting are augmented using vocal effects that garble the rapper's words into a melody of syrupy sounds; reduced annunciation causes words to blend together, and quick movements between monotone delivery and occasional octave leaps, which emphasize particular syllables, bring out textural sounds as the Auto-Tuning attempts to situate his expressions within a particular key. The sonic influence of past lean aestheticians comes out when Lil Wayne raps "and this how we do it, do it in our South."[38] The line "do it in our South" is affected not by Auto-Tune but via an effect that pitches Wayne's voice lower and slower, a clear callback to DJ Screw's use of pitch and tempo to "chop and screw" tracks. Right after representing this regional culture, Wayne mixes drank with some weed, describing the sedative effects: "One more ounce'd make me feel so great. Wait, now I can't feel my face."[39]

AUTO-TUNING OPIOID AESTHETICS

The timbre of mumble rap emphasizes sedation via muscle weakness, and through slurs, elision, and monotone delivery, the rappers themselves display a type of disability. This disability is a performative act, which parallels the idea that, as music scholar Kemi Adeyemi explains, "marginalized bodies produce marginalized sounds to communicate things that escape language."[40] This is expanded through technological mediation; studio effects add to the rapper's performance and continue to highlight the euphoric and disembodied effects of opioid abuse. The most obvious sonic intervention comes through

Auto-Tune, a digital voice processer that applies pitch correction to a singer's voice. This software analyzes a vocal performance in real time and shifts audio input to follow the framework of a specific key.

Instead of using this technology in a deceptive, hidden way, presenting a smooth vocal performance in a less-than-talented singer, trap and mumble rap emphasize the idiosyncratic sound qualities of Auto-Tune.[41] Music journalist Simon Reynolds describes this as a post-human technology where, "at the speediest retune settings, the gradual transitions between notes that a flesh-and-blood vocalist makes are eliminated. Instead, each and every note is pegged to an exact pitch, fluctuations are stripped out, and Auto-Tune forces instant jumps between notes. The result is that sound we know so well: an intimate stranger hailing from the uncanny valley between organic and synthetic, human and superhuman."[42] Auto-tune in this way is not a corrective but a creative distortion, which reveals potential vibrancy of life in the "breaks."[43]

Postproduction (i.e., once the vocalist is out of the recording booth) might call for Auto-Tune to "clean up" a performance. Yet in the case of Future, Young Thug, Lil Uzi Vert, and other mumble rappers, the vocal software is used as a live effect, one that is played with by the performer in real time. Future's long-time recording engineer Seth Firkins told Red Bull Music Academy that, "people forget, [Auto-Tune] is, in a sense, an instrument. It's not just some [effect]—it's an integral part of his emotion and his sound and his delivery, and how he expects things he says and notes he hits to be bent and twisted. . . . [Future] has steered away from [repetitive flows], and I think Auto-Tune has helped him, because every note is different in a sense. The delivery is different, and Auto-Tune has helped him achieve that."[44] This "misuse" of technology is a hallmark of other black musical forms, such as scratching and mixing of hip-hop turntablism.[45] The post-human and post-verbal aesthetics of Auto-Tuned mumble rap present an Afrofuturistic possibility, one where technologies of correction and standardization are instead used to produce unexpected and creative outcomes. As Johnathan Stern reminds us, "[technologies] cannot come into existence to simply fill a pre-existing role."[46]

"HEY, LET'S HAVE A VERY GOOD TIME": HEARING OPIOID AESTHETICS

The musical qualities of trap music have had a major influence on popular artists outside of hip hop, such as Katy Perry's 2013 song "Dark Horse," which featured Three 6 Mafia member Juicy J. Yet it is through mumble rap that we see how charismatic, musically adept, and creative artists use studio technologies and affected vocal styles to go beyond the lyrics to explore and employ the aesthetics of opioid use. Through their performance of alternative orality, mumble rappers engage with ideas of substance abuse and disability[47] while simultaneously providing an Afrofuturist aesthetic that reconfigures black voices and experiences.[48] The sounds of ultrapopular rappers Young Thug, Future, and Lil Uzi Vert have taken advantage of the creative potential of opioid aesthetics, and in this final section, we unpack these artists' hit singles from 2015 and 2017 to understand how this opioid culture has emerged as part of the national soundscape.

Young Thug—"Halftime"

Following a string of well-received mixtapes and singles, Young Thug released the debut commercial mixtape *Barter 6* in 2015. The album art, like the Instagram post discussed at the beginning of this essay, highlights the excesses of his lean abuse: set against a simple black background, a nude Young Thug is cast in a red spotlight, and the scrawled text, vertical orientation, and location of the title over the rapper's genitals implies that the rapper is urinating blood, one of the many side effects of opioid abuse.[49]

The album's eighth track, "Halftime," is a celebration of this abuse. The track opens with the synthesized sound of a plucked instrument accompanying Young Thug muttering, "Turn up, thugga, thugga, ayy, let's go."[50] In this intro section, we hear the liveness of the studio recording; the song's engineer did not clip off the ends of the rapper's first phrases in a digital audio workstation, and the listener hears Young Thug shuffling in the booth, therefore putting us into the soundworld of the recording studio. The lyrics begin with Young Thug mixing "half a perc [Percocet], half a xanny [Xanax]," with "half a pint [of promethazine and codeine cough syrup],"[51] and throughout the piece, we may recognize a correlation between the content and delivery of the lyrics. For example, in the opening lines the rapper elides "xanny" with "make it" to give greater weight and space to the idea of "half-time." Through Young Thug's vocal performance, producer Kip Hilson's woozy instrumental track, and the studio engineering of Alexander Tumay, opioid aesthetics are inextricably linked to the production of Young Thug's music.

Young Thug's rapping style takes advantage of Auto-Tune's melodic qualities through onomatopoeia; as he raps "just might pull up on my Spider,"[52] referencing a Ferrari 458 Spider, an overdubbed Young Thug screeches to emulate a fast turn or a donut. This creates a counter melody to the plucked synthesizer, one that lasts for nearly four bars of the piece. Further, the ad-libs Young Thug punctuates his lines with are noticeably dry, or lacking effects. While we are hearing one iteration of the rapper through the main lyrical content, other iterations of the same individual emerge to comment on and humorously critique the verse.

Tumay's recording techniques apply vocal effects live so that the artist can play with the post-human technologies of Auto-Tune, chorus, and delay. In "Halftime," this comes out forcefully in the chorus; as Young Thug belts and slurs the line "Hey, let's have a good time" in various permutations, Tumay applies a thick layer of chorus effects via the Antares Harmony Engine. In combination with Auto-Tune, this chorus effect highlights and reproduces the disembodied sound of opioid aesthetics by presenting a multiplicity of voices uniquely timbred and pitched, yet thickly coalesced and interwoven, from the soloist's performance.

Future—"Mask Off"

In 2017 Future released an eponymous fifth album, receiving average reviews yet tremendous commercial success. Critiqued for its lack of ambition, the album nevertheless went on to be certified platinum six months after its release, fueled by the viral hit "Mask Off."[53] In this song, Future boasts about luxurious lifestyles, highlighting the drug dealing that got him financial success as well as his copious use of drugs. The most striking element is the chorus, which features Future rapping "Percocet, molly, Percocet." The mixture of Percocet (oxycodone-acetaminophen) and molly, slang for the crystalline powder form of MDMA, combines downers and uppers in a potentially lethal situation. Delivered in a flat affect, Future's chorus sounds his anhedonia despite all the excesses of his lifestyle such as luxury cars, international flights, and gastronomic extravagance.

The effects of vocal processing and Future's affect make it difficult to decipher the ab-libs that follow each iteration of the chorus. On the website Genius.com, a wiki-style lyric site that allows users to contribute lyrics and discuss the metaphoric or cultural references within hip hop, users have debated whether the rapper states "Big foreigns," a reference to a car collection, or "Big Pharma," which would implicate pharmaceutical manufacturers as fueling the opioid epidemic. This website presents a literal version of Eidsheim's *acousmatic question* by encouraging listeners to share their interpretations of the performer's words and aesthetic.

Further technological mediations construct an opioid aesthetic that extends beyond mishearings and overt lyrics. Throughout "Mask Off," we are not listening to a single iteration of Future's vocals but three discrete voices placed spatially in the mix by audio engineer Seth Firkins. Future's main vocal track is centered in the mix, but a schizophonic texture is created through delay effects, which re-present Future's verse with a quarter-note delay. This is mixed in the left channel and balanced by the rapper's ad-libs positioned in the right channel. In the piece this technique is not used constantly but as a tactic to highlight the opioid aesthetics of particular phrases. Through a simultaneous iteration of multiple Futures, the listener is situated within the disembodied effects of the drugs he raps about.

Lil Uzi Vert—"XO Tour Llife3"

Lil Uzi Vert achieved mainstream success through the hit single "XO Tour Llife3," which peaked at number seven on the US Billboard Hot 100 list in 2017. The lyrics of the piece trace the downsides of Uzi's fame, particularly the impact it has had on personal relationships. In the chorus of the song, Uzi sings over and over, "All my friends are dead, push me to the edge."[54] Uzi's slurred delivery brings out the emotional impact of this line, and the insider listener knows from songs like "YSL" that the rapper often shouts out the names of deceased friends from his hometown of Philadelphia. However, in an interview, the track's producer TM88 claimed that this line was merely a reference to "dead presidents," or money.[55]

Yet other lyrics and their timbres suggest otherwise. In the first verse, Uzi raps "Xanny help the pain. Please, Xanny make it go away. I'm committed, not addicted, but it keeps control of me. All the pain, now I can't feel it. I swear that it's slowing me."[56] This line is delivered in a pleading tone, and through vocal fry, Uzi teases out melodic content from Auto-Tune. His lyrical use of opioids strains his voice while also sedating his annunciation. Of the rappers discussed in this piece, Lil Uzi Vert is most connected to issues of mental health, and in particular he speaks to issues that have affected the black American community. In 2017, the rapper responded to the overdose of Lil Peep by announcing he had quit his Xanax habit.

CONCLUSION

The recent deaths of ASAP Yams (2015), Lil Peep (2017), and Mac Miller (2018) have caused many in the hip-hop industry to question promoting the abuse of opioids and other prescription drugs. This has also outed some artists as using opioid aesthetics without using opioids themselves. As Future explained,

> I'm not like super drugged out or [a] drug addict. My music may portray
> a certain kind of image and I know it's some people that might be super

drugged out and they listen to the music like, "Ay thank you, you speaking for me" and then some people that's not [super drugged out] that feel like, "Man I don't have to do drugs, I can listen to Future and feel like I'm on something" and don't have to try [drugs].[57]

Similarly, the backlash over Young Thug's IV image spurred fans and media outlets to dig up a 2016 article that explained how the rapper receives vitamin injections once a month to supplement poor eating and exercise habits.[58] Yet the performance of abuse still reflects despondent experiences within black American communities. Using the symptoms of abuse as a creative force complicates essentialist perspectives about drug use.

While this discussion of opioid aesthetics begins to tease out issues of mental health and disability performance, I agree with Adeyemi, who succinctly explains,

We can examine how lean is Auto-Tuned, chopped and screwed, and lyricized until we're blue in the face. Sitting in the muck of lean-addled songs—theorizing how it feels to lean back and let our heads roll off our necks while we watch our surroundings fade and sway to purple— reveals a critically important rubric of black bodies, sounds, and affects that are wholly circumscribed by the entanglements of race, political economy, and the medical industrial complex. Reading black life against the sounds of lean subsequently makes the intersections of black labor, joy, *and* depression audible.[59]

My reading of the opioid aesthetics of trap music and mumble rap has suggested an alternative sonic space, one where the musician uses tactics of orality and technology to imbue the listener with their own feelings of euphoria, melancholy, and disembodiment. Through Gates's lens of signify(g) and Eidsheim's *acousmatic* correctives, we may hear aesthetics as operating on multiple levels, constructing a feedback loop between artist, engineer, and listener. The embodiment of opioid use is a sensorial tactic in which both performer and listener are entangled in a unique affect. In this way, opioid aesthetics work as a creative post-verbal, post-human signifier while also providing a critical lens to amplify the complexities of surviving and thriving in twenty-first-century America.

NOTES

1.   For more on the impact of lean and opioid use on social media, see Roy Cherian et al., "Representations of Codeine Misuse on Instagram: Content Analysis," *JMIR Public Health and Surveillance* 4, no. 1 (March 2018): e22.

2. Lean is known by many names, such as *syrup* and its slanged cousin *sizzurp*, or *purple drank* after the coloration of the mixture. *Lean* derives from the idea that getting high on the drug makes it difficult for the user to stand straight, which results in them leaning over.

3. Soon after it was posted, Young Thug pulled the image from Instagram. Jeffery Lamar Williams (@thuggerthugger1), "Fuck a double cup I wanna feel it faster," Instagram, December 31, 2017, https://www.instagram.com/thuggerthugger1.

4. This includes journalists such as Charley Locke, "Young Thug Isn't Rapping Gibberish, He's Evolving Language," *Wired*, June 6, 2018, www.wired.com/2015/10/young-thug -evolution-of-language/; and Simon Reynolds, "How Auto-Tune Revolutionized the Sound of Popular Music," *Pitchfork*, September 17, 2018, https://pitchfork.com /features/article/how-auto-tune-revolutionized-the-sound-of-popular-music/.

5. See Kemi Adeyemi, "Straight Leanin': Sounding Black Life at the Intersection of Hip-Hop and Big Pharma," *Sounding Out!* September 27, 2015, https://sound studiesblog.com/2015/09/21/hip-hop and big-pharma/; Justin Adams Burton, *Posthuman Rap* (New York: Oxford University Press, 2017); Calvin John Smiley, "Addict Rap?: The Shift from Drug Distributor to Drug Consumer in Hip Hop," *The Journal of Hip Hop Studies* 4, no. 1 (2017): 94–117; and Ben Westhoff, *Dirty South: OutKast, Lil Wayne, Soulja Boy, and the Southern Rappers Who Reinvented Hip-Hop* (Chicago: Chicago Review Press, 2011).

6. Burton, *Posthuman Rap*, 82.

7. For examples, see Kyle Adams, "Aspects of the Music/Text Relationship in Rap," *Music Theory Online* 14, no. 2 (2008); Adam Krims, *Rap Music and the Poetics of Identity* (Cambridge: Cambridge University Press, 2011); and Tricia Rose, *Black Noise: Rap Music and Black Culture in Contemporary America* (Hanover, CT: University Press of New England, 1994).

8. Hopsin, "No Words," *Pound Syndrome*, Funk Volume and Warner Bros., 2015.

9. Wiz Khalifa explains in Nathan Slavik, "Wiz Khalifa on Lil Yachty: 'We Call It Mumble Rap, If They Want to Stay around They'll Evolve,' " *DJBooth*, June 23, 2016, last updated October 10, 2018, https://djbooth.net/features/2016-06-23-wiz-khalifa-lil-yachty -mumble-rap.

10. Nina Sun Eidsheim, *The Race of Sound: Listening, Timbre, and Vocality in African American Music* (Durham, NC: Duke University Press, 2019), 9.

11. Roland Barthes and Stephen Heath, *Image, Music, Text: Essays* (New York: Hill and Wang, 2007), 269.

12. Following Eidsheim, artist Brendon Labelle has focused on the embodiment of vocal performance via orality, i.e., how elements such as facial muscles, vocal cords, and diaphragms impact the sounds produced, as well as how sounds are heard.

13. Nina Sun Eidsheim, "Sensing Voice Materiality and the Lived Body in Singing and Listening," *The Senses and Society* 6, no. 2 (2011): 133–55, abstract.

14. Signifyin(g) spelled this way foregrounds black American vernacular while simultaneously positioning this semiotic approach as an Afrological one. For more, see Henry Louis Gates Jr., *The Signifying Monkey: A Theory of African-American Literary Criticism* (New York: Oxford University Press, 1988).

15. Samuel A. Floyd, "Ring Shout! Literary Studies, Historical Studies, and Black Music Inquiry," *Black Music Research Journal* 11, no. 2 (1991): 265–87.

16. Floyd, "Ring Shout!," 52.

17. Steven Feld, "Pygmy POP. A Genealogy of Schizophonic Mimesis," *Yearbook for Traditional Music* 28 (1996): 1–35, https://doi.org/10.2307/767805.

18. This has a long history in the South, specifically Houston. In Marah Eakin's "Learn All about the Long, Lean History of 'Sizzurp' with This 7-Minute Audio Primer" (*AV Club*, August 23, 2017, https://news.avclub.com/learn-all-about-the-long-lean-history-of

-sizzurp-wit-1798237116), author Lance Scott Walker describes how Houston blues musicians in the 1960s would mix Robitussin into their beers.

19. Shaheem Reid, "Lil Wayne on Syrup: 'Everybody Wants Me to Stop . . . It Ain't That Easy,'" MTV News, February 28, 2008, www.mtv.com/news/1582520/lil-wayne-on -syrup-everybody-wants-me-to-stop-it-aint-that-easy/.

20. "Dysarthria," American Speech-Language-Hearing Association, accessed December 20, 2019, www.asha.org/public/speech/disorders/dysarthria/.

21. Mikey Fresh, "VIBE Interview: Mac Miller on His New Album 'Watching Movies': 'I Just Did What I Wanted,'" Vibe, February 24, 2015, https://www.vibe.com/2013/06 /vibe-interview-mac-miller-his-new-album-watching-movies-i-just-did-what-i-wanted/.

22. Will Stephenson, "Young Thug: Came from Nothing," The Fader, February 11, 2014, https://www.thefader.com/2014/02/11/young-thug-came-from-nothing.

23. Simon Frith, "What Is Bad Music?" in Bad Music: The Music We Love to Hate, eds. Christopher Washburne and Maiken Derno (New York: Routledge, 2004), 26.

24. Jasmine Alyse, "Is Mumble Rap Really Such a Terrible Thing?" Vibe, June 6, 2017, https://www.vibe.com/featured/mumble-rap-essay/.

25. Smiley, "Addict Rap?"

26. Alex S. Porco, "Throw Yo' Voice Out: Disability as a Desirable Practice in Hip-Hop Vocal Performance," in Disability Media Studies, eds. Elizabeth Ellcessor and Bill Kirkpatrick (New York: New York University Press, 2017), 96.

27. Porco, "Throw Yo' Voice Out," 96.

28. DJ Screw, "Who Knows the Feeling?" (1996).

29. Bilal Allah, "Givin It to Ya Slow: DJ Screw Interview," Rap Pages, November 1995, 84.

30. Westhoff, Dirty South.

31. Three 6 Mafia, UGK, "Sippin' on Some Syrup," When the Smoke Clears, Loud, 2000.

32. Three 6 Mafia, "Sippin' on Some Syrup."

33. Jayson Rodriguez, "Pimp C Died from Accidental Cough-Medicine Overdose, Sleep Condition: Autopsy," MTV News, February 4, 2008, www.mtv.com/news/1580916 /pimp-c-died-from-accidental-cough-medicine-overdose-sleep-condition-autopsy/.

34. Aspringer, "Lil Wayne Explains His Addiction." HipHopDX, February 29, 2008, https:// hiphopdx.com/news/id.6476/title.lil-wayne-explains-his-addiction#.

35. Lil Wayne, "Me and My Drank," Tha Carter after tha Carter (mixtape), 2008.

36. Lil Wayne, "Me and My Drank."

37. Lil Wayne, "Me and My Drank."

38. Lil Wayne, "Me and My Drank."

39. Lil Wayne, "Me and My Drank."

40. Adeyemi, "Straight Leanin'."

41. Alexander G. Weheliye, "Feenin: Posthuman Voices in Black Popular Music," Social Text 20, no. 2 (2002): 21–47.

42. Reynolds, "How Auto-Tune Revolutionized the Sound of Popular Music."

43. Fred Moten, In the Break: The Aesthetics of the Black Radical Tradition (Minneapolis: University of Minnesota Press, 2003).

44. Jordan Rothlein, "Seth Firkins on Being Future's Vocal Producer and the Power of Auto-Tune," Red Bull Music Academy Daily, August 24, 2017, https://daily.redbullmusic academy.com/2017/08/seth-firkins-interview#!.

45. Moten, In the Break.

46. Jonathan Sterne, "Bourdieu, Technique and Technology," Cultural Studies 17, no. 3–4 (2003): 373.

47. See Brandon LaBelle, "Raw Orality: Sound Poetry and Live Bodies," in Voice: Vocal Aesthetics in Digital Arts and Media, eds. Norie Neumark et al. (Boston: MIT Press, 2010), 147–71; and Porco, "Throw Yo' Voice Out."

48. See Kodwo Eshun, *More Brilliant than the Sun: Adventures in Sonic Fiction* (London: Verso, 1998); Weheliye, "Feenin"; and Eidsheim, *Sensing Sound*.

49. On the track "Thought It Was a Drought," Future raps, "I just took a piss, and I see codeine coming out." This song is a direct response to drug manufacturer Actavis's decision to stop producing promethazine/codeine cough syrup, and in the track, Future brags about his ability to access the drug even during the "drought." See Future, "Thought It Was a Drought," *Dirty Sprite 2*, A1 Recordings, Freebandz, and Epic, 2015.

50. Young Thug, "Halftime," *Barter 6*, 300 Entertainment, Atlantic, and YSL, 2015.

51. Young Thug, "Halftime."

52. Young Thug, "Halftime."

53. Lil Uzi Vert, "XO Tour Llif3," *Luv Is Rage 2*, Generation Now and Atlantic, 2017.

54. Lil Uzi Vert, "XO Tour Llif3."

55. Lauren Nostro, "The Making of Lil Uzi Vert's 'XO TOUR Llif3' with TM88," Genius, June 9, 2017, https://genius.com/a/the-making-of-lil-uzi-vert-s-xo-tour-llif3-with-tm88.

56. Lil Uzi Vert, "XO Tour Llif3."

57. Khari, "Future Says He's Not Really an Addict, Raps about Drugs Because It's 'a Catch,'" *The Source*, January 16, 2016, https://thesource.com/2016/01/16/future-says-hes-not-really-an-addict-raps-about-drugs-because-its-a-catch/.

58. Yoh Phillips, "Young Thug's Very Real, Impossible to Believe Lifestyle," *DJBooth*, February 19, 2016, last updated March 9, 2018, https://djbooth.net/features/2016-02-19-young-thug-lifestyle-myths.

59. Adeyemi, "Straight Leanin'."

PART III

NEW DAY DAWNING

RECOVERY, SOBRIETY, AND POST-OPIOID FUTURES

CHAPTER 15

Healing Open Wounds

Chelsea Jack

> Only by restoring the broken connections can we heal.
> —Wendell Berry, *The Unsettling of America*

AN OPEN WOUND

Chris Yeager began lobbying for cannabis reform in his home state of West Virginia after his younger brother, Jeremy, asphyxiated and passed away as a result of an opioid-related overdose on Christmas Eve in 2010.

"It's like an open wound," Chris said eight years later.[1]

We were talking in the backroom of a retail location for Appalachian Cannabis Company (ACC), his small, but growing, business, which he began in 2016. Chris legally farms and processes hemp, the statutory term for a recently legalized species of cannabis with low levels of the psychoactive compound tetrahydrocannabinol, or THC.[2] From his hemp crop, Chris extracts a differ-ent cannabis compound capturing the American imagination: cannabidiol, or CBD. CBD belongs to a group of chemicals called cannabinoids, which have been anecdotally and, in some cases, scientifically reported to have therapeutic potential, including pain and anxiety relief.[3] He retails these hemp-derived CBD products in West Virginia locations including Cross Lanes, Charleston, and Morgantown.

Producers and consumers alike have fueled enthusiasm for hemp by em-phasizing that, when it comes to pain and anxiety relief, CBD is (as one con-sumer told the *New York Times*) "a more nontoxic, natural route" than some synthetic and semisynthetic pharmaceuticals.[4] Chris's mission in starting ACC has been to fight the opioid overdose epidemic in West Virginia with the goal of making CBD products an available, acceptable, and a less risky alternative to prescription opioids.[5] As of August 2019, ACC included the following state-ment on their website: "We now provide an alternative to the practices that have placed our state first in the nation in terms of opioid addiction and over-dose deaths and last in economic growth and job opportunity."

After his brother's death, Chris began to notice how prevalent opioid use disorder and overdoses were in his community. "At this point, we—my family and I—were numb," Chris recalled. "I'm like, 'What in the world is going on?' I started to see other people, other friends, and it's becoming more widespread. That's the first time it hit so close to home for me." Opioid use disorder[6] and fatal opioid overdoses—fueled in part by large-scale pharmaceutical distribu-tion and overprescription—had reached (as the Centers for Disease Control de-scribed in 2011, a year after Jeremy's death) "epidemic levels."[7] From 1999 to 2013, the number of annual deaths involving prescription opioids quadrupled from 4,000 to 16,235, as did retail sales of prescription opioids.[8] Chris began seeing manifestations of the crisis in West Virginia after his brother's death, right around the same time that governmental public health agencies began sounding the alarm. "I started lobbying in front of the state legislature as soon as my brother passed away in 2010. The problem was only getting worse. I felt like something had to be done. That's what sparked the fire."

Chris's story begins with his brother's death and his subsequent decisions, first, to begin lobbying for medical cannabis and then, when it became legally possible, to farm hemp for CBD. Until the enactment of the 2014 farm bill, hemp cultivation was very restricted and subject to US drug law because of the plant's connection to marijuana.[9] However, with the 2014 farm bill, the federal government began slowly expanding the ability of individual states to support scientists and farmers in the legal cultivation of hemp as a commodity crop.[10] It was not until 2018 that hemp was redefined in relation to the Controlled Substances Act—specifically, hemp was reclassified from a Schedule 1 drug with no accepted medical benefit to an agricultural commodity—but, even still, regulations are confusing and evolving when it comes to the production of non-FDA approved hemp extracts, like nearly all CBD products, and foods infused with hemp-derived compounds. Even so, in cooperation with the West Virginia Department of Agriculture and pursuant of the 2014 farm bill, Chris joined a growing movement of hemp farmers and began producing, as well as retailing, hemp-derived products in 2017. It is a journey that began from a desire to provide alternative forms of healing to his community in the midst of the opioid crisis.

Chris's story is decidedly about building a post-opioid future by cele-brating cannabis cultivation, and it is also about cultivating human health through connections with, what many might consider, "natural" landscapes and substances. Both times I visited and interviewed Chris (first in July 2018 and then a year later in August 2019) it became clear how choosing a hemp-derived CBD extract, as a substitute for or as a supplement to pharmaceuticals, could be viewed as an experience with political, economic, and aesthetic dimensions. People are experimenting with medicinal alternatives, which is certainly a political and economic act, and furthermore, in opting out, they are choosing *storied* medicinal alternatives, which is an imaginative and aesthetic experience.[11] The chosen story, for producers and consumers alike, is not only about rejecting the establishment but also about returning to nature. "Nature," English literary critic Raymond Williams famously wrote, "is perhaps the most complex word in the language."[12] Unlike Williams, I will not trace how this complex word has been used historically across time and space, but, instead, I will look at how it quietly surfaced during oral history interviews with an important interlocutor as I began studying emerging hemp commodity chains in the United States.

NOTICING TOXIC SYSTEMS

Chris explained that his brother's death triggered a new way of seeing and making sense of the world around him. He "started to see other people, other friends" differently after his brother's death, which eventually pushed him to shift course and pursue reparative political action by lobbying for alternative modes of pain relief. He initially felt "numb"—anaesthetized—but that numbness gave way to new senses of urgency, curiosity, and will. "What in the world is going on?" he asked.

Rates of fatal opioid overdoses have been higher in West Virginia than in any other state, Chris told me, and so creative policy solutions are needed urgently in his community. He sees cannabis reform as one potential solution. Personal experience has taught him that cannabis and cannabinoids are effective forms of relief—from pain, anxiety, and trauma—without the same risks associated with prescription medications. Shortly after his brother passed, Chris, who is also a veteran of the US Marine Corps, was diagnosed with posttraumatic stress disorder (PTSD). He chose to self-medicate with cannabis because, in his words, "opioids had put a bad taste in [his] mouth" and he had become skeptical about how many veterans were being prescribed cocktails of powerful, and potentially risky, medications when they received health care through Veterans Affairs.[13]

For support, Chris joined his West Virginia chapter of NORML—the National Organization for the Reform of Marijuana Laws, which has advocated for cannabis reform since 1970 through individual state chapters. He even began traveling to the state legislature to push for reform: "I would suit up and say, 'I'm a military veteran. I use cannabis. I don't want to be a criminal. I don't have so much as a parking ticket on my record, and every day when I have to go out and illegally find a way to consume cannabis, I'm breaking the law. I don't think I should have to do that. I've fought for the right to have the choice.'"

Chris was part of a group of activists who would eventually push their political representatives to legalize medical cannabis in West Virginia in 2017. That victory was hard fought, and Chris experienced moments of serious political disillusionment throughout the process, especially as he realized how political power and wealth had concentrated in his home state. In the state that has reported some of the highest rates of opioid-related overdose deaths,[14] how could someone like Patrick Morrisey be elected attorney general in 2012, with his history of lobbying on behalf of Big Pharma?[15] Painful ironies like this signaled political corruption. He was equally frustrated by procedural limitations that seemed to constrain his ability as a citizen to enact change: "The political system has worn people down so much that they don't care. It has worn them down. They don't want you to come to the poll. We can't put cannabis on a ballot and vote on it. We don't allow voter referendum in West Virginia."

Political power felt concentrated in such a way that ordinary constituents, like Chris, felt disconnected from the representative bodies empowered to enact meaningful changes. He felt worn down—and not just by the legislature's resistance to acknowledge cannabis reform as a possible means of curbing the opioid crisis. He looked around and saw incomprehensible human loss, and it felt as if toxic systems in the state were conspiring to devastate human health. He began to notice how large-scale systems were negatively impacting not just human health but also environmental health.

At the end of 2013, Chris was drained by the political process, especially by resistance to cannabis reform within the House of Delegates, and he finally reached a tipping point. Two major life events prompted him and his family to make a huge change and move to Colorado, where Chris began learning about and working in the state's relatively established cannabis industry. Those two events were the loss of his father-in-law, who had been a friend and mentor, and the 2014 Elk River chemical spill. He took these events as signs telling him that they needed to make a change:

> My father-in-law passed away in December of 2013. For me that was symbolic. It was like the writing on the wall. I kept thinking, What are

we gonna do? I think we should go to Colorado. West Virginia—the legislature—is not there yet. I can't do this for another three years. I was talking to my father-in-law about this while he was alive, and we were gearing up for it. He passed away in December, and then they poisoned our water. . . . It was the MCHM chemical spill. . . . They dumped this stuff into our water. It was on the Elk River. That's literally like a baseball throw away from our home.

MCHM, 4-Methylcyclohexanemethanol, is an organic compound used in the processing and treatment of coal to reduce the amount of ash, and over 7,500 gallons of it leaked from a Freedom Industries storage tank into the ground and contaminated the Kanawha Valley water supply in the spring of 2014.[16] The spill impacted over three hundred thousand residents, including Chris and his family.

As Chris recalled the Elk River chemical spill, he described an attention to "writing on the wall," a sense of the world structured by human *and* environmental catastrophe prompting alternative action. This sense of catastrophe included the human losses of his brother and his father-in-law, and, beyond his closest human relations, it also included a loss of faith in his state's political processes, businesses around him, and, ultimately, the environmental loss of the Elk River. Knots began to untangle: profit-seeking companies—in the pharmaceutical industry, the coal industry, and the chemical industry— seemed to be constantly contaminating his community with toxic substances at the expense of human and environmental health.

Chris and his family moved to Denver, and he began working at a company called Starbuds, where he got his cannabis education: "I woke up, ate, lived, and breathed cannabis. It was a great opportunity, but when I was out there I still came back to West Virginia to apply for a permit and lobby during legislative sessions." Chris was referring to his authorization to grow and process industrial hemp, which had become a legal possibility after the enactment of the 2014 farm bill. The farm bill had called for the "legitimacy of industrial hemp research," which made it possible for individual states to begin pilot research programs on hemp through their state department of agriculture, and, in some states, that meant people like Chris could register to grow hemp through such programs.[17] He explained that the point of moving to Colorado had been to learn as much as he could and then one day return to West Virginia to pioneer a cannabis industry there. Chris and his family did eventually move back to Charleston. After acquiring his industrial hemp authorization through the West Virginia Department of Agriculture, he set up Appalachian Cannabis

Company in December 2016, and his first ACC retail location in Cross Lanes, West Virginia, went live on August 19, 2017.

When Chris described reading "the writing on the wall," he described a way of paying attention to the potential for catastrophe, with a focus on how man-made catastrophes shape human and environmental health. The invocation of Freedom Industries affords a serious discussion about a radical sense of freedom or liberation, not in terms of being able to pick up and move, but in terms of being able to liberate one's self and community from (what historian Philippe Pignarre and philosopher Isabelle Stengers have called) the "infernal alternatives" that unfettered capitalist modes of production present themselves with every day.[18] Liberation from infernal alternatives means exposing fabricated choices for what they are. Examples range from debates on job creation versus environmental regulation to the infernal bargain Americans make by handing over control of medicine research to profit-driven companies inherently concerned with the relative increase in revenue over current revenue, not health understood as sickness reduction.[19] What paths lead away from a politics where acceptance of fabricated choices is an imperative?[20] Chris's story invites us to consider such a path. He chose to heal by literally opening up the earth—exposing an open wound—and planting seeds in the ground to create a new beginning.

REBUILDING CONNECTIONS WITH THE ENVIRONMENT

When we met up at his Cross Lanes store in July 2018, Chris modestly described hemp farming as something that involved getting caught up in nature, meaning that it required affecting and being affected by nature. He started with a microfarm of seventy plants, and those seventy plants produced about fifty-five thousand seeds, which Chris and his team then planted in 2018. "We touch every one of those plants," he said, suggesting how much attention and devotion gets transferred in the hemp fields. As he described his own agricultural practices, Chris did not create a stereotypically pastoral picture or idealize the life of the farmer. He explained, instead, that farming involves multiples kinds of risks, many of which are environmental and beyond the control of individual farmers. Chris humbly acknowledged these, as do many hemp farmers and researchers who have navigated new terrain as they have participated in state research programs since the enactment of the 2014 farm bill. Those risks can frequently include harsh weather conditions, weed pressure, pest pressure (caterpillars, beetles, etc.), and pathogens (fungi or mold during the drying process), to say nothing of unanticipated anthropogenic hazards or accidents (such as an industrial chemical spill contaminating groundwater).[21] "With this plant—and I've been doing this for a while—it can get you. It can sink your ship," he cautioned. For Chris, engaging with the environment through agriculture meant that humans could be affected in unexpected ways by factors beyond human control, what Kant might have called "sublime" natural forces, which could lead to undesirable (though perhaps humbling) experiences in the process.[22] Despite these risks, as Chris described his own embodied agricultural practices, he envisioned how growing hemp and, perhaps one day, medical cannabis could lead to healed relationships between humans and their natural environment.

The legalization of medical cannabis in West Virginia, however, which should have been a major political victory for activists like Chris, has been anything but straight forward. Chris has remained skeptical about how the state has begun translating the West Virginia Medical Cannabis Act, S.B. 386, into a functioning program over the last two years. First and perhaps most obviously, many are frustrated because the bill was signed into law by Governor Jim Justice in April 2017 and, at that time, the state said that implementation of the program was expected to be complete by early 2019, with patient and caregiver identification cards necessary to obtain medical cannabis issued after July 1, 2019. These dates have come and gone, and, as of this writing in 2020, there is still no functioning medical cannabis program.

As Chris looked across the evolving regulatory landscape in West Virginia for growing and processing medical cannabis, he also saw requirements being introduced that might undercut a more engaged relationship with the environment. A medical cannabis advisory board of doctors, attorneys, patient advocates, and law enforcement has been established, Chris explained, to examine and analyze regulations for medical cannabis in the state and issue recommendations to the governor. At several points, the board had accepted and reviewed public comments about medical cannabis. "I would go out and tell them where the holes were in the regulations. I'd say, 'You want all the growers to grow inside, but you have no idea what that will do to our electrical grid. You should allow us to grow with our natural resources out in the sun, not contained.' " Chris was concerned that it would be wasteful to force medical cannabis growers indoors, primarily because the sun is an effective and powerful natural resource. At the heart of his concern is a question about the ethics of requiring that growers augment the built, human environment with energy-intensive indoor grows when a more sustainable option seems to be encouraging outdoor plots that utilize the power of the sun.[23]

Chris stressed the importance of the public offering comments and pushing back against unsavory regulations, because, if no one does, he believes the state might repeat old patterns of centralizing production with those in possession of the most capital at the expense of human and environmental well-being. He worries that regulators might introduce costly restrictions that prohibit ordinary people from growing or processing medical cannabis, and the result of their exclusion might be that medical cannabis becomes pharmaceuticalized, despite the devastation that has come from the state empowering the pharmaceutical industry in the past: "They [regulators] wanted to make it as restrictive as possible. They basically tried to bundle it up and hand it to the pharmaceutical companies. Put a price tag on growing and processing that normal people couldn't afford. 'Put it into a package, not flower, and put it in devices and sell it as oil.' You tell me how many West Virginians you think are going to be able to get that done." Economic, social, and environmental concerns flow together. Chris believes that economic and social justice could be prioritized by limiting capital-intensive requirements that might bar "normal people" from entering the game, like onerous packaging and processing requirements that might not only be costly to participants in the market but also, with respect to postconsumption impacts, the environment.

Concerns for environmental and economic justice converged again as Chris repeated a central irony in many narratives about life in West Virginia: "Why, when we are probably the richest state in terms of natural resources, are our people so dirt poor?" A careful reading of this statement would not rush to the conclusion that Chris supports the continuation of an environmental ethic based on the idea that humans should continue exploiting and extracting value from nature with no concern for mutual well-being. Instead, he seems to imply that, if mutual impoverishment has been the result of exploiting the natural environment, then we need to figure out what kind of human-environmental relationship will lead to mutual flourishing.

Chris contextualized his frustrations about the implementation of the medical cannabis program by identifying a familiar subtext of the proposed regulations: namely, a self-serving desire (of the state, of industry) to maintain inequitable concentrations of economic and political power such that particular stakeholders, including the pharmaceutical industry, can capitalize on new economic opportunities at the expense of "normal people." He imagines Big Pharma would want to prevent the decentralization of ownership and production when it comes to this promising new cash crop because it can provide relief for multiple physical and mental health conditions.

"They don't want you to have something that can help," said Chris. "If you can take one thing like cannabis and it can help you in nine different ways, why in the world would they want you to have that? They want to sell you something for your anxiety. They want to sell you something for the side effects from your anxiety medication. And when you can't sleep from that, they want to find something for that. If they can sell you the disease and the cure, they're making money all the way around every time."

Cannabis, Chris said, has the potential to thwart the centralized, special-ized, and standardized power of pharmaceutical manufacturing: it is a weed "that you can grow in your backyard." That is the "magical" part of the plant that Chris loves so much, especially compared to pharmaceuticals "grown in a lab," not a field. "It's not natural," Chris said about medicines synthesized in labs. "This plant, God designed this plant so that these greedy business people and politicians and pharmaceutical companies cannot control it. That's what scared them for years. If that genie gets out of the bottle, which it's out now, and grandma can grow her medicine in her garden—what do we need them for?"

To many, cannabis seems like a plant that has the potential to expose advertising and persuasion as symptoms of a competitive market economy that prioritizes profit over human health: "If they can sell you the disease and the cure, they're making money all the way around every time." These words are eerily similar to the words of caution that Wendell Berry shared in *The Unsettling of America* decades ago, in which he lamented how modern indus-trial society had "a series of radical disconnections," especially between human bodies and the earth, enabled by an economy that "proposes, not health, but vast 'cures' that further centralize power and increase profits."[24] Like Berry, Chris is sick of the state's permitting industry to profit on the devaluation of human health by generating increasing demand for potentially risky pharma-ceuticals, despite the fact that such profit-seeking actions have impoverished human health in many communities. It is painfully ironic, he suggests, that humans have allowed other humans to create these forms of poverty when the natural environment in the state of West Virginia seems to provide so many possibilities for ecological flourishing, if only humans could figure out how to engage with their environment in healthy ways.

UNMAKING IGNORANCE IN THE AGE OF PERSUASION

Despite legalization, hemp farmers will continue to face many uncertainties in the coming years, including the need for specialized machinery for plant-ing and harvesting hemp. That particular challenge, however, didn't stop ACC from fifty-five thousand seeds in the ground during the 2018 planting season. "We modified an old tobacco setter that had been out of commission for twenty-five years. It was rusty. It was crazy looking. We made modifica-tions. We ran test runs. We got it," he said proudly.

Chris posted a video to Facebook of the ACC crew operating the tobacco setter in a hemp plot last summer. At one point in the video, Chris is off camera, and he trains the lens onto another man, who is identified as a Marine Corps veteran (as Chris is). The man places small hemp plants "slow and steady" into the setter, which are then transferred into the soil. "Have you ever done anything like this?" Chris asks his fellow Marine. "Negative," the man responds, and they both laugh. "I don't think anybody has, not around here."

The narrative is one about pioneers at the frontier of a new agricultural commodity chain, but the presence of the tobacco setter subtly introduces contingent environmental and social histories into the video.[25] The viewer watches hemp farmers repurpose an artifact of the US tobacco industry, affording an opportunity to recall how that industry has created demand for an addictive substance at the expense of human and environmental health.[26] The devastating health impacts of tobacco consumption have been well-documented among humans, and increasing attention has been devoted to the study the environmental impacts of tobacco throughout its life cycle.[27] On the production side, these impacts include deforestation, heavy use of biocides, and depletion of soil nutrients, to say nothing of postconsumption impacts related to tobacco product wastes (cigarette butts and other tobacco product wastes are the most common form of litter worldwide).[28] The presence of the tobacco setter introduces the history of industrialized agriculture, which has had damaging consequences for the whole planet by creating dependencies on petroleum, biocides, and synthetic fertilizers that generate greenhouse gas emissions and contribute to climate change. Industrialized farming today is decidedly removed from the natural systems and processes that shape pastoral ideals.[29] But, with production sites typically out of sight and out of mind, many people do not know or talk about the consequences of what farming has become.

Intended or not, the ACC video affords viewers the opportunity to consider an object that gets you thinking about "the making and unmaking of ignorance," to borrow a phrase from historian Robert Proctor.[30] Proctor has argued that tobacco manufacturers spent the better part of the twentieth century producing doubt and ignorance about the hazards of smoking.[31] He characterized that state of affairs in this way: "We rule you, if we can fool you. No one has done this more effectively than the tobacco mongers, the masters of fomenting ignorance to combat knowledge. Health fears are assuaged by reassurances in the form of 'reasonable doubt'—a state of mind with both PR and legal value." The tobacco setter in the film conjures this past and present history into the imagination of the viewer.

The farmers in the video have repurposed this object to cultivate alternative forms of bodily relief for those situated in capitalist economies and a crop considered by many to have environmental benefits, including soil remediation and carbon sequestration (though some claim that these benefits are exaggerated); and yet, the tobacco setter, as an object, inspires aesthetic literacy and vigilance in a world where marketing—which, Proctor reminds us, "has always involved a certain persuasion bordering on deception"—rules.[32] Unlike seamless direct-to-consumer pharmaceutical ads or those identical orange prescription bottles, Chris's smartphone video is clunky, dizzying, and human. Real humans, with hands in need of steadying, are at work under the sun and close to their environment.

CANNABIS FUTURES

After his brother's death, Chris began to see troubling disconnections between consumers and producers, constituents and their elected officials, and people and their natural environments. Events like the 2014 Elk River chemical spill read like writing on the wall that something had to change. In the years that followed a series of human and environmental crises, Chris saw therapeutic potential in the cannabis industry. Hemp presented itself as a viable solution, not only in terms of yielding alternative medicines in the midst of the opioid crisis, but also in terms of helping people get back in touch with agriculture and the environment. Chris saw potential in this plant to improve the ways humans modify landscapes and the natural environment through agriculture.

Stories like Chris's are not common in popular discourse about the opioid crisis, insofar as his story is not about choosing sobriety or turning away from substances altogether after his brother's death—he became a cannabis farmer. At the heart of his story is a question about the politics of legitimacy when it comes to the lives of people and substances. Popular narratives about the opioid crisis do not often connect the same dots that Chris has, and yet his story invites us to see this crisis differently and to reconsider what areas are truly in crisis, from medicine to agriculture. His story serves as a helpful reminder too that, whether it comes to agricultural or pharmaceutical commodities, consumers must be discerning, if not demanding, to protect their own well-being.

Many hemp farmers growing for CBD are not only trying to promote therapeutic alternatives in the face of overprescribing and prescription drug-related overdoses; some are also advocating for alternative farming practices to prevent this emerging production from being absorbed into industrialized agricultural commodity chains, which they connect with myriad crises including climate change. Where I live in upstate New York, for example, many hemp farmers are emphasizing the importance of crop rotation (defined by the

Rodale Institute as planting different crops sequentially on the same field) to reduce weed pressure and to build the soil, as opposed to monoculture (planting the same crop sequentially on the same field), which often requires many synthetic inputs and compromises soil health.[33] For their part, consumers are seeking out hemp extract producers who are serious about regenerating the soil, rejecting unfettered capitalism, and restoring healing connections between humans and the environment.

NOTES

1. Chris Yeager, interview by Chelsea Jack, July 12, 2018, and August 22, 2019, at Appalachian Cannabis Company in Cross Lanes, West Virginia.
2. To be clear, hemp is a type of cannabis. Per the Agricultural Act of 2014 (P.L. 113–79, Section 7606), cannabis plants with very low levels of the psychoactive compound tetrahydrocannabinol (or THC, less than or equal to 0.3 percent) have earned the statutory classification of "industrial hemp," distinct from marijuana, which has higher levels of THC.
3. For more on evidence of health effects of cannabis and cannabinoids, see: National Academies of Sciences, Engineering, and Medicine (NAS), *The Health Effects of Cannabis and Cannabinoids* (Washington, DC: The National Academies Press, 2017), 29, 38. The report says: "CBD is pharmacologically active, however, and, therefore, classifying cannabis in terms of drug- and fiber-producing seems inaccurate. Both THC- and CBD-types are considered drug-types, and both cultivars could theoretically be exploited to produce fiber" (45).
4. Alex Williams, "Why is CBD Everywhere?" *New York Times*, October 27, 2018, https://www.nytimes.com/2018/10/27/style/cbd-benefits.html.
5. The therapeutic potential of cannabis, as part of the solution to the opioid crisis, has received increased scholarly attention. See Paul J. Larkin Jr. and Bertha K. Madras, "Opioids, Overdoses, and Cannabis: Is Marijuana an Effective Therapeutic Response to the Opioid Abuse Epidemic?," *Georgetown Journal of Law and Public Policy* 17, no. 2 (2019): 555–98; M. A. Bachhuber et al., "Medical Cannabis Laws and Opioid Analgesic Overdose Mortality in the United States, 1999–2010," *JAMA Internal Medicine*, 174, no. 10 (2014): 1668–73; J. Elikottil et al., "The Analgesic Potential of Cannabinoids," *Journal of Opioid Management* 5, no. 6 (2009): 341–57.
6. The term *opioid use disorder* has been used following *The Diagnostic and Statistical Manual of Mental Disorders*, and the point is to avoid moralizing language (like "abuse") while also avoiding the analytical shortcomings of distinguishing opioid use as "medical" versus "nonmedical," given how these lines can blur in the context of prescription opioid use. For more on talking about substance use: Colleen Walsh, "Revising the Language of Addiction," *Harvard Gazette*, August 28, 2017, www.news.harvard.edu/gazette/story/2017/08/revising-the-language-of-addiction/. For more on overprescription in West Virginia: Eric Eyre, "Drug Firms Shipped 20.8M Pain Pills to WV Town with 2,900 People," *Charleston [WV] Gazette-Mail*, January 29, 2018, https://www.wvgazettemail.com/news/health/drug-firms-shipped-m-pain-pills-to-wv-town-with/article_ef04190c-1763-5a0c-a77a-7da0ff06455b.html.
7. "Prescription Painkiller Overdoses at Epidemic Levels," Centers for Disease Control and Prevention Newsroom, US Department of Health and Human Services, November 1, 2011, www.cdc.gov/media/releases/2011/p1101_flu_pain_killer_overdose.html.
8. This data has been published in Anna Lembke, *Drug Dealer, MD* (Baltimore: Johns Hopkins University Press, 2016). This time period is inclusive of the date when Chris

experienced the loss of his brother. However, more recent data can be found here: Puja Seth et al., "Overdose Deaths Involving Opioids, Cocaine, and Psychostimulants—United States, 2015–2016" *MMWR Morbidity and Mortality Weekly Report* 67 (2018): 349–58.

9. Individual states and people have fought to cultivate cannabis, despite federal insistence that the plant be subject to the same controls as marijuana, per the Controlled Substances Act of 1970. See: Renée Johnson, "Hemp as an Agricultural Commodity," Congressional Research Service Report, June 22, 2018, 18–19, https://fas.org/sgp/crs/misc/RL32725.pdf.

10. See note 3 above.

11. I am making a similar argument to the one that Michael Pollan made about the rise of "Supermarket Pastoral," though I'm not necessarily suggesting that producers and people in advertising are evoking nature to dupe consumers (*The Omnivore's Dilemma: A Natural History of Four Meals* [New York: Penguin Books, 2006], 134–84).

12. Raymond Williams, *Keywords: A Vocabulary of Culture and Society* (New York: Oxford University Press, 1983), 219–24.

13. It has been argued that "prescription opioid (PO) misuse represents a major health risk for many service members and veterans" (Andrew Golub and Alex S. Bennett, "Prescription Opioid Initiation, Correlates, and Consequences among a Sample of OEF/OIF Military Personnel," *Substance Use and Misuse* 48, no. 10 [2013]: 811–20). See also: K. H. Seal et al., "Association of Mental Health Disorders with Prescription Opioids and High-Risk Opioid Use in US Veterans of Iraq and Afghanistan," *JAMA*, 307, no. 9 (2012): 940–47; Geetanjoli Banerjee et al., "Non-medical Use of Prescription Opioids Is Associated with Heroin Initiation among US Veterans: A Prospective Cohort Study," *Addiction* 111, no. 11 (2016): 2021–31.

14. "In 2016, West Virginia had the highest rate of opioid-related overdose deaths in the United States—a rate of 43.4 deaths per 100,000—and up from a low 1.8 deaths per 100,000 in 1999. The number of overdose deaths peaked at 733 deaths in 2016 with the majority of deaths attributed to synthetic opioids and heroin. Since 2010, deaths related to synthetic opioid deaths quadrupled from 102 to 435 deaths and deaths related to heroin rose from 28 to 235 deaths" (National Institute on Drug Abuse, "West Virginia Opioid Summary," last updated March 2019, https://www.drugabuse.gov/drugs-abuse/opioids/opioid-summaries-by-state/west-virginia-opioid-summary).

15. Jim Axelrod and Ashley Velie, "West Virginia AG's Past Work with Drug Companies Questioned," CBS News, June 2, 2016, https://www.cbsnews.com/news/questions-raised-about-west-virginia-attorney-generals-past-with-drug-companies/.

16. Alexandra Field, Meridith Edwards, and Catherine Shoichet, "West Virginia Chemical Spill Shines Spotlight on Loose Regulation," CNN, January 13, 2014, https://www.cnn.com/2014/01/13/us/west-virigina-chemical-contamination/.

17. See note 3 above and Johnson, "Hemp as an Agricultural Commodity."

18. Philippe Pignarre and Isabelle Stengers, "Infernal Alternatives," in *Capitalist Sorcery: Breaking the Spell*, translated and edited by Andrew Goffey (New York: Palgrave Macmillan, 2011), 23–30. These concerns are written about in relation to the US pharmaceutical industry and lobby, and Joseph Dumit has built on Pignarre's and Stengers's ideas in his work on the pharmaceutical industry as well. For more see, Joseph Dumit, "The Infernal Alternatives of Corporate Pharmaceutical Research: Abandoning Psychiatry," *Medical Anthropology* 37, no. 1 (2018): 59–74.

19. Pignarre and Stengers, "Infernal Alternatives"; Dumit, "The Infernal Alternatives of Corporate Pharmaceutical Research."

20. Pignarre and Stengers have illustrated this point beautifully: "We now find these alternatives everywhere. To adapt, to 'reform' the welfare state has become an ardent obligation. Sacrifices are necessary otherwise the financing of retirement will no longer

be assured. Or social security payments will become a bottomless pit! *Accepting* has become an imperative. Europe has to *accept* GM foods, or it will lose its competitive edge in the global marketplace, and its researchers will disappear down the brain-drain! We must accept the need to keep illegal immigrants out by every means available—let's not be squeamish or there will be a social catastrophe, the collapse of our systems of social security, the rise of the extreme right!" ("Infernal Alternatives," 24).

21. These risks have been reported to me by other hemp farmers and included in Commissioner of Agriculture and Consumer Services, *Annual Report on the Status and Progress of the Industrial Hemp Research Program*, Virginia Department of Agriculture and Consumer Services, December 2018, https://rga.lis.virginia.gov/Published/2018 /RD563/PDF.

22. On the "sublime": Immanuel Kant, *Observations on the Feeling of the Beautiful and Sublime* (Berkeley, CA: University of California Press, 2004 [1764]); Immanuel Kant, *Critique of Judgement* (Oxford: Oxford University Press, 2009 [1790]). On agriculture and aesthetics: Pauline von Bonsdorff, "Agriculture, Aesthetic Appreciation and the Worlds of Nature," *Contemporary Aesthetics* 3 (2005): n.p.

23. For more information on this pending regulation, see "Notice of an Amendment to an Emergency Rule," West Virginia Secretary of State, September 12, 2019, http://apps .sos.wv.gov/adlaw/csr/readfile.aspx.

24. Wendell Berry, "The Body and the Earth," in *The Unsettling of America* (Berkeley, CA: Counterpoint Press, 2015), 143.

25. Dipesh Chakrabarty's notion of historical "contingency" might be helpful here ("The Climate of History: Four Theses," *Critical Inquiry* 35, no. 2 [2009]: 197–222).

26. For more on the environmental and health impacts of tobacco, see Thomas E. Novotny et al., "The Environmental and Health Impacts of Tobacco Agriculture, Cigarette Manufacture and Consumption," *Bulletin of the World Health Organization* 93 (2015): 877–80, https://www.who.int/bulletin/volumes/93/12/15-152744/en/.

27. Novotny et al., "The Environmental and Health Impacts of Tobacco Agriculture, Cigarette Manufacture and Consumption."

28. Natacha Lecours et al., "Environmental Health Impacts of Tobacco Farming: A Review of the Literature," *Tobacco Control* 21 (2012): 191–96. For more on this topic, see: T. E. Novotny and E. Slaughter, "Tobacco Product Waste: An Environmental Approach to Reduce Tobacco Consumption," *Current Environmental Health Reports* 1 (2014): 208.

29. This is something that writer Michael Pollan has described extensively in his book *The Omnivore's Dilemma: A Natural History of Four Meals* (New York: Penguin Books, 2006).

30. See Robert Proctor, *Agnotology: The Making and Unmaking of Ignorance* (Stanford, CA: Stanford University Press, 2008), 1–20.

31. Proctor, *Agnotology*, 1–20.

32. Jerome Cherney and Ernest Small have argued that these benefits might be exaggerated. See Jerome H. Cherney and Ernest Small, "Industrial Hemp in North America: Production, Politics and Potential," *Agronomy* 6, no. 4 (2016): 58.

33. "Crop Rotations," Rodale Institute, accessed September 27, 2019, https:// rodaleinstitute.org/why-organic/organic-farming-practices/crop-rotations/.

CHAPTER 16

Pain Is One Dance Partner: *Move* with It

Anne Lloyd Willett

INTRODUCTION

My water broke on Christmas morning, five weeks before my due date. It was my first pregnancy, and I was both overjoyed and uncertain about stepping into this unknown world of motherhood. Despite my nausea, I relished in my pregnancy. There was nothing imaginable to the feeling of new life inside me. I rubbed my tummy often, played Mozart for my little guy, and spoke to him all the time. In meetings at work, I felt a giggle on the edge of my lips knowing that I had snuck someone else into the meeting, someone who was privy to the confidential information being shared. I felt very connected, and I wasn't nervous about the early delivery. Somehow, I knew life was unfolding perfectly. And I suppose, in a way, it was.

My son Jackson was home after two days in the hospital, and he grew remarkably, bumping up to the top of the charts in weight and height. I recall so many precious moments of holding my dear son, staring in awe and watching him wiggle his body and stare intently back at me. I began a journal—*Letters from the Heart of Mom*—where I wrote personal notes to him telling him about his beauty, his life, my love, and how it was all playing out through his childhood and teenage years. There was nothing that could capture the unbelievable love I felt for this child.

Exactly twenty-one and half years after my water broke that Christmas morning, my younger son awakened me in the middle of the night. He had been spending the night with his father. He gently nudged me and gave me a kiss. Startled, I knew immediately something terrible had happened. Jackson had passed away.

We had all gone bowling just a few hours before—my former husband, our two sons, Jackson's roommate, and myself. It was a celebration. Even though he rarely partook in the sport, Jackson won all the games. There were smiles. There was also an elephant in the room. Jackson had been prescribed an opioid following a knee injury he incurred at college, ultimately leading to his death.

Just a year after my son passed away, my other son had to have an emergency appendectomy while in college in New York. When you've already lost a child, the *mother bear* comes out tenfold. My son had one of the doctors from Mount Sinai Beth Israel call to give me an overview of the procedure they planned. I told the doctor about his older brother being prescribed an opioid for an injury that had led him down a path of destruction and demise and that I did not want any such drugs prescribed following the appendectomy. The doctor seemed understanding, saying he is very aware of the prevailing opioid epidemic. The next day, my son communicated with me through FaceTime and showed me his prescription for Percocet. My son, who was born wise and has grown even wiser through the death of his brother, said, "Mom, our medical world is a mess." He went on to share that he didn't experience pain, except for some slight discomfort from where the intravenous injection had been, and that he didn't even need the Tylenol they also recommended. Three of his friends were with him when he received the prescription; two of them cautioned against it while one of them encouraged him to take it since the doctor had prescribed it. My son told me he realized his friends represented the general population of young people, that some are awake to the dangers while others are naive and thinking that what the doctor says is always best. He also said that he could imagine kids in his university who would offer good money to buy the pills or, even worse, steal them.

As a mother, I have been fully exposed to a crisis that permeates our society, and I am *awake* to it all!

Jackson's death was the beginning of a long, arduous journey through mourning, letting go of how I thought life would be, and moving in new directions. There came a moment when I sat on the floor of my living room dividing my son's ashes, which would be scattered in significant places. I was numb and raw, and when I touched what was left of my son's body, I knew that my work was being called to a higher level. I did not want to take on the opioid crisis. It is a dark subject that requires understanding the pharmaceutical companies that use lavish meals and other perks to convince doctors to promote their highly addictive drugs, the government officials and lobbyists who have conflicts of interest with Big Pharma, the pharmaceutical distributors that pump massive quantities of opioids to pill mills, and the insurance companies and pharmacists who are caught in the middle of it all. But understanding the opioid epidemic also requires an understanding of pain and the ways that people deal with it.

The body is the vessel that houses the unique soul. It speaks to us often, wanting us to listen and to *hear*. Pain is something to be with. It is one messenger. Instead of quickly shooting the messenger with pills or unnecessary surgeries, the key is to *listen*. The pain is what we must dance with and allow us to move along our path. It is through body and movement that we are confronted to become awake and aware. It is through body and movement that we become able to tune into our path and better align with our soul's mission in some way. The pain that I feel in my body as a result of the death of my son awakens me to *move* in order to develop a better understanding of what is promoting our pain, how the body is speaking to us, and the power of *movement* as we *dance our own dance*.

As a movement therapist and well-being coach, my work facilitates connections between mind, body, and spirit and brings people to a new awareness of their bodies, their pain, and their journeys. My son's death has brought my work to a new level. This essay empowers people to look at pain differently and to move from pain management focused on anesthetics (often with harm) toward a more kinesthetic and aesthetic experience of it.

WHY SO MUCH PAIN?

> These pains you feel are messengers. Listen to them.
>
> —Rumi

I have over thirty-five years of experience in counseling, coaching, nutrition, wellness, and teaching movement. As a counselor in my early days, I saw people experiencing deep emotional pain. As a teacher of movement, I see many encountering physical pain. Through my work then primarily as a counselor and my work now that focuses more on movement and the body, I have come to believe that there is no difference in these pains. The body houses the spirit. If there is pain in spirit, there is pain in body and vice versa. It is all connected. So why is pain something we hear so much about? More than ever, people are experiencing back pain as well as deep emotional pain. At the same time, pain is very unique and personal, and there is no panacea. The pain of losing my son seemed tenfold to those near me. They couldn't fathom such a pain. It was their worst nightmare; for me, it was simply part of my life. It entered my life as a pain for a reason, something for *me* to understand and to *move* with and through.

Merriam-Webster defines *pain* as "usually localized physical suffering associated with bodily disorder (such as disease or an injury) . . . a basic bodily sensation induced by a noxious stimulus received by naked nerve endings, characterized by physical discomfort (such as pricking, throbbing, or aching) and typically leading to evasive action," or "acute mental or emotional distress or suffering."

Further definition is required for the word *evasive* or *evade*, which means "to slip away; to take refuge in escape or avoidance."

Pain is real. Though it is not something we want to *slip away* from. It is something to be with, to *dance* with on some level, something that we can learn from and move from. It is part of our story. No one is free from it, and pain can awaken us in some way.

Pain is very complicated. It can vary from nerve pain, joint pain, or emotional pain. It can differ widely in intensity, frequency, and timing of onset. There are doctors, scientists, and others who research it, and no one can completely grasp the complexity. It has been studied through the lens of pain and brain connection. It has been observed through placebo studies that show pain can be reduced with no known medication. It has been puzzling with phantom pain occurrences, where pain remains constant even after a limb is removed. There are many who undergo back or hip surgery believed to eliminate the problem, and yet, they remain in pain. Pain is a mystery and cannot be completely understood.

Pain as we know it today is a construct we have created. It has become ingrained in our lives as part of our busy, stressful patterns, sedentary lifestyles, fear-inducing media, and medical world. Stress does not connote something bad. It can be *eustress*, as Hans Selye first described, a positive type of stress. Regardless, any type of stress creates a bodily response. Our adrenaline, cortisol, and norepinephrine get fired. Our bodies don't know whether they are running from a lion, from a pile of emails, or from an overzealous to-do list. More than ever, we are creating our own stress, and it is chronic. We have no boundaries between our phones, computers, and phone watches. We embrace our phones as if they are another limb, hunkered forward looking down at them as we move on the streets, in the elevators, or even in our cars. We drive fast, honk more, and rush about our busy daily lives. Amidst the hum of stress, our lifestyles promote stillness in the body. We breathe poorly as we hold the stress in our bodies. We sit in cars and buses. We sit at desks, in chairs. Or we bring our desks to standing where we still remain in a holding pattern, just a different one. We run to

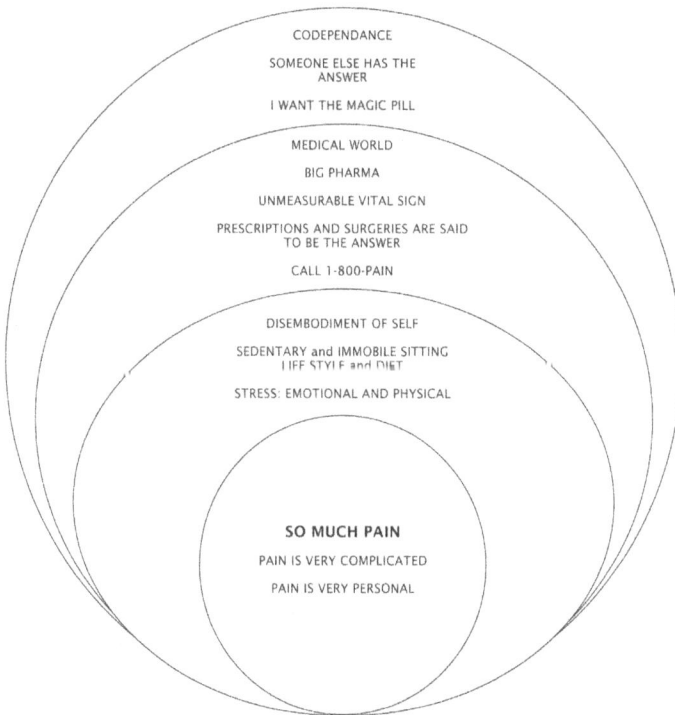

CODEPENDANCE

SOMEONE ELSE HAS THE
ANSWER

I WANT THE MAGIC PILL

MEDICAL WORLD

BIG PHARMA

UNMEASURABLE VITAL SIGN

PRESCRIPTIONS AND SURGERIES ARE SAID
TO BE THE ANSWER

CALL 1-800-PAIN

DISEMBODIMENT OF SELF

SEDENTARY and IMMOBILE SITTING
LIFE STYLE and DIET

STRESS: EMOTIONAL AND PHYSICAL

SO MUCH PAIN

PAIN IS VERY COMPLICATED

PAIN IS VERY PERSONAL

Fig. 17.1. Complexity of pain.

the gym for a hard workout, then back to our sitting we go. We have little reason to get down on the floor to fully use our hip or knee joints. We rarely spiral our bodies. Even our car cameras take the place of us circling our torsos back to look over our shoulder. Compounding it all, we tune into media every chance we get through papers, articles, television, and internet surfing to learn more about the broken world we live in. There seem to be more shootings, more suicides, more political chaos than ever before.

The construct of pain has been further exacerbated by the medical world. Beginning in the late 1990s and early 2000s, pain became a vital sign for medical practitioners—the fifth vital sign joining heart rate, blood pressure, respiratory rate, and temperature.[1] Pain cannot be objectively measured as the other vital signs can, and I believe pain has been introduced as something that is *suggested* on some level. Also, it has become something that *needs* to be addressed in ways that are not necessarily sound practices or beneficial in the long run. It carries some urgency with it when doctors and even some hospitals are evaluated on how well they quell their patients' pain.

I hear many people talk about getting hip or knee replacements, noting doctors' recommendations—"It is what you do when you get older"—as if it is a matter of fact. What they don't realize is that it is not a replacement; it is a prosthetic. It is artificial. Over time, it will wear out, and the surgery taxes the body, from the anesthesia to the disruption of fascia, the body's connective tissue *web* that connects the body from head to toe. Are the surgeries and the pills that accompany them absolutely necessary? And what about all the medical tests from MRIs to yearly screenings that instill fear and promote what may be unnecessary procedures? Most of us have some abnormalities in our bodies that we will die *with* and not from. A doctor shared with me that he often sees spinal imperfections when evaluating his patients for cancer. Since they are not complaining of back pain and his primary focus is on their cancer, he does not point out the disk issues. If the patient did know of the blemish, would it lead to a pain that is *suggested* on some level or, more radically, lead to a demand for surgery (and, of course, accompanying pills) to fix the imperfection?

A medical world that focuses on surgeries, procedures, and prescription drugs often leads to what I call *anesthesia kinesthesia*, or the masking of our own body awareness and movement through some sort of numbing effect. Are surgeries and procedures and pills truly saving lives in all cases, or, in some cases, are they simply instilling fear while diverting us from the message our bodies are sending us? I have worked with many clients who are very afraid. They are afraid of pain, afraid of moving. Fear exacerbates the situation by dialing up the cortisol levels, taking us away from rational thought to a mode of fight or flight. People go to their doctors in fear. They make decisions about their bodies based on fear. It is a perfect stage set for pharmaceutical companies to swoop in and rescue you from your pain with their highly addictive drugs that can wreak havoc on the body ecosystem.

A pharmacist told me that one in three people take at least one (and most take more than one) prescription drug. If this is true or even close to true, what does that say? There are drugs that can help in some way. Drugs may stabilize a condition, though they don't get to the root cause or underlying problem. There are many drugs that create more harm than good. Does drug research always include the scientific method? Who is backing the studies that may be scanty ones at best, perhaps with conflicts of interest? What are these drugs doing to our bodies, to our health?

When you watch the nightly news, you will see that almost three-quarters of the commercials are for drugs and many of them are for drugs to counter the side effects or inadequacy of the other drugs. More drugs to help with the drugs. The advertising depicts a happy scenario in which the individual is smiling with joy, while the audio gives all the side effects that often include death. Many of us are visual learners and, therefore, we may not even *hear* what is being described as dangerous and even fatal side effects. Instead, what is salient in the commercial is the smiling face depicting delight.

I often think that, if people read every single word of the fine print about the side effects, they would not take the drug. So many questions can be raised when you study the contraindications. Why would an antidepressant have a side effect of suicidal thoughts? And why would someone take an anti-inflammatory without exploring why the inflammation is there in the first place? Are these drugs leading to a permeating of our digestive tract somewhere along the way, allowing unwanted bacteria into the rest of the body and breaking down a *wall* we do want? Are these drugs wreaking havoc on our bodies ultimately creating more *pain*?

The drug model supports the common thought that there is something *out there* that can *fix me* and make me feel happy. At the same time, part of this perfect storm swirling in the escalation of pain is the disempowered individual disconnected from self and looking to someone or something else to fix them. We depend on doctors and pharmacists as we run to them to take us out of our misery. In many cases, we have lost personal responsibility for our own health and well-being and have placed the onus on someone outside us to take us out of our pain. Yet so much of the answer lies within. Hippocrates is credited with saying, "The natural healing force within each of us is the greatest force in getting well." It points to the ability we have to assist in our own healing. Does our pain call for a shift in our life in some way? Is it giving us a clue? Is there something we can do differently as we move forward in the journey? Is there a new pattern of living, a new practice we can embrace—whether it's eliminating toxic people; altering the manner in which we move; *turning off* for a while whether it be turning off the news or electronics; changing jobs; drinking less alcohol; eating healthier; changing up daily repetitive motion; embracing a more active life in our everyday living; or taking more time to relax and breathe? Is the pain urging us to stop running from something and instead to pause, ponder, and *be with* what is in our lives? To breathe and make a life course correction? Is pain a part of our journey and something that we are to learn and grow from in some way? Rather than running to the outside for answers, pause. The answer in part lies within, often right there in front of us. In the process of codependence with our doctors, we miss out on the role we play in the choreography of our own lives.

Pain is part of our mainstream consciousness. We see legal advertising written on buses, "Call 1-800-PAIN." We read about it every day, we obsess over it, and our medical and pharmaceutical systems have brought it to the forefront of our lives. At the same time, our bodies are full of stress, stillness, and fear. We focus mostly on our symptom suppression and dis-ease management. Pain as we know it today is something we created; it is also a construct we can undo. We can begin to look at our patterns of living and see pain as a messenger, as one dance partner in this journey we call life.

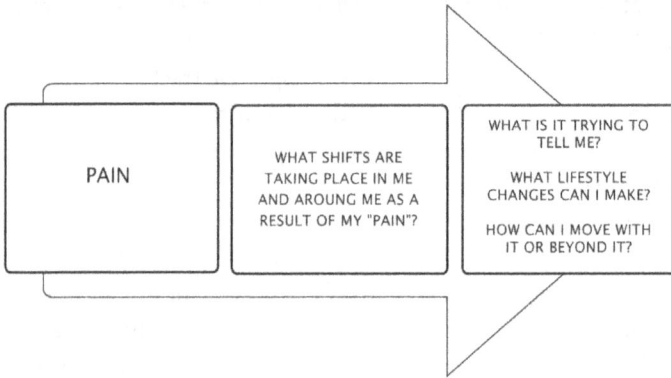

Fig. 17.2. Viewing pain as a messenger.

MOVING BEYOND THE BROKEN MODEL

You never change things by fighting the existing reality. To change something, build a new model that makes the existing model obsolete.

—Buckminster Fuller

Sometimes we might want to tell ourselves to skip taking an aspirin or calling the doctor in the morning. Our medical model is broken. By broken, I mean it is not sustainable and does not always comprise the best and most sound practices for the greater good. Many are in pain. More than ever, people are searching for an answer most often outside of themselves, and unfortunately, they are relying on medical models that need fixing. Doctors are practicing. They are *practitioners* in a world where their curriculum barely includes nutrition, a foundation for health. They are courted by Big Pharma in many ways, an industry that has its own agenda. Doctors often operate within a mode of fear because they are easily sued and work within a broken health insurance model. They don't necessarily have time nor take the time to read the fine print of all the scientific research. They do not always have the best answer.

What happened to prevention and wellness? Imagine waking up in the morning and asking yourself, What am I going to do today to take care of my body and my spirit? Rather than waking up anticipating some pain or experiencing fear of a disease, instead you note the wellness you are feeling on some level even if for a few moments. You are grateful for your health and your own self-care. You embrace joy knowing you take responsibility for your own health and you have practices in your daily life that will truly nourish you in some way. Or, if you are experiencing disease (dis-ease), you are well-informed and aware of your choices in how to best proceed to wellness for *you*, and you don't feel the need to react quickly in a fear-based response.

There is a shift to move beyond the broken model. A focus on quantum physics and integrated body systems has led to newly emerging or reemerging models of health care. These focus on prevention as well as treatment and include functional medicine, integrative medicine, energy medicine, epigenetics, stem cell therapy, nutritional sciences, microbiome health, fecal testing and transplants, fascial health, homeopathy, cranial sacral therapy, essential oils, tai chi, manual therapy, acupuncture, therapeutic touch, and movement therapies such as yoga and Pilates among others. Alternative approaches to wellness may have been squashed with the Flexner Report of 1910, but they are returning alongside the research affirming them as viable options and supplements to health care.

Western medicine has its value. There are pills and surgeries that are helpful to healing and that work for many. There are also *other* ways of looking at anatomy and the body. There is merit to approaching the body as an interconnected and dynamic set of systems where there is no one-size-fits-all when it comes to health and medicine. What works for you may not work for your neighbor, whether it be diet or cancer treatment. It isn't about Western medicine versus Eastern medicine or traditional versus alternative approaches. It is about *global medicine* and *global health*—approaching wellness with a larger perspective of the body and a focus on individualized care, understanding that each body is not an apparatus but a dynamic ecosystem comprised of human cells as well as trillions of other microbiota.

The body is breathing, flowing, moving, adapting, and changing every single moment; each one has unique genes, microbiome, lifestyle, and geography. We have choices when it comes to our bodies and health. At the same time, we must become active agents of our own health, focusing first on prevention and well-being. It begins with tuning into our distinctive bodies.

THE BODY IS THE BEAUTIFUL VESSEL

> O body swayed to music, O brightening glance,
> How can we know the dancer from the dance?
>
> —William Butler Yeats

Not long ago, I attended my first cadaver study. Lead by an amazingly knowledgeable doctor who has been leading cadaver studies for twenty-five years, it entailed five days of me dissecting the human body with scalpel in hand, going layer by layer from the skin through every organ in the body. I worked with three untreated cadavers, which means they had not undergone embalming though were preserved by refrigeration only, thereby allowing me to see more color and movement in the body. It changed my life profoundly—as a teacher of movement, as a life coach and counselor, as a human being—and I will forever be integrating the experience into my work. I had observed the body through live human surgeries, though this time, I explored and witnessed firsthand the depth, connections, and intricacies of the beautiful human body. I also saw the uniqueness of each body. No two are alike. And the body illustrations we see in the books don't come close to depicting the real thing. More than ever I believe there is no way any pharmaceutical company can create a drug that takes into account the individuality and complexity of the human body, all the glands and organs, as well as the processes (function, formation, and chemical) that take place in any given moment in the body. I believe that, most often, the drugs can do more harm than good. Not only do we see the harm listed in the potential side effects, we wait and wonder about the long-term effects that are rarely, if ever, studied.

The body is not a machine. Close your eyes and imagine blood, water, and other fluids running throughout every nook and cranny of your body, your heart beating, your organs gently swaying, new cells emerging, and old ones dying and being carried away. The body is vibrant, living, moving energy. I recently saw a documentary on the universe. One of the scientists noted that we really only understand 5 percent of all that exists beyond Earth. Being very immersed in learning about the body, reading historical and current medical information, and seeing how unique each body is in front of me when I work,

I conclude the same holds true for the body. The body is a miracle. We understand many things about it, yet it remains a mystery on some level. Moreover, each body is a unique separate ecosystem of human cells plus trillions of non-human cells. When it comes to caring for a body, what works for one person does not necessarily hold true for another. Each day, we get conflicting information about what is good or not good for us. It can be mind boggling. We are all in the same incubator trying to find our way through life. We are connected, yet we are unique with each body holding an individual vibrant entity and its own soul. The person who best understands the 5 percent of the body is the person whose body it is.

The body is the vessel, and it speaks to us all the time. It whispers, and eventually it screams. The key is to listen. I believe the body is the barometer that helps navigate us though our connected individual journeys. It tells us when we are hungry, when we need to poop. It even tells us when we need to leave the room or maybe make a change in our lives, big or small. When your body experiences pain or discomfort or tightness, what is it suggesting? My right hip is a gripping point for me. Whenever I am feeling stressed or upset or working too hard, I bring my thoughts to my right hip, and sure enough it is always holding tight. At one time, my tight hip led to knee pain. A doctor suggested knee surgery even though he claimed not to know what the cause might be. No surgery for me, and I now know to *check in* with my body and breathe, relax, or make a shift in some way. My right hip gives me a lot of information. I was child number five, a large baby with a small-frame mother. When I see baby photos of me, with my legs especially, my right one is turned in. I was likely gripping that right hip beginning in utero. Pulling on that right hip is a pattern I continued through adulthood. It wasn't until my thirties that I realized it was part of my story and a great messenger for me.

It is about *practicing bodyfulness*, which means tuning into your body and paying attention to its signals. This concept came to me when I was sitting in a talk on mindfulness. Significant is that I was *sitting* for about two hours; I noticed my hip started hurting, and I lost focus on the speaker's words. There has been so much talk on mindfulness, which is a bit of a misnomer. Being full of the mind can be confusing. When I was a counselor, I realized that talk therapy could only get one so far. Thoughts are something we create and repeat in our head as part of our story. Oftentimes, thoughts are something that don't even belong to us. They are something we bring into existence. In and out of the head they go. Rather than focus on the mind, I discovered the beauty of focusing on the body. The body houses the spirit. The soul speaks to us through the body. What is the body saying when we get a cramp, when we feel tired, when we have a headache, when we feel stiff, or when we have a stomachache? The answer can be we are breathing bad air, or we are working too much, sitting too much, or not moving in a healthy way. We might need to lose some weight or change our diet, or it could be that we need to rid ourselves of toxic people in our lives or make a job change.

Several years ago, I began studying fascia.[2] Fascia is said to be the body's largest organ that runs from head to toe and comprises elastin fibers and collagen fibers as well as a gelatinous ground substance, or extracellular matrix, that transports metabolic material throughout the body. It infuses every blood vessel, organ, nerve, muscle, and bone down to the cellular level. It is a continuum through the body capable of penetrating, dividing, supporting, responding, and connecting all parts of the body with respect to function and structure.

It is the system of all systems as it touches everything from our lymphatic system to our digestive system to our nervous system to our cells, a superhighway of sorts. Think of it as this beautifully woven fibrous web of gluey gel and cells circulating gas and cells and food and waste and information for our existence. It is viewed and researched in ways that include being a pathway for cancer transmission, a tool for the cleansing and renewal of the body, and a conduit for energy, and it has been shown to have a relationship to pain. Fascia plays a key factor in everything from understanding human emotion to training for Olympic sport competition.

At one time thought by doctors to be the mere stuffing, fascia is now taking a bigger role in our understanding of the body. The Fascia Research Congress (FRC) was first held at Harvard Medical School in 2007. The intention was to bring together the world's top fascial scientists to present their research to those of us in the field—those of us working with the client—whether it be a doctor, a massage therapist, or a movement specialist. FRC has been held in international cities every two to three years since then, and the research and knowledge has expanded significantly. When I first attended the Fascia Research Congress, I was in the presence of brilliant people from all over the world that included medical doctors, doctors of osteopathy, doctors of veterinary medicine, doctors of medicine in dentistry and dental surgery, PhDs, manual therapists, movement therapists, as well as scientists and researchers. Notably, there was not a hierarchy—no one smarter or better than the other. We comprised a group of individuals each dedicated to our work however that manifests for each of us—each of us sharing what we have learned in practice and research and each of us dedicated to the highest knowledge and the best practices. We all work with clients in some way to facilitate health and wellness of the body, the vessel. It was amazing to see that so many are moving beyond the old medical model. More than ever we understand the complexity and integration of the body and realize how fascia plays an important role.

For me, I focus on movement. By moving the body and in turn stimulating the fascia, we encourage flow in the body of integrated and self-regulating systems. Furthermore, I believe that it is fascia that holds the *story*. It is by listening to the body and discovering through movement that we gain valuable insight into one's life, the individual story, and learn how best to navigate through it all. It is not about reaching for a pill to mask what the body is trying to tell us.

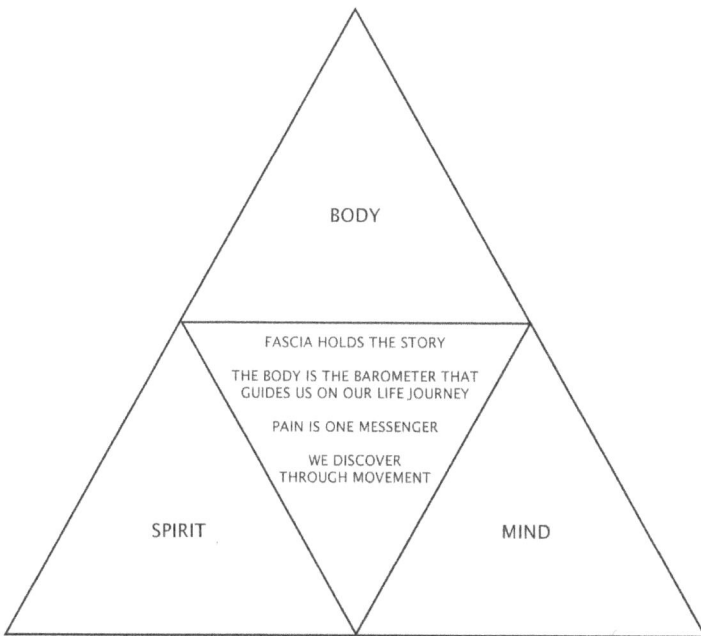

Fig. 17.3. It's all connected.

IT'S ALL ABOUT MOVEMENT

> Movement is life, and life is movement,
> and we get out of it what we put into it.
> —Ron Fletcher

We are training our fascial system all the time for better or worse. Think of it as a type of memory-foam mattress. Nonmovement, repetitive movement, surgeries, and pills that impact the ecosystem all affect our fascial system. Healthy fascia is vibrant and moving, whereas unhealthy fascia is matted, full of adhesions, and held. Imagine little puddles in the body getting muddied the longer they stand still. In one cadaver I worked with, there had been surgery around the right side of the body, there were lots of adhesions, and the hip had no mobility at all. Whether this beautiful soul had restricted movement due to the scarring or due to immobility, the story was the same—a body locked up with no hip movement and likely pain.

We are a sedentary lot, and we need to wake up to the impact it has on our lives and on our health. The key is to move. Unfortunately, too often the pain instills fear that brings about less movement that further induces more pain. My passion is the body, and my job is to facilitate people to move in new ways where they experience *aha moments* of connection as well as trust in their bodies. My clients range in age from twelve to ninety-eight. In my work, I draw from Pilates, yoga, dance, creative movement, breath therapy, stretch therapy, relaxation, and meditation.

When a client comes to my studio, I begin by asking about how the body is feeling. I then give them a movement sequence. The sequence takes their bodies in all directions and allows them to actually feel and connect to the body at that moment. I then ask again how the body is feeling. Interestingly, their answers from when they first come in and after they move may differ. Through the warm-up movement, they become aware that how they *thought* their bodies were and how they *actually* feel are different. They may feel tighter than imagined. They may feel less pain than they anticipated. From there, I spend the rest of the session moving them on equipment, at the barre, and on the floor focusing on areas of tightness or disconnect that they noticed as well as what I saw in the warm-up. Each session is about a *journey* of exploration—in body sensation as well as potential movement—moving in ways that they may not have moved before.

Some realize how immobile they are in daily life. For many, they discover they can move in ways they never imagined. If they have pain, they may notice their pain may be coming from some place other than where it is manifesting in the body, or even find that their pain awakens them to something else and leads them to make a change in some way. Through movement, they make discoveries about their lives. Movement often uncovers areas where they need to make course corrections, whether it be a different gait, a new mattress, or a new partner. For my athletes, they begin to understand the power of their bodies and how fascia plays a role. I facilitate my clients to embrace body-awareness and self-care and to build upon their strengths and abilities through the power of movement.

The work can be confronting. Though, most often, people come to me eager to *wake up* in their bodies through movement. Building on my over thirty-five years of experience in body and movement, I never stop learning. I only teach from a place of knowing and personal connection to each individual client. I am simply the facilitator. My clients are the ones who make it happen through self-awareness, discovery, and making changes in their movement and lives.

Clients leave the sessions with a good workout or stretch session. Ongoing sessions can lead to much more. Some examples of what I have seen through my years of teaching and facilitating clients to make discoveries through movement include:

- A young mother diagnosed with breast cancer who learned to breathe and move in new ways and to make changes in her life that are healthier for her
- A tennis athlete who learned to eliminate shoulder pain by moving in ways that involve his whole body rather than primarily upper body
- Multiple clients who have found relief from digestive tract issues through breath and spinal articulation
- A pregnant woman who learned to use breath and gentle stretching to facilitate ease in her delivery as well as ease in navigating through life as a young mother
- A man who discovered that his back pain reflected his overly stressful life and that he needed to *slow down*
- A man who incorporated better breathing into his life when sitting at his desk or when lifting weights
- A man who realized that his back pain began when his parents got divorced and wondered if he never dealt with his sadness
- A young athlete who learned to connect to his entire body for more powerful movement

- A woman who began to better trust her body and what it is saying and to make adjustments rather than running to the doctor for answers
- A man who learned to move differently and to make changes in his life to alleviate knee pain and avoid surgery
- A woman who learned to make adjustments in her life and her movement to end chronic hip pain and avoid surgery
- A woman who discovered how beautiful and strong she was before going on a hiking trip overseas
- A woman who came to understand that spending money to learn to take good care of her body was far more beneficial than spending money to treat her pains
- A man who noticed that his shoes were tight and that he rarely moved his feet or toes
- A young student who learned she needed to take better care of herself in the midst of her heavy academic and athletic workload
- A woman who found how to incorporate breath and wiggly movement during her job that involved sitting all day

My clients come to me for one-on-one sessions, and we move and breathe. I tell them the key for them is to always walk out of the session with something new, whether it be an insight into their daily movement or a new way of moving. One tool I give my clients early on to bring home with them is the *wiggle*. *Wiggle often* is what I suggest to my clients. It can be fast or slow, and it is something to do throughout the day. It is about moving and taking the body in different directions. The wiggle can involve smaller movements, those that are less conspicuous as you sit in an office meeting, or they can be large and involve getting up and down off the floor in order to move the hip and knee joints. It can last a few seconds or several minutes. It can include dancing in the living room or even in the car listening to good music while waiting for someone. It is fun to see how each person has their own version of the wiggle. The beauty of the wiggle is that it aligns with the body's desire to move. It encourages constant movement and brings awareness to practicing *bodyfulness*.

Underneath the wiggle is the *internal wiggle*, which is the breath. Most of us don't take the time to focus on our breath, and we grab just enough oxygen to get through our day, thereby operating off of a stale air system. It was a poignant moment when I was observing a surgery as part of my research and noticed how much the body parts moved as a result of the breath. There is so much movement in the breath alone. Through the movement of breath, the organs

Take a moment yourself to WIGGLE. If you are sitting, start by moving your toes, then your hips. Explore other movement of your fingers, wrists, shoulders, and ribcage. Bring it to standing and explore more. Look over your right shoulder then your left. Spiral your body further if you can. Lift your arms over your head. Get down on the floor and rise back up and repeat a few times. Play with your movement - making it big or small or contrived or silly and free-form. Turn on music if you want and make the wiggle a dance.

What do you notice when you take time to wiggle?

Fig. 17.4. The practice to *wiggle often*.

get a gentle massage and a wiggle. I know so many who have digestive issues, breathing issues, trouble relaxing, or difficulty sleeping. Breath therapy alone helps them in some way. Breath is movement and creates a lovely internal dance between the fascia and all the organs. The breath feeds us. The breath also calms.

It is all about movement and practicing *bodyfulness*. We have the ability to

Take a moment to imagine the movement of your breath. Begin by visualizing the diaphragm muscle (research if you don't know what it is). It is a beautiful jellyfish-like muscle below your breasts that pulls down on the inhale and slides up on the exhale, a movement which for many seems counterintuitive. As you breathe, notice how the diaphragm pulls down toward the dense liver on the right side, the stomach on the left side and other organs, and then on the exhale comes up to kiss the heart creating gentle movement among the organs as well as a gentle pull on the spine and a noticeable movement throughout your entire torso.

What do you notice when you take time to visualize your breath?

Fig. 17.5. The practice to focus on breath.

incorporate it into our everyday lives. Movement begins with a gentle internal wiggle of the organs and of the systems through focused breath. On top of the breath, an intentional wiggling of the body creates movement beyond the movement of the breath. Wiggling through breath and body can be done anytime and anywhere. It is empowering to breathe with intention and to wiggle the body often. The body, inside and out, wants to move throughout the day. It is part of our cleansing, renewal, and vitality. It is easy to wiggle—to breathe, to move, to dance. The work comes in making it a practice.

Practicing bodyfulness every day takes intention to:

- Take moments to breathe fully to allow the inside of the body to wiggle
- Step out of sedentary styles and wiggle the body often
- Take the time to periodically *check in* on the body throughout the day
- Listen to what the body might be saying, to what it needs
- Respond

SUMMARY

> When we try to pick out anything by itself,
> we find it hitched to everything else in the Universe.
> —John Muir

That day when I combed my hands through the ashes of my eldest son, what was once my handsome, sensitive, beautiful boy, I didn't cry. For several moments I was very still, caught up in the surrealism of it all. I look back on that moment in time that was dark and incomprehensible as being a pivotal one. Right then, I got a huge affirmation that the work I do is not only powerful but also what the world needs right now. I know that my son did not die in vain and that he is with me from here on out, teaching me and guiding me in my work. It is very challenging for me to work alongside my pain. I also know I have no choice. It is my dance. This is my life, and this is my gift. When a new educational book arrives or I sign up for another workshop that involves the body or movement, my younger son asks me if I'll ever know enough. No one can ever truly understand each beautiful and amazing body, though I will always have an insatiable appetite for learning and applying all I know to my work as a teacher of movement. I will never stop learning about the body and movement. I know that this is my calling and I am aligned with something beyond me.

Practice *bodyfulness*. Listen to your body, let it guide you. The spirit is always talking through the body. Wiggle often. It is through wiggling that our bodies stay *humming* and vibrant. Move more. We are created to move. It is through movement that we are confronted and become *awake*. It is through movement that we make discoveries, become aware of who we are and what we need to take care of ourselves. It is through movement that we get clues for how to traverse through the journey.

Pain is just one dance partner. It isn't the pain itself that dictates our quality of life; it's how we respond when it shows up. What is your discomfort or pain saying? *Move* with it in some way before fearfully running to the outside for answers. *Dance* with it, at least one dance, before quickly shooting the messenger with surgery or a pill.

NOTES

1.   David W. Baker, "History of the Joint Commission's Pain Standards: Lessons for Today's Prescription Opioid Epidemic," *JAMA* 317, no. 11 (2017): 1117–18, https:// jamanetwork.com/journals/jama/fullarticle/2606790; Baker, *The Joint Commission's Pain Standards: Origin and Evolution* (Oak Terrace, IL: The Joint Commission Division of Healthcare Quality Evaluation, 2017), https://www.jointcommission.org/assets/1/6 /Pain_Std_History_Web_Version_05122017.pdf; N. Levy, J. Sturgess, and P. Mills, " 'Pain as the Fifth Vital Sign' and Dependence on the Numerical Pain Scale Is Being Abandoned in the US: Why?," *British Journal of Anesthesia* 130, no. 3 (2018): 435–38, https://doi.org/10.1016/j.bja.2017.11.098; Teresa A. Rummans, M. Caroline Burton, and Nancy L. Dawson, "How Good Intentions Contributed to Bad Outcomes: The Opioid Crisis," *Mayo Clinic Proceedings* 93, no. 3 (2017): 344–50, https://www.mayoclinic proceedings.org/article/S0025-6196(17)30923-0/fulltext; Joan Stephenson, "Veterans' Pain a Vital Sign," *JAMA* 281, no. 11 (1999): 978, https://jamanetwork.com /journals/jama/fullarticle/189053.
2.   See FasciaResearchSociety.org, FasciaResearch.de, and FasciaResearchCongress.org. In addition, consult Jean-Claude Guimberteau and Colin Armstrong, *Architecture of Human Living Fascia: The Extracellular Matrix and Cells Revealed through Endoscopy* (Pencaitland, Scotland: Handspring Publishing, 2015); David Lesondak, *Fascia: What It Is and Why It Matters* (Pencaitland, Scotland: Handspring Publishing, 2018); Daniele-Claude Martin, *Living Biotensegrity: Interplay of Tension and Compression in the Body* (Munich: Kiener, 2016); Thomas W. Myers, *Anatomy Trains: Myofascial Meridians for Manual and Movement Therapists* (London: Churchill Livingston Elsevier, 2014); Graham Scarr, *Biotensegrity: The Structural Basis of Life* (Pencaitland, Scotland: Handspring Publishing, 2014); Carla Stecco, *Functional Atlas of the Human Fascial System* (London: Churchill Livingston Elsevier, 2015).

CHAPTER 17

Images of Opioid Addiction, Recovery, and Privilege in Mainstream Hip Hop

Paige Zalman

On September 7, 2018, twenty-six-year-old Malcom James McCormick, better known as hip-hop artist Mac Miller, died following a drug overdose involving fentanyl, cocaine, and ethanol.[1] According to his personal assistant, Miller, like many people addicted to opioids, "struggle[d] with sobriety and when he 'slip[ped]' he consume[d] [substances] in excess."[2] Miller's struggles with addiction and substance abuse were documented in his music, including his chillingly prophetic "Perfect Circle/God Speed" (2015), in which he observes: "They don't want me to OD and have to talk to my mother / Tell her they could have done more to help me / And she'd be crying saying that she'd do anything to have me back." The song's blues-inspired opening includes a chorus of background singers intermittently cooing "oohs," a slow-moving bass guitar riff, piano interjections, and electric guitar effects over a lazy drum groove that matches Miller's subdued flow—reminiscent, perhaps, of the lazy speech patterns of a person under the influence. The song's second half, where the above quote is heard, features a slow R&B-inspired groove with a soaring falsetto vocalist singing in the background to the accompaniment of high synthesizer chords, evoking the sounds of a church organ even as he refers to his out-of-control drug abuse ("these white lines" and "them pills that I'm popping") and the toxic masculinity that likely prevented him from seeking adequate help for his deadly addiction. While both the music and Mac Miller's voice are more animated in the song's second half, which ends with the rapper stating that he has finally "opened up his eyes" and bidding "good morning" to his listeners, the work is a heartbreaking, lasting reminder that this young man—a beloved artist, son, and friend—will never wake up again due to his addiction to opioids.

Mac Miller's losing battle with opioid addiction is exemplary of a larger phenomenon in the United States today, and unfortunately, any sort of lasting reprieve from such an addiction is a luxury that often only the privileged can afford. In this essay, I explore recent representations of opioid addiction that exist within mainstream hip hop, using case studies that are exemplary of larger trends in both the hip-hop community and the community of people struggling with opioid addiction across the United States. But rather than simply offering an analysis of the musical and lyrical techniques that these artists use, I wish to consider the ways that privilege—which exists as a consequence of one's social class, race and ethnicity, gender identity, sexuality, and other factors—figures into these artists' varied engagements with opioid addiction in their work. Using close readings of individual songs and biographical analysis, this essay argues that one's lack of privilege might compound the difficulties faced by opioid addicts in their attempts to seek help and receive treatment. To illustrate these issues of privilege, I draw upon Nadine Hubbs's idea of the "narrating class," which she defines as middle-class Americans that are "the analysts and experts, the language, representation, and knowledge specialists for the whole society. . . . whose identity and privilege depend precisely on its distinction from the working class."[3] Privilege plays a large role not only in determining one's ability to be honest about needing help but also in determining one's ability to find and receive adequate treatment for opioid addiction in the form of rehab or some other institutional assistance. Privilege can often also determine which addicts will have the means to maintain a long-term drug-free lifestyle once outside the safety of these institutions. The process of maintaining long-term abstinence from drugs is often referred to as "recovery" because it involves not only continued abstinence but also addressing one's "emotional, physical, and spiritual health."[4] As a consequence of privilege's significant role in shaping one's access to both rehab and long-term recovery, my consideration of the following case studies in mainstream hip hop will explore the artists' backgrounds and musical engagement with both drugs and addiction treatment in an effort to better understand the links between treatment availability and social factors such as race, class, and gender.

PRIVILEGE AND RECOVERY

Rehabilitation and treatment services are limited in the United States, with around 10 percent of all opioid-addicted patients receiving treatment of any kind.[5] But, as comedian-journalist John Oliver noted in a May 2018 segment of *Last Week Tonight*, media representations of rehab often paint rosy pictures of exotic venues, spa-like amenities, and insurance-funded relaxation.[6] Yet there appears to be little evidence that such facilities are effective, largely because they often do not offer evidence-based interventions and can lead to potential relapses.[7] For people occupying a lower socioeconomic status, treatment for drug addiction can be even more difficult to obtain. A 2018 *New York Times* article relays how some patients—particularly those "without money or private health insurance"—must travel long distances every day to wait for a dose of methadone that will stave off cravings for opiates and mitigate withdrawal symptoms, while wealthier middle- and upper-class people in recovery can utilize treatments such as buprenorphine or Suboxone, which they receive from a doctor and requires "no additional commute, no security check, no waiting, no line for the plastic cup [of methadone]."[8] This phenomenon is not only true in New York but appears to be true across the country. Though data about addiction and recovery is limited, a 2006 survey by the Substance Abuse and Mental Health Services Administration revealed that 92 percent of patients receiving buprenorphine were white, while a 2018 press release by the Centers for Disease Control and Prevention reported widespread "overdose deaths . . . in all categories of drugs examined for men and women, people ages 15 and older, all races and ethnicities, and across all levels of urbanization."[9] Additionally, in the year 2016 alone, it appears that the largest increase in overdose deaths occurred in the black community, leading the *New York Times* to suggest that "the common perception of the [opioid] epidemic as an almost entirely white problem rooted in overprescription of painkillers is no longer accurate."[10] Yet a bias toward white-centered narratives around the opioid crisis remains the norm. Unlike the crack cocaine epidemic of the 1980s and 1990s, when African American addicts were blamed and imprisoned for their addictions and mainstream news outlets painted images of gangs and inner-city crime, the opioid epidemic's impacts in middle-class white communities—the narrating class—has allowed for the description of drug addiction as a disease to take hold.[11] Calls for compassion and medical treatment have even led Presidents Obama and Trump to call opioid addiction a public health crisis.[12]

But, even with such changing narratives, ideas about addicted women, and especially addicted mothers, have hardly changed. Although stereotypes from the crack epidemic represented "crack babies," "crack moms," and even "crack whores" as a racialized problem, opiate-addicted infants of all races are being born at an alarming rate.[13] But while most addicted individuals are free to seek treatment for opioid addiction without legal repercussions, assuming that these individuals have the necessary financial means to do so, women could be prosecuted if they attempt to seek help for an addiction while pregnant. Yet if pregnant women do not seek treatment, it could lead to severe complications in the pregnancy, including the death of the mother or the unborn baby. This dilemma is even worse for poor women and black women, who, according to one study, are more likely than other women to be arrested for using while pregnant.[14]

In summary, only a small percentage of Americans that need treatment for opioid addiction actually receive it. For those that do find treatment, studies show that race and class strongly influence whether one is able to go to an inpatient rehab facility and receive drug replacement therapies from a family doctor or if one must instead commute long hours and wait in line at a methadone clinic. Additionally, people of color struggling with opioid addiction are more likely to experience legal repercussions related to their drug use, while women could face prosecution for endangering the life of an unborn child.

HIP-HOP ARTISTS AND THE OPIOID CRISIS

Images of opioid addiction and recovery within mainstream hip hop allow one entry point into further understanding the inherent privilege of recovery. The genre itself, having emerged during the 1970s as a platform through which the alienated were able to have a voice, has been disparaged numerous times for its glamorization of crime, violence, and drug use (while the numerous possible positive attributes of hip hop are generally ignored).[15] However, hip hop has become one of the most popular genres both in the US and globally, helping to place hip hop in a unique position of influence over young people, one of the age demographics hit hardest by the opioid epidemic.[16] In recent years, hip hop has increasingly incorporated opioid use as thematic content, and, as a genre that now has artists and fans of all economic classes and races, hip hop's social inclusivity makes it an ideal genre with which to examine the impacts of the opioid crisis in music. Eminem, Lil Wayne, Nicki Minaj, and Macklemore all engage with opioid use or recovery in their music in varying ways, and I argue that the content of these musical portrayals is contingent on each artist's individual level of privilege as determined by their proximity to the narrating class. As such, it can be instructive to situate each of these artists within a broader sociocultural context so as to better understand how privilege might influence the ways that they engage with opioid use in their music.

Eminem, one of the best-selling musical artists of all time, is praised especially for his intricate rhyming lyrics and varied subject matter, which is sometimes humorous.[17] But his upbringing was traumatic; he describes pieces of it in his single "Cleanin' Out My Closet," chronicling his father's absence, his mother's prescription drug abuse, his family's frequent moves into government housing, and his experiences of child abuse. Though he embodies some qualities of privilege in the United States, such as being white and male (thereby placing him closer to the narrating class), Eminem's traumatic childhood and his experiences with poverty worked against him for a large portion of his life, contributing to his own struggles with opioid addiction, which he has documented candidly in his lyrics. After seeking help in 2008, Eminem has since frequently used his long-term recovery as inspiration for his music instead.

Unlike Eminem, Lil Wayne does not appear to have sought help for his speculated addiction, and he certainly has not attempted to rap about recovery, even if his music does demonstrate some negative aspects of drug abuse. At a further disadvantage than Eminem due to his own difficult childhood experiences with an absent father and poverty, compounded by being African American in a society that privileges whiteness, Wayne has also been arrested and jailed for possession of both drugs and firearms, while his contemporary Eminem merely received probation for his own weapons and assault convictions. As Michelle Alexander notes in *The New Jim Crow: Mass Incarceration in the Age of Colorblindness*, such racial biases are common in the US justice system, in which an African American man like Wayne is more likely than the white Eminem to experience legal issues related to drug possession and to receive such a harsh punishment for his offenses.[18] Additionally, Wayne's lack of racial privilege—even as a moneyed hip-hop artist—might hinder his abilities to seek help for his suspected addiction due to the increased stigma faced by addicts of color from both white society and from other African Americans.[19] As of September 2018, Wayne continued to glamorize opioid use in his music— his most recent album, *Tha Carter V*, explicitly refers to his appreciation for Percocet in the tracks "Problems" and "Mess," and he also claims he is "geekin' like Brittany" in the song "Demons," a reference to the actress Brittany Murphy who, in 2009, famously succumbed to a fatal mixture of pneumonia and the opioid hydrocodone, among other drugs.[20]

A life mixing hip hop and opioids can be even more difficult for female artists of color like Nicki Minaj. Hailed as "the most influential female rapper of all time," she is known for her fast, animated rapping style, wearing colorful wigs and clothing, and her numerous theatrical alter egos.[21] But these alter egos are not simply for show; she claims that she began to adopt these identities as a coping mechanism during her difficult childhood.[22] She was born in Trinidad but immigrated to the United States at age five.[23] Her father was abusive and addicted to drugs, and in one instance, he attempted to burn the family house down to kill Minaj's mother.[24] Her childhood is reminiscent of similar struggles with abuse faced by Eminem, and she is a person of color like Lil Wayne, but Minaj's privilege status is further compounded by her gender. Indeed, Minaj has been infamously outspoken about the hardships faced by black female artists and has received significant criticism for her stances.[25] For a member of a minority group already facing so much inequity, seeking help for an opioid addiction would likely only cause further damage to her already heavily criticized image. Though Minaj has never admitted to an addiction, podcast host Joe Budden has accused her of abusing pills because her ex-boyfriend and fellow rapper Meek Mill went public about his own struggles being addicted to Percocet when he and Minaj were still together.[26] Whether these rumors are true or merely an attempt to bring down a strong, outspoken, and empowered women is unclear, though Minaj's glamorization of substance abuse in her music is disquieting nonetheless.

Although she exists well outside the narrating class, Minaj's glamorization of opioid use in her music is a tactic that seemingly elevates her social status. She usually romanticizes using opioids by portraying them as another facet of the glamorous lifestyle she purports to lead, one that matches her glitzy wardrobe and grandiose personality. For instance, "Miami" (2018) seemingly depicts a recent visit to the Florida city, where she claims to have insider knowledge about where to find cheap recreational opioids and benzodiazepines, another addictive narcotic: "Just the other day I was out in Miami / Got the low-low on them Percs, low-low on them Xannies." Minaj then emphasizes her lavish lifestyle by bragging that she is "filthy rich" and further asserts herself as superior with a humorous reference to the powerful teen clique from the cult classic *Mean Girls* ("None of you bum bitches can sit with me and Gretchen"). Sonically, the track opens with an electronic, psychedelic ambiance before the beat drops and the first chorus begins. Below Minaj's rapping is a danceable drum groove coupled with undulating electronics and effects typical of her style. Ultimately, "Miami" is a party anthem significant because its casual depiction of opioid usage is symbolic of Minaj's prestige and status in the hip-hop world in spite of her exclusion from the narrating class.

While Minaj evokes opioid usage as a status symbol, Lil Wayne uses opioids as a coping mechanism—in lieu of psychiatric help, a privilege in itself—to mourn the deaths of his friends. In "Me and My Drank," released on his *Tha Carter after Tha Carter* (2008), he describes his love for lean, the opioid-infused cough syrup mixture, while simultaneously mourning the deaths of rappers Pimp C and DJ Screw, both of whom died from complications with abusing cough syrup with codeine. Despite the fact that the drug killed his friends, Wayne states, "I'mma do this for you" and continues to rap about how much he loves "[his] drank," professing adoration for his friends' murder weapon.[27] "Me and My Drank" features Wayne's signature rap style, which has a distinct drawling quality in that his words are somewhat slurred at times, exacerbated further by heavy Auto-Tune effects and giving the impression that the rapper is under the influence of his beloved drank even as he records the song. Though there are numerous healthy ways one might cope with death, people living outside the narrating class often face hardship or stigma pursuing grief counseling or other psychiatric help in addition to addiction treatment, which perhaps plays a part in Wayne's dangerous coping mechanisms.

Prior to his more recent album *Recovery* (2010), in which he raps about getting clean and overcoming his opioid addiction, Eminem described using drugs to cope with loss in the song "Déjà Vu" from his 2009 album *Relapse*. Over a rock drum pattern and strummed guitar riff, we hear an EMT reporting the condition of an overdosing patient—likely Eminem himself—who is unresponsive, pale, and diaphoretic, having aspirated on his own vomit. The speaker attempts to justify his addictions to Vicodin and alcohol in numerous ways, citing the death of his friend and fellow rapper Proof and his insomnia as contributing factors, and remarks that his drug and alcohol use are limited and under control. Despite these bargains, his biological and adopted daughters find him overdosed on the bathroom floor, a traumatic sight that Eminem himself had likely witnessed with his own mother, revealing addiction's vicious and intergenerational impacts. Though more recent songs like "Not Afraid" and "Going through Changes" portray a more hopeful Eminem that has overcome addiction, "Déjà Vu" demonstrates the lasting impact of childhood trauma and the ways that someone like Eminem, who grew up in poverty but is now a famous musician, is still affected by those childhood experiences and the lack of class privilege that he experienced as a child.

Lil Wayne's "I Feel Like Dying" (2007) is also brutally candid about the downside of drug abuse, though Wayne withholds significantly more than Eminem, whose closer proximity to the narrating class prevents him from facing as much stigma. Over an upbeat drum groove, the chorus of "I Feel Like Dying" is a sample of Karma's "Once": "Only once the drugs are done / do I feel like dying / I feel like dying." Wayne raps the verses, describing how drugs can cause these suicidal thoughts: "Jumping off of a mountain into a sea of codeine / I'm at the top of the top, but still I climb / . . . I feel like flying, then I feel like frying / Then—." The Karma sample then answers "I feel like dying" as the chorus returns. These lyrics are surely a reflection of Wayne's own experiences, whose frequent use of cough syrup and other drugs has been heavily publicized and whose numerous health problems have led to widespread speculation about the nature of his addiction.[28] But the song is surprisingly upbeat, a stark contrast to the sorrow expressed in the lyrics. Additionally, the only voice that sings "I feel like dying" is Karma's, not Wayne's, evidence that Wayne might not be able to acknowledge his problems. Perhaps he does not believe that he has a problem; more likely, perhaps the stigma of admitting addiction and seeking help would be unbearable. For instance, Miles White compares male rappers to African American prizefighters like Muhammad Ali and Jack Johnson, writing that, like boxing, "rap . . . is also an arena where black males perform ritualized aggression and metaphoric violence through language." He also points out that, as with black minstrel performers in the first half of the twentieth century, rappers adapted the derogatory "thug" image because there is demand for depictions of black men as dangerous and hypersexualized.[29] If Wayne were to admit that he needs help with an addiction, he would no longer fit into these boxes and would likely be ostracized from the hip-hop community. While Eminem can rap candidly about his addiction problems, Wayne's lack of privilege prevents him from the same kind of honesty.

Like Wayne, Nicki Minaj also appears to rely on opioids as a method for coping with life's difficulties in her song "Here I Am" (2010). The song features electronic effects, a slow tempo, and uncharacteristically serious subject matter that is emphasized by a recurring piano riff and Minaj's soaring singing voice underneath her spoken verses. Minaj wrote in a November 2010 Facebook post that she originally intended to title this song "Letter to the Media" because, in it, she laments the fact that certain critics "only see the worst in" her and admits that their criticisms hurt.[30] Her solution to that pain, however, is to numb herself by using the same opioids that she glamorizes in "Miami": "And I might pop a couple of them Perco-C's / Yeah, that'll make me transform to Hercules." Minaj's music suggests that Percocet helps her feel powerful, whether through social power as in "Miami" or the power to quiet negative feelings as in "Here I Am." In her drug use, her marginalized status as a woman of color outside of the narrating class is seemingly erased. Unfortunately, this facade likely keeps her from seeking help for her addiction problems. Like Wayne, Minaj as a black woman in hip hop faces significantly more stigma than white male artists like Eminem. She appears to be judged more harshly due to her lack of privilege and thereby would face more difficult consequences if she were to admit that she needed help.

MACKLEMORE: THE PRIVILEGED SPEAKS

Unlike the other three artists, Macklemore, a contentious figure in hip hop who grew up in a white middle-class family in Seattle, comes directly from the perspective of the narrating class. White fans love him, even anti-hip-hop parents, but he has faced pushback from many for trying too hard to appear "woke" by calling out white privilege while continuing to benefit exorbitantly from that same privilege he denounces in tracks like "White Privilege" (2005) and "White Privilege II" (2016).[31] He became famous for the classist hit "Thrift Shop" (2012), in which he brags about slumming and buying cheap used clothing, flaunting the cultural mobility that members of the narrating class often enjoy. Along with being skyrocketed to fame as a white artist and afforded musical opportunities that a black artist might not be, Macklemore has also benefitted from the privilege to both seek help for his addiction as well as to speak out about the opioid epidemic. Like his music that directly embraces his narrating class privilege, a subject on which he acknowledges he is not "the expert" but about which he hopes to "start a conversation," his music about recovery from addiction, too, capitalizes on the same privilege that afforded him his fame and success, while others without those privileges struggle with opioid addiction and often die.[32]

In an attempt to use his privilege to create political change, Macklemore blames powerful institutions for the opioid crisis in his music, pointing his finger specifically at the pharmaceutical industry, US Congress, and doctors who prescribe opioids without regard for how the drug may affect their patients. His single "Drug Dealer," featuring singer Ariana Deboo, was featured on a 2016 MTV documentary called *Prescription for Change: Ending America's Opioid Crisis*, during which President Obama and Macklemore sit down to discuss the opioid epidemic. Deboo's sung chorus proclaims that her "drug dealer was a doctor" who got drugs "from Big Pharma" and "tried to kill me for a dollar," while Macklemore's rapped verses contain incendiary comments such as referring to members of Congress as "murderers who will never face the judge." Much like Wayne's "I Feel Like Dying," Macklemore emphasizes the nature of the love-hate relationship an addict has with drugs in the third verse, stating that he is "best friends with the thing that's killing me." Yet the track ends on a hopeful note with the Serenity Prayer, which is frequently associated with recovery from drug addiction and often begins and ends twelve-step meetings.

Of my four case studies, Macklemore is the only artists to belong to the narrating class from birth, and it is clear that his privilege empowers him, more so than any of the others, to not only rap candidly about his own struggles with addiction but also to take it upon himself to incite change on a societal level.

CONCLUSION

Hip hop at its core was created as a music to empower the disempowered. It was born from a lifestyle involving drugs, guns, and gang violence, a lifestyle that is almost inescapable for thousands of Americans living in poverty either because it may seem like one of the only lucrative options or because it might be the only way that people can survive in those impoverished areas. But the genre also emphasizes a fake opulence centered around being the best, being wealthy, and being sexually desired—in the examples above, these ideas are demonstrated by Nicki Minaj's music most but are also very present in much of Lil Wayne's music. The creative ingenuity of these privilege-bearing artistic personas likely extends into these artists' own lives and lifestyles, undermining efforts toward developing a recovery lifestyle based upon transparency and vulnerability. But if hiding shameful secrets and difficult emotions through a glamorous facade has become second nature to many of these artists—if lying is the way they have learned to cope with life—an honest, long-term recovery will be even more difficult to attain.

This public performance of lavishness and poise might extend to the lives of hip hop's listeners, as reflected in Elaine Sheldon McMillion's documentary *Recovery Boys* (2018), which focuses on a recovery community in north-central West Virginia. During one particularly poignant moment, the group of recovering addicts in rehab drive to work at a nearby coal mine while listening to "Stuntin' " by rapper DecadeZ. Though the song is not about drug use, it explores the term *stunt*, which is slang for showing off, usually through expensive material possessions and wealth. Juxtaposed with the devastating circumstances in which the young men have found themselves and the heart-wrenching poverty of rural West Virginia one glimpses through the documentary, viewers can be sure that these boys are not in any position to "stunt" in this time in their lives, and they likely never have been. But for people in recovery, facades are dangerous, and soon after this scene, the group relapses and hides the truth until they are confronted by the directors of the rehab center.

Privilege is power in the opioid epidemic. Although privilege does not guarantee survival—take the opening example of Mac Miller's tragic death, for instance—seeking treatment and maintaining an honest, long-term recovery is much more attainable for those who have the financial means and social support to do so. We see this phenomenon clearly in hip hop: artists like Lil Wayne and Nicki Minaj refuse to admit that they need help despite heated speculation about their addictions, whereas Eminem has evolved from justifying drug use in his music to creating music about recovery. Macklemore, who has always experienced the privilege of the narrating class, is in a different category altogether. While he clearly tries to use his privilege in positive ways, his music nonetheless demonstrates the powerful advantage that his privilege has afforded him in overcoming opioid addiction, especially compared to the others. Ultimately, these case studies demonstrate the powerful impacts that race, gender, and class can have on one's ability to pursue opioid addiction treatment and lasting recovery and our continued need to consider these impacts as the opioid crisis worsens.

NOTES

1. Andrew Flanagan, "Mac Miller Died from Overdose Involving Fentanyl, Coroner Finds," *Music News*, NPR, November 5, 2018, https://www.npr.org/2018/11/05/664369522/mac-miller-died-from-overdose-involving-fentanyl.
2. Flanagan, "Mac Miller Died from Overdose Involving Fentanyl."
3. Nadine Hubbs, *Rednecks, Queers, and Country Music* (Berkeley: University of California Press, 2014), 37.
4. "Recovery Is Possible," Office of Addiction Services and Supports, https://www.oasas.ny.gov/recovery/recovery-possible.
5. Beth Macy, *Dopesick: Dealers, Doctors, and the Drug Company That Addicted America* (New York: Little, Brown, 2018), 243.
6. Florida is home to many rehab centers, likely due to the fact that the first big "pill mill" was also born in the state. See John Temple, *American Pain: How a Young Felon and His Ring of Doctors Unleashed America's Deadliest Drug Epidemic* (Guilford, CT: Lyons, 2015).
7. For more on evidence-based treatment of addiction, see Wim Van Den Brink and Christian Haasen, "Evidence-Based Treatment of Opioid-Dependent Patients," *The Canadian Journal of Psychiatry* 51, no. 10 (2006): 635–46; Heath B. McAnally, *Opioid Dependence: A Clinical and Epidemiologic Approach* (Cham, Switzerland: Springer, 2018); and Alan David Kaye, Nalini Vadivelu, and Richard D. Urman, eds., *Substance Abuse: Inpatient and Outpatient Management for Every Clinician* (New York: Springer, 2015). Even many evidence-based treatments are imperfect, as pharmaceuticals such as Suboxone and methadone, which are intended to stave off cravings, have the potential to be abused.
8. Jose A. Del Real, "Opioid Addiction Knows No Color, but Its Treatment Does," *New York Times*, January 12, 2018, https://www.nytimes.com/2018/01/12/nyregion/opioid-addiction-knows-no-color-but-its-treatment-does.html. Additionally, Macy has explored the difficulties of connecting people with addiction to care providers, whether it be psychological treatment or drug-replacement therapies like methadone or Suboxone (Macy, *Dopesick*, 269–96).
9. On buprenorphine, see Real, "Opioid Addiction Knows No Color," and Abby Goodnough, "When an Iowa Family Doctor Takes on the Opioid Epidemic," *New York Times*, June 23, 2018, https://www.nytimes.com/2018/06/23/health/opioid-addiction-suboxone-treatment.html. On overdose deaths, see "U.S. Drug Overdose Deaths Continue to Rise; Increase Fueled by Synthetic Opioids," Centers for Disease Control and Prevention,

press release, March 29, 2018, https://www.cdc.gov/media/releases/2018/p0329-drug
-overdose-deaths.html.

10. Josh Katz and Abby Goodnough, "The Opioid Crisis Is Getting Worse, Particularly for
    Black Americans," *New York Times*, December 22, 2017, https://www.nytimes.com
    /interactive/2017/12/22/upshot/opioid-deaths-are-spreading-rapidly-into-black
    -america.html.

11. Nick Glunt, "Empathy for Drug Addicts Growing—Local Experts Say Public Perception
    Is Changing Because Heroin, Painkiller Epidemic Is Affecting Every Facet of Society,
    Regardless of Race, Region," *Akron Beacon Journal*, April 30, 2016.

12. Glunt, "Empathy for Drug Addicts Growing"; Julie Hirschfeld Davis, "Trump Declares
    Opioid Crisis a 'Health Emergency' but Requests No Funds," *New York Times*, October
    26, 2017, https://www.nytimes.com/2017/10/26/us/politics/trump-opioid-crisis.html.

13. Jennifer Egan, "Children of the Opioid Epidemic," *New York Times Magazine*, May 9,
    2018, https://www.nytimes.com/2018/05/09/magazine/children-of-the-opioid
    -epidemic.html.

14. Egan, "Children of the Opioid Epidemic." See also: "Gazette Editorial: Opioid Scourge
    Felt by Newborns, Child Welfare, Soon in School," *Charleston [WV] Gazette-Mail*, June
    26, 2018; Macy, *Dopesick*, 189–231.

15. See, for instance, Monica Denise Griffin, "The Rap on Rap Music: The Social
    Construction of African-American Identity" (PhD diss., University of Virginia, 1998);
    Bakari Kitwana, *The Rap on Gangsta Rap: Who Run It? Gangsta Rap and Visions of Black
    Violence* (Chicago: Third World Press, 1995); Noah Berlatsky, ed., *Rap Music* (Farmington
    Hills, MI: Greenhaven, 2013); and Bryan J. McCann, "Contesting the Mark of
    Criminality: Race, Place, and the Prerogative of Violence in N.W.A.'s Straight Outta
    Compton," *Critical Studies in Media Communication* 29, no. 5 (2012): 378–79.

16. Jenna Payesko, "Boomers, Millennials Affected the Most by Opioid Epidemic," *MD
    Magazine*, November 28, 2017, https://www.mdmag.com/medical-news/boomers
    -millennials-affected-the-most-by-opioid-epidemic.

17. Paul Edwards, *How to Rap: The Art and Science of the Hip-Hop MC* (Chicago: Chicago
    Review Press, 2009).

18. Michelle Alexander, *The New Jim Crow: Incarceration in the Age of Colorblindness* (New
    York: New Press, 2012), 98–100.

19. "African American Mental Health," National Alliance on Mental Illness, last updated
    2019, https://www.nami.org/Find-Support/Diverse-Communities/African-Americans.

20. *Geeking* is a colloquial term that describes a user that is heavily intoxicated.

21. Jon Caramanica, "A Singular Influence," *New York Times*, March 30, 2012, https://www
    .nytimes.com/2012/04/01/arts/music/nicki-minaj-is-the-influential-leader-of-hip-hop
    .html; Jochan Embley, "From Nas to Drake, the Most Influential Hip Hop Artists of All
    Time," *Evening Standard*, June 29, 2018, https://www.standard.co.uk/go/london/music
    /the-most-influential-hip-hop-artists-of-all-time-a3863356.html.

22. Hermione Hoby, "Nicki Minaj: 'I Am Doing Everything the Boys Can—Plus More . . . ,'"
    The Guardian, November 27, 2010, https://www.theguardian.com/music/2010/nov/28
    /nicki-minaj-interview-hermione-hoby.

23. Minaj was an undocumented immigrant when she came to the US as a child and has
    been very outspoken against President Trump's strict immigration policies and his
    separation of immigrant children from their parents (Michael Rothman, "Rapper Nicki
    Minaj Shares Her Personal Story as a 5-Year-Old 'Illegal Immigrant,'" ABC News, June
    21, 2018, https://abcnews.go.com/GMA/Culture/rapper-nicki-minaj-shares-personal
    -story-year-illegal/story?id=56057816.

24. Hoby, "Nicki Minaj," *The Guardian*.

25. Sparking an infamous controversy with Miley Cyrus, Minaj tweeted in May 2015 that
    she was "tired" because "black women influence pop culture so much but are rarely

rewarded for it." For the original tweet, see Nicki Minaj (@nickiminaj), "I'm not always confident," Twitter, July 21, 2015, 3:14 p.m., https://twitter.com/nickiminaj/status /623617003153035264. For a detailed summary of the controversy, see Vanessa Grigoriadis, "The Passion of Nicki Minaj," *New York Times Magazine*, October 7, 2015, https://www.nytimes.com/2015/10/11/magazine/the-passion-of-nicki-minaj.html.

26. Diamond Alexis, "Joe Budden Accused Nicki Minaj of Drug Abuse, and Fans are Outraged," BET, July 5, 2018, https://www.bet.com/music/2018/07/05/joe-budden -nicki-minaj-drug-abuse.html. See also "Cardi B's Sister: Nicki Minaj is a Drug Addict!," MTO News, September 30, 2018, https://mtonews.com/cardi-bs-sister-nicki-minaj-is-a -drug-addict.

27. In addition to Pimp C and DJ Screw, another rapper whose death Wayne mourns in "Me and My Drank" is that of Big Moe, who also rapped about his love for purple drank. However, before Moe died in 2007, he wrote a song called "Leave Drank Alone," in which he stated that he was quitting using drank because of its role in the death of DJ Screw. At the end of this song, he raps that he is trying to "take it one day at a time," a phrase heard often in recovery circles.

28. Wayne has been hospitalized for seizures several times, and though he claims that the medical issues are due to epilepsy and exhaustion, many speculate that the condition is caused by his heavy drug usage because seizures can be an effect of opioid overdose (Daniel Summers, "The Cocktail That's Killing Lil Wayne," *Daily Beast*, June 18, 2016, https://www.thedailybeast.com/the-cocktail-thats-killing-lil-wayne). Wayne has previously lied about a preteen suicide attempt during which he shot himself, maintaining instead that he was just a stupid kid who did not realize that the gun would go off (Sha Be Allah, "Lil Wayne Admits When He Shot Himself It Was Really a Suicide Attempt on 'Tha Carter V,' " *Source*, October 3, 2018, http://thesource.com/2018/10/03 /listen-lil-wayne-admits-when-he-shot-himself-it-was-really-a-suicide-attempt-on-tha -carter-v/).

29. Miles White, *From Jim Crow to Jay-Z: Race, Rap, and the Performance of Masculinity* (Urbana: University of Illinois Press, 2011), 68.

30. Nicki Minaj, "Pink Friday Diaries: Here I Am is the 2nd song I recorded for the album," Facebook, November 16, 2010, https://www.facebook.com/nickiminaj/posts/1613965 67230254.

31. Audie Cornish, " 'This Song Is Uncomfortable': Macklemore and Jamila Woods on 'White Privilege,' " *All Things Considered*, NPR, January 29, 2016, https://www.npr .org/2016/01/29/464707970/-this-song-is-uncomfortable-macklemore-on-the -contradictions-of-white-privilege; Gene Demby, "I Guess We Gotta Talk about Macklemore's 'White Privilege' Song," *Code Switch*, NPR, January 29, 2016, https:// www.npr.org/sections/codeswitch/2016/01/29/464752853/i-guess-we-gotta-talk -about-macklemores-white-privilege-song.

32. Cornish, "This Song Is Uncomfortable."

CHAPTER 18

The Voices of Hope—A Recovery Community Choir: Redefining Self, Community, and Success

Natalie Shaffer

I. OUR SECRETS KEEP US SICK

"Fuck this orange juice! I'm going to get high." The rawness of the statement churned in my stomach. My eyes swelled with tears as I empathized with the pain and fear present under the surface of the words that came from recounting the difficulty of not being able to open a container of orange juice after the plastic ring broke on first attempt, a seemingly simplistic task. My inability to produce that level of understanding with addicted loved ones in my life provided stark contrast to the amount of space I could provide these strangers to be human. In fact, this speaker did not get high and called a mentor and friend instead. The support offered by peers in the circle as they spoke astounded me. As I sat observing an open Narcotics Anonymous meeting in a dark and stuffy basement of a local church, on what seemed like the hottest night of July yet, I felt compassion come over me, replace the anger, offer perspective.

Like most individuals I know in West Virginia, my life was touched by the disease of addiction, both in ways I could understand and am still coming to recognize. I was one of those people who never entertained the thought of staying in West Virginia past high school. I knew the accepted narrative around success in the Mountain State was, if you wanted to make something of yourself, you had to leave and do it fast before you got stuck. So I did. After graduating from West Virginia Wesleyan College, I spent years away from the lush forests and electric autumns of my home, away from friends, and away from the familiar. I found myself "forced" to return due the nonrenewal of a job contract and a mother freshly diagnosed with stage IV breast cancer. I returned viewing West Virginia as a necessary pit stop on the way to my next successful endeavor.

During those years away, roughly 2006 to 2011, the use and prescription of opioids increased in astronomical percentages. The resultant heroin usage, as it was simply cheaper to obtain on the street, became a commonplace conversation in my home state. A study conducted in February 2019 using data collected from the West Virginia University Medicine health care system found the hospitalization rate for opioid overdoses increased 13 percent on average each year in a similar fashion to the opioid overdose death rate for the state, 12 percent, between 2008 and 2016. During the same time, the percentage of patients with a repeat opioid overdose increased annually by 13 percent on average.[1] Drug overdose deaths more than doubled in the United States between 2000 and 2016, and since 2010, West Virginia has found itself at the center of the crisis with the highest opioid overdose death rate of 52.0 per 100,000, more than 250 percent higher than the national rate of 19.8 per 100,000 in the United States.[2] In 2019, more than 80 percent of the overdose deaths in West Virginia were attributed to opioids.[3]

I knew none of those statistics when I returned to Morgantown, West Virginia. After settling back in, I entered what would become a long-term relationship with a brilliant and charismatic athlete. A few years later, they sustained a back injury during a soccer match and were placed on high-dose opioid medication following their surgery. During this recovery their grandmother passed away, and they learned their team, and livelihood at the time, would not offer them a spot the following season due to the injury. Physical, emotional, and spiritual emptiness ushered in a new age of what I now can label as "active addiction" into our home. Eventually they came to identify as an addict, sought help, and oscillated between periods of being "in" and "out" of recovery. As I fought to finish a graduate degree, pay all our bills, and "make sure they were not using" (i.e., babysat another adult), resentment festered on both sides that could not be dissolved. I was irritable, unreasonable, and angry. They were all of those things too. At the advice of a friend, there I sat in an NA meeting, on an uncomfortable folding chair, listening to what other addicts do to get through the day and unlearning the story of what addiction looked like.

II. REPLACING EXISTING CULTURAL NARRATIVES

The cultural narrative I knew pertaining to addicts was that they were "bad" people who made the "wrong choice" of using and deserved what they got as a result. I knew from the personal experience of watching a disease take over and tear down another remarkable human being's life, remove their passion, and erase their connection to anything and anyone other than drugs that this narrative was not accurate. It was just easier. I knew from listening to the stories shared in various twelve-step meetings filled with dignity, authenticity, and courage that these were not "bad" people. In fact, most of the individuals I met had more self-awareness and genuine intention behind their actions than the "good" people I knew and interacted with on a regular basis. But these were all thoughts I struggled to reconcile in my personal life. My professional and academic life seemed as far removed from addiction as possible, a good arm's length, a safe distance. After all, I had experience putting distance between myself and things others viewed as shameful or unacceptable.

I was back in a graduate program at West Virginia University in March of 2017 and attempting to finish writing my uninspired thesis on violence in American opera and new second degree in choral conducting when I traveled to the American Choral Directors Association National Conference in Minneapolis, Minnesota, and had the pleasure of attending a session presented by Dr. Kristina MacMullen of the Ohio State University titled "A Voice of Reason: Social Justice, the Greater Good, and Why We Sing." She shared her experience identifying an issue of social injustice in her community, human trafficking, and the steps she took to generate a platform to educate and inspire others by creating a multimedia choral concert as part of a three-day summit hosted at the Ohio State University.[4] I knew this session would become the new focus of my thesis and, perhaps more importantly, that this was the work I wanted to do.

Serious injustice, broken families, and struggling communities are not new developments in West Virginia. An increase in political activism coupled with the prevalence of social media use keeps the discussion of social justice issues like addiction in the forefront of news cycles and everyday conversations about what someone saw on Facebook. While lawmakers and religious leaders suggest fragments of possible solutions, I find an innovative possibility emerging from the work of musicians, specifically conductors in social justice and community choirs. These choirs provide participants the opportunity to cross cultural boundaries, define collective and personal identity, process trauma, and influence their larger community. As Julia Balén observes, singing with this type of choir is more than a pastime; it is a meaningful form of "protest through celebration."[5] Gregory F. Barz holds a similar view, which expands on the opportunity choral music making provides to create and offer a counternarrative to the existing cultural story.[6] Both agree that without specifically identifying the current "master narrative," to use Balén's term, there is no chance of successfully constructing or presenting a new, and often more realistic, story that could bring about the change many hope to see in their communities.

At the same time I was finishing my thesis, I found myself offered the opportunity to take over as director of a homeless choir. The choir began earlier that year at the request of a local free medical clinic, Milan Puskar Health Right, in a conversation with my conducting advisor. Health Right was looking to expand activities at their local drop-in center, the Friendship House, as a means of promoting harm reduction and social engagement among their clients. I was involved from the beginning as an assistant and enjoyed attending weekly rehearsals with the group. After hearing about my change of thesis subject and passionate interest in social justice through choral music, my advisor suggested I take over their role as artistic director of the yet unnamed choir. As the group and I continued to work together, we began to trust one another. Over time, I learned their stories. As I listened, I came to realize addiction was at center of nearly every narrative. It became exceedingly clear that this issue of social justice, present in both my personal and professional life, would become the focus of my work in collaborative social justice through choral musicking. Musicking as defined by Christopher Small is to take part in any capacity in a musical performance, whether by performing, listening, rehearsing, practicing, providing material for performance, by dancing.[7]

West Virginia's associations with addiction and drug use are generally well known due to national media coverage and popular documentaries like Netflix's 2017 *Heroin(e)* and 2018's *Recovery Boys*. In West Virginia, the master narrative related to addiction was clearly positioned around the binaries of good and bad, of acceptable and unacceptable, and encased the whole issue with a sense of shame and secrecy. Sociologist and music educator Estelle Jorgensen's research examines the importance of considering the role of cultural institutions and societal norms in the creation of "right and wrong" and "good and bad" to assist in identifying the benefits of upholding structures that create and perpetuate social inequity.[8] In other words, and through a lens of critical theory, contemporary distinctions between "what is just" versus "what is evil" are often grossly influenced by the ruling institutions of society that commonly stand to benefit from the continuation of existing power structures in some manner. That master narrative, therefore, or the accepted truth behind it, of what is just and noble should be examined rather than complacently accepted. Understanding which actions belong in those categories is perhaps less important than comprehending the rationale behind the creation of the categories. The knowledge of who profits, and how, provides important understanding to those individuals creating strategic approaches to social justice and crafting counternarratives to existing cultural norms.

III. GETTING IN THE WORK, NOT IN THE WAY

The following is one of the most helpful quotes I came across while researching collaborative social justice: "The pursuit of social justice presupposes an interest in creating or fostering a more humane society." [9] The reminder that there are individuals who do not have an interest in working toward a more civilized society is both infuriating, at times, and an immensely helpful reminder. The "homeless" choir I have the pleasure of working with came to be known as the Voices of Hope Choir, a community choir for those experiencing homelessness, addiction, mental illness, and their allies. I assumed everyone would be on board with my elaborate plans of constructing and presenting a counternarrative concerning addiction and want to push full steam ahead. Many of the members are happy simply coming and singing once a week for an hour. That is the best they can do, and that is all they can afford to give of themselves. Their mental energy is conserved for meeting their tangible needs for the remainder of the day and not for the betterment of society. I can hardly find fault with that and would be blind to my own privilege to expect more.

Some of the members are social workers and healthcare providers from Health Right who come next door to participate with us. They spend their entire workday attempting to bring about a more humane existence for others. They, too, reserve the right to not want to march into a city council meeting every month and explain why refusing to install new benches out of fear that homeless people will start sleeping on them, or addicts will pass out on them, in a nice part of town is less than humane and then sing a song as proof of the inherent worth of each choir member. The work is hard and tiring, and not everyone signed up for that.

The second issue of particular merit as a person interested in "doing justice" in a truly helpful way is the problem of speaking for others. Linda Alcoff clearly articulates the belief that "both the study of and the advocacy for the oppressed must come to be done principally by the oppressed themselves." [10] Although the nonoppressed members of society often hold the position and status to call attention and begin correcting injustice, they should be ready to step out of the way for the oppressed to be heard. The rationale behind this line of thinking is the insight that "we [society] must acknowledge the significant effect of the distance between the speaker's social location and those being spoken for." [11] Respectfully engaging with other humans and presenting a topic accurately with the humility to acknowledge the large space (and thus potential for inaccurate interpretation) between speaker and subject is challenging. For example, I notice when the Voices of Hope Choir performs there are often audience members who want to chat with me during intermission or after the show. They ask what I think they can do to be supportive or helpful and for interesting details about the stories of other members of the group but do not speak to any of the choir members personally. In these moments, I find myself being hyperaware of the disconnect of my social location to that of most of my choir and try to foster conversation with them directly. To hear someone's story, that exchange of personal information, or to hold space while someone explains what they need and remain open when it disagrees with what you think would help requires vulnerability. Again, the work is difficult, and not everyone signs up.

American folklorist Elaine Lawless uses reflexive ethnography throughout her process to include "who we are as we do ethnography, where we are as we write up these ethnographies, and where we are as we offer our interpretations of these materials we study. We are obligated to present ourselves in our texts as we are in our work: humans seeking understanding, engaged in dialogue and interpretation with others."[12] So as I move forward with sharing the experience of directing Voices of Hope, I acknowledge the influence of my background in the interpretation of my experience and the humans with whom I interact. I also engage the voice of a recovering addict and my assistant director Ryan Fieldman to provide additional reflection from a direct source.

The Voices of Hope meet once a week on Wednesday mornings for an hour of rehearsal. We originally met in the sanctuary of a local church where a community kitchen serves lunch each weekday for anyone who is hungry. The idea behind the location was simply that at-risk members of the community would likely be going to that location for food beginning at eleven o'clock, so by holding rehearsal at ten o'clock they may come check it out. There were pros and cons to the meeting location, but ultimately the group voted to move it to the Friendship House, the drop-in center supported by Milan Puskar Health Right. The building is a two-story rental space that provides a large meeting room, bathroom, two offices, computer area, small meeting room, kitchen area, and storage closet upstairs and a recreation/living room, a couple private rooms with cots for a nap, and additional living space downstairs. The majority of choir members were individuals who frequented the Friendship House, and it was more convenient to meet there. Ryan noted that he felt the new location drew more people in, as it is difficult to hear a room full of people singing and laughing and not want to be a part of that. He elaborated that for himself and others it seemed that, no matter what kind of stuff they were "sitting in," usually rehearsal kind of wakes them up.

An additional reason for the location change was the evolution of accompaniment for the group. Originally, I played piano for most of the songs, and some music therapy students from West Virginia University would drop by now and then and play guitar or *cajon* with us. As the group began to grow, there was an influx of guitar players and even a couple individuals who played bass or drums. Rather than bring up the guitars from the Friendship House and drums from my studio each week, meeting at the House made it possible to leave our instruments in one location and afforded a quick set up. Ryan reflected that, while it is more convenient to be at the Friendship House, there are times that he misses the church space. The stone floors and vaulted ceilings, the grand piano, and beautiful wooden pews provided an atmosphere that highlighted how special this hour of the week was and how worthy all participants were to be there. Like other elements of the group, I remain flexible on location and am open to returning to the church space if the group is interested.

I knew nothing formally about directing a choir of people dealing with homelessness, mental health issues, and addiction, so like any academic worth their salt, I started researching. I read about the Dallas Street Choir in Dallas, Texas, founded by Dr. Jonathan Palant in 2014, and discovered some basic ideas about incentive programs, repertoire selection, and behavior expectations. It was from an email exchange with Dr. Palant that I realized I would need to make song lyric sheets simple and ensure they were printed in a large font, as many members would have vision issues and most would not have corrective lenses to assist their reading. The general setup of his group rehearsals would not work for us, so I continued researching. I came across the website for the Voices of Our City Choir in San Diego and its founding directors Steph Johnson and Rob Thorsen. Their vision statement and mission explanation provided a basic example that I showed the Voices of Hope members as we crafted our own. They also provided an education and advocacy model that I shared with Ryan and other core group members. These are members who are present at nearly every rehearsal and feel a sense of accountability to the choir and to the other individuals who attend on a regular basis.

The transient nature of the choir's members offers perhaps the largest hurdle when it comes to planning and performing from a director's viewpoint. The core group of individuals supporting Voices of Hope make it possible to invite new members each week and help everyone feel up to speed. At this point the core members are Ryan Fieldman, assistant director and peer recovery coach; Caitlin Scott, director of The Friendship House; Diane Green, business manager of Milan Puskar Health Right; Jacob Eye, peer recovery coach; Wes Bergen, local minister; and Jordan Hunter, a social worker for Health Right. These individuals set up chairs, arrange rides when we perform outside of walking distance, run rehearsal if I am not present, and create accompaniment for some of our pieces. Because each of them comes to the group with a different background and level of understanding of addiction, homelessness, and music, their voices offer insight, ideas, and necessary feedback throughout the process. That is not to say that their voices are valued over other members. I encourage anyone to suggest repertoire, provide feedback about performance events and rehearsal, and simply check in emotionally if they feel so inclined.

Our rehearsals work like any other choir I have directed in the past. We begin with warm-ups. For individuals not familiar with choir, these can sometimes feel foreign, silly, and unrelated to just singing some songs. Some members come to Voices of Hope with years singing experience in school choirs and jump right into this practice. Others attend multiple rehearsals before they are willing to participate in warm-ups. Ryan feels that warms-ups are one of the most functional things we do during choir because they get everybody centered. When we make our way through the breathing exercises and get everyone focused on just enjoying that hour, he sees a change. He observes that whatever was going on mentally seems to dissipate and by the end of the hour choir members seem noticeably calmer: "Everyone seems to be getting along." As a director, this is the main time I can actively work on technical aspects of singing like breath support, relaxation in the jaw and neck, intonation, and counting. Some members requested the opportunity to learn the basics of reading music, so I use the end of our warm-up period to introduce basic rhythms that we read and clap and basic pitch patterns that we work out using numbers rather than solfège (do-re-mi) syllables.

When teaching a new song to the group, I primarily work by rote. This instruction strategy is efficient for us as I get to model proper breathing, vowel shape, and phrasing for them rather than try and explain all those parts. Once we have worked on a piece for a while, I invite any members who feel confident to sing with me and newcomers to echo back. Some pieces that were suggested by members, like Jim Croce's "I Got a Name," were not familiar to me and full of variations on the written melody. In this case I asked a member who knew the song well to do their best to sing parts for us, and I amended my score accordingly to be prepared to lead in the future. I believe the experience of watching me not knowing everything was comforting and equalizing, as well. For melismatic passages, I simply use hand motions to convey the melodic contour. Some members have asked to start using sheet music, so they follow the shape there while others follow my hand. Our binders are organized alphabetically and contain a simple lyric sheet as well as a copy of sheet music for each song in our repertoire. A table of contents became necessary as some members became easily frustrated with the alphabetical order, so amending the binders to include page numbers and a table of contents served us well. At this point, Voices of Hope has standards that we keep in rotation all the time in both rehearsal and performance and seasonal pieces that are new and added to the end of the binder. We divide our year into fall semester (August–November), holiday (December), spring semester (January–May), and summer (June and July).

The Voices of Hope has successfully hosted members of the city council and the mayor at the Friendship House, introduced these government leaders to individuals who frequent the drop-in center, and performed some of our favorite songs including "Hotel California" by the Eagles, "Linger" by the Cranberries, and "Let It Be" by the Beatles. Choir members voiced their desire to be a part of the Morgantown Art Walk last fall, so we set up outside the Friendship House and prepared three different sets to perform throughout the evening. Passersby could sit and listen or explore the drop-in center, which was left open so people could view the client-created art that adorned the walls. Choir members invited friends and family to come see them perform, meet the group, and to sing "Take Me Home, Country Roads" by John Denver with us. Ryan recalled the sense of belonging and fellowship present among members as they rushed to set up chairs, hang additional lighting outside, and prepare refreshments for visitors on both occasions.

On two other occasions, the Voices of Hope has performed at a local church, the minster of which plays bass guitar for the group. Some members foster deep-seated resentments against organized religion, and others center their lives around spiritual practices that are not based in a Western Christian faith. This created two issues we discussed as a group: repertoire and performance venues. There are a few songs in the group's repertoire that are based in Christian tradition, a mashup of "Amazing Grace" and "House of the Rising Sun," the call-and-response campfire song "Over My Head," and a gospel medley created by group members that flows from "Amazing Grace" into "This Little Light of Mine" and ends with "Down by the Riverside." I found it immensely important to not only say that members did not have to sing these songs but to be positive in fostering discussion about them and reinforcing whatever decision came from that discourse. Some members stated they had a god of their understanding and were fine substituting that in their minds as we sang because they liked the songs. Some said they preferred not to sing them but would play an instrument, and others were fine with whatever the group decided. Each of those songs stayed in rotation and are not practiced any more or less than others.

The second part of the discussion came from the invitation from a church to come sing and share a meal. This is another area where I believe getting out of the established hierarchy of a director serving as a dictator in all matters related to the choir has been beneficial to this group. Creating space for an open dialogue about who would or would not be comfortable attending a performance in a church service and then sharing a meal could not have happened at the onset of the group. This was not something I would have given the group to consider before we came to know one another and build trust. Ryan shared that everyone seemed to feel heard, and the decision of the group to accept the invitation did not lead to feelings of dismissal or frustration by anyone who was initially uncomfortable. For us, it also helped that many members knew Wes, the minister, from weekly rehearsals as bass guitarist and appreciated his accepting and laid-back style.

I do not want to paint the picture that every discussion goes smoothly and along my time frame. Nor do I want to portray our rehearsals to be the epitome of efficiency, professionalism, and collaboration. We strive to adhere to our guidelines and vision statement, "Rewriting the narrative around homelessness and addiction in our community through music making, group participation, and advocacy," and we are completely human in that attempt. When writing our first song together, our version of Bob Marley's "Three Little Birds," I planned for one rehearsal to be enough time to complete lyrics for three verses and one chorus together. I thought we would use a whiteboard and work together seamlessly to create our song. That process took four weeks and almost inspired a fight as some members felt their voices were not being heard in the process of creating lyrics. Do we have days where we warm up, run through eights songs, and leave feeling totally accomplished? Definitely. Do we have days where everyone is stressed out, talking over top of one another, arguing about whether a passage should say "she said" or "and said," or passing out in a chair at the back of the room because they used right before they came by? Yes, we do. And the members keep coming back. So do I.

As Ryan and I discussed why our recipe seems to work, we identified the emotional and physical reactions to the rehearsal and performance processes. Ryan, a recovering addict and peer recovery specialist for Health Right, shared his experience that any kind of connection is going to help. His basic understanding is that, neurologically speaking, enjoyable group activity that offers human connection releases endorphins, and the brain will in return produce dopamine:

> And it just feels you know . . . people may not be able to describe it the same way I just did, but it just feels good. It's like a natural high. So I mean maybe it's a sneaky way of saying like, hey, there is something else that like can make you feel this way. And I think if people are able to consistently do those things, then they just kind of inherently learn that like, hey, there's other ways I can make myself feel good, you know? It's like ok, well . . . there's the seed, and maybe something will grow from that.

Other members have shared at the conclusion of rehearsals that choir was the best hour they had in weeks. Some members sit quietly crying or in reflection while others sing around them; some members get angry or frustrated and leave rehearsal only to return and apologize to the group. The open space created at rehearsals coupled with the ability to gently hold one another accountable are both building a sense of community.

A specific moment I saw this community pull together was at a family-friendly holiday event hosted by the West Virginia Black Bears baseball team. The Voices of Hope was invited for the second year to sing carols while families made crafts, had cookies, and took photos with Santa. The holidays can be a challenging time for individuals in recovery and for those experiencing homelessness, as memories and intense feelings of nostalgia and grief can cloud present reality and lead to disconnection. As we practiced a variety of carols and secular favorites, members shared which were their favorites and personal stories from their past holidays, both positive and negative. When we attended the event, a member who had not sung with us long, in early recovery from addiction and recently released from incarceration, told us they invited their ex-partner to stop by and bring their daughter. They shared with the group that the child was born while they were in prison, and because of the rules and itinerary of their recovery house, they had only met their daughter once. Near the end of the event, the member found them and spent a few minutes holding their daughter and speaking kindly to their ex. Group members stood back taking pictures and sharing in the joy that their friend could spend this small amount of time with their family. They offered support after the child left, and sadness crept across the member's face. The new member smiled through his tears and thanked everyone for their kindness and sharing their stories of estranged loved ones. One member replied, "We are all a lot of things, but we are also members of the Voices of Hope, and this is kind of what we do."

IV. OFF THE PAGE

I am grateful to say the Voices of Hope choir has become the first living and breathing incarnation of my thesis research. If I am being completely transparent, the origin of that project was quite self-serving. With my long-held interest in choral music and social justice, this idea combined two passions and offered a path to career authenticity. I recognized a need in my immediate community related to addiction, and I was not sure the best way I, a choir director, could be effective at making a difference. I saw addiction and, not being an addict myself, wanted to show up but not be in the way. There is no possibility of divorcing my personal history with the disease from my interest in this research and desire to lead this choir. Moreover, I cannot attempt to sever emotional ties with West Virginia to become a more objective voice or pretend I am not acutely aware that, for now, this work anchors me in the state and challenges my learned success narrative.

I collected my knowledge of the disease in a way I hoped others would not need to experience it in order to gain empathy. My unlearning of the dismissive narrative that addicts are horrible people and not worthy of compassion or respect allows me to see the people buried alive within the disease: those experiencing a dis-ease of self and with life around them. These are human beings with inherent dignity and worth, in transition, as they are pressed beneath strata of guilt and pain, like coal.

I intended to validate the application of choral musicking as a means of creating community, fostering personal healing, and promoting social change first in that research document and now off the page. At times, our vision statement—"Rewriting the narrative around homelessness and addiction in our community through music making, group participation, and advocacy"— seems lofty, but it is what we do. On the advocacy front, the Voices of Hope performances open channels of communication with city leaders, state legislators, and members of local law enforcement and judicial systems as we invite them to sing with us at the Friendship House or offer holiday carols at their doorsteps. A different face of addiction is shared with the outside community as we sing, laugh, and generally get down during family-friendly events downtown or organize a fundraising concert with all proceeds going to the Morgantown Community Kitchen that has fed them many times and to which they would like to give something back. We have attended city council meetings as a group, not to perform, but to support one another in voicing concerns about topics from bench installation, Narcan accessibility, and safety.

Some of the seemingly smaller scale and less tangible accomplishments occur in our group participation and musicking. Milan Puskar Health Right considers the Voices of Hope part of their harm-reduction approach to recovery. Rehearsal is an hour of singing and generally some time in fellowship before and after during which members are not using. Any measurable amount of time in which their clients are not actively harming themselves is an achievement. The Friendship House views Voices of Hope as one of its most successful groups, where members continually bring friends with them to try out choir and are always ready to share why they participate. I view it as a successful group because members tell me things like, "Well it was either come to choir or sit at home and shoot some smack, so I brought my ass down here," and then flash me a smile like a child who is fully aware of their level of orneriness. I am not conceited enough to believe my choir is keeping this addict from using all day or ever again, but I do share in their joy and freedom of engaging with life, without drugs, and truly enjoying those moments. Recovery involves building a tool kit of people, places, and things that help keep you sober, grounded, and accountable. For some members choir is simply enjoyment, and for others it is a functional tool.

Success in the twelve-step recovery programs is a life that is happy, joyous, and free. As I redefine success with Voices of Hope and in my career through that lens, I am happy to see collaborative social justice, the truly effective kind, evolving from choral musicking. We are building community, both insular and external, through connections centered around choral music, which, I hope, will continue to foster social change. Social change and the notion of social justice, working toward a society where every individual is honored as they are at that moment, equates to a sense of freedom. The path to solutions is already present in the voices of those individuals around me. As we keep connecting those voices to community members in positions of leadership or with talents and means to collaborate with them, changes will occur. Most imperative to me is the reminder that the changes may be solely within the members of my group and myself but not the community at large, and that is still a West Virginia success story.

NOTES

1. Sara Warfield et al., "Opioid-Related Outcomes in West Virginia, 2008–2016," *American Journal of Public Health* 109, no. 2 (2018): 303–5, https://ajph.aphapublications.org/doi/abs/10.2105/AJPH.2018.304845.
2. Warfield et al, "Opioid-Related Outcomes."
3. J. D. Thornton et al., "Pharmacists' Readiness to Provide Naloxone in Community Pharmacies in West Virginia," National Center for Biotechnology Information, National Institutes of Health, February 2, 2017, https://www.ncbi.nlm.nih.gov/pubmed/2816 3027.
4. Kristina MacMullen, "CONCEPT: Freedom," Creativity, Kristina MacMullen, 2018, https://www.kristinamacmullen.com/creativity.

5. Julia Balén, *A Queerly Joyful Noise* (New Brunswick, NJ: Rutgers University Press, 2017).
6. Gregory Barz, *Singing for Life: HIV/AIDS and Music in Uganda* (New York: Routledge, 2006).
7. Christopher Small, *Musicking: The Meanings of Performing and Listening* (Middletown, CT: Wesleyan University Press, 1998).
8. Estelle R. Jorgensen, "Intersecting Social Justices and Music Education," in *The Oxford Handbook of Social Justice in Music Education*, ed. Paul Woodford (New York: Oxford University Press, 2015), 6–28.
9. Paul Woodford et al., "Preface: Why Social Justice and Music Education?" in *The Oxford Handbook of Social Justice in Music Education*, ed. Paul Woodford (New York: Oxford University Pres, 2015), 1–12.
10. Linda Alcoff, "The Problem of Speaking for Others," *Cultural Critique*, no. 20 (Winter 1991–1992): 8.
11. Alcoff, "The Problem of Speaking for Others," 7.
12. Elaine Lawless, "I Was Afraid Someone like You . . . an Outsider . . . Would Misunderstand," *The Journal of American Folklore* 105, no. 417 (1992): 302.

Contributors

JONAS N. T. BECKER is an interdisciplinary visual artist whose work spans video installation, photography, sculpture, and community engagement. Their work explores how beliefs form around specific sites and geographies. They are interested in these landscapes as an intersection of personal identity, cultural mythologies, and political power. They are an assistant professor of photography at the School of the Art Institute of Chicago.

AMANDA M. CALEB is a professor at Misericordia University with a joint appointment in English and medical and health humanities. With a variety of research interests focused on individual accounts of illness and public policy, she has published on topics including the heterotopic Victorian sickroom, Darwinian views of female intelligence, the rhetoric of British eugenics, and the value of narrative medicine for people with dementia.

LEIGH H. EDWARDS is a professor of English at Florida State University. A scholar of media studies and popular culture, she focuses on representations of gender and race in popular music, on television, and in new media. Her most recent book is *Dolly Parton, Gender, and Country Music* (Indiana University Press, 2018).

CHRISTOPHER GARLAND is an assistant professor in the department of writing and linguistics at Georgia Southern University. His writing has appeared in the *Journal of Social and Economic Studies*, *Contemporary French and Francophone Studies*, *Writing Visual Culture*, and *Mediascape*, as well as in the edited collections *Hollywood's Africa after 1994* (Ohio University Press) and *Haiti and the Americas* (University Press of Mississippi).

CRYSTAL GOOD is hard to put in just one box. She prefers: artist, advocate, and entrepreneur. She is a member of the Affrilachian (African American

Appalachian) Poets, a group of writers and artists whose creations and existence combat the erasure of African American identity in the Appalachian region, an Irene McKinney Scholar, and the author of *Valley Girl*. Crystal lives by a philosophy of "one day at a time" and is thankful for the recovery fellowship of which she is a member and to whom she gives credit for opening the door to her personal healing.

ASHLEIGH HARDIN is an assistant professor of English and director of writing at the University of Saint Francis in Fort Wayne, Indiana. She has written and presented on the role of narrative in cultural understandings of addiction before and during the War on Drugs.

MICHAEL HENSON is author of four books of fiction and four of poetry. His most recent book, *Maggie Boylan*, was designated a 2018 Great Group Read by the Women's National Book Association and was a finalist for the Appalachian Studies Association's Weatherford Award.

CHELSEA JACK is a PhD student in the anthropology department at Yale University and a National Science Foundation GRFP Fellow. Her fields of interest include medicine and healing, agriculture, and environmental history.

JORDAN LOVEJOY is a PhD candidate in English and folklore at the Ohio State University. Her dissertation project explores the cultural and environmental memory of floods in Appalachian life and literature.

SUSAN McDONALD is an associate professor at Misericordia University and serves as the chair of the social work department. Her areas of interest are narrative therapy and trauma, and she has published on topics including narrating practices with children and adolescents and narrative medicine with older adults.

TATIANA PROROKOVA-KONRAD is a postdoctoral researcher at the department of English and American studies, University of Vienna, Austria. Her research interests include war studies, ecocriticism, disability studies, gender studies, and race studies. She is the author of *Docu-Fictions of War: U.S. Interventionism in Film and Literature* (University of Nebraska Press, 2019) and a coeditor of *Cultures of War in Graphic Novels: Violence, Trauma, and Memory* (Rutgers University Press, 2018).

AUSTIN T. RICHEY is a PhD candidate in ethnomusicology at Eastman School of Music in Rochester, New York. His dissertation research is based in his hometown of Detroit, Michigan, where he highlights the resonances between diasporic African musical, dance, and visual arts and Detroit-specific musical genres, such as Motown and techno. Contemporary culture makers in Detroit compose a unique sonic Afro-modernity through the blend of multiple black musical histories, and in the process, they present new narratives on culture and revitalization in this historically multifaceted American city.

NATALIE SHAFFER, a recent graduate of West Virginia University with master's of music degrees in both music history and conducting, currently serves as an adjunct professor of music at West Virginia University and Glenville State College. She functions as both ethnic/multicultural chair and social justice chair for the West Virginia chapter of the American Choral Directors Association and serves as director of music ministry at Avery United Methodist Church in Morgantown, West Virginia. Her research into collaborative social justice through choral musicking resulted in her current position as artistic director with the Voices of Hope community choir.

ETHAN SHARP is an independent scholar, grant writer, and consultant for arts organizations. He received a PhD in folklore from Indiana University and previously taught at the University of Texas–Pan American, Georgia State University, and the University of Kentucky. He has published articles on the public culture of drug trafficking and substance use disorders in Mexico and is currently conducting oral history research with recovery advocates in Kentucky with a grant from the Kentucky Oral History Commission.

TRAVIS D. STIMELING is an associate professor of musicology at West Virginia University. A scholar whose work focuses on commercial country music, Appalachian traditional musics, and environmental protest, he is the author most recently of *Songwriting in Contemporary West Virginia: Profiles and Reflections* (West Virginia University Press, 2018).

ANNE LLOYD WILLETT is a movement therapist and international teacher and presenter with over thirty-five years of experience in wellness and movement. She weaves in a fully integrated body-mind-spirit approach that incorporates holistic medicine, coaching, Pilates, yoga, fascia, human microbiome, nutrition, dance, breath therapy and stretch therapy. She owns a movement studio in Chattanooga, Tennessee. You can learn more at AnneLloydWillett.com.

JACQUELINE YAHN is an assistant professor of education at Ohio University's Eastern Campus where she coordinates the middle childhood education program. Her work as a practitioner focuses on engaging university partnerships with schools and communities in northern Appalachia, and her research as a scholar focuses on policy and leadership issues in rural schools and communities. Her most recent work is "Power and Powerlessness in the Shale Valley Schools: Fracking for Funding" (*West Virginia Law Review 120*, no. 3, 2018).

PAIGE ZALMAN holds a master of arts degree in musicology from West Virginia University. Her research interests include popular music, music and gender, and music and contemporary politics. Her original research has also appeared in the scholarly journal *American Music*.

Index

www.ingramcontent.com/pod-product-compliance
Lightning Source LLC
Chambersburg PA
CBHW050337270326
41926CB00016B/3501